D0382068

Saying It's So

Sport and Society

Series Editors
Benjamin G. Rader
Randy Roberts

A list of books in the series appears at the end of this book.

Saying It's So

A Cultural History of the Black Sox Scandal

Daniel A. Nathan

University of Illinois Press
Urbana and Chicago

Manufactured in the United States of America
C 5 4 3 2 1

∞ This book is printed on acid-free paper.

Library of Congress Cataloging-in-Publication Data
Nathan, Daniel A.
Saying it's so : a cultural history of the Black Sox scandal /
Daniel A. Nathan.
p. cm. — (Sport and society)
Includes bibliographical references (p.) and index.
ISBN 0-252-02765-5 (cloth : alk. paper)
1. Chicago White Sox (Baseball team)—History. 2. World
Series (Baseball) (1919) 3. Baseball—Corrupt practices—
United States—History. I. Title. II. Series.
GV875.C58N38 2003
796.357'64'0977311—dc21 2002001360

Contents

Acknowledgments vii

Introduction 1

1. History's First Draft: News, Narrative, and the Black Sox Scandal 11
2. "Fix These Faces in Your Memory": The Black Sox Scandal and American Collective Memories 58
3. The Novel as History, a Novel History: Bernard Malamud's *The Natural* and Eliot Asinof's *Eight Men Out* 92
4. Off the Bench: Historians Take a Swing at the Black Sox Scandal 119
5. Idyll and Iconoclasm: Retelling the Black Sox Scandal in the Eighties 149
6. Dreaming and Scheming: The Black Sox Scandal at the End of the Twentieth Century 190

Conclusion 217

Notes 223
Index 277

Illustrations follow page 118

Acknowledgments

Many people, more than I can mention here, helped me write this book. My debts range far and wide, and it is with great pleasure that I acknowledge the following people.

The earliest drafts of this project were written in Iowa, where many friends provided me with invaluable support and access to their critical skills. They include Joyce Atkinson, Dallas Clemmons, Alison Kibler, Paul Gutjahr, Scott Juengel, Larry McCauley, Eric Neel, Pete Simonson, Rob Urstein, and Elliott Vanskike.

Thanks are also due to Susan Birrell, Kathleen Diffley, Rich Horwitz, Bob Kelley, Tina Parratt, John Raeburn, and Al Stone, all of whom I worked with at the University of Iowa. I am especially grateful to Susan, whose intelligence is surpassed only by her decency, generosity, and good humor. I need to acknowledge and thank two earlier mentors, Lloyd Michaels and Jeanne Braham, who taught me the importance of a good, close reading, vigorous writing, and scholarly inquiry.

My friends at Miami University in Oxford, Ohio, were (and remain) incredibly supportive and generous. In particular, I need to thank Shel Anderson, Andrew Cayton, Mary Kupiec Cayton, Carla Corroto, Sheila Croucher, Kathy Franz, Celeste Friend, Charlotte Newman Goldy, Carolyn Haynes, Jack Kirby, Denise McCoskey, Mary McDonald, Margie McLellan, Elaine Miller, Kate Rousmaniere, Peggy Shaffer, Steve Waksman, Allan Winkler, and Emily Zakin. During our years together, I am sure that most of these people heard more about the Black Sox and baseball history than they ever wanted to. In addition, Allan Winkler's editorial suggestions made this book tighter and more readable. Much more important, his example is inspiring.

In various ways, Ferit Güven, Sofi Nur Miller Güven, Grace Kelley, Chris King, Deb King, Sean Snaith, Gene Cox, Elise Megremis, Dan Malec-Kosak, Kelly Malec-Kosak, and the Three Daves—aka Dave Wiggins, Dave Zang, and Elliott Gorn—all helped me keep my eye on the ball and enjoy life.

Many thanks to Dick Crepeau, Steve Gietschier, and the rest of the baseball cohort of the North American Society for Sport History, an organization that has been very supportive of my work. The research staffs at the Chicago Historical Society and the Baseball Hall of Fame Library, two remarkable institutions, were also helpful. Thanks, too, to Kevin Grace of the University of Cincinnati's Archives and Rare Books Department for his friendship and generosity.

At Skidmore College, Mary Lynn, Nancy Osberg-Otrembiak, Greg Pfitzer, Jerry Philogene, and Joanna Zangrando have been incredibly supportive and exemplary colleagues. I also need to thank Eliot Asinof for his hospitality, Bill Jauss for sharing his memories with me on a beautiful day at Comiskey Park, and all of the other people whom I interviewed for this book.

Ben Rader, Randy Roberts, Dick Wentworth, and two anonymous reviewers all offered constructive criticism that improved this book.

Blessed with tremendous familial support, I want to thank Jon Nathan, my brother, for the patience he exhibited when I had computer woes; Sol Nathan and Irene Nathan, my grandparents, for their weekly phone calls and unconditional love; and my parents—Ron Matthews and Jerry Matthews and Irv Nathan and Judy Walter—for their example and encouragement, which came in many forms. The editorial pen that my father took to the manuscript that became this book is but one indication of how he made it better. No one could ask for more supportive parents.

Finally, my deepest gratitude is owed to Susan Taylor, my partner in all things, for her patience, for helping me to keep matters of consequence in focus, and for Benjamin Erik Nathan.

* * *

Portions of chapter 1 previously appeared in "Anti-Semitism and the Black Sox Scandal," *Nine: A Journal of Baseball History and Social Policy Perspectives* 4:1 (Fall 1995). Distributed by the University of Nebraska Press. Reprinted by permission.

Portions of chapter 6 previously appeared in my coauthored essay(with Mary G. McDonald) "Yearning for Yesteryear: Cal Ripken Jr., The Streak, and the Politics of Nostalgia," *American Studies* 42:1 (Spring 2001). © Mid-America American Studies Association, 2001. Reprinted by permission.

Saying It's So

Introduction

In early October 1919, the Chicago White Sox lost the World Series to the Cincinnati Reds, five games to three. By most accounts, the underdog Reds should not have beaten the Sox, who had won the World Series in 1917. In 1920, several prominent White Sox players testified before a Cook County grand jury that they had conspired with gamblers to lose the series. All told, eight ballplayers—most famously, the outfielder "Shoeless" Joe Jackson—were implicated. Shock waves of disbelief and indignation rippled across the country. Although eventually acquitted of conspiracy charges, the eight men, their names forever sullied, were banished from the game by baseball commissioner Judge Kenesaw Mountain Landis. "I don't know whether the whole truth of what went on there among the White Sox will ever come out," lamented Edd Roush, a Hall of Fame outfielder and the last surviving member of the 1919 Cincinnati Reds, more than forty years later. "Even today nobody really knows exactly what took place. Whatever it was, though, it was a dirty rotten shame."[1]

The Black Sox scandal has remained firmly entrenched in American memories and imaginations. In its day it was reported on the front page of virtually every major newspaper in the country. The scandal and its participants continue to be the subjects of magazine articles and receive attention in academic and popular histories, novels, dramas, feature films, television documentaries, and Web sites. Collectively, these and numerous other cultural narratives and texts, according to the paleontologist (and occasional baseball writer) Stephen Jay Gould, "illustrate the continuing hold that the Black Sox Scandal has upon the hearts and minds of baseball fans and, more widely, upon anyone fascinated with American history or human drama at its best."[2] This book examines how that drama has been represented and remembered—by journalists, novelists, historians, filmmakers, creators of other forms of popular culture, and a small sample of baseball fans. It is an interdisciplinary cultural history of a singular moment that has persisted in our collective consciousness for more than eighty years. One of my principal arguments is that how people have thought about and depicted the Black Sox scandal reflects something revealing (and sometimes important) about their identity, their values, and their historical moment. Thus, *Saying It's So* is less about baseball history than it is about cultural values and the way people make meaning.

The Event

It is probably wise to provide a more detailed summary of the scandal for the benefit of those unfamiliar with it and as a refresher for those who are. Two caveats: First, a more complete history than what is offered here would include how the scandal was embedded in various social and historical contexts, most obviously the game's long association with gambling and management-labor relations. Second, my version should not be mistaken for an "objective" account of the affair. Like all historians, I see the past from particular perspectives that affect my understanding of it and thus my storytelling.

Traditionally, Black Sox scandal narratives begin in the fall of 1919, when the Chicago White Sox of the American League faced the Cincinnati Reds of the National League in the World Series.[3] Led by the outfielder Joe Jackson, the pitcher Eddie Cicotte, and the second baseman Eddie Collins, the White Sox were expected to beat the Reds because they had won the series two years before with the same nucleus of ballplayers and because at the time the American League was generally thought to be superior to the National League. Despite being favored, the White Sox played poorly. They lost four of the first five games, rallied to win two in a row, but lost the best-of-nine series on October 9 when the Reds scored four runs in the first inning on their way to a 10-5 victory.[4] Many Chicagoans, perhaps especially the White Sox team owner, Charles A. Comiskey, and the first-year manager, William "Kid" Gleason, were disappointed and frustrated by the Sox's performance. Often brilliant during the regular season, Cicotte and Claude "Lefty" Williams were unusually erratic on the pitching mound, and Collins, the first baseman Arnold "Chick" Gandil, the shortstop Charles "Swede" Risberg, and the centerfielder Oscar "Hap" Felsch generally played poorly. On the other hand, Jackson, the third baseman George "Buck" Weaver, and the rookie pitcher Dick Kerr were impressive: Jackson had a World Series record twelve hits (including the only home run) and a .375

batting average, Weaver hit .324 and fielded well, and Kerr won two games and maintained a 1.42 earned run average.[5]

Before, during, and after the series, rumors circulated that some Sox had conspired with gamblers and had not played to the best of their ability. Comiskey responded that the rumors were "yarns spun out of the bitterness over losing wagers" and declared that he would offer a reward (some sources say $20,000, others say $10,000) for information confirming team members' crookedness.[6] Although he was apparently presented with information indicating that the rumors had some factual basis, Comiskey—advised by his friend Alfred Austrian, a prominent Chicago attorney—chose to do nothing. That winter, the journalist Hugh Fullerton published a series of newspaper articles suggesting that the series had been tampered with by gamblers; nonetheless, the White Sox management sent contracts for the upcoming season to all the men thought to be involved in the plot. With the exception of Gandil, who chose to remain in California rather than play for Comiskey, the 1920 White Sox essentially fielded the same squad as the previous year.

During the spring and summer of 1920, the White Sox generally played well (if sometimes erratically) and contended for the American League pennant. In early September, as the team battled the Cleveland Indians for first place and as Babe Ruth of the New York Yankees was in the midst of shattering the record for home runs in a single season, it was reported that gamblers had tried to fix the August 31 game between the Chicago Cubs and the Philadelphia Phillies. The story led to a Cook County grand jury investigation that quickly moved beyond the Cubs-Phillies game and examined baseball and gambling in general and the rumors regarding the White Sox and the 1919 World Series in particular. For the next two-and-a-half weeks, a host of witnesses—Comiskey, the American League president (and Comiskey nemesis) Ban Johnson, the former Cubs owner Charles Weeghman, the gambler Monte Tennes, the noted Broadway celebrity George M. Cohan, the Major League ballplayers John "Rube" Benton and Charles "Buck" Herzog, among others—testified about the purported fixing of the series.

Then on September 28 the *Philadelphia North American* reported that a former boxer named Billy Maharg admitted that he and "Sleepy" Bill Burns, a former Major League pitcher, were involved "in the conspiracy that resulted in eight members of the Chicago American League team 'throwing' games to Cincinnati in last year's World Series."[7] The next day Eddie Cicotte testified before the Cook County grand jury for over two hours and confessed that he had received $10,000 before the World Series to play to lose, which he did. Later that afternoon, Joe Jackson testified that he knew of the plot and accepted $5,000 in bribe money (he was initially promised $20,000 by Chick Gandil), but that he had played to win.[8] It is an apocryphal and now modified story, but supposedly a disillusioned street urchin on the steps of the courthouse confronted Jackson after his testimony. "It ain't true is it, Joe?" the youngster asked. Jackson reportedly replied, "Yes, kid, I'm afraid it is."[9] (After the story circulated, Jackson consistently denied that the exchange had occurred.)[10] The next day, Lefty Williams and Hap Felsch confessed—Williams to Alfred Austrian and Felsch to a Chicago reporter—that they too had conspired with gamblers to lose the series. Said Felsch: "Well, the beans are all spilled and I think that I am through with baseball. I got my five thousand and I suppose the others got theirs too. If you say anything about me don't make it appear that I'm trying to put up an alibi. I'm not. I'm as guilty as any of them. We all were in it alike."[11] Despite the confessions, it was unclear who did not play to the best of his ability during the series, who had accepted money from gamblers, who knew what and when. Ultimately, in late October, eight players—including Gandil, whom Cicotte described as the plot's "master of ceremonies," and Buck Weaver, who acknowledged that he knew of the scheme but denied being involved in it—and five alleged gamblers were indicted on a variety of conspiracy charges.[12] The infamous New York gambler Arnold Rothstein, often regarded as the affair's principal fixer, was not among them. A few weeks later, anxious team owners hired the respected if flamboyant federal judge Kenesaw Mountain Landis to serve as organized baseball's first commissioner.[13]

After much delay, partly due to a change of administration in the Illinois State's Attorney's Office, the Black Sox arraignment took place in mid-February 1921 and the trial finally began in mid-July. It was an unusual, even farcical legal proceeding. First, the novelty of Major Leaguers on trial caused a great deal of public excitement and media interest. Indeed, one day a riot was narrowly averted "when 500 men and boys besieged the entrance of the courtroom seeking admission," reported the *Chicago Herald and Examiner.*[14] To add to the drama, the prosecution announced that the ballplayers' original confessions and their immunity waivers had mysteriously disappeared from the state's attorney's office. As a result, Cicotte, Jackson, and Williams promptly recanted their confessions, which were nonetheless read into the record by court reporters. From a legal standpoint, it did not seem to matter. The very nature of the indictments, which outlined five separate conspiracies, made it difficult for the prosecution to convict the defendants. Furthermore, the judge's instructions to the jury—he explained that the state had to prove that it was the intent of the defendants to defraud the alleged victims identified in the indictments and the public, not merely to intentionally lose the World Series—made a guilty verdict unlikely. On August 2, 1921, the indicted ballplayers and gamblers were acquitted of all charges. It took the jury one ballot and less than three hours to reach its verdict.[15] While it was a somewhat predictable and anticlimactic decision, the defendants, their attorneys, and many baseball fans in the courtroom were jubilant. The next day, however, Landis declared that all ballplayers involved in the incident—Joe Jackson, Buck Weaver, Eddie Cicotte, Chick Gandil, Hap Felsch, Lefty Williams, Swede Risberg, and Fred McMullin of the White Sox as well as Joe Gedeon of the St. Louis Browns, who knew of the fix—would be permanently ineligible to play organized baseball.[16] Landis was widely hailed for his decision; it has never been reversed.

The Tale

Many have observed that this infamous scandal represents a moment of crisis and transformation. In addition to fostering changes within the organization of the game, the Black Sox affair may have affected the way many Americans perceived not just the national pastime but also the nation. One critic, George Grella, has even suggested that the scandal "may have been more important than World War I in educating the nation in the dubious lessons of disenchantment."[17] In a similar vein, the literary critic Cordelia Candelaria maintains that the scandal "marks a crucial milestone in U.S. sociohistory. Before the scandal, baseball's contamination by business and gambling were regarded as minor but necessary evils in a supposedly free-market economy. Afterwards, the painfully disillusioned public could no longer keep up the pretense of the sport's arcadian purity."[18] The historian Donald Honig simply maintains that the Black Sox have become "to baseball history what Benedict Arnold is to American history."[19] Some of these claims are hyperbolic, but the fact remains that many people are still interested in the fixed World Series.

My interest can be traced to a long-misplaced book of baseball history that I read as a boy. At the time, the story of the fixed World Series was unbelievable and improbable to me; ballplayers not playing to win was inconceivable. When I returned to the story a few years ago, I, naive then, was disturbed by the idea that a celebrated social institution like the World Series, which some critics and fans refer to as a sacred ritual, was so easily corrupted. Today, the scandal is a site where my eclectic intellectual interests converge, and I am motivated by the combination of wonderment and incredulity that the event continues to evoke. One producer of ESPN Classic's 2001 documentary on the Black Sox scandal put it well: "It is hard to believe that something that large in scope, which happened in the modern century in front of the nation's press could be so shrouded in mystery, even to this day."[20] More important, it seems to me that the Black Sox scandal throws into relief questions about historical representation, narrative, and collective memory. This book uses the Big Fix as a portal of sorts into these issues and considers what versions of the Black Sox scandal reveal about those who created them and the respective eras in which they were produced.

Writers and thinkers ranging from Walt Whitman and Mark Twain to Jacques Barzun and George F. Will have proposed that baseball is intimately and indelibly linked with American ideals and values, history and culture. In one way or another, most people who have written about baseball as a cultural text have suggested that the game's symbols and rituals, its heroes, history, and mythology, reveal something significant about American belief systems, values, and ideologies. In fact, a few critics have noted that Barzun's oft-repeated maxim, "Whoever wants to know the heart and mind of America had better learn baseball," has contributed to the increased scholarly attention the game now receives.[21] In his essay "The Creation Myths of Cooperstown" (1989), Stephen Jay Gould recognizes that "baseball is a major item of our culture, and it does have a long and interesting history." He also notes, "Any item or institution with these two properties must generate a set of myths and stories (perhaps even some truths) about its beginnings."[22] The same is true of its moments of crisis.

Still, this only partly explains why the Black Sox scandal, a relatively insignificant historical incident resulting in no deaths and no profound social or cultural changes, has persisted in American memories and imaginations. What is it about this moment that elicits seemingly continuous retelling? Why do Americans continue to reproduce and consume narratives of the Big Fix? Moreover, what are the dominant reconstructions of the Black Sox scandal and the ideological implications of those versions of the past? What do the retellings suggest about the relationships between different versions of a historical story? What do they tell us about American collective memories? What do they say about the tension between narrative representation and social reality? And, even more broadly, what do they reveal about the relationships between the present and the past?

A variety of writers have explored some of these issues. In *Shoeless Joe and Ragtime Baseball* (1992), Harvey Frommer posits that "it is all of the unanswered questions as well as a powerful sense that justice miscarried, that the ignorant were duped by the clever, that the powerless suffered and the strong prevailed, that makes the story of Shoeless Joe and his teammates live on."[23] The historian David Q. Voigt argues that the scandal's mythological function—which he describes as the "single sin myth"—explains its historical endurance: "The myth of baseball's single sin proclaims that the game has known but one case of proven dishonesty, yet the early years of the game were pockmarked with countless rumors of bribery and cheating similar to this episode."[24] Voigt contends that the baseball establishment, led by Judge Kenesaw Mountain Landis, had an obvious vested interest in promoting the Black Sox scandal as a singular transgression. Following Voigt's lead, the literary critic Christian K. Messenger argues that the "Black Sox remain the primal cautionary tale of American sports' ensnarement by money and greed. Here all the abuses of the economics of sport are in evidence."[25] The political columnist George Will simply comments, "When scandal touched baseball, it touched a national nerve."[26]

Partly due to nostalgia, romanticism, and the seemingly didactic quality of the players' fate, the Black Sox scandal has long been a cultural moment that has warranted retelling. But by retelling it, cultural narrators or storytellers—be they journalists, historians, novelists, dramatists, or filmmakers—have in no small measure recreated the event. They have engaged in a dialogue between the past and the present that simultaneously debunks, romanticizes, and reconfigures our understanding of the historical event known as the Black Sox scandal. As one would expect, each narrator portrays the incident somewhat differently and uses it for different ends. Writing in another context, the novelist Evan Connell notes that when "values change, so does one's evaluation of the past and one's impression of long gone actors. New myths replace the old."[27] One objective of this book is to trace the changing values expressed in Black Sox narratives over the years.

Narrating from disparate contexts and ideological positions, the storytellers examined here bridge their own private concerns and interests with the same moment of public crisis. In the process, each offers a decidedly different interpretation—of the event itself and its cultural significance. Within this struggle for cultural meaning, the historical "accuracy" or "truth" of a narrative is less important to me than its construction, which inevitably reshapes, omits, distorts, conflates, and reorganizes the past. Here Michael Schudson's observation in *Watergate in American Memory: How We Remember, Forget, and Reconstruct the Past* (1992) is useful: "The contest among differing perspectives is important, and my subject lies in examining the construction, revision, cultural transmission, and enduring influence of these different perspectives."[28] I am not interested in narrative versions of the Black Sox scandal for their own sake, though they are noteworthy. Rather, I am interested in exploring what they reveal about narrative, collective memory, and their intimate and complicated relationships with a dramatic moment in baseball history.

It is important to be explicit about my critical presuppositions. In this account, I am not interested in determining the "truth" of the scandal, which was inevitably left behind in the shadowy hotel rooms, bars, and pool halls that the implicated White Sox and their assorted alleged accomplices frequented in 1919. One result of the temporal distance that separates us from the Black Sox scandal is that it is inaccessible except in some textual form. In this respect my thinking parallels Keith Jenkins's in *Re-Thinking History* (1991), in which he writes, "The past and history are different things."[29] Jenkins argues that the past has occurred, that history is what historians write, and "that 'history' is really 'histories,' for at this point we ought to stop thinking of history as though it were a simple and rather obvious thing and recognise that there is a multiplicity of types of history whose only common feature is that their ostensible object of enquiry is 'the past.'"[30] Working from this presupposition does not deny the integrity of the past or of historical knowledge. Furthermore, it does not suggest, as Schudson is afraid it does, "that there is only discourse and no independent world to which discourse is beholden."[31] But it does force us to reexamine history as a human construct, a starting point that challenges us to recognize the contexts in and purposes for which it is written. It requires us to be ever mindful that the past is in important ways lost and that history is always an account by someone for someone.

It is also important to add that no cultural text or historical narrative is absolutely authoritative. Albert E. Stone makes this point in *The Return of Nat Turner: History, Literature, and Cultural Politics in Sixties America* (1992). In the process of examining the cultural reactivation that William Styron's novel *The Confessions of Nat Turner* (1967) instigated, Stone contends that it is dangerous to endow "either literary or historical works with fixed or authoritative meanings."[32] Moreover, Stone asserts, "we must not grant history priority over literature—or vice versa."[33] Because he insists that all texts are "complex symbolic acts and artifacts," Stone suggests that we should take seriously all responses to dramatic historical moments like Turner's uprising, be they literary, cinematic, journalistic, folkloric, or mythic.[34] Read within this context, the Black Sox scandal and its various representations take on a new appearance. Not only do versions of the episode reveal that the past is reconstructed to accord with specific present (usually dominant) interests and values but also that they have ideological subtexts reflecting something about the authors and the text's moment of creation. This should be acknowledged since one objective of this book is to locate, describe, critique, and put in context the ideological subtexts inscribed within Black Sox scandal narratives.

One of my underlying assumptions is that cultural perspective and context go a long way toward determining meaning. Accounts of the affair are best understood if they are examined from the moment in which they were initially produced and read. Although I agree with the cultural historian Robert Darnton that "reading has reemerged as the central fact of literature," it should be clear that I am not proposing a reader-response study.[35] Instead, I examine closely the other end of the "social transaction," namely the texts themselves, particularly their reconstruction and the various contexts that produced and surrounded them. Just as the scandal is most profitably understood within the context of social, labor, and baseball history, the narratives that recreate it need to be put into their contexts. When they are recognized as products that cannot be divorced from their specific social and cultural circumstances, I believe they reveal more about those who constructed them and their intended audiences than about the scandal itself.

As the reader will soon learn, this book is not a seamless historical narrative; in places, it might even be described as disjointed. There are several reasons for this. Years ago, a colleague convinced me that seamless historical narratives—fluid, often beautifully written works that smooth out the rumpled, indeterminate nature of their subjects—can charm or mislead (perhaps even deceive or trick) readers "into thinking that history is," as he put it, "a continuous whole with a positivistic and self-evident nature," when it is not. Such works seem to be stories without storytellers; they seem more intelligible and tidy than the past was. In actuality, as most historians would acknowledge, the narrative fluidity of the best histories is a testament to the rhetorical skill of their respective authors, for the past is always more ambiguous, complicated, and disordered than the prose used to describe and analyze it. This is certainly the case with the Big Fix. Consequently, I have self-consciously written a cultural history that reveals my handiwork, seams and all. Rather than give my history what the philosopher of history Hayden White refers to as "illusory coherence," I have tried to replicate the complicated nature of the event and the ways in which representations and memories of it complement and compete with each other.[36]

Finally, it is important to note that the ongoing Black Sox scandal narrative is less a unique cultural phenomenon than an emblematic one. There have been, of course, scores of highly controversial moments in American history that have been retold in many different mediums to the point of generating mythology. Watergate, for instance, has surely forged a secure place in our collective memories. Much like the Pocahontas narrative, the Salem witch trials, Nat Turner's slave revolt, the battle at the Alamo, the battle of the Little Big Horn, the *Titanic* disaster, the bombing of Pearl Harbor, the Rosenberg espionage case, and the assassination of President Kennedy, the Black Sox scandal has successfully resisted fading into obscurity. The fixed World Series of 1919 has remained poignant in part because it involves an institution that has been consistently used to illustrate so-called American values and ideals. But the scandal's remarkable endurance can also be attributed to the fact that the narratives that recreate it often complicate simplistic black-and-white conceptions of historical representation and social relations. In other words, a study of representations of the Black Sox scandal enriches our understanding of how cultural and historical meaning is produced.

1

History's First Draft: News, Narrative, and the Black Sox Scandal

"Reducing events to stories and getting stories into print," writes the historian Robert Darnton, "is a matter of cultural fit—of narrative conventions and newsroom traditions that work as a way of imposing form on the booming, buzzing confusion of the day's events."[1] For the journalists who first tried to reduce the 1919 World Series scandal to articles, the "buzzing confusion" must have been extraordinary. Though there had been rumors that the series was crooked—some circulated even before it began—it remained a difficult story to write and publish. There was no hard evidence of any wrongdoing and few editors or publishers were eager to print articles revealing the dirty underbelly of the national pastime. Moreover, as they must have sensed, the Black Sox scandal, as the game-fixing affair soon came to be known, was a remarkably complicated affair. "What actually happened has never been established with complete certainty," writes the historian William K. Klingaman. "Conflicting evidence, stories that changed from day to day, confessions that were later retracted, all muddy the water sufficiently to keep many of the exact details shrouded in a fog of mystery."[2] Having read histories of the episode, biographies of its participants, and contemporary accounts of the Big Fix and subsequent trial, I too am unable to determine precisely what occurred, who participated and to what extent, who knew what and when. This much, however, is clear: from the very beginning the Black Sox scandal was constructed by the press as a labyrinthine story of deception, betrayal, and moral disorder. In the media's hands, it was a story that touched on issues at the heart of American culture.

Although published in a variety of forums (which represented subtly different interests) and read by heterogeneous audiences, the scandal's most significant early narratives appeared in daily metropolitan newspapers. These narratives are important for at least three reasons. First, they vividly illustrate the process of transforming an event into news, throwing into relief the ways in which the press narrated (what it believed to be) a crisis. Second, they illuminate how the Black Sox scandal served as a vehicle for adducing a number of apparently discrete cultural preoccupations of the early twentieth-century United States: the "cleanliness crusade," crime, anti-Semitism, middle-class masculinity, social class, labor relations, and the role of the mass media in a burgeoning society. Finally, these narratives have exercised a remarkably influential and lasting effect on how the Black Sox scandal has been retold, rewritten, and remembered. In spite of its numerous retellings, storytellers have labored to escape the pull of the episode's earliest versions. Closely read with over eighty years of hindsight—paying special attention to the symbols, metaphors, allusions, and narrative forms used to shape the event—the print media's coverage of the game-fixing scandal not only offers preferred ways of seeing American sport and society in the early twenties but also reminds us that "news is not what happened in the immediate past but rather someone's story about what happened."[3]

My approach to this material—primarily daily news stories and editorials—is impressionistic yet thorough. One of my critical presuppositions is that the news media, within the structure of a highly organized bureaucracy, construct a reading of events and the social world in which they occur that is far from mimetic but that reflects (and reproduces) some of the assumptions, values, beliefs, and needs of its audiences. A close reading of approximately a year's worth of Black Sox scandal news items in myriad newspapers has solidified my belief that what appears in newsprint are usually "tissue-thin slices of reality," to use James W. Carey's wonderful phrase.[4] That is, the news does bear some semblance to what someone (perhaps a participant, an eyewitness, a spokesperson, an "expert," or the journalist) thinks has happened. Rather than suggest that those who construct the news are not adept at doing so—for they are—I presuppose that how journalists and editors craft the news is essential to understanding its cultural and historical significance. So although the news offers us privileged renditions of social reality, it does not offer us transparent, unproblematic versions of it.

The sources used to write this chapter were drawn almost exclusively from daily metropolitan newspapers, primarily papers in Chicago (for obvious reasons) and New York (which was, then as now, a significant site in the production of the news). But because I am interested in how regional perspectives differ from each other, as well as from more distant national views of the episode, I also sampled how the game-fixing scandal was reported in Atlanta, Boston, Cincinnati, Cleveland, Detroit, Kansas City, Pittsburgh, Los Angeles, New Orleans, and Washington, D.C.—that is, most cities that had a Major League team at the time and several that did not. Nonetheless, due to various constraints, I inevitably focus on a small and selective portion of the press coverage. As one would expect, not all the multiple voices in the American news media at the time are represented here, such as African American newspapers, the immigrant and foreign-language press, and socialist and labor papers. The media's treatment of the scandal was not monolithic and my history is not—and cannot be—comprehensive.[5]

Historical Contexts

The period immediately after World War I is often characterized as a time of unprecedented prosperity and wild consumption, hedonistic moral relativism and reckless irresponsibility—the "Roaring Twenties," the "Jazz Age," and the "Lawless Decade." The historian Daniel H. Borus notes that "the decade is known as a mélange of new fads and mores, uncontrolled consumption, and political conservatism. One can hardly envision the twenties without thinking of flappers, prohibition, bathtub gin, rumrunning, radio, movies, all manners of crazes (flagpole sitting remains inexplicable), petting, and fundamentalists."[6] Taken alone, this is, as Borus notes, a hackneyed, superficial, and misleading rendition. Despite (or because of) popular historical stereotypes, it is important to remember that the third decade of the twentieth century was an extraordinarily tumultuous period. During the early twenties American society entered a period of prosperity, transformation, and anxiety. While the modern era arguably debuted before World War I, the cataclysm of the war left much of the world fundamentally shaken.[7] For some artists and intellectuals, the unparalleled brutality of the conflict—over 25 million casualties, much of Europe devastated both physically and economically—signified the end of Western Civilization.[8] At the very least, an uncertain dawn had broken.

For many Americans, after the initial euphoria of the armistice, the immediate postwar period was a time of disappointment. Inflation, mass unemployment, labor disputes and strikes, a Red Scare and the suppression of civil liberties, and race riots in northern cities unsettled a triumphant country. There was also widespread uneasiness about population and urban growth, race and gender relations, increased urbanization and bureaucratization, and significant economic and technological changes.

Long before the war, metropolitan newspapers were firmly entrenched and powerful social and economic institutions. Mass media historians more or less agree that the modern newspaper took shape in the 1830s and 1840s.[9] But it was during the 1880s and 1890s, due in part to technological advances—such as the development of bigger, faster printing presses, cheaper paper production, and improved news gathering and distribution methods—and the aggressive competition among publishers such as Joseph Pulitzer, William Randolph Hearst, and Adolph Ochs, that newspapers emerged as preeminent cultural institutions. Moreover, many of them substantially enlarged their circulations; for example, Pulitzer's *New York World* increased its circulation from 15,000 in 1883 to 250,000 in just four years.[10] "Not only were individual papers growing bigger than ever before," notes the media critic and historian Andie Tucher, "they were beginning to look more like each other than ever before."[11] One result of the confluence of these and other forces was that by the turn of the century metropolitan newspapers enjoyed unprecedented hegemony over the construction and dissemination of information. Newspapers not only brought the world into view but also interpreted it for their readers. As the editor and popular historian Frederick Lewis Allen put it in 1922, newspapers "are the eyes through which largely we see the life of our times."[12]

By the twenties, the number of newspapers declined, but their overall circulation and social importance increased as newspaper chains and conglomerates dominated the industry.[13] Furthermore, the news reporting formulas established and employed by metropolitan papers provided models for provincial publishers and editors. Thus the mainstream popular press affected the news received by people who lived well beyond the reach of metropolitan circulations. As for sportswriting, though it had existed in various forms since the mid-nineteenth century, it was not until the early twenties—when sport itself was fulfilling increasingly significant social roles—that sports journalism became fully enmeshed in American culture.[14] By that time, the sports page, which had begun to take shape in the 1880s with the rise of "yellow journalism" and special Sunday editions, had evolved into a full-fledged sports section in most metropolitan daily newspapers and had transformed some of its most notable writers—Ring Lardner, Grantland Rice, Damon Runyon, and a few others—into national celebrities. The media historian Robert W. McChesney argues that by the twenties publishers and editors realized that sport aptly served their needs: it was ideologically nonthreatening, "did not antagonize any element of the desired readership," and "lent itself to all sorts of civic boosterism on the part of the newspaper. As sport gave cohesiveness and identity to a community, a newspaper's coverage and promotion of sport could be considered a significant contribution to its metropolis. Finally, coverage of sport never called into question the dominant social relations."[15] All of this suggests the influence metropolitan newspapers had in shaping the attitudes, values, and beliefs of many Americans. Despite the rapid growth of mass media forms such as the cinema, news magazines, and popular opinion magazines, the newspaper remained the nation's primary mass communication institution at the beginning of the twenties.

Concurrently, professional baseball was a well-established, widely popular social institution. "Probably at no other time," argues the historian Harold Seymour, "did baseball enjoy a stronger emotional grip upon Americans" than during the first decades of the twentieth century.[16] After nearly fifty years, professional baseball had finally achieved institutional stability and social acceptance. Less than three months before the White Sox and the Reds met in the 1919 World Series, the philosopher Morris R. Cohen argued in the *Dial* that baseball was the country's civil religion: "I know full well that baseball is a boy's game, and a professional sport, and that a properly cultured, serious person always feels like apologizing for attending a baseball game instead of a Strauss concert, or a lecture on the customs of the Fiji Islanders. But I still maintain that, by all the canons of our modern books on comparative religion, baseball is a religion, and the only one that is not sectarian but national."[17] In addition, the historian Steven A. Riess notes that by the twenties many people viewed baseball "as an edifying institution which taught traditional nineteenth-century frontier qualities, such as courage, honesty, individualism, patience, and temperance, as well as certain contemporary values, like teamwork."[18] According to the ideology that professional baseball promoted about itself, the game embodied the nation's pastoral heritage, self-reliant individualism, and democratic cooperation, and thus it conveyed traditional American values to its participants and spectators. Tremendously popular with people (mostly men and boys) from various regional, socioeconomic, and ethnic backgrounds, baseball "was probably more successful in helping socialize and integrate Americans than ever before," argues Riess.[19] Although baseball had to compete with college football and professional boxing for popular and media attention as American sport entered its so-called Golden Age, the game successfully retained its standing as the national pastime.

But like many things, baseball was not always what it claimed or appeared to be. The game could hardly be a fountainhead of democracy when African American players could not play with white men—to say nothing of the exclusion of women. Additionally, when baseball owners were confronted with an expensive work force, they essentially turned ballplayers into indentured servants via the infamous "reserve clause," a gentlemen's agreement codified in 1879 that effectively bound players to their teams indefinitely.[20] Just as important, the professional game's integrity was questioned long before the Black Sox scandal. Baseball and gambling had been allied from the beginning. In *The Fix Is In: A History of Baseball Gambling and Game Fixing Scandals* (1995), Daniel E. Ginsburg maintains: "Suspicion of 'fixes' began early in the 1860s, as the game grew in popularity."[21] Even before the National League was founded in 1876, professional gamblers plagued the game. In 1865, for example, three members of the New York Mutuals intentionally lost a game against Brooklyn's Eckford Club.[22] Twelve years later, the Louisville scandal, in which four members of the Louisville Grays confessed to conspiring with gamblers to lose games, "received tremendous play throughout the nation, and it was the first time that proof positive had been produced against players who were then forever expelled from the game."[23] Considering the baseball magnates' consistently shoddy treatment of their employees, it should not be surprising that baseball games were fixed before the 1919 series. Riess puts the matter succinctly: "A substantial disparity existed between the ideology of baseball, which sought to present the sport in the best possible context, and the realities of the game. The baseball creed constituted a cultural fiction; that is, the baseball ideology was regarded as an accurate description of the sport, and, even though it was inaccurate, the conventional wisdom influenced the way people behaved and thought. It did not matter that the ideology strayed from the truth."[24] It is in these social and cultural contexts that the Black Sox scandal and its earliest narratives are best understood.

Hugh Fullerton and Harbingers of Scandal

On October 9, 1919, shortly after the White Sox outfielder Joe Jackson grounded out to the Reds second baseman Morrie Rath to end the World Series, Hugh Fullerton—a diligent, inquisitive, widely respected reporter—set about making his deadline for the *Chicago Herald and Examiner.* First, however, Fullerton apparently met briefly with the White Sox owner, Charles A. Comiskey, and the White Sox manager, William "Kid" Gleason, in Comiskey's office. "Some years before," writes Eliot Asinof in *Eight Men Out: The Black Sox and the 1919 World Series* (1963), "Comiskey had given Fullerton his first job and he felt a great loyalty to him. So it was not just to get a story that he went to the Old Roman's office after the final game: he wanted to share Comiskey's grief."[25] Fullerton had predicted that the White Sox would beat the Reds, five games to three; that he was wrong was no doubt irksome, since he had a reputation as a knowledgeable sports prognosticator. Not long after he had made his prediction, but before the games began, Fullerton and his fellow scribes heard rumors that the series was fixed. Agitated and fearful, Fullerton enlisted the assistance of the former New

York Giants pitching great Christy Mathewson, who was covering the series for the *New York World.* "They arranged to sit together in the press box and go over every doubtful play," notes Asinof. "And just for the record, Fullerton decided he would pencil a circle on his score card around every play that was really suspect."[26] By the end of the series, Fullerton had identified seven questionable plays. It is unclear what exactly was said in Comiskey's office that October afternoon. The following day Fullerton warned in his column: "There will be a great deal written and talked about this world's series. There will be a lot of inside stuff that never will be printed, but the truth will remain that the team which was the hardest working, which fought hardest, and which stuck together to the end won. The team which excelled in mechanical skill, which had the ability, individually, to win, was beaten." Superb teamwork and effort had overcome the odds (which were unusually volatile just before the series began) and a seemingly superior opponent. The White Sox played so poorly, Fullerton wrote, "that an evil minded person might believe the stories that have been circulated during the series. The fact is that this series was lost in the first game, and lost through over confidence. Forget the suspicious and evil minded yarns that may be circulated." The Reds were not really the better team, Fullerton stressed, but "they play ball together, fight together and hustle together, and remember that a flivver that keeps running beats a Rolls Royce that is missing several cylinders." Despite these attempts to explain the Reds' victory, Fullerton did hint that something was amiss with the series. "Yesterday's game in all probability is the last that ever will be played in any world's series," wrote Fullerton cryptically. "If the club owners and those who have the interests of the game at heart have listened during this series they will call off the annual inter-league contests." Finally, Fullerton assured his readers that, despite a strong nucleus, the White Sox would field a significantly different team in 1920: "There are seven men on the team who will not be there when the gong sounds next Spring and some of them will not be in either major league." Fullerton did not elaborate or explain, but added that the "unbeaten faction of the beaten White Sox did not quit."[27] Purposefully oblique, Fullerton stopped short of suggesting that another faction had conspired to lose the series.

Months passed, the baseball establishment did not take Fullerton's warnings seriously, and nothing was done to quell the rumors. Fullerton persisted.[28] He wrote an impassioned series of articles charging that Major League Baseball was in the throes of a crisis. Unable to convince the *Chicago Herald and Examiner* to publish his articles—they were apparently deemed too risky to publish, in part due to libel laws and in part because upending baseball's image as a hallowed national institution might hinder the sale of newspapers—Fullerton eventually convinced editors at Joseph Pulitzer's *New York Evening World* to run them. On December 15, as the baseball magnates conducted their winter meetings, page three of the *New York Evening World* blared: "Is Big League Baseball Being Run for Gamblers, with the Players in the Deal?" Fullerton declared:

> Professional baseball has reached a crisis. The major leagues, both owners and players, are on trial. Charges of crookedness among the owners, accusations of cheating, of tampering with each other's teams, with attempting to syndicate and control baseball, are bandied about openly. Charges that gamblers have succeeded in bribing ballplayers, that games have been bought and sold, that players are in the pay of professional gamblers and that even the World's Series was tampered with are made without attempt at refutation by the men who have their fortunes invested in baseball.

Fullerton put the matter bluntly: "The time has come for straight talk. How can club owners expect writers, editors and fans to have any faith in them or their game if they make no effort to clean up the scandal?" Although he noted that numerous problems plagued professional baseball, Fullerton maintained that the "most serious assaults on the good name of the game have been made during and since the World's Series between the Reds and the White Sox. In Chicago, St. Louis and other cities the stories have been discussed, names used, alleged facts stated until half the people believe there was something wrong with the series." Certainly Fullerton took such talk seriously. He noted that the "public has for years had little faith and much disgust in the officials and club owners of the major league clubs. But never before have players been so freely charged with cheating." Rather than lend credence to the allegations of malfeasance on the part of the ballplayers, Fullerton argued that the "fault for this condition lies primarily with the owners. Their commercialism is directly responsible for the same spirit among the athletes and their failure to punish even the appearance of evil has led to the present situation, for the entire scandal could have been prevented and the future of the game made safe by drastic action in the Hal Chase case."[29] (In 1918, Chase, a talented but notoriously corrupt first baseman, was suspended for allegedly betting on a game and attempting to bribe a teammate. During the off-season, National League president John Heydler acquitted and reinstated Chase due to a lack of evidence.)[30]

Careful not to directly accuse anyone of wrongdoing, Fullerton wrote that others had charged "that several members of the Chicago White Sox team entered into a conspiracy with certain gamblers to throw the series. I have steadfastly refused to believe this possible. Some of the men whose names are used are my friends and men I would trust anywhere, yet the story is told openly, with so much circumstantial evidence and with so many names, places and dates, that one is bewildered." Bewildered though he may have been, Fullerton concluded quite reasonably: "If these men are guilty, they should be expelled as Patrick expelled the snakes and [William] Hulbert [the former president of the National League] expelled the baseball crooks of years ago. If they are innocent, they should be allowed to prove it, and the persons who are responsible for the charges should be driven out of the sport forever."[31] Despite Fullerton's challenge and despite how "widely read" were the articles, notes the historian David Q. Voigt, the pieces "were discounted as improbable muckraking. One critic objected that Fullerton was 'always scoffing at the honesty of an institution, no matter how sacred.'"[32] This response is relatively mild compared with how some people reacted to Fullerton's articles. In fact, his stories provoked a firestorm of rebuttals from the baseball establishment.[33]

In retrospect, it is clear that no one wrote more prescient and influential articles about the 1919 World Series and the Black Sox scandal than Hugh Fullerton. For one thing, he was correct: something was amiss with the World Series and a great deal would be written about it, probably more than he could have imagined. Furthermore, Fullerton's stories remind us that it matters who writes our news. More than just observers or go-betweens for a reading public or cogs in the bureaucracy that manufactures news, reporters are often implicated—sometimes subtly, sometimes more explicitly—in the construction of the events they cover. Like other storytellers, reporters are often an integral part of the narratives they tell. In addition, a reporter's authority frequently endures and inevitably shapes the ways in which events are later understood. In this way reporters are actively involved in the production of history. As one critic argues: "The popular historians of baseball are the journalists, figures of such power that it can be said, fairly, that the history of baseball is more their story than the story of those who played the game."[34] If this is the case, perhaps Fullerton deserves even more credit than he is usually given for his role in exposing the Big Fix. Not only did Fullerton's stories anticipate the game-fixing revelations—indeed, his stories helped bring the conspiracy to the public—but they also position us to examine how the event was narrated by the media at the time. His stories began the process of crafting the scandal as a tragic morality play (as opposed to a comedy or an inconsequential human interest story), as an unfolding drama that mattered to much of the nation. Regardless of how improbable they may have seemed to some people, Fullerton's stories were auspicious harbingers of things to come.[35]

Seeing the Scandal

In many ways the Black Sox scandal provides us with a fine example of an ideal news story, for it combined "celebrity with scandal in an action that can be simply stated but provides the possibility of endless speculation."[36] The World Series game-fixing affair had all of the above, which explains why from late September 1920 to early August 1921 millions of words were written about it in newspapers all over the country. Yet when reports about the alleged game fixing first broke in late September 1920, people did not actually need to read the stories to understand its importance: they could immediately *see* its significance. In the beginning, accounts of the thrown games and the clandestine meetings between the ballplayers and gamblers were not relegated to the sports section—they were printed on the front page, often in conjunction with bold, banner headlines. For approximately a week in late September and early October, the size of the headlines—one of the most obvious ways the hierarchy of news is expressed—proclaimed the event's significance, at least within the context of the newspaper. There is, of course, some truth to the old adage that "a headline is not an act of journalism, it is an act of marketing."[37] But that does not really matter here. What is important is that daily newspapers made it clear—visually—that the baseball scandal mattered.

One way this was conveyed was by giving the game-fixing stories the most prominent space in the newspaper. On September 29, 1920, the day after Cicotte and Jackson testified before the Cook County grand jury, many newspapers used headline sizes usually reserved for the outbreak of war or the assassination of a prominent political leader. (In this way the press coverage of the World Series scandal can be viewed as part of a continuum of spectacular coverage rather than as a singular phenomenon.) The *New York Times*, "the closest thing America had to a national newspaper," proclaimed across its three far-right columns: "EIGHT WHITE SOX PLAYERS ARE INDICTED ON CHARGE OF FIXING 1919 WORLD SERIES; CICOTTE GOT $10,000 AND JACKSON $5,000."[38] That same day, the *New York Tribune* ran the following headline across the right half of its front page: "Eight White Sox Are Indicted; Cicotte and Jackson Confess Gamblers Paid Them $15,000." The *New York World*, which Joseph Pulitzer had made hugely successful, printed "CICOTTE AND JACKSON BARE SALE OF GAMES; 8 WHITE SOX INDICTED" on top of its two far-right columns. Not to be outdone, the upstart *New York Daily News*, which proclaimed itself to be "New York's Picture Newspaper," ran the headline "EDDIE CICOTTE ADMITS BRIBE" all the way across its front page; it also printed individual photographs of the eight implicated ballplayers.

Of course, the scandal was big news in places besides New York City. The *Boston Daily Globe* provided photographs of the "Eight Alleged Baseball Crooks" while its headline—"TWO WHITE SOX STARS ADMIT THROWING BIG 1919 SERIES"—ran across two-thirds of its front page. The *Baltimore Sun* announced in bold, capital letters: "TWO WHITE SOX PLAYERS CONFESS; 8 ARE INDICTED; COMISKEY CLEANS OUT TEAM." The front page of the September 28, 1920, evening edition of the *Atlanta Journal* proclaimed: "8 WHITE SOX PLAYERS INDICTED." The *New Orleans Times-Picayune* headline the following day declared: "EDDIE CICOTTE AND JOE JACKSON CONFESS GREATEST SCANDAL IN BASEBALL HISTORY." (It should be noted that in some cities the game-fixing news was regarded more coolly. The *Washington Post* resisted some of the hype; its September 29 headline occupied only one column and simply read "SOX STARS ARE HELD." Three thousand miles to the west, the *Los Angeles Times* merely reported, "White Sox Indicted.")

But in Chicago, as one would expect considering that thousands of local readers had a partisan interest, the headlines on September 29 were extraordinary. The front page of the *Chicago Tribune,* which immodestly referred to itself as "The World's Greatest Newspaper," screamed "TWO SOX CONFESS" in huge letters; to the right, a subheading read, "Eight Indicted; Inquiry Goes On." The *Chicago Herald and Examiner,* owned by William Randolph Hearst and one of the *Chicago Tribune*'s leading rivals, matched the *Tribune* headline for headline. In enormous letters across the entire front page, the *Herald and Examiner* headline exclaimed: "EIGHT SOX INDICTED CICOTTE AND JACKSON CONFESS COMISKEY SUSPENDS 7 STAR PLAYERS." That same day, the *Chicago Daily News,* another of Chicago's well-established papers, proclaimed in its late edition, all the way across the front page, "FELSCH, WILLIAMS CONFESS; INDICT FIXERS." To further impress upon its readers the significance of the indictments, the *Chicago Daily News* published a cartoon entitled "The Harvest Moon" in the middle of its front page. The cartoon depicts approximately a dozen shadowy figures ("gamblers" and "crooks") carrying sacks (with dollar signs on them) over their shoulders; surveying the scene, with surprise and dismay, is an anthropomorphized moon marked with baseball seams.

Not surprisingly, newspaper headlines emphasized local connections to the scandal whenever possible. The *Cleveland Plain Dealer* viewed the affair in terms of its effect on the Indians, who were in a tight race with the White Sox for the 1920 pennant. "JACKSON AND CICOTTE ADMIT GUILT," exclaimed its September 29, 1920, headline, "CLEVELAND ALMOST SURE OF PENNANT." Elsewhere, community newspapers noted roles their native sons may have played in the game fixing. The *Boston Daily Globe* announced on its front page, "JURY INDICTS BOSTON MAN," a reference to the gambler Joseph "Sport" Sullivan. The day before, the *Des Moines Register* had reported, "DES MOINES GAMBLERS IN SOX RAID," a reference to David Zelcer (sometimes spelled Zelser), who was apparently an associate of some of the men who allegedly carried out the conspiracy.[39]

These examples suggest that for people who only had time to glance at their morning newspaper over breakfast or who hurriedly passed by newsstands, there was no uncertainty about the day's lead story. The Black Sox scandal was literally bigger news than the upcoming presidential election or the political violence in Ireland. Newspaper headlines, in other words, signified that the game-fixing revelations were scandalous and that the unfolding events were a major civic spectacle and catastrophe.

In addition to dramatic, attention-grabbing headlines, most newspapers underlined the importance of the scandal via other visual signifiers. At first, newspapers were littered with photographs and cartoons about the affair. For most of the week leading up to the indictments the *Chicago Tribune* published photographs of Charles Comiskey, American League president Ban Johnson, many of the players alleged to have participated in the fix, and the Cook County grand jury.[40] The populist-minded *Chicago Herald and Examiner* printed even more photographs than its cross-town rival. The day after Cicotte's confession, the *New York Tribune* published individual portraits of all the implicated players.[41] That same day, the *Cincinnati Enquirer,* the *New Orleans Times-Picayune,* the *Cleveland Plain Dealer,* and the *Boston Daily Globe* featured a cluster of players' portraits on their front pages. While these (and other) photos certainly augmented the written texts they accompanied, they should be viewed as another category of news that further promoted the Big Fix as a singular and sensational moment.

Many cartoons devoted to the episode performed a similar function in late September and early October. The *Chicago Tribune,* for example, printed a "before-and-after" cartoon on its front page. In its first panel (subtitled "Our National Sport as It Has Been Regarded"), two men, obviously enjoying themselves, are at a baseball game. One says to the other: "The beauty about baseball is that it's always been kept straight and clean." In the second panel ("It Now Joins the 'Black Eye Club'") a bruised and battered anthropomorphized baseball is being introduced to other social outcasts: a black-eyed boxer, a jockey, a politician, and a financier. The same paper has another notable illustration. "It May Sicken Him of That Dish" portrays a nervous-looking fan preparing to spoon a hard-boiled egg (labeled "Organized Baseball") whose foul smell (the words *gambling* and *scandal* emanate from the cracked egg) gives him nervous pause.[42] The *Chicago Herald and Examiner* published a cartoon featuring a fan gasping as a baseball-headed figure falls off the pedestal of clean sport.[43] The *New York Tribune* printed an elaborate four-paneled cartoon featuring a man wearing glasses reading his newspaper at a breakfast table. Unperturbed by headlines of "fixes" in government and finance, the bespectacled man is outraged by the rumors that baseball games were fixed.[44] The *St. Louis Star* ran a cartoon with a cigar-chomping gambler digging a grave for baseball's coffin. In the background, headstones for boxing and horse racing loom prominently.[45] Like the photos, these cartoons alerted readers that the baseball scandal was important and deserved their attention.

The Color of Scandal

The World Series game-fixing scandal also owed some of its prominence to the poetry of its sobriquet: the Black Sox scandal. Even people who had only a dim sense of baseball or the World Series affair could (and still do) sense the ignominy of the phrase. Though it is difficult to pinpoint the precise origin of the expression, the phrase merits consideration. One of the first times it appeared was on October 1, 1920, in the *Chicago Herald and Examiner,* where it was used in the headline to Charles Dryden's sports column: "Here's Hope for Black Sox Let 'Em Grow Beards and Change Names."[46] Dryden, it is worth noting, did not use the expression in his column, which suggests that it was probably the creation of an editor or a production worker at the newspaper.

The expression gained currency as the scandal dragged on. In the fall of 1920 it was used sporadically, but by the spring and summer of 1921 newspapers nationwide used it regularly. From the outset, however, nearly every journalist, editorialist, and cartoonist who reported or commented on the story represented the implicated players and the scandal in terms of *blackness.* Newspapers consistently referred to the implicated ballplayers as "black sheep" and to the day that Cicotte and Jackson testified as "baseball's black day."[47] "Any kind of gambling on baseball is bad," said the noted Broadway celebrity George M. Cohan (who reportedly lost money on the series), "and this affair has given the game a mighty bad black eye."[48] A few days later, the *Chicago Daily News* ran a cartoon on its front page entitled "Contrast in Black and White" in which a batter (labeled an "Honest Ballplayer") is at home plate with a giant black splotch (labeled "Scandal Blot") behind him.[49] The semiotics of the word *black* are not difficult to perceive in these examples. In its long-standing Western cultural tradition, the word *black* has unmistakably pejorative connotations: it signifies corruption, immorality, and guilt. It is a readily available cultural marker and metaphor for depravity.[50] Furthermore, the consistent use of blackness to describe the scandal and those implicated in it drew upon (and reproduced) racist uses of language, despite the fact that *colored* and *Negro* were the words most commonly used to describe African American people at the time. Dependent upon conventional tropes and characterizations, the press certainly used them when reporting on the scandal.

Cleanliness and Contamination

Since the implicated White Sox players supposedly "blackened" baseball's reputation, it is not surprising that there were so many allusions in the media to "cleaning up" the game. At one point or another, virtually every commentator used this idea. Neither a cliché nor a dead metaphor, the cleanliness trope was one of the primary ways people—reporters, participants, and readers—made sense of the episode. These calls to cleanse baseball need to be understood within the broader context of the "cleanliness craze" led by progressive reformers, who inherited the impulse from their Victorian forebears. Today, Upton Sinclair's famous muckraking novel *The Jungle* (1906), which exposed the horrors of the Chicago meat-packing industry and spurred its reform, is one of the best-known examples of this impulse. By the beginning of the twentieth century, writes Suellen Hoy in *Chasing Dirt: The American Pursuit of Cleanliness* (1995), "middle-class Americans idealized cleanliness as their 'great virtue.'"[51] Twenty years later, by the time of the Black Sox scandal, Hoy maintains that "public and private cleanliness were the American norm, ubiquitously honored if not everywhere faithfully practiced."[52] Certainly those concerned with the well-being of baseball evoked the rhetoric of cleanliness, even before the scandal was revealed.

On September 19, 1920, the *Chicago Tribune* published a letter written by Fred Loomis, a respected local businessman and "one of Chicago's most enthusiastic baseball followers." Loomis, like many baseball fans, wanted to know if there was any substance to the widespread and persistent rumors that the White Sox had deliberately lost the series. Startled by the rumors, Loomis wrote: "Up to this time baseball has been accepted by the public as the one clean sport above reproach in every particular and engaged in by men, both owners and players, whose honesty and integrity have been beyond suspicion or reproach." To protect baseball's sanctity, Loomis argued, "the game must be cleaned up and it must be cleaned up at once."[53] On the same page was an article that complemented Loomis's letter. "During the last few months," the *Chicago Tribune* reported, "a number of [White Sox] players, feeling the sting of this distrust of their faith and integrity, have expressed a desire to have the entire affair cleaned up so that the innocent ones may be restored to good standing and the guilty, if any, be expelled."[54] In many ways, these responses—and many of those to follow—were appropriate. For as the anthropologist Mary Douglas argues: "Dirt offends against order. Eliminating it is not a negative movement, but a positive effort to organise the environment."[55] The implicated ballplayers, in other words, had so stained the national pastime that the lords of the game, the press, and some of the public supported their expulsion.

During September and October 1920, newspapers all over the country consistently used the metaphor of "cleaning up" the national pastime. Two days before Cicotte and Jackson testified before the Cook County grand jury, Harvey Woodruff, the sports editor of the *Chicago Tribune,* wrote: "Seldom has a grand jury been intrusted with a greater responsibility. Baseball, as the national sport, is worth all this effort to keep it clean and wholesome—free from all crookedness."[56] The following day, both the *New York Times* and the *New York Tribune* followed suit. "The game itself will suffer temporarily as a result of the public's confidence being shaken," the *New York Times* editors observed, "but the sport will thrive under cleaner conditions."[57] The sports columnist W. O. M'Geehan of the *New York Tribune* maintained: "All sportsmen, all lovers of clean sport, hope that the investigation will be thorough and carried through until it is settled for once and all as to whether or not the series" was fixed. M'Geehan was forthright about the matter: "The game must be cleaned up," he insisted.[58] Two days later, the *New York World* contended that the public "had always believed that baseball was a clean sport. It will not return to that belief until it knows that the last taint has been removed."[59] This was abundantly clear to the baseball magnates.

The baseball establishment repeatedly expressed concern for cleanliness within its ranks. Hard hit by the game-fixing revelations, Comiskey announced: "I would rather close my ball-park than send nine men on the field with one of them holding a dishonest thought toward clean baseball."[60] "I am willing to do anything I can to clean up the game," insisted John McGraw, the fiery manager of the New York Giants. "I think it is the duty of managers to clean up their own clubs."[61] John Heydler, president of the National League and the man who, just the year before, had cleared the corrupt first baseman Hal Chase to play for the New York Giants, avowed: "Baseball must be cleaned at any cost."[62] Ban Johnson, president of the

American League and a Comiskey nemesis, said of the scandal: "I'm glad it's all cleaned up."[63] (Johnson spoke wishfully and prematurely, for the resolution would not come for almost a year.) Some in the press viewed this indignation and righteousness with circumspection. The *Cincinnati Enquirer,* for instance, printed a cartoon in which a Cook County grand juror is sweeping "gambling filth" out of a doorway marked "Organized Baseball." To the left, Heydler (who is holding "The Old [Hal] Chase White Wash Brush") and Johnson look on in surprise as Johnson says, "Oh, dear, oh, dear, I never dreamt of it!"[64] Later, as the legal system continued to pursue the allegations, the syndicated columnist Damon Runyon wryly observed, "As long as the affair is out of baseball hands there is hope that it will eventually be thoroughly cleaned up."[65] (At the time, Judge Kenesaw Mountain Landis had not yet been given baseball's reins.)

Several men associated with the Cook County baseball investigation also employed the cleanliness trope. Henry Brigham, the grand jury foreman, declared: "I hope the cleaning process of this investigation will extend to all the sore spots in the sporting world."[66] Less than a week later, Judge Charles McDonald, who presided over the investigation, intoned: "I believe you men [the grand jurors and prosecutors] are doing a patriotic duty in cleaning up the baseball situation."[67] In fact, the discourse of cleanliness was so pervasive that some ballplayers used it. Eddie Cicotte testified that taking "that dirty, crooked money" caused him "hours of mental torture" and left him "with an unclean mind." Keeping his secret, deceiving "the boys who had stayed straight and clean and honest," was excruciating, said Cicotte. Possibly speaking metaphorically, Joe Jackson testified that the $5,000 he received was given to him in a "dirty envelope."[68]

The conventional wisdom of the day was that a dirty, unkempt house was an affront to decency and bred vice and that baseball demanded better, cleaner accommodations. The *Washington Post* editors were hopeful that a "drastic housecleaning throughout the baseball world would quickly follow any proof of wrongdoing."[69] In the Queen City of the West, the *Cincinnati Enquirer* reported that the "grand jury has shown that baseball needs a thorough house cleaning from top to bottom."[70] Similar sentiment was expressed elsewhere in Ohio. The *Cleveland Plain Dealer,* which noted that the scandal "puts no stain upon Cleveland's achievement of winning this year's league pennant," further editorialized: "Unless the national game be given a house-cleaning from top to bottom, unless every crooked influence is rooted out and kept out, baseball, popular as it is today, will not long survive the shock of these disclosures."[71] Frightened by the media and public outcry, team owners accelerated their reorganization of the game's governing structure. An opponent of any plan that would limit his authority, Ban Johnson sought delays: "I believe in a thorough housecleaning before starting to remodel the house."[72] Despite his protestations and warnings—Johnson apparently described Judge Landis as a "pompous fraud"—the team owners remodeled their house anyway and installed Landis as its sole commissioner, thereby effectively leaving Johnson out in the cold.[73]

For almost a year, the press reiterated these metaphors and images. In June 1921, a few weeks before the trial began, Landis proclaimed: "Honesty in baseball is necessary for its continuance as the great American game and it must be kept clean at all hazards."[74] During the trial, one prosecutor argued that "Comiskey wants to keep the game clean for the American public and I tell you now that if the owners don't get busy when rottenness crops out baseball won't last long." Like many others, he contended that the indicted ballplayers had "dragged the game through the mire and in their blindness deliberately fouled their own nest."[75] Clearly, for many Americans in the early twenties, cleanliness and "whiteness" equaled virtue.

Since the implicated ballplayers had allegedly soiled themselves and their profession, the authorities believed they had to be laundered to cleanse the national pastime. One defense attorney noted: "This trial is a laundry for the American League and it wants the jury to run the washing machine."[76] To the prosecution's consternation, the jury did not cooperate: on August 2, 1921, the indicted ballplayers and gamblers were acquitted of all charges. The *New York Daily News* headline blared "BLACK SOX WASHED WHITE" all the way across its front page.[77] The Associated Press declared that the Black Sox had been "laundered officially."[78] The *Atlanta Journal* sports columnist Morgan Blake insisted that, rather than being truly laundered, "the Dirty Sox were only dry cleaned. The perfume remains."[79] Two days after the trial, the *Chicago Daily News* printed a cartoon on its front page entitled "A Difference of Opinion." A heavy-set woman (whose back has the lettering "Jury Verdict") attempts to bring "Clean and White" laundry (also labeled the "Ex-Sox") into a house. Blocking her entry to the door is Landis, who proclaims: "They look just th' same to me as they did before."[80] The *New York Times* editors responded to the acquittal with sarcasm: "The Chicago Sox are once more whiter than snow. A jury has said that they are not guilty, so that settles that."[81] Despite being acquitted, the Black Sox were widely considered polluters. Moreover, they were doubly depraved, for they not only crossed the line that demarcated propriety and sportsmanship from illegitimacy and corruption but also endangered the integrity of others via guilt by association.

For many in the press and the baseball establishment, the threat of contamination was palpable. Gambling and corruption (as opposed to an exploitative labor arrangement and poor working conditions) were the dreaded diseases plaguing professional baseball and contaminating an otherwise healthy and admirable national institution. (This, of course, was a convenient fiction.) Nearly a year before the World Series game-fixing rumors were substantiated, one noted baseball writer, John B. Sheridan, argued that any ballplayer who would throw a game would "infect the entire fabric of baseball."[82] Crooked ballplayers and gamblers, the *Sporting News* editorialized (almost three months before the scandal broke), were poisoning baseball's system.[83] After the game fixing was made public, the *Brooklyn Eagle* simply described the scandal as "a nauseous mess that for a moment beclouds the greatest professional sport in the world."[84]

That "moment" would last for over a year and the press continued to use contamination metaphors, as if professional baseball were a sick organism in need of dramatic, life-saving treatment. The *New York Times*, for example, remarked: "Let whatever rottenness that has infested the game be brought into public view that it may be the better eradicated."[85] Once the source of baseball's contamination was identified—and there was virtually unanimous agreement that it was gambling—pundits promptly set about offering remedies. The consensus was that baseball needed to be purged and purified. Editors at the *Chicago Tribune* maintained that if the Cook County grand jurors and prosecutors "can purge the game of any taint of scandal they will have accomplished a great deal."[86] For its part, the *Chicago Herald and Examiner* tried to reassure its readers: "The courage and prompt action of baseball owners will, let us hope, save the game from the cancerous blight of professional gambling."[87] Ever the moralist, Ban Johnson insisted: "Baseball must be cleaned of all the poison that was injected into its system by a few petty gamblers and several easily tempted players, and I will not rest content until the general public says of the national game that the wound has been thoroughly healed and the guilty have been sufficiently punished."[88] Baseball, "infected with fraud," according to the *Detroit Free Press*, could not sustain its hold on the national imagination, and thus its profitability, unless it underwent some type of purification.[89] To reconstitute its status as a symbolically significant national institution, Major League Baseball had to excise the "dangerous lesion" afflicting it.[90]

The Great Double Cross

One of the most influential ways the media conveyed the Black Sox scandal to readers was as a crime story of seemingly epic proportions. Narrating the event in this manner brought the principals and issues into dramatic focus and effectively simplified a complicated episode. Nonfiction crime stories (to say nothing of detective and mystery stories) had already been selling well in the United States for more than a hundred years.[91] According to Andie Tucher, crime news was a staple of the penny press in the 1830s because "it was easy and inexpensive to gather; it was pleasant and familiar to readers already conversant with street literature; it provided New Yorkers [and others] with useful and important information about the way their city worked; and it would meet no serious competition from the established press."[92] Soon thereafter the established press began in earnest to publish crime stories, which no doubt contributed to mounting circulation rates. By the twenties, two veteran journalists agreed that crime "is the most interesting of all news themes—judged by circulation gains and popular interest."[93] In this way, as in many others, the media's treatment of the World Series scandal should be viewed as part of a continuum rather than as a break from tradition. Still, the Big Fix was an exemplary crime narrative. It had all the necessary components of the conventional crime story formula: calculating villains (the implicated ballplayers and the professional gamblers), unsuspecting victims (Comiskey, boys, and the nation), and virtuous heroes (the journalists, the prosecutors, the baseball officials and players who were trying to get to the bottom of the scandal); it had a dastardly deed (the manipulation of a nearly sacred national institution), a tearful confession (Eddie Cicotte apparently wept on the stand), and an uncertain conclusion (it was unclear if the game-fixing and conspiracy allegations could be proven in court).

First and foremost, the language the press used to tell the "story of the most gigantic sporting swindle in the history of America," as the *New York Tribune* put it, made it clear that the Black Sox affair was *the* crime story of the moment.[94] The *Chicago Tribune* described the tale told by one of the fix's many bit players as "a drama that a scenario writer might well name 'The Great Double Cross.'"[95] Cliff Abbo of the *New Orleans Times-Picayune* wrote that the affair was "one of the most colossal attempts at wholesale burglary perpetrated by any clique of gamblers or dishonest participants."[96] The nationally syndicated sportswriter Grantland Rice, who exerted a great deal of influence in shaping preferred ways of understanding American sport, opined that the individuals "mixed up in this crookedness are worse than thieves and burglars. They are the ultimate scum of the universe, and even the spotted civilization of the present time has no place for them outside of a penitentiary."[97] Clearly beyond the pale of respectable society, the indicted ballplayers and gamblers were quickly vilified and transformed into national objects of disgrace. "Some degree of respect can be entertained for a thief in the night when compared with this collection of so-called humans," continued Abbo. "It is like the comparison of the sweet-scented lilac with the fetid, decomposed carcass of a skunk."[98] The men caught up in the Big Fix were thought to be so heinous, so despicable, that many journalists were compelled to evoke historical analogies to convey their presumed treachery.

More than any other historical figure, Benedict Arnold was invoked to describe the perpetrators. A notable story carried all over the country reported that a coterie of newsboys in Boston had condemned "the Chicago baseball players whose corruption in the last world series, they said, struck a 'murderous blow at the kids' game.'" The newsboys, who probably expressed the sentiment of many others, referred to the implicated players as "the Benedict Arnolds of baseball."[99] Morgan Blake of the *Atlanta Journal* added: "Every ball player who is honest, every fan who loves the game for the game's sake will always despise them. In the history of the game they will be likened to Judas and Benedict Arnold. The most contemptible character on earth is the man who betrays his friends."[100] The next day, Charles Dryden, the sports columnist of the *Chicago Herald and Examiner,* "hand-picked [a] Benedict Arnold All-Star team" comprised mostly of the accused White Sox players, and the *Pittsburgh Post* ran a story entitled "'Benedict Arnolds' of Baseball Slink from View of Oldtimers, Who Can't Believe Disclosures."[101] Months later, during the criminal trial, the *Chicago Herald and Examiner* ran a photograph of men and boys in the courtroom listening to testimony that portrayed "their heroes of the diamond as worse than Benedict Arnold or Judas Iscariot."[102] Like Benedict Arnold and Judas, the Black Sox were loathed (arguably inordinately) in part because they had been trusted and admired by those they had betrayed.

Because crime stories call for justice, the Black Sox scandal ended up in a courtroom, even though State's Attorney Maclay Hoyne admitted from the beginning that he was "uncertain whether any crime has been committed."[103] Legal action was taken largely because of the perception that the public demanded it. After months of delay, and after weeks of exasperating jury selection, the Black Sox trial finally commenced in mid-July 1921.[104] Many months before, George Phair of the *Chicago Herald and Examiner* penned a poem in anticipation of the trial:

> The game of ball will soon be heard
> Throughout the favored land
> The umpire soon will raise his voice
> And issue his command
> The batter soon will amble up
> And take the witness stand.[105]

On the last point at least, Phair was wrong: none of the accused men testified on his own behalf. And despite the confessions and waivers of immunity proffered by three indicted players before the grand jury the previous fall—which had mysteriously disappeared by the time the case came to trial—the prosecution had difficulty establishing that a criminal conspiracy had occurred.[106] As one defense attorney argued: "It is true there has been some evidence of transactions with gamblers, but to find the defendants guilty the state had to establish there was a conspiracy, as the indictments charged. And this they have signally failed to do."[107] The presiding judge, Hugo M. Friend, instructed the jury that the law required proof of intent to defraud the public and the alleged victims identified in the indictments, not just of intent to throw baseball games. After the jury acquitted all the charged ballplayers and gamblers, the *Chicago Tribune* reported that "the verdict was greeted with cheers" and that the courtroom "was like a love feast" due to all the handshaking, back slapping, and other public displays of affection.[108] The celebration, it would turn out, was premature.

Since the press constructed the fixed World Series as a crime story—even if technically a crime had not been committed—it made perfect sense that a federal judge was given the last word. Immediately after the verdict was announced, Landis declared: "Regardless of the verdict of juries, no player who throws a ball game, no player that undertakes or promises to throw a ball game, no player that sits in a conference with a bunch of crooked players and gamblers where the ways and means of throwing a game are discussed, and does not promptly tell his club about it, will ever play professional baseball."[109] That said, Landis eliminated the affair's irksome loose ends and gave the incident some closure. Although he did not investigate the alleged crime or preside over the case, Landis effectively "solved" the problem the acquittals presented the baseball establishment. Through his action the verdict became an acquittal only in a technical sense. Not surprisingly, Landis was widely hailed for his decisive action. "Judge Landis took his position to give organized baseball a character bath," the *Chicago Tribune* editors observed. "With the Black Sox back in the game the bath would have looked worse than if it had been drawn from the Missouri river in flood time."[110] That same day, the *Cleveland Plain Dealer* noted that the "thanks of the baseball world are due Judge Landis for his prompt declaration."[111] In a similar vein, the *Cincinnati Enquirer* printed a cartoon with the eight Black Sox, dripping with "Legal Whitewash," huddled on a rock in the middle of the ocean. Landis, on a ship named *Organized Baseball,* is sailing away in the distance and says, "Not a chance."[112]

Writing in a different context, the literary critic Peter Hühm notes that most "detective stories start out with a community in a state of stable order. Soon a crime (usually a murder) occurs, which the police are unable to clear up. The insoluble crime acts as a destabilizing event, because the system of norms and rules regulating life in the community has proved powerless in one crucial instance and is therefore discredited."[113] It is not difficult to transpose this schema onto the Black Sox scandal. Professional baseball had been trying hard to promote itself as a stable, virtuous national institution reflecting all that was good in American society. Then, seemingly from nowhere, a heinous and apparently aberrant development was revealed. Try as they might, the legal authorities could not effectively solve the credibility problems this "destabilizing event" produced. In this way the Big Fix, like many formulaic crime stories Hühm discusses, became an occasion to reconstitute order and power, and it provided openings for various ideological reaffirmations.

Finally, Hühm argues that after the authorities admit that the crime (and the criminal) has stumped them, "the detective takes over the case, embarks on a course of thorough investigations, and finally identifies the criminal, explaining his solution at length," and in the process "restores the disrupted social order and reaffirms the validity of the system of norms."[114] At first glance, it might appear that Hugh Fullerton played this role, but in the end Fullerton did not have much power to exert. Furthermore, most of Fullerton's colleagues were not interested in giving him his fair share of credit for bringing the affair to light. Instead, for many in the media, Judge Landis was a far more convenient and attractive hero, particularly as the scandal approached its uncertain conclusion. When the episode was in need of closure, Landis provided it with a dramatic flourish—thus ending what a Chicago journalist described as "one of the most startling and tangled tales of graft and interlocking double-crossing ever unfolded in the Criminal courts building."[115] It was quite a claim considering Chicago's reputation for corruption.

Lean-Faced and Long-Nosed Gamblers

The media's portrayal of some of the scandal's "calculating villains" deserves more attention. Usually, loss and disappointment precipitate a search for objects of blame. Moreover, in moments of crisis it is common for the powerless or the unpopular to be scapegoated. In some such moments in this country, even though anti-Semitism has not led to pogroms, Jewish conspirators have been found behind problems.[116] Given the nation's nativist temperament during the early twentieth century and the conspicuous presence of professional gamblers from Jewish backgrounds at the 1919 World Series, it is not surprising that an undercurrent of anti-Semitism is detectable in the media's Black Sox scandal coverage.[117]

At the outset, rather than hastily vilify and accuse gamblers of tampering with the series, the press essentially ignored the rumors that implicated them. There were, however, some notable exceptions. As early as October 1919, the *Sporting News* editorialized: "There are no lengths to which the crop of lean-faced and long-nosed gamblers of these degenerate days will go."[118] A short time later, after Hugh Fullerton wrote critically of some players' performances, the *Sporting News* responded that just "because a lot of dirty, long-nosed, thick-lipped, and strong-smelling gamblers butted into the World Series—an American event, by the way—and some of said gentlemen got crossed, stories were peddled that there was something wrong with the way the games were played."[119] This often-cited passage is notable for its stonewalling the possibility of a fix, its reactionary tone, its use of stereotypical anti-Semitic imagery, and its insinuation that Jewish gamblers were somehow less, or even un-, American because they may have meddled with a virtually sacred national institution. It is also worth mentioning that as the scandal took shape the *Sporting News*'s response became more even-handed, though no less bigoted. Surveying the implicated gamblers, the *Sporting News* reminded its readers that "it does look like most of the [Abe] Attell gang—but then we're all American born, and don't forget that a [Joseph 'Sport'] Sullivan is involved as well as a[n] [Arnold] Rothstein."[120]

Later, when the story finally broke, many newspapers not so subtly implied that Jewish outsiders were responsible for despoiling the national pastime. Although there were few explicit references to their Jewish backgrounds, the noted underworld figures Arnold Rothstein and Abe Attell (aka "The Big Bankroll" and "The Little Champ," respectively) figured prominently in the coverage. More specifically, they were commonly personified as a dual threat: not only had they allegedly assaulted the integrity of organized baseball with gambling and commercialism but they also had threatened some of the traditional American values for which the game stood, such as meritocracy, equality, and openness.

It is now generally agreed upon that Arnold Rothstein—one of the best-known and most powerful New York gangsters and the inspiration for Meyer Wolfsheim in F. Scott Fitzgerald's *The Great Gatsby* (1925)—did *not* fix the 1919 World Series. "Rothstein's name, his reputation, and his reputed wealth were all used to influence the crooked baseball players," writes his biographer Leo Katcher. "But Rothstein, knowing this, kept apart from the actual fix. He just let it happen."[121] Nevertheless, like virtually everyone associated with the affair, Rothstein was no innocent. He knew of the fix early on and profited greatly from it. Katcher speculates that Rothstein won at least $350,000 on the series.[122] Whether he deserved it or not, Rothstein was (and remains) closely associated with the scandal. As F. Scott Fitzgerald famously suggested, he was widely believed to have been "the man who fixed the World Series" and played "with the faith of fifty million people—with the single-mindedness of a burglar blowing a safe."[123] After being consistently mentioned in the early Black Sox scandal narratives as a possible "fixer," Rothstein publicly denied being involved. When he voluntarily presented himself before the Cook County grand jury—in part because the rumors linking him to the scandal brought his illicit businesses unwanted attention—Rothstein deflected the media glare by implicating his sometime associate Abe Attell.[124] "My friends know that I have never been connected with a crooked deal in my life," Rothstein said. "I have been victimized more than once and have been forced to bear the burden as best I could."[125] But as Katcher notes: "No one really believed in his innocence, only in his cleverness."[126]

Few believed in Abe Attell's innocence, either. The featherweight boxing champion of the world between 1900 and 1912, Attell was instrumental in fixing the series. An associate and occasional bodyguard for Rothstein, Attell apparently deceived several small-time gamblers and White Sox players into believing that Rothstein was backing their venture. When the scandal was exposed, Attell's name was, like Rothstein's, constantly coupled with the plot and his whereabouts were newsworthy throughout the affair. As one would expect, Attell at first denied being involved. "I never handed any money to the White Sox players," Attell claimed. "I never acted as a fixer."[127] Years later, though, Attell seemed to be proud of his association with the Black Sox scandal. In 1926, he bragged to sportswriters, "I was the payoff man."[128] In spite of his complicity, Attell, like almost all the gamblers, escaped prosecution, in no small part due to Rothstein's assistance. Although he was indicted by the grand jury, attempts to extradite the New Yorker were unsuccessful.[129] It was Attell who succinctly observed that the episode "was a game of cheaters cheating cheaters."[130]

Perhaps the press's most virulently anti-Semitic stories emanated from Henry Ford's *Dearborn Independent.* One of the best-known and wealthiest men in the United States, Ford helped to revolutionize mass industrial production and to popularize the country's consumer culture. But by the twenties Ford was also "America's best known anti-Semite."[131] During most of the twenties, Ford's newspaper published articles (reprints were quickly collected in book form) that revealed obviously far-fetched Jewish conspiracies and accused "Jews of utilizing communism, banking, labor unions, alcohol, gambling, jazz music, newspapers, and the movies to attack and weaken America, its culture and people."[132] The combination of the Black Sox scandal's cast of prominent Jewish characters and Ford's awareness that baseball's popularity was at least partially rooted in its embodiment of traditional American values simply added fuel to his anti-Semitic fire.

In September 1921, Ford's newspaper published two long articles that addressed the Big Fix, "Jewish Gamblers Corrupt American Baseball" and "The Jewish Degradation of American Baseball."[133] The anonymous writer put the matter bluntly: "If fans wish to know the trouble with American baseball, they have it in three words—too much Jew." Noting that the World Series scandal "was curiously notable for its Jewish character," the writer suggested that the implicated ballplayers were simply "Gentile boobs" and "Jewish dupes" who were only involved in the game fixing because they "had listened to the suggestions of a Jew." In this bigoted diatribe the author also argued that baseball had passed into the hands of an assortment of Jews (those in the upper levels of baseball management, as well as professional gamblers) who were conspiring to turn the national pastime into a commercial, rather than a sporting, enterprise. "If baseball is to be saved," Ford's writer instructed, "it must be taken out of their hands until they have shown themselves capable of promoting sport for sports' sake."[134] The historian Peter Levine correctly notes that the articles displayed "little knowledge of the history of the game but an unfortunately good grasp of racist stereotyping and anti-Semitism."[135]

Of course Rothstein and Attell drew much of the *Dearborn Independent*'s wrath. Described as "a slick Jew" and "the man higher up" in the scandal, Rothstein was "either the vilest crook or the most abused man in America." As for Attell, the articles alternately described him as a "Jew gambler" and as the "king bee" of the scandal. Expressing the conventional wisdom of the day, the anonymous writer added: "Attell is of such a character that he ought to be barred from the grounds of any sport."[136] Levine judiciously points out that "Ford was wrong to interpret Attell and Rothstein's involvement in the Black Sox scandal as evidence of an international Jewish conspiracy to corrupt Anglo-Saxon institutions. Wrong about the responsibility of Jews for turning baseball into commercial enterprise, Ford was correct in noting that America's national pastime was big business."[137]

There is little argument about whether Rothstein and Attell were involved in the Black Sox scandal: they most certainly were, though possibly to a lesser extent than is generally believed. Rothstein's role in the fix was probably limited to damage control, while Attell's role is often expediently minimized or exaggerated. Still, despite their involvement, Rothstein and Attell (along with several other lesser Jewish gamblers) were portrayed by the media as the Big Fix's driving force in large part because their ethnicity fit the popular cultural stereotype of the deceitful, dishonest, and money-hungry Jew. Rather than unduly castigate the players (who probably initiated the scheme) or the labor conditions and relations that engendered the game fixing, the media focused on the menace that professional gamblers (often code for Jewish gamblers) posed. By using Rothstein and Attell to reinforce a potent ethnic stereotype, the media were able to personify the pair as the source of baseball's tragedy and moral disorder.

A Melodrama of Beset Manhood

In the daily press, the scandal emerged as an extraordinarily dramatic narrative written by men, about men, and (presumably) for men and boys. In a sense, it was something akin to a masculine melodrama.[138] By revealing the ugly reality behind baseball's virtuous facade, the scandal made a mockery of the "manly" values the game supposedly provided young men and boys. In the process, it provided a stage on which the era's version of (white) middle-class masculinity was challenged, vigorously defended, and ultimately reconstituted. The affair's leading actors were cast in various well-known roles. The implicated players were simultaneously cast as wayward boys (i.e., failed men) and as avaricious ingrates. In sharp contrast to his Black Sox teammates, the second baseman Eddie Collins (sometimes referred to as one of the "Clean Sox" because he was uninvolved in and untainted by the scandal) continued to personify baseball's All-American masculine ideal. Charles A. Comiskey was depicted as a betrayed and martyred patriarch. Judge Kenesaw Mountain Landis was rendered as a stern, unforgiving patriarch and as baseball's moral savior. Taken collectively, these men and the ways in which they were represented throw into relief ideas about manhood in the early twenties.

Important cultural and social changes that affected American manhood had been under way since the mid-nineteenth century. Mass industrialization, urbanization, immigration, and the closing of the frontier fundamentally altered the American social landscape. One result was that ideas about masculinity were challenged and, some scholars argue, thrown into crisis.[139] Long-standing conceptions of manhood had to be reevaluated and modified. "With no frontier to conquer, with physical strength becoming less relevant in work, and with urban boys being raised and taught by women," writes the sociologist Michael A. Messner, "it was feared that males were becoming 'soft,' that society itself was becoming 'feminized.'"[140] Consequently, play, leisured entertainment, and, eventually, competitive sport began to occupy a more important role in the construction of masculinity, particularly its middle-class variants. Reformers, physical educators, and other leaders now frequently hailed sports as salutary, for both physical and moral reasons: it built strong bodies *and* character, *mens sana in corpore sano* for a new generation. This ideology translated into a simple equation: sport turned boys into healthy, respectable men. In this regard, baseball, already well established as the national pastime by the end of the nineteenth century, was exemplary. In fact, the historian Melvin L. Adelman adduces the culture's firm belief that as "a teacher and tester of manhood, baseball was not merely a game but a valuable educational tool."[141] This attitude was perhaps best articulated by William McKeever in *Training the Boy* (1913): "No boy can grow to a perfectly normal manhood today without the benefits of at least a small amount of baseball."[142] If baseball, as participatory and spectator sport, contributed to the construction and maintenance of hegemonic masculinity, the Black Sox scandal certainly threatened, or at least disrupted, that version of manhood.

Nonetheless, many observers continued to maintain that baseball was, as the *Chicago Tribune* editorialized in September 1920, "a healthful sport for boys and an interesting entertainment for men."[143] Despite the fix rumors and revelations, baseball was still a site where young men could test their manhood. It was still a culturally sanctioned activity that offered boys a chance to demonstrate their emerging masculinity to their peers. A few men close to the baseball game-fixing investigation and prosecution articulated the game's salutary qualities. Foreman Henry H. Brigham asserted that "the grand jurors are fully agreed that baseball has been a constructive moral influence to American life. Every normal boy learns to play and to love baseball." The jurors were convinced, Brigham said, that baseball contributed to the "manliness" and "to the character building process of almost every American youth. What a crumbling of ideals takes place, therefore, when the few professional crooks pollute the national game."[144] Months later, Edward Prindeville, one of the prosecutors, argued that the case before the jury dealt "with a class of men who are involved in the great national game, which all red-blooded men follow." Outraged by the ballplayers' apparent duplicity and fraud, Prindeville claimed that the "public, the club owners, and even the small boy playing on the sand lots have been swindled. That is why these defendants are charged with conspiracy."[145] It is also partly why they captivated the imaginations of newspaper readers nationwide.

Fallen Idols

It is often noted that baseball is a game of inches: the line that demarcates a strike from a ball, a home run from a fly out, is often remarkably narrow. For most of the 1920 season, the White Sox players aware of the game fixing may have felt as if they were constantly toeing the fine line between glory and infamy. As professional ballplayers at a time when baseball was the undisputed national pastime, many of the White Sox team members—especially those from the 1917 club—enjoyed celebrity far beyond Chicago. They were often lauded as great athletes who exemplified middle-class virtues like the work ethic and meritocracy. Many Americans thought of them as self-reliant, rugged heroes. For some worshipful Chicagoans, they were "the gods of baseball."[146] Such adulation turned to shock and disappointment in the face of their alleged perfidy. On the other hand, many respectable people still considered ballplayers in general to be little more than uncouth toughs and hayseeds, a sentiment that can sometimes be seen in the media.

The accused players were frequently described as "boys," which was almost always intended as a derisive appellation—they were not quite "men" or appropriately "manly." This was not an innocent or culturally insignificant use of language. The historian Warren Goldstein notes that during the mid-nineteenth century one "way of distinguishing baseball as a legitimate and serious activity for grown workmen was to insist on its manliness and to bar 'boyish' conduct from the game."[147] Goldstein observes that, for many men in the mid-nineteenth-century baseball fraternity, the "realm of 'manliness' was defined by what lay outside it; anything that was not 'manly' was roundly condemned."[148] In many ways this dynamic still existed at the time of the scandal. Consistently calling the indicted White Sox players—all of whom were over twenty-five—"boys" was a way of denigrating their manhood; it was a rhetorical strategy that denied them respectability and simultaneously bolstered middle-class masculinity in general.[149]

Friend and foe alike called them "boys." The great Babe Ruth, who was nearing the completion of a record-setting season, said of his colleagues: "I hope that the worst that can be proved against any of these men is that they were the tools of gamblers, who may have blinded some of the boys by offers of big money to throw games."[150] Others were less equivocal than Ruth: "It is plainly evident that some of these boys yielded to the influence of those whose names will doubtless follow in the list of defendants later on," remarked Henry Brigham after Cicotte and Jackson testified before the grand jury. "I sympathize with some of them. They were foolish, unsophisticated country boys who yielded to the temptations placed in their paths by the experienced gamblers."[151] In a similar vein, Robert Edgren of the *New York Evening World* editorialized:

> It is to be hoped that the Department of Justice will run down those responsible for the debauchery of baseball players. As a rule baseball players are not men of good education or keen intelligence. They are men of splendid physique and not too much brain. Most of them are little more than grownup boys. Baseball develops only the boyish side of their character. In the bigger things of life they are simple and unsophisticated. Most of them are young and their experience of life limited to the ball field. That has made them easy victims of shrewd, smooth, entirely unscrupulous gamblers.[152]

Despite its numerous oversimplifications and generalizations, this appraisal of baseball players was common. Months later, as the Black Sox trial neared its conclusion, even one of the defense attorneys referred to the players in similarly disparaging language, so pervasive was its currency. "These boys are not fallen idols or broken idols. Send them back to Comiskey Park and listen to the applause that will come from the grand stand," said James O'Brien on his clients' behalf.[153] That all the implicated ballplayers were working-class men from rural communities or the immigrant cities, poorly educated, and unrefined by most middle-class standards is immaterial here. What matters is that once the ballplayers were accused of game fixing, the media often portrayed these previously heroic athletes as loutish, distasteful dolts instead of as men entitled to the benefit of the doubt pending their day in court.

The media were concerned with how real boys perceived and were affected by the Black Sox scandal. The *New York Times* editorialized:

> Jackson and Felsch and Cicotte and Weaver and the rest of them were heroes to the boys of America. They belonged to the goodly fellowship that includes pirates and Indian fighters, super-detectives and, more recently, aces of the air service. To hear that they sold a world series is as bad news to the boys of America as if one of our modern historians should discover that Daniel Boone had been bought by the Indians to lose his fights in Kentucky, or that Paul Jones had thrown the Serapis–Bonhomme Richard battle for British gold.
>
> On city corner lots, in small towns and country villages, on diamonds improvised by farm lads in the stubble-field, millions of boys have spent the energy of their growing years in the wild hope that some day they, too, might take their places in the fellowship of the big-league elect. Most of them eventually outgrew the ambition, but it did them no harm. And now they find that some of their heroes were only crooks, and contemptible, whimpering crooks at that.[154]

Many newspapers expressed similar sentiments. The *New York Daily News* ran an impassioned article by Billy Sunday, the ballplayer-turned-vaudevillian-revivalist, that evoked similar themes but with a melodramatic twist. "The heart of the average American boy will cherish bitter enmity toward the dastardly gambling interests that corrupted his baseball idols," Sunday preached. "But no boy will say today he has lost faith in baseball." Sunday continued: "Thousands of youthful players on the city lots and members of country town teams from coast to coast will see in the baseball scandal only proof of the things they have always believed: That you can't play the game crooked and win. That 'murder will out.' And that you can't mix in bad company and get away with it."[155] For Sunday and many others, the Black Sox scandal was an occasion to reaffirm timeworn adages and ideologies. The *Chicago Herald and Examiner* recognized that the task of reconstituting the country's battered morality (and masculinity) would be arduous: "How many ministers preaching the clean life, how many honest men of business, trying to build up standards of honesty among their employees, how many fathers talking the principles of fairness and justice to their sons, will be required to overcome the effect of that direct blow at decency in the nation's sport?"[156] Taking a somewhat different tack, the *Cincinnati Enquirer* printed a cartoon that expressed the sense of loss and disillusionment many boys presumably felt. Entitled "The Fallen Idol," the cartoon featured a boy in knickers standing before a demolished statue captioned "Baseball Star Who Sold Out."[157]

Of course, the notion that the indicted ballplayers destroyed the faith of millions of boys is best exemplified by the apocryphal story most often associated with the Black Sox scandal. On September 29, 1920, the *Chicago Herald and Examiner* printed the following:

> As [Joe] Jackson stepped out of the [Criminal Courts] building [after testifying], one little urchin in the crowd grabbed him by his coat sleeve.
>
> "It ain't true is it, Joe?" he said.
>
> "Yes, kid, I'm afraid it is," Jackson replied.
>
> "Well, I'd never have thought it," the boy exclaimed.[158]

Other newspapers and two wire services reported the same basic story all over the country. Somehow, this improbable exchange was quickly modified and distilled into a single, and now often-used, expression: "Say it ain't so, Joe." It must be noted that Jackson always denied that anything like this had ever occurred.[159]

It is possible that Hugh Fullerton deserves the credit—or the blame—for launching this celebrated, if dubious, moment into American folklore and mythology. After the *Chicago Herald and Examiner* published its account, Fullerton wrote his own, highly embellished version of the scene for the *New York Evening World:*

> There came a day when a crook spread money before this ignorant idol and he fell. For a few dollars, which perhaps seemed a fortune to him, he sold his honor, and when the inevitable came, when the truth stood revealed, Joe Jackson went before a body of men and told the story of his own infamy.
>
> While he related the sordid details to the stern-faced, shocked men, there gathered outside the big stone building a group of boys. Their faces were serious. More serious than those who listened inside to the shame of the nation's sport. There was no shouting, no scuffling. They did not talk of baseball or of anything else. A great fear and a great hope fought for mastery within each kid's heart. It couldn't be true.
>
> After an hour, a man, guarded like a felon by other men, emerged from the door. He did not swagger. He slunk along between his guardians, and the kids, with wide eyes and tightened throats, watched, and one, bolder than the others, pressed forward and said:
>
> "It ain't so, Joe, is it?"
>
> Jackson gulped back a sob, the shame of utter shame flushed his brown face. He choked an instant.
>
> "Yes, kid, I'm afraid it is."
>
> And the world of faith crushed around the heads of the kids. Their idol lay in the dust, their faith destroyed. Nothing was true, nothing was honest. There was no Santa Claus. Then, and not until then, did Jackson, hurrying away to escape the sight of the faces of the kids, understand the enormity of what he had done.[160]

This remarkable fiction greatly contributed to the idea that the fixed World Series was an utterly shattering event for American boys. In Fullerton's nimble hands, a perplexed, innocent street urchin became a spokesman for millions of distraught men and boys. Among other things, he personified painful disillusionment and became a focal point for those who insisted that Jackson, Cicotte, and all the rest were beneath contempt.

Unmistakably vitriolic, the media's treatment of the eight Black Sox was severe. It cast the indicted ballplayers as traitors, outlaws, snakes, rats, and other objects of derision. Early on, Morgan Blake of the *Atlanta Journal* was convinced that the guilty ballplayers "will be banished from the game. They will be men without a country. Wherever baseball is loved in America, and that is everywhere within the confines of the union, they will be spit upon." Blake was certain that the Black Sox had earned themselves "the everlasting contempt of their fellow man."[161] The *Philadelphia Bulletin* equated any ballplayer who would conspire to lose games with "the soldier or sailor who would sell out his country and its flag in time of war."[162] Shocked that the implicated ballplayers had apparently double-crossed their colleagues, Harvey Woodruff of the *Chicago Tribune* observed that even "the unwritten code [of 'the criminal class'] prescribes death to traitors within its own ranks."[163] The *Cincinnati Enquirer* put the matter bluntly: "The crooks must be handled without gloves and no decent and fair-minded man can possibly have a word to say for them. They are outlaws from honorable society from this time forth."[164] Charles Dryden of the *Chicago Herald and Examiner* reminded his readers of a biblical parable: "In holy writ we read of the kindly man who found a half frozen snake by the roadside. He placed it in his bosom and when the snake got warmed up and recovered its pep it bit the man who nurtured it. That incident occurred several thousand years ago, but the world has changed very little in that lapse of time. In the modern parable, or whatever it is, we behold Mr. Comiskey the quivering hero of the bleeding heart and hand. The serpent he had warmed and fed for years bit him twice."[165] Noting that the Big Fix was an affront to sportsmanship, the *Chicago Tribune* opined: "Whining, accusing, denying, pleading, the crooks and gamblers seek to crawl out of the mess into which their greed and baseness have led them. Like rats they seek to desert the ship which they fear is sinking. Like rats they seek to climb over each other to the open-air, squealing and fighting as they scramble."[166] Weeks later, these editors lamented: "We have deluded ourselves that it [baseball] was a good, wholesome thing for the American people. It was a waste of time. It developed the worst sportsmanship of which the American people are capable. It was vicarious exercise and skill for thousands of soft, idle citizens who ought to have been hoeing beans and picking potato bugs."[167] Even though the paper had renounced baseball, all was not lost, for its editorial concluded on a whimsical note: "We swear never to go to another game—until the Cubs or the Sox open in the spring next year." This final comment was one of the few which suggested that baseball would survive the scandal.

In general, the media expressed little sympathy or compassion for the beleaguered ballplayers. The *Chicago Herald and Examiner* editors' comment that the "players who face disbarment from organized baseball as the result of the revelations so far are not altogether without sympathy" was atypical.[168] Moreover, the press rarely presumed the White Sox players to be innocent. The *Washington Post* was one of the few newspapers that resisted the urge to condemn the indicted White Sox before all the evidence was available. Washingtonians were advised "to bear in mind that indictments do not change the status of accused men. They are still presumably innocent in the eyes of the law, and they are entitled to the benefit of the doubt pending their trial."[169] If there was a moment during the affair that the press portrayed the accused with some measure of sympathy, it was when Cicotte testified about his participation. "Cicotte told it [his story] to the grand jury in tears and in shame, slowly, haltingly, hanging his head, now and then pausing to wipe his streaming eyes," wrote the *Chicago Tribune*'s reporter.[170] Papers all over the country quoted Cicotte's tear-stained testimony at length. According to the *New York Tribune,* Cicotte said, "I've lived a thousand years in the last twelve months. . . . I would not have done that thing for a million dollars. I didn't need the money. My salary was $10,000 a year and my job was secure."[171] Noting that "Cicotte wept," the *Cincinnati Enquirer* quoted Cicotte as having said: "I would give anything in the world if I could undo my acts in the last world series. I've played a crooked game and I have lost and I am here to tell the whole truth."[172] These and other versions of his testimony cast Cicotte as either a pitiable or a contemptible figure, depending upon one's perspective. For the most part, though, the press had little patience for what one writer called "all this sob stuff."[173] Of more importance, the media made no attempt to investigate the confluence of factors—such as the poor management-labor relations between Comiskey and his employees and the long-standing association between professional baseball and gambling—that fostered the fix. Rather than carefully consider the ways in which asymmetric power relations and an exploitative labor arrangement may have contributed to the episode, the press portrayed the implicated ballplayers as shameless "boys" best characterized by their "stupidity, moral obliquity and greed."[174]

Eddie Collins, a Clean Sox

The Black Sox scandal immediately (and forever) tainted the eight implicated players, but the White Sox captain and second baseman Eddie Collins maintained his reputation for integrity and excellence. If anything, the scandal enhanced his standing as a man of conviction and moral rectitude, as the very personification of the era's ideal athletic hero. A steady hitter, an intelligent base runner, and a brilliant infielder, Collins joined the White Sox in 1914 after Comiskey purchased his contract from the Philadelphia Athletics for $50,000. "Compact, combative, and a Columbia University graduate," writes the historian Charles C. Alexander, "Collins was so self-confident on and off the playing field that his teammates called him 'Cocky.'"[175] While he did not endear himself to most of his teammates,[176] Collins was well known for his aggressive and consistent play and was a favorite with many fans. Foremost among them was the novelist James T. Farrell. After learning of Collins's death in 1951, Farrell reminisced that as a boy he "dreamed of becoming another Eddie Collins and of succeeding him as second baseman on the Chicago White Sox."[177] Farrell probably spoke for many young men and boys when he noted that "as a player and a sportsman [Collins] became my model. He helped to form me into what I am. He played an important role in my life."[178] According to Farrell, "he was an alert, smart and clean baseball player. I tried to play the same way as he did. And in 1920, when the 'Black Sox' scandal was exposed, I was proud that he was not one of the eight White Sox players accused of having thrown the 1919 World Series to the Cincinnati Reds. When I read in the newspaper that one of the accused players had said that he had not even approached Collins with the proposition to throw games, I became very proud. Not only was he a great player: he was incorruptible."[179] Farrell's view of Collins was not singular. Collins was, and was cast by the media as, a powerful role model. Not surprisingly, then, when the scandal was revealed, Collins emerged as the foremost "Clean Sox" or "Square Sox."[180] He not only represented those White Sox who had played to win but also embodied the virtues that baseball and its heroes were thought to instill in the country's youth: honesty, responsibility, and sportsmanship. A man of professional accomplishment and honor, Collins represented a kind of masculine ideal.

Immediately after the game-fixing allegations were made public, the media reported that the unindicted players, led by Collins, were relieved to be out from under a cloud of suspicion. On September 29, 1920, a *Chicago Tribune* headline read: "Shadow Lifted, 'Square Guys' of Sox Celebrate."[181] That same day, the *Chicago Daily News* printed photographs of the "Twelve Sox Players Whom Money Could Not Buy" and reported that the "'remains' of the Sox baseball team weren't chewing on the persimmon of sorrow. Not by a long shot." Now that the Black Sox had been suspended, Collins "was full of pep" and "the ball park clubhouse was more cheerful to-day than it has been for a long time."[182] Morgan Blake of the *Atlanta Journal* surely spoke for many fans: "It is gratifying to note that Eddie Collins emerges from the scandal unscathed. Eddie was really the most popular member of the team and greatest second baseman of all times. He is a college man, who was trained in college athletics where a man would rather lose his life than throw a game."[183] Although he remained popular and his reputation for honesty and sportsmanship went unchallenged, Collins could not single-handedly keep the White Sox in the 1920 American League pennant race. Without its suspended players, the White Sox was simply not a good team. This apparently did not matter to some members of the media, who were more concerned with the team's innocence than its success. "Our pure White Sox lost a ball game today," reported the *Chicago Herald and Examiner,* "but lost on the square."[184] As the leader of the so-called "square shooters," Collins personified clean baseball and exemplified middle-class standards of integrity and success.

In 1922, after the Black Sox scandal had lost its currency as news, the *New Republic* observed that Collins "is still out there playing as near perfect ball as is permitted mortal man in a universe where error seems to be the order of the day."[185] Long after his playing days were behind him, after being inducted into the Baseball Hall of Fame in 1939, and after becoming the vice president and general manager of the Boston Red Sox, Collins continued to be singled out for his achievements and character because they corresponded with middle-class conceptions of ideal manhood. Still, he was (and is) probably best remembered as a symbol of the "virtuous" ballplayers caught in the maelstrom of the Big Fix.[186]

A Severe Blow to the Old Roman

The son of an Irish immigrant, Charles A. Comiskey was a testament to baseball's power to nurture an industrious boy into a successful man.[187] Having climbed the baseball ladder all the way from player to team president and owner of the Chicago White Sox, Comiskey was among the game's most respected men. For many, he personified the fulfillment of the American dream of self-reliance, wealth, and power. Widely known as "The Noblest Roman of Baseball" or the "Old Roman," Comiskey was considered to be "one of the first imaginative and creative minds in professional baseball."[188] According to the historian Donald Honig, "he was the epitome of the self-made man, having made all the waystation stops, a survivor and an achiever in a chancy, rugged environment."[189] In G. W. Axelson's biography, *"Commy": The Life Story of Charles A. Comiskey* (1919), Comiskey himself declared "that the world has given me a square deal—possibly more than I am entitled to" and credited his numerous accomplishments to a combination of hard work, good luck, and supportive friends.[190] "Formerly sport was not regarded as a proper calling for young men," said Comiskey on the eve of the 1919 World Series. "It is beginning to assume its rightful place in society. To me baseball is as honorable as any other business. It is the most honest pastime in the world."[191] By his example and message, Comiskey was a powerful role model for working- and middle-class American boys and men. That he could also be self-important, penurious, manipulative, and ruthless was not well reported by journalists (with whom Comiskey always maintained good relations) or well known to baseball fans.

Indeed, the press and the public deeply sympathized with Comiskey after the game-fixing allegations came to light. Cast by the media as a betrayed, indignant, and wounded patriarch, Comiskey played the role well. A few days before Cicotte and Jackson testified, Comiskey remarked: "If any of my players are not honest, I'll fire them, no matter who they are, and if I can't get honest players to fill their places I'LL CLOSE THE GATES OF THE PARK that I have spent a lifetime to build and in which in the declining years of my life I take the greatest measure of pride and pleasure."[192] Chicago newspapers reported that the sixty-one-year-old Comiskey was physically sick due to the scandal. As one *Chicago Tribune* headline put it: "Comiskey Hard Hit by Perfidy of His Players."[193] "It's been tough, but I feel better to-day. I'm glad the worst is over," Comiskey commented. "I'm glad I've got the team cleaned up. And I feel better. The boys that are left are straight. They've never thrown a game and they never will."[194] The next day the *Chicago Tribune* observed: "After twenty-four hours to recover from the shock, [Comiskey] appeared to be more like himself than on the day before. Although stricken with sorrow over the disclosures of crookedness in the ranks of his players, he appeared decidedly hopeful for the future of baseball, now that the confessions of the culprits had paved the way to cleaning up the game."[195] The solace and support Comiskey received from all over the country no doubt raised his spirits. "Sympathy for Charles A. Comiskey, White Sox president, who wrecked his once mighty ball club following disclosures of crookedness in the last world's series, isn't confined to Chicago alone," the *Chicago Herald and Examiner* reported. "Just about every state in the Union has been heard from now as a result of the 'I'm for Commy' movement started by the *Herald and Examiner* sporting department."[196] James O'Leary of the *Boston Evening Globe* wrote that Comiskey "has the sympathy of everybody who has known him as a player and owner for more than 30 years. He did much for the game in both capacities, and to have this calamity befall him in the declining years of his life, is a severe blow to the 'Old Roman,' and a foul blow, at that."[197] A day later, editors at the *Cincinnati Enquirer* observed: "Immeasurable sympathy goes out to that 'old Roman' of the game, Comiskey, and to the square members of his team, who were so close to winning the pennant prize, the reward contested for throughout the season and almost within grasp."[198] The *Los Angeles Times* lamented: "Poor old Comiskey! The noblest Roman was double-crossed by those who were bound to him by every tie of honor and interest. To keep baseball clean, to play the game squarely were the dominant purposes of his life; and now to have the one big scandal of the national sport in the midst of his own family makes it real tragedy."[199]

Besides offering Comiskey compassion and condolences, commentators also showered him with gratitude and testimonials, as if his professional life were suddenly over. The *Cleveland Plain Dealer* noted that Comiskey "merits the thanks of the American public for the prompt action taken to clean his own organization of those who had disgraced it, even though it means the virtual dissolution of his team for the moment."[200] Lauding Comiskey's selflessness and sacrifice in the face of the crisis, the editors of the *Chicago Herald and Examiner* argued that "the master stroke of his long and honorable baseball career [was] when he tossed away $500,000 worth of ball players that the national game might be kept clean."[201] All over the country, Comiskey was hailed as "one of the cleanest sportsman in baseball."[202] He was, the *Cincinnati Enquirer* maintained, "a man of the highest honor and sportsmanship."[203] The *Kansas City Star* drove the point home in an editorial that Comiskey "is and has been for more than forty years an outstanding figure in the baseball world. In both the troublous and the peaceful years of baseball he has stood first for all that is clean and honest. And he has endeared himself to the hearts of his countrymen by his courageous and manly course in dealing with crookedness. He has spent a lifetime making baseball a bigger and cleaner game."[204] Seen as a beloved sportsman and as a man of integrity and honor, Comiskey could in no way be held culpable for the Big Fix. According to the media, Comiskey was the victim, not the victimizer. Furthermore, other baseball magnates were made of less noble stuff. Comiskey, observed Hugh Fullerton, "was one man who gave more thought to the sport than to the money." Fullerton continued: "His players were accused. He stood to lose more than all the others. Yet he insisted on proving or disproving the charges against his men. Hoping they would be disproved he proved them, and when the proof was furnished he expelled players worth a quarter of a million dollars to him from his club, and forced their indictment for conspiracy."[205] No matter whether this version of Comiskey's actions is accurate, this is a concise rendition of the dominant way in which the media depicted his involvement. According to Eliot Asinof, Comiskey suspected that a plot was underway before the series was concluded but did little to prevent it. The following spring and summer, when the rumors of game fixing had been conveniently muted, "Comiskey counted his money and let them lie."[206] Asinof also points out that only when the scandal reached the press did Comiskey suspend the accused ballplayers. The historian Robert F. Burke argues that "in his own way Comiskey deserved as much or more condemnation than his corrupt players. In spite of his knowledge of their activity in 1919, he had concealed it for the sake of success on the field and at the gate in 1920."[207] At the time of the scandal, however, Fullerton's view of the venerable White Sox owner prevailed. Fullerton and many other observers were convinced that "in the hands of men like Comiskey," professional baseball would be "safe and clean."[208]

Judge Landis: "A Synonym for a Square Deal"

Much like Comiskey, Judge Kenesaw Mountain Landis was often celebrated as a self-made man. A high school dropout who became a federal judge, Landis acquired a reputation for integrity and decisiveness—"a synonym for a square deal."[209] An ardent moralist, a staunch prohibitionist, a zealous patriot, and a passionate baseball fan, Landis was, at best, an unorthodox and capricious judge whose decisions were often reversed on appeal. Referring both to his time as a judge and as baseball commissioner, the historian Harold Seymour maintains that "Landis's career refutes the cliché that in America laws, not men, govern the land."[210] According to the columnist Heywood Broun, Landis "typified the heights to which dramatic talent may carry a man in America if only he has the foresight not to go on the stage."[211] An egoist and a showman with a stern face, Landis was unanimously elected baseball's first commissioner by nervous team owners a month after the Black Sox scandal was exposed, and he remained in that position, ruling with nearly absolute authority, until his death twenty-four years later.[212] One of his first and most memorable acts as baseball commissioner was to place the indicted White Sox players on baseball's ineligible list, a purgatory from which they have never escaped. During his reign, Landis's actions and mere presence assured "the public that a firm patriarchal hand of justice ruled over the nation's pastime."[213] Landis was often short-tempered, mean-spirited, hypocritical, egomaniacal, and despotic, but his version of rough justice lent baseball the appearance of propriety and integrity it needed. "In retrospect," comments the sportswriter Ron Fimrite, "he seems like baseball's George Washington, a wise and all-powerful figure who, assuming an office no one had ever had before, kept a floundering enterprise together, cleansing it of corruption and divisiveness."[214] And like Washington, Landis and his reputation for honesty and righteousness have only been further mythologized over the years.

Due to Landis's time on the bench, his reputation was firmly in place well before the Big Fix. Yet the ways in which the press portrayed him during and following the affair certainly enhanced it. After he accepted the job as commissioner, which would pay him $50,000 annually for seven years, Landis explained why he did so to Clark Griffith, the owner of the Washington Senators and an old friend:

> Alone with Griffith in his office, Landis took him over to the window. "Griff," the judge said, "I'm going to tell you just why I took this job. See those kids down there on the street? See that airplane propeller on the wall? Well, that explains my acceptance. You see, that propeller was on the plane in which my son, Major Reed Landis, flew while overseas. Reed and I went to one of the World Series games in Brooklyn. Outside the gate was a bunch of little kids playing around. Reed turned to me and said: 'Dad wouldn't it be a shame to have the game of these little kids broken up? Wouldn't it be awful to take baseball away from them?' Well, while you gentlemen were talking to me, I looked up at this propeller and thought of Reed. Then I thought of his remark in Brooklyn. Griff, we've got to keep baseball on a high standard for the sake of the youngsters—that's why I took the job, because I want to help."[215]

Despite this melodramatic anecdote, Landis was probably sincere in his desire to cleanse and preserve the national pastime for the benefit of American boys. In fact, he would later argue: "Baseball is something more than a game to an American boy; it is his training field for life work. Destroy his faith in its squareness and honesty and you have destroyed something more; you have planted suspicion of all things in his heart."[216] Not surprisingly, news that Landis had been offered and had accepted the baseball commissioner position was greeted with fanfare and delight. On November 13, the *Chicago Herald and Examiner* ran a front page headline that exclaimed: "LANDIS TAKES BASEBALL JOB." According to the paper, hiring Landis was "the most substantial move ever made in baseball." In Landis, the magnates had hired someone "recognized everywhere as a man of absolute integrity and sterling judgment. Under his direction that national game should be restored to the full confidence of the public."[217] The consensus, among the media and the public, was that Landis would bring unprecedented integrity, honor, and order to professional baseball. Or, as Eliot Asinof puts it: "Landis was hailed as a hero, a savior, a mighty power for the forces of honesty and clean sport."[218] All that and more—for Landis provided professional baseball with a patina of integrity for the next twenty-four years.

During most of the scandal, Landis was relegated to the sidelines. As the case inched its way through the legal system, he generally kept quiet. But in June 1921, during the trial jury selection process, Landis could not maintain his silence and declared: "Honesty in baseball is necessary for its continuance as the great American game and it must be kept clean at all hazards."[219] Anticipating the trial's verdict and a post-acquittal confrontation between the soon-to-be legally innocent ballplayers and Major League Baseball, W. J. Macbeth of the *New York Tribune* wrote: "Presuming all [the ballplayers] are acquitted it will give Judge K. M. Landis an opportunity to prove himself the saviour of baseball. I am sure the Commissioner will never tolerate the presence of any one against whom suspicion pointed so strongly appearing in organized baseball."[220] Macbeth was correct on both points, for when the indicted ballplayers were acquitted, Landis wasted no time or words in laying down his version of justice. His decree was definitive, absolute, and warmly received nationwide. A *Kansas City Star* headline read: "ALL AGREE WITH LANDIS." One baseball official said: "I knew that Judge Landis would render a fair, impartial and just decision in the case of the accused Whitesox [*sic*]." "Judge Landis did the right thing when he barred the acquitted Whitesox [*sic*] from baseball," concluded the president of the International League.[221] Not so implicit in the media's portrayal of Landis was that by banishing the tainted ballplayers, and thus restoring the disrupted social order, he had reaffirmed professional baseball's position as a respectable social institution whose ethical standards were demonstrably superior to those of the law. In addition, his granite-like presence helped reconstitute the traditional, idealized version of middle-class manhood that the scandal had damaged. Another way Landis accomplished this, argues one critic, was by treating ballplayers "as PINS, persons in need of supervision and fatherly guidance."[222] Portrayed as a tough-loving, immovable patriarch, Landis personified rugged, wholesome American masculinity, and, in the words of Donald Honig, was a "menacing threat to any who would try to subvert the sanctity of the old ball game."[223]

Persistence

Intricately bound up with notions about middle-class masculinity, the Black Sox scandal did not go gently into the night, despite Landis's stern ruling. Like many newspapers and Americans, the editors of the *Chicago Herald and Examiner* were deeply troubled by the verdict. They were certain the court's judgment

> affects every boy in America. Very few of them have any clear conception of the league of nations, or the Penrose bill to make Secretary Mellon the arbiter of our financial destiny, or the problems of the Pacific. But all of them, from Maine to Oregon, will soon learn the verdict in this trial. They will draw their own conclusions.
>
> How much preaching and practice by parents, principals and parsons will be required to efface the effect of the conclusions they draw?[224]

The alliterative quality of its last sentence aside, this editorial is notable because it bespeaks the anxiety about masculinity—both boyhood and manhood—that the baseball scandal tapped into and highlighted. The Big Fix was a meaningful social drama for many Americans because it brought their concerns about middle-class standards of appropriate behavior to center stage. That, in the end, the dishonorable, offending actors were expelled, that Eddie Collins remained untainted, that Charles Comiskey survived with his reputation for integrity intact, and that Judge Landis had given professional baseball his imprimatur of moral rectitude probably made it a satisfying spectacle.

"Yes, We Take *The Tribune,* but We Don't Take It Seriously"

Looking at these newspaper accounts in hindsight is one thing, but it is equally important to consider how intended readers may have made sense of the stories. Unfortunately for historians, as Robert Darnton points out, "reading is not a distinct thing, like a constitution or a social order, that can be tracked through time. It is an activity involving a peculiar relation."[225] Reading is a complicated, poorly understood, frequently idiosyncratic, and seemingly ineffable activity. It is, moreover, usually performed simultaneously by different audiences. Worse, readers seldom leave traces for historians to use as evidence. "Except for surviving chance observations and marginal comments in the works themselves," writes the literary critic Cathy N. Davidson, "it is virtually impossible to know how past readers evaluated and understood particular books."[226] Considering the disposable and quotidian quality of newspapers and the manner in which they are preserved on microfilm, there is no possibility of discovering any "chance observations and marginal comments" on or about the initial Black Sox scandal narratives. Still, because cultural meaning is always negotiated and contested, it seems to me that at least some readers and audiences need to be accounted for here. One way to do that is to consider how readers responded to news stories in the form of letters to the editor. It is, of course, difficult to know how representative letters to the editor are, but they nonetheless provide us with opportunities to examine how some people made sense of the media's narratives. Obviously, newspapers (unavoidably) shape and mediate such letters—through selection, editing, placement, and sometimes outright fabrication—so such letters cannot provide us with unmediated or unambiguous access to "authentic" forms of knowledge.

At first glance, how the press reported the public's responses to the Black Sox scandal and how actual letter writers (or those interviewed on the street) responded to the scandal differed only slightly. According to the media, the episode produced widespread disbelief and outrage. Many people, especially baseball fans, did not initially believe the reports that the World Series had been tampered with. "As for the possibility that the series was actually fixed, most people refused to admit it," contends the historian Richard C. Crepeau. "Certain things were beyond reproach, they felt."[227] (Years later, recollecting the first reports that some White Sox players had thrown games, James T. Farrell wrote that, at the time, he "didn't want to believe it.")[228] Many people were startled by the news. The venerable Grantland Rice observed, "There are thousands upon thousands of loyal fans who have been badly stunned."[229] Harvey Woodruff of the *Chicago Tribune* reported: "Fans, on the whole, are shocked by the cumulating chain of circumstantial evidence—stories which in the main have been known to insiders for a year."[230] A few days later, Woodruff wrote that baseball fans everywhere "are shocked and stunned. What had seemed to them impossible, almost unthinkable, has been proven true."[231] The shock waves of disbelief quickly ebbed in the face of sworn confessions, which (unsurprisingly) produced a great deal of anger.

This fury suggests that many people were "successfully" or "correctly" decoding/interpreting the media's Black Sox narratives—that is, readers generally were not reading against the grain. It is common to find letters to the editor like the one that advocated wiping from "the records [the] names of all [the] players found guilty in this great atrocity."[232] Another letter implored the authorities to "give the crooked Sox everything they can have shoved at them. Crooks, double-crossers—then they squeal to get out of it. Put them in stripes."[233] When the *New York Daily News* asked passersby how the ballplayers should be punished, one Brooklynite said, "They ought to be tarred and feathered. A man who gives the greatest sport ever developed a black eye should be given all that's coming to him." Another respondent replied that they "ought never to be allowed to play baseball again. Baseball is too valuable an institution to be ruined by a lot of crooks. Run them out."[234] The *Chicago Tribune*'s "Inquiring Reporter" asked people in the street a different question—"How does the baseball scandal influence your interest or faith in the game?"—but got similar answers. One respondent said, "I will still have the same faith in the game. Because a few players are crooked that does not mean that they all are. You will find crooks in every game and baseball is no exception. I think it's going to help baseball rather than hurt it. They will clean [out] all the crooks, then we can have real clean games." "If the grand jury goes through with this investigation," replied someone else, "baseball will be rid for all time of crooks and gambling. The players will be afraid to accept any bribes, and for that reason I am going to have more faith than ever in the game. It's the game I like, not the players." One man answered: "They took horse racing away from us, also boxing, and if baseball is not kept straight we will probably lose that, too. It's the only game left, and both the players and the gamblers if found guilty, should be sent to prison. It will make a fan sort of suspicious, though, every time an error is made. I won't have quite as much faith in it. How can I?"[235] People other than journalists were clearly angry with and disappointed in the ballplayers. But their responses to the Big Fix also suggest that the tropes the media used—blackness and cleanliness, for instance—were in wide circulation and were readily available metaphors for news consumers.

It is interesting to note that for a few people the Black Sox scandal merely confirmed their suspicions about professional baseball's integrity. "How long is the memory of a baseball fan?" asked one letter to the editor of the *Chicago Tribune:*

> Not very long, I fancy, after hearing the plaudits that greet the appearance on the field of our slacker heroes. How many fans recall that our sterling Comiskey vowed that a certain famous batter [Joe Jackson], who, like many other professional athletes, sought refuge in the shipyards [during World War I], never again would play for the Sox? How many fans recall what a scanty few of our diamond stars were in the service even under the compulsion of the draft, or what a pitifully small number went into the army or navy voluntarily? There is not a trade, a profession, or any calling that has not ten times a better showing to its credit than was made during the war by the members of the sport world who are continually held up as popular idols. And now it is coming out that the yellowness of the draft dodger is tinged with the black of the crook. What more could be expected?[236]

For a minority of onlookers, the World Series scandal was not a debacle and it did not produce anger or disillusionment; it merely substantiated their cynicism and contempt for professional baseball. Many more letter writers, however, especially in Chicago, minimized the long-term effects of the game-fixing disclosures and tried hard to reestablish baseball's status as the national pastime. For example, a letter to the editor of the *Chicago Tribune* asked: "Do we close a bank because the cashier robs it? What have a few crooked ball players got to do with the great game of baseball—the greatest melting pot in the country?"[237] A month later, someone else, certain that the indicted ballplayers should be punished, but less certain that they would be, wrote: "Why should a chicken thief be brought to justice and these men let go. If they did not steal, our laws better be revised. Recalling Comiskey's threat during the war 'to keep Jackson out of my park for all time to come,' I am wondering who will press the charges unless the fans demand it."[238] Clearly in need of guardians, baseball could not be trusted to police itself.

One reason so many of these letters come from the *Chicago Tribune* is that in mid-December, several months after the scandal ceased to be front-page news, "The World's Greatest Newspaper" conducted a poll to determine whether "the White Sox players who threw the world's series of 1919 [have] been punished enough" or whether they should "be brought to trial and sent to prison."[239] The best answers under fifty words would be published. The "Fate of the Crooked Sox" survey offers us a fascinating collection of letters that reflect the spectrum of fans' positions. At one end of the spectrum were many replies like the following: "If a man in my employ, in whom I place the greatest confidence and whom I pay a liberal salary, deliberately double-crosses me, I do not consider justice has been done by simply discharging him. Let's forget the sob stuff and land them where they belong."[240] Much like the journalistic accounts that depicted the implicated players as contemptible social pariahs, this response suggests that the ballplayers should be judged and punished according to the severity of their duplicity; it implies that no crime is so great as the crime of betrayal. Or, as one respondent put it, the accused attempted "to tear down a monument that it took a lifetime for the 'Old Roman' to build; they threw down the greatest bunch of supporters a ball team ever had; they threw away their own self-respect and the right to any consideration whatever."[241] At the other end of the spectrum, quite a few fans answered in more moderate terms. One man commented: "The treachery of the crooked players has brought disfavor and contempt. Let them have their liberty of body, for shame and disgrace will haunt them through life."[242] Another insisted: "As far as the public knows, we actually have the goods on only three White Sox players—those who confessed. The others who claim they are not guilty should be brought to trial, and if found 'not guilty' should be reinstated, and if guilty their conscience and a public blacklist will be punishment to last a lifetime. How happy, though, some of us dyed-in-the-wool Sox fans would be if at least some of the supposed black ones were found, after all, to be white."[243] Although this is, it seems to me, one of the more sensible letters the paper published, its unabashed partisanship was uncommon. It is also worth noting that this was the final letter the *Tribune* printed as part of its survey. In the end, the poll results were somewhat surprising. After more than a week of voting, on December 19, 1920, the *Tribune* had received 110 ballots in favor of criminal prosecution and 183 ballots that indicated no further action was appropriate. "The vote presented many interesting phases," the *Tribune* reported. "In the early returns the ballots were nearly 3 to 1 that the players already had suffered enough. Of these ballots a surprisingly large number were from women, and several from ministers. Not a single voter in either class was affirmative for prison sentences." The *Tribune*'s analysis of its poll continued:

> It was noteworthy also that the country vote was much stronger proportionately for criminal prosecution than that of city fans. Does that indicate a higher standard of morality in the country, or that city fans cannot forget entirely their old admiration for their one time favorites?
>
> Many letters contained scathing criticisms of the club owners and rulers of baseball—in fact, this was quite general—and held that the players were no more guilty than those who employed and ruled them.
>
> It was somewhat surprising, however, to note the number who suggested that the players be returned to the game under probation and given another chance. This was not even contemplated in the question. Such expressions were all from city fans, whose opinion was influenced, perhaps, by the desire to see a winner and the fact that it will take several years to replace the stars who are stars no more.

This analysis suggests that numerous fans did (or could) not divorce themselves from their loyalty to the players, that they recognized the culpability of the owners and the baseball establishment for the scandal, and—by imagining and articulating alternative ways of responding—that they were able to resist the dominant, preferred readings of the episode that the media had constructed. Or, as one letter writer explained, "Yes, we take *The Tribune,* but we don't take it seriously."[244]

As the scandal dragged on, more fan letters expressed sympathy for the players and often maintained that they were the pawns of gamblers and the judicial system. These letters usually articulated the point of view that the players should be duly punished if convicted on conspiracy charges, but that they had probably endured enough misery. The press itself almost never expressed this viewpoint. In March 1921, the *Chicago Herald and Examiner* published a letter to the editor that may have articulated the way others felt:

> I am for the White Sox first, last and always, and would like to be heard from on the 'Black Sox' question. I pulled for them as strong as for any of the White Sox, and I hate to have my judgment questioned regarding the picking of an honest and dishonest man. If this is the land of the free, why should not these men be accorded the privileges of a free man? Why postpone their trial from one day to another if the state has such a clear case against them? If they are guilty, punish them all, but don't forget to punish also the higher ups; but if they are innocent, let the world know it just as when their suspected guilt was first discovered.[245]

Months later, the *Chicago Herald and Examiner* received a letter which began, "I am in no sense a baseball apologist, but is it not unfair to harp on 'crooked ball players' when a comparison proves they average just as high in honesty and reliability as those of any other occupation or profession?" Claiming to have access to reliable social scientific data, the letter writer argued that "dishonesty and graft are social diseases that reach every calling and profession in very near the same proportion. A proper understanding of this principle, which I myself am convinced is perfectly sound and incontestable, leaves no room for one profession or calling to cry out against the dishonesty and graft of those in other occupations."[246] The implicated ballplayers were little more than a few of the bad apples any profession must expect to have in its barrel. Also, they were afflicted with a "social disease" and thus were not as morally reprehensible as the press had portrayed them. A few weeks later, a letter writer to the same paper maintained that a great deal "has been said about the 'Black Sox' in the last year that was really disgusting. They deserved to be reprimanded completely, but not to such an extent as to blacklist the guilty players and prevent them from making a living. Every one knows these players are guilty and should be reprimanded, but why push the matter so rigidly when others rob millions of people out of millions of dollars." Indeed, the author wondered: "Why are professional gunmen and women who have practically been condemned for a crime a thousand times worse than the players committed allowed to go free? Were any of these women prevented from making a living? No! Why is the rent hog who has driven many a family to the streets and charged exorbitant rents allowed to go free?" The writer concluded, "When comparing the cases of the Black Sox and the others, I cannot see where justice is being done. The only people who are grumbling are the gamblers who lost heavily and who should be held responsible for the blotch on baseball."[247] Evidence is meager, but it seems unlikely that this was a lone voice.

Only some of the many people with opinions on the 1919 World Series scandal were heard from in newspapers at the time, and their letters were necessarily mediated, carefully selected, and edited. It is therefore impossible to know how most readers made sense of the media's Black Sox narratives. This is as inevitable as it is disappointing. Read by heterogeneous audiences, news stories and editorials about the Black Sox scandal were obviously interpreted and understood in myriad ways: affirmatively, uncritically, passively, skeptically, and resistantly, among many other possibilities. A creative process about which it is difficult to generalize, reading, argues the literary critic Robert Scholes, "consists of bringing texts together. It is a constructive activity, a kind of writing."[248] Exactly how this was done, how contemporary readers rewrote and made sense of the narratives they read in daily newspapers, is necessarily elusive.

More Typical than Terrible

As one might expect, the Black Sox scandal weighed heavily on some people for many years. Ring Lardner, one of the era's most prominent columnists, was reportedly scarred by the event.[249] His colleague and friend Grantland Rice wrote in the mid-1950s that the fixed World Series was one of only two sports scandals that really concerned him (the other was the 1951 college basketball point-shaving affair).[250] Westbrook Pegler, the caustic sportswriter-turned-right-wing-crank, was also troubled. In 1932, Pegler wrote in his nationally syndicated column: "The fake world series of 1919 produced some of the worst newspaper reporting that the American press ever has been guilty of and why all of us who were detailed to cover the show were not fired for missing the greatest sport story in 20 years is something I have never understood. We were terrible."[251] Perhaps they were terrible, but journalists certainly did not "miss" the story. Although most reporters and editors initially dismissed or ignored the fix rumors, once the scandal broke newspapers exploited the Black Sox story for everything it was worth for nearly a year. Moreover, coverage was probably more typical than terrible. The press described the scandal in the ways available to it, reflecting, refracting, and reproducing many of the assumptions and anxieties, needs and desires of Americans. Furthermore, the press rendered the scandal in the ways that it believed satisfied its audiences and in ways that repositioned it as a credible, authoritative, and profitable institution. That is, the Black Sox scandal stories the media told precisely dovetailed with their vision of their social world.

2

"Fix These Faces in Your Memory": The Black Sox Scandal and American Collective Memories

A week after the Black Sox scandal became a national front-page sensation, the *Sporting News,* then commonly referred to as "Baseball's Bible," ran photographs of the "eight men who were charged with selling out" the game. The headline implored: "FIX THESE FACES IN YOUR MEMORY." The pictured ballplayers are wearing their uniforms and stern expressions. Encircled by his teammates, the veteran White Sox pitcher Eddie Cicotte, the first player to confess to throwing the World Series, occupies a special place of disgrace in the middle of the collection. The caption reads:

> These are the White Sox players who committed the astounding and contemptible crime of selling out the baseball world in the 1919 World's Series, not only of defrauding the public, but themselves passing up the honors of a world's championship for bribe money paid them by gamblers who are no less contemptible than that [*sic*] of the players. Four of them are guilty by their own confessions and the evidence against the other four is so conclusive that their denials only add to the contempt in which they are held. They have been dismissed from baseball and whether or not they go to jail their punishment will be such that other crooked players, if there be any left in the game, will hesitate to ever again throw down baseball. Some of the eight have been great stars in their day, but they will be remembered from now on only for the depths of depravity to which they could sink.[1]

Vitriolic in its denunciation of the implicated players and gamblers, the *Sporting News* simultaneously anticipated and promoted the dominant way in which the Black Sox scandal would be remembered for generations: eight ballplayers had defiled the national pastime, they were to be punished accordingly, their legacy was nothing less than shame. Over the years, even if people did not in fact remember the faces or the names of the individual Black Sox, the event was inscribed in memory, both private and collective. In this way the *Sporting News* headline was realized: the fixers were indeed fixed in American memories.

Eventually, all news stories fade and are displaced and Black Sox stories were no exception. After the implicated White Sox players were acquitted in early August 1921—and the newly appointed baseball commissioner, Judge Kenesaw Mountain Landis, immediately dashed any hopes they may have had about being reinstated—the media promptly moved on. Nevertheless, memories of the Big Fix lived on in the immediately following decades. They did so partly due to the domineering presence of Judge Landis, who played an instrumental role in restoring the appearance of propriety to the national pastime. Hired to restore some much-needed integrity and order to the game, Landis also led the movement to repress memories of the Black Sox embarrassment. At the same time, the continued presence of the disgraced players kept the memory of the episode active in local communities for many years. To a lesser extent, it is also possible to make sense of the scandal's continued presence in American memories as a masculine narrative and phenomenon; that is, to view it as a story about men, told by men, to socialize young men and boys, for from the beginning the scandal was recognized as a minor crisis for American middle-class masculinity. For many baseball fans, all across the country, the fixed World Series was an extraordinarily dramatic rupture not easily forgotten. But perhaps most important, as the years passed and the events either faded or ossified in individual recollections, the Big Fix was incorporated and frequently reinscribed in American collective memories.

My interest here is to examine how the Black Sox scandal was remembered before it was turned into popular literature and history at midcentury and to reflect on how those memories expressed the needs and desires of their propagators and illuminated particular cultural moments. By exploring some ways that memories of the affair endured in the three following decades—in the "twilight zone that lies between living memory and written history," to use C. Vann Woodward's wonderful phrase—I further trace the historical development of the Black Sox scandal as a cultural phenomenon.[2] Loosely organized chronologically, this chapter traces and probes some of the more interesting moments from the twenties through the early fifties when the Black Sox scandal was articulated or revealed. My readings are eclectic, wide-ranging, fragmentary, and necessarily conditional: such is the nature of memory, private and collective.

What Is Collective Memory?

Collective memory in general and American collective memory in particular are complicated and contentious subjects. For some postmodern critics, who maintain that culture "is no longer a unitary, fixed category, but a decentered, fragmentary assemblage of conflicting voices and institutions," collective memory, with its implied consensus, is a dubious phenomenon.[3] From this perspective, collective memory suggests a degree of coherency and unity that most societies lack. At the same time, there are those who maintain that Americans in particular have little to no sense of memory, that we are chronic amnesiacs. The political columnist Meg Greenfield writes, only somewhat hyperbolically, that "we have no collective memory, none. If it happened more than six hours ago, it is gone."[4] Even for those like myself who work from the presupposition that there is memory on a collective scale—that is, memory beyond the individual level—collective memory is difficult to define. Referred to by some as popular memory, by others as social or collective memory, and by still others as public memory, the idea that groups of people remember (and forget) the past in meaningful ways has attracted the attention of scholars from numerous disciplines without coalescing into a widely accepted definition.

Used in this book, collective memory is a way of expressing sets of ideas, images, and feelings about the past that resonate among people who share a common orientation or allegiance. Collective memory is a cultural construction, an elaborate network of narratives and texts (which include objects and ceremonial performances) that represents or explains the past. Collective memory is not an autonomous, static force, but is instead a dynamic phenomenon produced and modified by individuals and institutions in specific contexts. "In each construction of a memory," argues the historian David Thelen, whether personal or collective, "people reshape, omit, distort, combine, and reorganize details from the past in an active and subjective way. They mix pieces from the present with elements from different periods in the past."[5] For these reasons there is nothing "natural" or "authentic" about collective memory. As many historians and cultural critics have argued, more often than not people and societies construct versions of the past that conform to their respective beliefs about the present; collective memory is one of the names given to those constructions, which come in various forms.

More so than anyone, the French sociologist Maurice Halbwachs has informed my understanding of collective memory.[6] In the posthumously published *The Collective Memory* ([1950] 1980), Halbwachs argues that memory—both collective and individual (for Halbwachs they are virtually inseparable)—is socially constructed and present-oriented, an instrument of reconfiguration (as opposed to retrieval) and social power. According to Halbwachs, "a remembrance is in very large measure a reconstruction of the past achieved with data borrowed from the present, a reconstruction prepared, furthermore, by reconstructions of earlier periods wherein past images had already been altered."[7] Halbwachs asserts that memory is invariably fragmentary and provisional, dynamic and ongoing, always an act or a process as opposed to an objective, static record to be recalled. Indeed, we should remember that, as the historian Patrick H. Hutton puts it, Halbwachs's "main purpose as an historian was to show how unreliable memory is as a guide to the realities of the past."[8] For Halbwachs, it is only through membership in social groups—kinship, religious, ethnic, and class, for instance—that individuals are able to acquire and recall memories. As he puts it: "There is no universal memory. Every collective memory requires the support of a group delimited in space and time."[9] Halbwachs notes that when it comes to memory, "we are never alone."[10] Actually, Halbwachs argues for a plurality of collective memories. He suggests that "just as people are members of many different groups at the same time, so the memory of the same fact can be placed within many frameworks, which result from distinct collective memories."[11] For Halbwachs, then, collective memory responds to the present needs of a coherent body of people at a specific sociohistorical moment.[12]

In many ways, collective memory is similar to other evocations of the past in that it is always selective and fragmentary, provisional and incomplete, socially constructed and anchored in the present. If Halbwachs and his followers overstated the presentist nature of collective memory, there was probably some utility in doing so at the time. From their perspective, historians and critics had too long regarded memory as a simple record, as a reified piece of the past, as a recollection rather than as an active reconstruction.[13] It is no longer plausible to think of memory in these terms; Rankean dreams of narrating "how it really was" have fallen on hard times. In their place we are left with a postmodern cornucopia of memories and histories—which is not to suggest that collective memory is "a terrain where anything goes."[14] On the contrary, collective memory is a cultural terrain where certain narratives and images are routinely scrutinized, debated, and reevaluated. In this way collective memory, like other phenomena that engage cultural politics, occupies space that is frequently contested and deliberated.

Finally, anyone considering collective memory historically must confront the question of evidence. Memory, of course, infrequently leaves tangible traces for future historians to study. Indeed, memory is "one of the most evanescent forms of evidence," writes the historian James Wilkinson.[15] "At present, history is a courtroom where the exclusionary rule, formerly strictly enforced, has been discarded. Evidence is everywhere," Wilkinson argues. "Never have historians had so much evidence at their disposal; never has there been so much mistrust about what the evidence shows." Although Wilkinson is correct that there is "tension between the desire to know and the availability of materials from which to derive that knowledge," traces of Black Sox scandal memories do exist in various forms, such as newspaper and magazine articles, obituaries and cemeteries, photographs and paintings, memoirs and music, fiction and folklore.[16] Yet no matter what our sources suggest we cannot be certain what most people actually believed and felt about the Big Fix; we can only examine the impressions of the 1919 World Series scandal that a small number of people recorded. Consequently, my focus here is on the producers, not the consumers, of Black Sox scandal narratives and images. Since memorialists cannot render the past in ways that are implausible—only with great difficulty can someone "sell" versions of the past that do not interest people, conform to their expectations, or satisfy their needs and desires—I work from the assumption that the (re)production of Black Sox scandal memories is related to the public's perception of the event and its participants.

Kenesaw Mountain Landis: Baseball's Czar and Memory Marker

The most visible reminder of the Big Fix in the decades following the event was certainly Judge Kenesaw Mountain Landis. One of the few legitimate beneficiaries of the affair, Landis was unanimously elected by Major League Baseball team owners to a seven-year term (at $50,000 a year) as baseball's first commissioner in November 1920, less than a month after the grand jury handed down its indictments.[17] For most Americans, the flamboyant and intensely patriotic Landis signified tough justice, patriarchal discipline, and incorruptible integrity. "With his country accent, his snow-white hair, string ties, and penchant for cursing, Kenesaw Mountain Landis was a Latter-Day Roy Bean," muses the folklorist Tristram P. Coffin. "Educated in a somewhat informal manner; short-fused, but a soft touch; a hater of minority groups, socialists, and communists; a VFW-type patriot, he appealed to the conservative, the traditional, the old-fashioned who found him a square bastion against the rioters, city slickers, and pay-off boys of megalopolitan life. And he did take the American law into his own hands, distributing his version of justice in the most ancient of ways."[18] Due to these characteristics, his stern demeanor, and his skillful self-promotion, Landis was seen by many as the game's moral savior and guardian. Or, as Coffin puts it: "This sophisticated version of Roy Bean served baseball as an ethical hero. And as is the case with many such heroes, his reputation for integrity and wisdom has long since outrun his reputation for whimsy, cantankerousness, and extra-legality."[19] Landis's election simultaneously represented a new beginning and a return to so-called traditional values; he was to exorcise the memory of an embarrassing episode even as it unfolded and to ensure that scandal never again tainted the national pastime. Paradoxically, although his very presence activated Black Sox scandal memories, Landis led the movement to suppress those memories. For twenty-four years he served as the czar of baseball and as a kind of memory marker for the Black Sox scandal. In some ways, it was his professional raison d'être.

Landis began his work enthusiastically. Though he accepted baseball's commissionership in November 1920, he did not formally take charge until the following January.[20] As spring training rolled around in mid-March and the legal proceedings against the eight indicted ballplayers dragged on, Landis declared: "Baseball can protect itself regardless: all the indicted players have today been placed on the ineligible list!"[21] Landis apparently did not know or care that Comiskey had already suspended the players the previous September.[22] Either way, it was important for Landis to be seen as decisive and uncompromising in this matter, even at the risk of redundancy. Five months later, in early August, the Black Sox and their alleged gambling associates were acquitted. The players, of course, were ecstatic, as were many White Sox fans. When the players were found not guilty, writes Eliot Asinof, a "roar went up in the courtroom."[23] One defense attorney noted: "The verdict is a complete vindication of the most mistreated ballplayers in history."[24] Much of the media, however, was incensed. The Associated Press reported that the news was greeted with "surprise, disappointment and chagrin" by sports editors and writers, adding that the judgment was a "travesty" nearly as "stunning and disturbing as the original disclosures."[25] Landis, in his often-quoted statement, did not just banish the players from baseball but also reminded the public about his power: "Just keep in mind that regardless of the verdict of juries, baseball is entirely competent to protect itself against the crooks both inside and outside the game."[26]

Ultimately, this was the only response that mattered. Landis offered no leniency, no second chances. Seemingly contemptuous of the very judicial system of which he was still a member, Landis evoked extralegal authority to do what the law did not: purge the Black Sox from the game and, by implication, legitimate society—though not from personal and nascent collective memories. By expelling the acquitted ballplayers he ensured that their pariah status would remain permanent. Moreover, just as the game's magnates had hoped, he established himself as someone who would not tolerate dishonesty. For many, writes Asinof, he was "a hero, a savior, a mighty power for the forces of honesty and clean sport."[27] Landis, in short, provided baseball with the stern paternal guidance and masculine vigor that it (apparently) lacked, a deficiency that some argued had provided an opening to corrupt gamblers and crooked ballplayers in the first place. Frequently referred to as baseball's dictator, Landis can also be seen as baseball's surrogate father-figure, a strict disciplinarian who would not stand for insubordination or moral laxity from wayward ballplayers (i.e., "boys"). Even for those who did not follow the game closely, the masculine nature of Landis's persona and presence was unmistakable.

After the 1919 game-fixing scandal was finally resolved, "nobody was more eager than Kenesaw Mountain Landis for the ghosts of baseball past to vanish for good," comments the historian Charles C. Alexander.[28] Unfortunately, the ghosts of baseball past and present continued to haunt the game, and as a result Landis was busy squelching a variety of (mostly minor) scandals, many of which reactivated still fresh Black Sox memories. In fact, even before he offered his famous decree, Landis was working as baseball's moral guardian. In March 1921, he expelled Gene Paulette, a utility player with the St. Louis Cardinals, for associating with gamblers and allegedly offering to throw games. "My only regret," claimed Landis, "is that the real culprits, the gamblers, cannot be reached by this office."[29] A month later, Landis placed Benny Kauff of the New York Giants on baseball's ineligible list when he was charged with involvement in a stolen automobile syndicate. Although no baseball-related charges were brought against Kauff, who had testified as a witness at the Cook County grand jury the previous year, Landis ruled that Kauff's "mere presence in the line-up would inevitably burden patrons of the game with grave apprehension as to its integrity."[30] Kauff was eventually found not guilty, but was never reinstated.[31]

The following year, Landis banned the pitcher Phil Douglas for apparently offering to desert the New York Giants during the pennant race if members of the St. Louis Cardinals would pay him off. The Douglas expulsion was a national sensation, one the *New York Times* hyperbolically described as "the biggest scandal in the history of baseball."[32] Two years later, Landis banished Jimmy O'Connell and Albert "Cozy" Dolan of the Giants for their participation in an alleged scheme to bribe the Philadelphia Phillies shortstop Heinie Sand. Since the O'Connell-Dolan affair occurred "while memories of the Black Sox scandal were still fresh," writes the historian Harold Seymour, it "reawakened doubts about the integrity of Organized Baseball."[33] Indeed, "the story was almost as much a sensation to the country as the White Sox scandal," notes J. G. Taylor Spink.[34] Throughout the off-season, the O'Connell-Dolan affair received a great deal of media attention and critical commentary, some of which suggested that the incident could be as devastating to the game's image as the Black Sox scandal had been.[35]

An even more startling revelation was made in November 1926, when Hubert "Dutch" Leonard, a retired pitcher, charged that the perennial stars Ty Cobb and Tris Speaker, along with the former Cleveland outfielder and onetime Boston Red Sox pitching sensation Joe Wood, threw games played between Detroit and Cleveland late in the 1919 season. According to the writer Daniel E. Ginsburg: "The exposure and publication of the details of the scandal on December 21 rocked the nation. Not since the Black Sox scandal had stars of this magnitude been involved in a baseball gambling scandal. However, unlike the Black Sox case, the public rallied to the defense of the beleaguered stars."[36] Landis resolved the Cobb-Speaker affair in late January 1927 by declaring them innocent of game-fixing charges and returning them to the game's good graces.[37] Finally, soon after the Cobb-Speaker incident was revealed, baseball was shaken by another game-fixing charge: this time, Charles "Swede" Risberg, a leader of the 1919 World Series fix, claimed that the 1917 White Sox had pooled their money and paid the Detroit Tigers $1,100 to throw two doubleheaders late in the season. An investigation revealed that money had indeed been collected for the Tigers, but it was determined that the money was not a bribe but a gift to the Detroit pitchers for beating Boston three games to four in a previous series.[38] "It was an act of impropriety, reprehensible and censurable," Landis commented, "but not an act of criminality."[39] Although Landis would preside over numerous other disagreeable and annoying incidents, none involved a player charged with throwing, or attempting to throw, a game. Landis, it would seem, had successfully cleansed the game of its unsavory elements.

In and of themselves, these incidents are not terribly important. In viewing them collectively, however, one could argue that gambling interests did in fact continue to pose a threat to the integrity of the game and that Landis performed a vital function in maintaining baseball's integrity. There is, no doubt, some truth to this. But it is just as plausible that Landis's stern presence and severe (and sometimes capricious) punishments promoted heightened sensitivities to previously acceptable (though ethically suspect) behavior and that, thus, such behavior was more frequently reported to management and by the media. In this way Landis, sitting on high, dispensing a form of frontier justice, intermittently brought Black Sox memories back to the forefront of the country's collective consciousness because it served his purposes to do so. I am not suggesting that Landis, "suspicious to the point of paranoia about gambling," fabricated game-fixing or ethical crises so that he could then rectify them.[40] Rather, I am suggesting that the skillful way in which he framed these minor incidents ensured the public, the baseball players, and the team owners that he was ever vigilant and ruthless in his pursuit of maintaining order. As J. G. Taylor Spink observes: "There is no doubt that Landis put the fear of God, and the fear of Commissioner Landis, into the ball players. The great mass of players always have been inherently honest, but if there were any likely to stray the very fact that they knew the white-haired Landis sat in the Commissioner's seat kept them on the path of righteousness."[41] To consolidate and reaffirm his institutional power and ethical standing, and to reposition baseball as a national institution with a special hold on American imaginations, Landis had to make vivid public examples of the Black Sox and all the (alleged) miscreants who followed them. In other words, he shrewdly activated and used Black Sox scandal memories to promote himself as a despot and to advocate a particular code of conduct.

If remembrance of the past begins with the remembrance of people, no one was more important than Judge Landis in maintaining Big Fix memories from the twenties to 1944, when he died. Perhaps intuitively aware that memory needs to be sustained by repetition and public rituals, Landis not only roared loudly whenever baseball was (supposedly) imperiled but also made his presence conspicuous in other ways. Every October for twenty-three years the ever-watchful Landis could be found in the commissioner's box at the World Series, his chin resting on the railing. Of course, the memories he helped reactivate, the narrative he implicitly retold about the scandal and its aftermath, served his own interests. Landis initially used the 1919 scandal to establish his discretionary power and thereafter used memories of it to protect and solidify his position; in the process he legitimized patriarchal dominance and promoted a middle-class version of appropriate manliness. Landis saw to it that baseball's historical links with the traditional values most commonly associated with middle-class masculinity (such as respectability, integrity, and self-control) were not further damaged by scandal. As a result most people believed that "Landis ruled wisely, courageously, and fairly throughout his twenty-three-year reign. Few Americans of the era matched his esteem and popularity," notes the historian Jules Tygiel.[42]

Landis's obituaries suggest the respect he commanded. "He had a special gift for penetrating the wrappings of passion and sentimentality and irrelevance to the core of right and wrong in any issue," editorialized the *Chicago Herald-American,* "and having done that, he had the calm assurance to decide for the right exactly as he saw it. Another name for that kind of assurance is integrity."[43] Yet another name for that kind of assurance is hubris. "At times he may have been arbitrary, self-willed, and even unfair, but he 'called 'em as he saw 'em,' and he turned over to his successor a game cleansed of the nasty spots which followed World War I," concludes J. G. Taylor Spink. "He put the fear of God into weak characters who otherwise might have been inclined to violate their trust."[44] Although that sense of fear could be put to other uses, it was an essential element in keeping Black Sox scandal memories alive.[45] Obviously the players (eventually) got the message. But so too did the fans; public confidence in the game was largely restored and baseball experienced a period of relative tranquility, in spite of the ravaging effects of the Great Depression.[46] Often referred to as the only successful dictator in American history, Landis elicited tremendous respect and admiration—indeed, gratitude—for helping restore baseball to its exalted place as the national pastime. More than fifty years after his death, the image of the stern, sharp-eyed old man protecting baseball by lording over it remains with us.

"With the Single-Mindedness of a Burglar Blowing a Safe"

A great deal has been made about the allusion to the Black Sox scandal in F. Scott Fitzgerald's *The Great Gatsby* (1925).[47] Since many critics view the novel as a microcosm of a failed society, it is entirely appropriate that the 1919 World Series scandal appears in it. After learning that the enigmatic and boorish gambler Meyer Wolfsheim—Jay Gatsby's mysterious benefactor—was "the man who fixed the World Series back in 1919," Fitzgerald's narrator, Nick Carraway, muses: "The idea staggered me. I remembered, of course, that the World Series had been fixed in 1919, but if I had thought of it at all I would have thought of it as a thing that merely *happened,* the end of some inevitable chain. It never occurred to me that one man could start to play with the faith of fifty million people—with the single-mindedness of a burglar blowing a safe."[48] For some readers, the scene reverberates throughout the novel, for it is one of the earliest indicators that the dashing Gatsby is not what he appears to be. Thereafter his underworld connections undermine his legitimacy and taint him. The literary critic John Lauricella argues that "the moment is so well-known and so strongly characteristic of Nick and Gatsby that it may be read as the novel's signature scene."[49] According to Lauricella, "Gatsby's 'gonnegtion' with Meyer Wolfsheim, criminal meddler in America's National Game, is an index of the corrupt means this decadent romantic (i)dealist twists to serve his incorruptible dream."[50] Although it is worth noting the symbolic importance that Fitzgerald attributes to the scandal, the process and implications of this specific remembrance are my focus.

By using the Big Fix less than five years after its conclusion, Fitzgerald could provide his first readers with an essentially contemporary framework to understand Gatsby's duplicity and amorality (or immorality). For Fitzgerald and his initial audience, the Black Sox scandal was a living memory; it still had immediacy and moral resonance. Indeed, we can take Nick Carraway's understanding of the event to represent widely held public perceptions and assumptions. After their luncheon exchange, Carraway begins to recognize that Meyer Wolfsheim—commonly believed to have been modeled on the gambler Arnold Rothstein—is, at least in part, the source of Gatsby's affluence and apparent success. It is due to Wolfsheim, a "small, flat-nosed Jew" with roving "tiny eyes" and eccentric speech patterns and habits (such as wearing cuff links made of human molars), that Gatsby has attained a semblance of the American Dream; at the same time, Wolfsheim is responsible for the nation's loss of innocence. As far as the latter is concerned, Fitzgerald, like most of the sportswriters who broke the scandal story, probably overstates the influence Wolfsheim/Rothstein wielded.[51]

The historical facts are less important than tracing Fitzgerald's contribution to the maintenance of the Big Fix in collective memories. For Fitzgerald, Meyer Wolfsheim—an uncouth underworld figure, an outsider, a caricature of an ethnic stereotype—is responsible for the corruption of the national pastime as well as the novel's hero. Wolfsheim is the sinister tempter who (presumably) transforms the self-made Gatsby from a courageous (and penniless) war hero into a profligate bootlegger. Gatsby is certainly a rogue, albeit a romantic one, long before he meets Wolfsheim, but Wolfsheim nurtures him, provides him with illicit opportunities and "gonnegtions," and feeds his unattainable dream. "Wolfsheim has a subordinate and yet very important role to play in the novel," the critic Josephine Z. Kopf argues. "Like the classical usurer, he is the power behind the scenes in Gatsby's life."[52] More to the point, Fitzgerald suggests that Wolfsheim has significantly helped corrupt, enervate, and, in effect, emasculate Gatsby. Like the Black Sox before him, Gatsby is done in by Wolfsheim. Wolfsheim makes Gatsby—he says he raised Gatsby "up out of nothing, right out of the gutter" (172)—and in the process destroys him. Kopf puts it succinctly: "Fitzgerald needed an evil manipulator; [and] the villainous Jew served his purpose well."[53] Fitzgerald, in short, reinscribes Wolfsheim/Rothstein in collective memories as the principal cause of the Black Sox scandal, an event he famously suggests challenged the faith of fifty million Americans, including presumably Nick Carraway, if not Fitzgerald himself. For Fitzgerald, "a student of history" who "recognized what baseball had come to mean to America," the Black Sox scandal can be seen as a site of moral failure and financial success, as a vivid example of the ambiguous wasteland that he believed the United States had become.[54]

In Memoriam: Charles Comiskey and Kid Gleason

In late October 1931, as most of the nation slid further into economic disarray, Charles Comiskey died at age seventy-two. Comiskey was eulogized in the most respectful terms imaginable. "The obituary is, in some respects, a model for other news stories," notes the media historian and critic Michael Schudson. "Everyone dies, but whose death is worthy of coverage?"[55] The death of one of the few men in baseball history to rise from the ranks of the players to team ownership and the man arguably most devastated by the Black Sox scandal eleven years before was obviously newsworthy. Triumph and tragedy, especially when they are commingled, sells newspapers. Such a pattern emerges in Comiskey's obituaries, which certainly reactivated Black Sox scandal memories.

In death, Comiskey was widely hailed as a self-made man of unsullied integrity who greatly advanced the American League and the national pastime and was among Chicago's leading citizens. According to Judge Landis, Comiskey had an unusual combination of "integrity, fidelity, and industry. His career is suggestive of that of so many eminent Americans who rise from humble beginnings to what the world appraises great success."[56] A chorus of journalists and prominent men—including President Herbert Hoover—concurred by offering testimonials that Comiskey would have relished.[57] "The career of Charley Comiskey, the Old Roman of baseball," wrote John Kieran of the *New York Times,* "was a romance of sport, a Horatio Alger tale of a poor boy who, by his own skill, courage, and intelligence, rose to fame and fortune."[58] "Great men have come and great men have gone," the sports editor Edward Geiger eulogized, "but, all things equal, Comiskey leaves behind a record unique in the typical American game, a record for doing good athletically, morally and socially, a record of which any living person might well be proud."[59] The *Chicago Herald and Examiner* reported: "Hundreds of messages of condolences began arriving at the [Comiskey] home after the news of Comiskey's death was made public.

Expressions of sympathy will reach thousands, for the 'Old Roman' was one of the most beloved and picturesque figures baseball ever produced. His friends were legion and ranged from kings to those of the lowest estates."[60] As these examples suggest, to his eulogizers Comiskey was a genuinely great man, a hard-working pioneer, an intelligent and charitable baseball magnate held in the highest esteem, the very personification of the American success story.

Many eulogizers also suggested that, perhaps as much as his advanced age and lingering heart condition, Comiskey's physical decline and death could be attributed to the Black Sox affair. "Ever since the Black Sox scandal—a disgraceful affair in which seven men are alleged to have sold out their employer in the 1919 world series—Comiskey had been a changed man," commented Harry Neily in the *Chicago American.* "The disgrace of being the owner of the only ball team in modern times to sell out to gamblers weighed heavily upon him." Neily continued: "He could not understand how a man of his long and honorable career should be the victim of such skullduggery. It was a hard blow."[61] Evidently "shattered in spirit and health" after the Big Fix was made public, Comiskey soon thereafter withdrew from the White Sox's daily operations.[62] A subheading in the *Sporting News*'s story about Comiskey's passing put the matter succinctly: "Old Roman's Health Failed after Exposure of 1919 Series."[63] Warren Brown, a sports columnist for the *Chicago Herald and Examiner,* observed that Comiskey had at least one great team and "one that plumbed the very depths of baseball." Unfortunately, Brown noted, "It was one of the two tragedies of Comiskey's life that these two were actually one and the same team." The blow the Black Sox debacle delivered "was not a fair one. It was delivered well below the belt, and the greatest of fighters could hardly be expected to cope with that sort of foul attack." In the end, the scandal, "combined with the death of his wife, shattered Comiskey's health." Moreover, Brown concluded, "it shattered the morale of the entire institution he had built up, so that the White Sox, since the disintegration of that tampered team, have never been the same."[64] Apparently the victim of a lethal combination of deception, betrayal, and heartbreak, Comiskey, argued his eulogizers, was the Big Fix's most ravaged and least deserving victim.

Inevitably, eulogizers of popular and respected public figures celebrate and sanitize the deceased and their accomplishments. Obituaries usually present the deceased in the most flattering light possible, out of respect for the dead and their family and friends. But obituaries sometimes remind readers of their own history or connect them to notable historical events. Obituaries can mark time for entire communities of readers. Comiskey's obituaries provided an intersection of collective and personal memories about the Black Sox scandal. For many people, especially Chicagoans, Comiskey's obituaries were probably a long-expected and melancholy postscript to the World Series scandal; for others, they were an occasion to remember or learn about a venerated American and a singular sports episode.

Two days into 1933, William "Kid" Gleason, the White Sox's manager during the 1919 World Series, died at the age of sixty-seven after a long illness. Gleason's passing did not elicit the voluminous media attention Comiskey's death had received, but eulogizers employed a similar narrative to describe Gleason's post–Black Sox scandal years. The *New York Times* noted: "After the revelations of the 1919 world's series between the White Sox and the Cincinnati Reds reached the public, the shock of that scandal which involved his players kept Gleason on a sick bed for a long period. His life was despaired of more than once." Gleason, whom the paper described as "one of the most picturesque figures in baseball," apparently never fully recovered from the shock of the World Series scandal, despite "his great vitality."[65]

At the time of his death, Gleason, like virtually everyone caught in the web of the scandal, was firmly ensconced in Black Sox memories. Thirty years later, Eliot Asinof would maintain that Gleason was "fully aware of how severe a blow he had suffered. He had tried to cover it up with toughness, to forget the old and build up the new. But memories of the betrayal smothered him."[66] Portrayed as a victim of treachery, Gleason remains a depressing example of how the Big Fix made bystanders suffer.[67]

"Reinstate Shoeless Joe!"

Not long after Charles Comiskey and Kid Gleason died, Joe Jackson once again made the news. In 1933, John Mauldin, the mayor of Greenville, South Carolina, led a drive to clear Jackson's name so that the former outfielder could manage a local semiprofessional team without endangering the future Major League eligibility of his players. Even twelve years after the Black Sox banishment, guilt by association—or perhaps moral contamination—was apparently still a concern. Thanks to Mauldin's efforts and Jackson's popularity, the drive collected over five thousand signatures on a petition addressed to commissioner Landis. "In mid-December," writes Donald Gropman, one of Jackson's biographers, "amid a flurry of news reports, Mauldin mailed the petition and an application for Joe's reinstatement to the Commissioner's office."[68]

Later that month, before Landis decided on the application, the *New York World-Telegram* published an unattributed article, "Reinstate Shoeless Joe!"

which took an uncommon position. The story opened by revealing Edward Barrow, the New York Yankees business manager and former manager of the Boston Red Sox, as Jackson's supporter. Barrow, the article continued, "said that he was in favor of letting Jackson earn a living in baseball again, and letting him run an industrial league team in Greenville, S.C." Barrow argued that Jackson "has done a long and sufficient penance, and that it would be the human thing to lift the bars and let him run that club in Greenville. After all, it is not in organized baseball, and no harm would be done to anybody." Barrow added, "As a matter of fact, I don't see why Buck Weaver, Happy Felsch and Eddie Cicotte should not be reinstated along with Jackson. They have paid for their indiscretion, and as long as we do not have them in any organized league, what possible injury could they do to the game?" The article concluded by noting that a "canvass of other leaders in the major leagues, including Judge Kenesaw M. Landis, brought a terrific silence. Barrow alone gave voice to the Christmas spirit, and held out the hand of human sympathy for Shoeless Joe."[69] Probably motivated in part by holiday goodwill, Barrow and the unattributed author of the story expressed a viewpoint—in a word, clemency—out of step with the times.

Perhaps what is most notable about Barrow's comments is the impassioned rebuttal they provoked. "Before the ink was dry on the Barrow article," notes Gropman, "it was attacked by Westbrook Pegler, whose syndicated column appeared in almost two hundred newspapers with a total readership of twelve million."[70] An acerbic former sportswriter, Pegler, whose work at this time had not yet lapsed into repetitive and nasty attacks on labor unions, New Dealers, and President Franklin D. Roosevelt and his family, expressed the dominant way the Black Sox scandal and the players' fate was understood.[71] Pegler argued: "The movement to obtain a writ of amnesty for Shoeless Joe Jackson, the old ball player who was ruled out of the game amid great public horror in 1919, reminds me that sin does not pay and that I had better be good or I will get mine. It was a dreadful thing that Shoeless Joe did in the world series of 1919 between the White Sox, of which he was a member, and the Cincinnati Reds." After the facts were brought to light, "justice was terrible and swift," in Pegler's appraisal. Jackson and his implicated teammates had betrayed "a sacred public trust" and as a result "were held up to public scorn all over the country. The public was aghast about it all, and the conspirators slunk away and tried to hide." At the time, Pegler continued, Americans "were furious against the men who had betrayed their confidence in the world series, which is the annual autumn blue ribbon classic of the great national game." According to Pegler, most Americans "have never forgiven the perfidy of the White Sox, who marred the brightest illusion and shook the innocent confidence of American youth. That was the real evil of it. Little, dry-faced kids in the street, who believed in baseball and made heroes of such as Joe Jackson, read in the papers that the world series had been a fake, and there is no way of telling what effect it had on their lives." For Pegler, the matter at hand obviously went far beyond the confines of baseball. He positioned himself as a stern moralist who was unequivocally "against the proposal to reinstate Jackson, feeling that he and the others should be made horrible examples. Show them any consideration and you will set an example which might lead to grafting in public office, contempt for the public intelligence and the degradation of government." He concluded: "Will the citizens condone misconduct in the high places of American life or will they not?"[72] It is not surprising that Pegler framed Jackson's fate as a question of morality (as opposed to labor relations, for instance). In fact, though it was more vitriolic than most, Pegler's response to Jackson was representative of how the Black Sox scandal was most frequently remembered and perceived at the time.

An (Elusive) Boyhood Parable

When we consider the ways in which Big Fix memories persisted during these years, it is important not to ignore individual or personal memories of the event. After all, as Maurice Halbwachs notes, "it is individuals as group members who remember."[73] And although private memories are necessarily idiosyncratic, selective, and fluid, they are not inconsequential or devoid of meaning. Of course, they are also very difficult to document. Unless they are transcribed or frequently articulated, they are usually lost to history.

Initially, I suspected that one way the Black Sox scandal persisted in American memories was as a kind of masculine narrative transmitted from one generation of (mostly male) baseball fans to the next. Like Aesop's fables, the story of the Black Sox scandal could be told in an explicitly didactic manner, perhaps especially so for young men and boys interested in sports. From one perspective, it was a story about men behaving badly, corruption, and its consequences. As the film critic Richard Schickel puts it: "There was a time when the Black Sox Scandal was central to the moral education of young American males. The fact that it involved baseball players—members of the 1919 Chicago White Sox—who conspired with gamblers to throw the World Series (no less) struck at the very center of boyhood. The fact that the consequence of the act was so dire—permanent banishment from baseball—in comparison with the paltry rewards (a few thousand dollars to each man) imparted ironic force to the story." "Haunting in its humanity and unambiguous in its morality," Schickel continues, "this story was turned by fathers into a parable that helped set several generations of sons on the path of righteousness."[74] There is some evidence to support this idea. For example, Alf Walle's "'I'm Afraid It Is, Kid': The Social Dynamics of a Baseball Story" (1979) suggests that the Black Sox scandal narrative was indeed a common (and gendered) folk tale.[75]

Briefly, Walle analyzes two versions of the legendary "Say it ain't so, Joe," exchange that "are completely opposite in tone and message" and argues that folklore "performers will, although possibly unwittingly, transform folklore as it is transmitted and make it meaningful within a current context and to the specific segment of society to which it is addressed."[76] The two renditions Walle examines are best described as the "Little Kid" and the "Kid Gleason" versions. In the former, a boy approaches Joe Jackson on the courthouse steps after Jackson has testified about the 1919 World Series and says, "Say it ain't so, Joe," to which Jackson replies, "I'm afraid it is, kid." "As a youth during the 1950s and 1960s," explains Walle, "I heard this version of the courthouse exchange from my peers, my Boy Scout troop leader, and my football coach, among others."[77] In the latter version, William "Kid" Gleason, the White Sox manager, approaches Jackson and asks the same question, to which Jackson replies, "I'm afraid it is, Kid." Walle notes that he heard this treatment of the exchange "only from the old men who habitually played checkers around the courthouse square of my hometown. This version was becoming obsolete during my youth, but certain of these old men not only remembered it, but constantly retold it."[78] By diagramming the divergent structural components and meanings of these accounts, Walle illustrates how a virtually identical ten-word conversation can be transformed into two diametrically opposed narratives. In the first account, Walle notes, Jackson "is an authority figure, a heroic personality, and a model for youth to emulate";[79] he is a moral failure who loses the respect of the younger generation. In the second account, Jackson "is the youthful understudy and surrogate son of Kid Gleason, the old pro and symbolic father"; in this version of the story, Jackson is ostracized because he "breaks the sacred trust of sportsmanship and proves to be unworthy of respect."[80]

Walle's article is important because it suggests that the Black Sox scandal was still being used as a masculine cautionary tale some forty years later and because it exemplifies how an event or a story (whether historical or apocryphal) can be put to various (even conflicting) uses. "Over the years," Walle concludes, "people familiar with the actual event passed from the scene, and individuals who learned the tale from oral tradition slowly transformed its meaning and message"; more often than not those people were men who recognized the utility of the Black Sox story to instruct boys about the unforgiving way of the world, about disappointment and justice (or injustice), about what it means to be a responsible man.[81]

Emboldened by Schickel and Walle, I set out to gather anecdotal evidence that corroborated this use. I suspected that there were more men (and maybe some women) who had been told about the scandal in the way Schickel and Walle describe. Obviously I did not expect to track down and interview many people old enough to remember the actual scandal, though there are some. Rather, considering the aims of my project, I was more interested in talking to people who came of age in the late twenties, thirties, forties, and early fifties—that is, people who had no direct or living memory of the event, but who learned about it from someone else. With this in mind, I interviewed or corresponded with nearly a hundred people, mostly middle-class white men in their midsixties and older. (I recognize that my sample is too small and selective to be statistically meaningful, but the stories and silences I heard are revealing nonetheless.) My informants were from all over the country: Akron, Baltimore, Boston, Cincinnati, Cleveland, Dayton, Milwaukee, New Haven, New York City, Omaha, Orlando, Toledo, Washington, D.C., and, of course, Chicago, both the North Side and the South Side. I met some of them through friends and family; I met others at professional meetings and via the Internet (primarily thanks to the Society for American Baseball Research listserv); and I met some at Comiskey Park in Chicago and Cinergy Field (formerly known as Riverfront Stadium) in Cincinnati.

For the most part, people seemed to enjoy talking to me about baseball, their youth, and the past. Similar to the men and women David Cataneo interviewed in *Hornsby Hit One over My Head: A Fans' Oral History of Baseball* (1997), most of the people I spoke with were knowledgeable and enthusiastic about the game.[82] Almost without exception, they had fond baseball memories; this is not surprising, for baseball oozes and promotes nostalgia. Predictably, several men I interviewed mentioned that their fathers had introduced them to the game and cultivated their interest in it. Many knew about the Black Sox scandal and had opinions about whether Joe Jackson should be in the Baseball Hall of Fame. In all of these ways my informants reconfirmed Carl Becker's argument that "everyman is his own historian."[83] (It is worth noting that two men I interviewed had met ballplayers who had played in the 1919 World Series. One who grew up in a southwest suburb of Chicago met George "Buck" Weaver in 1945 at a baseball school run by the Chicago Park District.[84] Bill Gleason, a South Side

Chicagoan and respected sports journalist, spoke at length with the White Sox catcher and Hall of Famer Ray Schalk, one of the so-called Clean Sox. He recalled that "if you ever said the Black Sox or the scandal to Schalk that ended the conversation.")[85]

Yet generally the people I spoke and corresponded with had great difficulty remembering how they had learned about the Big Fix. Some said that they heard about it by "word of mouth" in the streets and on the sandlots; others said that they read about it in newspapers, baseball almanacs, and periodicals like the *Sporting News* and *Baseball Digest.* A few people remembered specifically which texts they had read. One man I interviewed said he probably learned about the Black Sox scandal from Warren Brown's popular history *The Chicago White Sox* (1952).[86] Another informant reported that he learned about the scandal from Nelson Algren's short story "The Silver-Colored Yesterday," which was anthologized in Charles Einstein's *The Fireside Book of Baseball* (1956).[87] Two respondents thought they learned about the scandal from *The Great Gatsby.*[88] More commonly, though, my informants replied that they did not know how they had learned about the scandal. One man, the historian Melvin L. Adelman, spoke for many when he explained, "I feel like I've always known about the Black Sox scandal."[89]

Unfortunately, no one recalled being told about the episode as a masculine cautionary tale or as an explicitly gendered narrative. Bill Gleason said, "I was born two years after the scandal broke, but my father and all his friends were White Sox fans and they talked about it quite freely."[90] And yet he did not remember his father or his father's friends ever discussing the Big Fix—which was for them a moment of betrayal—in a didactic or moralizing manner. Bill Jauss, a *Chicago Tribune* reporter whom I met at Comiskey Park, came the closest to telling me the story I had expected:

> I lived on the North Side, so my Dad introduced me to baseball by taking me to Wrigley Field when I was seven or eight years old. But my uncle Harry, even though he lived down the street from us, was an unreconstituted South Sider. He took me to my first White Sox games, and he took me to my first Negro League games, when the leagues were segregated. . . .
>
> Uncle Harry is the guy who first told me about the Black Sox scandal. Now you got to understand, you know how kids are that age. "Why did they fake the World Series, Uncle Harry?" And Uncle Harry says, "Because old man Comiskey was so cheap."
>
> This was around World War II, [when] I was eleven or twelve years old. And this is my uncle telling me that old man Comiskey was cheap. Later on I learned and I read that all owners were cheap and all baseball players were playing for peon wages. But that was the way I first heard about it. And then he explained to me—it just crushed him . . . this man had grown up a South Sider and a White

Sox fan—he was sort of like my Dad, who was a diehard Republican, and when Richard Nixon turned out to be a crook my Dad never forgave him. He went to his grave despising Richard Nixon. Uncle Harry for a long time resisted the White Sox, but then ultimately he came back and became a Sox fan again. Now I don't know how typical he was of White Sox fans his age—I imagine quite a bit, because later I studied the attendance figures for the White Sox after the scandal and they went way in the can for a long time.

I asked my Uncle Harry, "How could they"—I didn't use these words—but, "How could they jeopardize these big salaries (thinking in terms of 1942) just to gamble a few games?" And he said, "Bill, they didn't make that kind of money in those days." Sure enough, they were working for $2,500 or something like that. I didn't learn until later that Joe Jackson was semiliterate and very gullible.[91]

Jauss's story was the most extensive and interesting I heard regarding this issue, though he did not suggest that the story his uncle told him was supposed to be didactic. Still, it expresses a sense of bewilderment, disillusionment, and class consciousness that none of my other respondents articulated. It is also significant that a male authority figure, one who seemed to have some enmity toward Comiskey and some measure of understanding and perhaps compassion for the implicated ballplayers, told Jauss about the Big Fix. Over fifty years later, a great deal of Uncle Harry's attitude survives in his nephew. This seems to be an instance where the power of private storytelling has prevailed.

In general, however, my (admittedly narrow) oral history suggests that Schickel overstates the extent to which the Black Sox scandal was a narrative "turned by fathers [or other male authority figures] into a parable that helped set several generations of sons on the path of righteousness." By the twenties, the mass media (primarily daily newspapers and periodicals like the *Sporting News* and *Baseball Digest*) and other privileged storytellers (principally fiction writers like Fitzgerald and Algren) appear to have taken up the cultural work of preserving the scandal in collective and private memories. This does not mean that the episode was not a common folk story or a cautionary tale passed from one generation of baseball fans to the next. I still suspect that it was in some places, perhaps especially on Chicago's South Side and in Black Sox hometowns. But documentation that proves this is scarce, and so the moral and educational value of the story remains indeterminate.

"Remember the Black Sox?"

One of the most interesting Black Sox scandal narratives during these years was John Lardner's "Remember the Black Sox?" which was published in

April 1938 by the *Saturday Evening Post*.[92] Lardner's article offered readers what was at the time the most extensive account of the 1919 game-fixing debacle. Unlike most previous authors, Lardner aspired to do what Eliot Asinof later more fully accomplished in *Eight Men Out,* that is, to weave together a multitude of obscure, seemingly unrelated threads and in the process offer a (seemingly) comprehensive reconstruction of the scandal. At the same time, as its questioning title suggests, Lardner's article provided readers with an invitation to reexamine their personal memories of an event almost twenty years distant, all the while reinscribing the event in collective memories. Such memory relies upon repetition.

Lardner—although only twenty-five at this time, he would become a widely admired *Newsweek* columnist and a critic for the *New Yorker*—began his narrative by recreating the preseries atmosphere in Cincinnati and by introducing some of the affair's principal actors. He noted, for instance, that the series engendered a tremendous amount of open gambling and that the "players [were believed to be] heroic, as they never had been before" (14). After the White Sox suffered a surprising and humiliating loss in game one, Lardner wrote that "the country at large didn't know for another twelve months that the fix was in—the biggest, sloppiest, crudest fix of a sporting event that was known to man. It was a makeshift job; compounded in equal parts of bluff and welsh and cold gall, with no contributor or agent-contributor knowing what the man next to him was up to, and very seldom bothering to find out" (15). It was, Lardner noted, "a haphazard business, all right, comical in some of its aspects, but it nearly wrecked baseball for all eternity" (15). Lardner described the revelations of baseball's crookedness as "a real and ugly shock" (15) to a nation that did not take its baseball lightly.

> The public came within a whisker's width of never seeing another box score, never heckling another umpire, never warming another hot stove. It was close—too close for comfort. And though the baseball magnates of 1938 like to think of 1919 as a tightly sealed chapter, and though the Hall of Fame at Cooperstown is closed, actually if not officially, to Joe Jackson, Buck Weaver, and Eddie Cicotte—well, we're wallowing in baseball luxury now. We can afford to look back at the abyss after eighteen years of hard, steady climbing. (15)

Lardner then reconstructed some of the machinations that led to the fixed games. He probed the gambler's so-called plan, rehashed the bitter dissension that racked the White Sox, mentioned the ways in which Comiskey covered up the affair, and noted the election of Landis as baseball's first commissioner. He also devoted considerable attention to the players. "It's obvious today," Lardner concluded, "that some of them [the banished ballplayers], fix or no fix, were never paid money to throw a game. That all of them are serving life sentences without trial. That, with one or two exceptions, none of them belongs in the same league with [Benedict] Arnold . . . or Guy Fawkes" (85). Writing from a safe distance, Lardner could afford to give the vilified Black Sox some understanding. Finally, Lardner asked (and answered) two questions that no doubt interested many readers: Where are the Black Sox now? and Will any be enshrined in the newly founded Baseball Hall of Fame? Lardner reported that they were scattered all over the country, in some instances still pleading their innocence but essentially disgraced—with the notable exception of Joe Jackson, who remained a hero to the textile workers and boys of Greenville, South Carolina. According to Lardner, there were no rules that said "that the baseball writers cannot vote the Sox to the Hall, if they feel in their hearts that they belong there. There will never be a ruling until some outlaw collects enough votes to qualify him for the holy tablets, and the magnates hope very earnestly that no such emergency will arise" (85). Contrary to the baseball establishment at the time, which actively suppressed memories of the affair, Lardner implicitly argued that the Black Sox scandal was a travesty worth remembering, a moment that could impart valuable lessons about what happened to those who (supposedly) defiled a national institution, who damaged a public trust.

Lardner's essay is notable for many reasons, most obviously because the author's father, the misanthropic humorist Ring Lardner, one of the best-known writers in the United States during the latter half of his career, covered the 1919 World Series. According to one of Ring Lardner's biographers, "after the integrity of the games was conclusively undermined by the Black Sox scandal of 1919 he turned, in disgust and sorrow, to other subjects."[93] Eliot Asinof maintains that the "scandal scarred him leaving a wound that would remain tender for the rest of his life. Significantly, he never wrote a column on the fix or a word about any of its participants."[94] Although John Lardner was only eight years old when the Black Sox scandal broke, it was within this family context that he presumably first learned about the event. In a sense, Lardner's article (which was published less than five years after his father's death) can be read as a case of a son revisiting and reexamining—perhaps even rewriting—his father's past; the son was free to explore where his father chose not (or could not bring himself) to tread. For those interested in Oedipal interpretations of history and Harold Bloom's "anxiety of influence," this Lardner's article is a minor bonanza.[95]

As John Lardner himself suggested, "Remember the Black Sox?" appeared when the fixed World Series could be addressed safely, without fear of further damaging baseball's reputation. By the time the *Saturday Evening Post* bought Lardner's article (for $750), baseball had weathered the scandal's backlash and the worst of the Depression and could finally confront its demons.[96] Moreover, by 1938 many (some?) boys and young men had been raised on the "Say it ain't so, Joe," parable. The melancholy story of Joe Jackson and his teammates had quickly ascended to mythic status. An independent thinker and journalist—indeed, the sportswriter Red Smith later called him "a bona fide original"—Lardner told the Black Sox scandal in such a way that the fixers are severely punished for hitting "the baseball public between the eyes" (84).[97] But he also implied that some (perhaps most) of the White Sox did not deserve all the ignominy thrust upon them. For instance, Lardner asked: "Was the ball club underpaid? That's the excuse which many critics give for what happened in 1919. Commy [Comiskey] was a powerful, upright man, a baseball pioneer, but his best friends could not call him a lavish spender—not with the hired help" (82). Lardner observed that few "players had five-figure incomes prior to 1920. But Commy's [pay] scale was lower than most, and his players were better than any" (82). In this way Lardner began to historicize the Big Fix and the complex conditions that fostered it; in the process he offered a (slightly) more complicated version of the event than any proffered to that point.

Although a hybridized narrative—for the most part a conventional morality play with a strain or two of protorevisionist history woven into it—Lardner's "Remember the Black Sox?" is in many ways representative of most Black Sox scandal stories written between the twenties and the early fifties: it vilified the gamblers for the calamity; it condemned the ballplayers for their duplicity, disloyalty, and stupidity; it suggested that the whole episode is safely consigned to the past; and it noted that baseball's present and future had been purged of such perfidy. Consequently, one could argue that Lardner's story buttressed the master narrative about the fixed World Series that the baseball establishment promoted as official history. But Lardner also suggested that remembering the Black Sox scandal necessarily engages memories of supposedly heroic men who dramatically failed a generation of American boys and were made to suffer tremendously for it. Subtly didactic, "Remember the Black Sox?" reminded its readers that the love of money is the root of all (or at least most) evil and that justice is in short supply, thereby reaffirming the need to keep to the straight and narrow. Boys will be boys (even if they are actually men), Lardner suggested, but some sins are simply unpardonable.

Nelson Algren's Black Sox Blues

More so than most of his peers, Nelson Algren wailed the Black Sox blues with passion and power. Referred to as the "poet of the Chicago slums" by the editor Malcolm Cowley and (more derisively) as "the bard of the stumblebum" by the literary critic Leslie Fiedler, Algren was an impressionistic social realist who had an abiding interest in sport.[98] Two of his novels, *Never Come Morning* (1942) and the posthumously published *The Devil's Stocking* (1983), have prizefighters as protagonists. But the Big Fix captivated Algren's imagination, for over the course of his lengthy career Algren would sporadically return to the subject. Algren used the Black Sox as a way of reconnecting with the past—sometimes nostalgically, sometimes with a more critical perspective—and thus in a small way he helped reinscribe the event and its participants in American collective memories. But before we turn to some of his Black Sox narratives, it is important to offer a brief sketch of the man Ernest Hemingway once rated "second only to William Faulkner as America's greatest novelist."[99]

Born to second-generation Americans in 1909, Nelson Algren Abraham (his full given name, which he legally changed in 1944) spent most of his childhood and adolescence in Chicago.[100] The youngest of three children, Algren was an underachiever as a student, more interested in athletics than books. Still, in 1927 Algren matriculated to the University of Illinois. After graduating in 1931 with a degree in journalism, the aspiring writer "began tinkering with his name," writes his biographer Betina Drew.[101] Due to the Great Depression, Algren had a difficult time finding work with a newspaper. As a result, "he drifted to New Orleans and later to the Southwest, riding box cars and taking odd jobs when he could find them."[102] A great deal of that experience became fodder for his first novel, *Somebody in Boots* (1935). After spending a few months in a Texas jail for stealing a typewriter, Algren returned to Chicago, where he frequented leftist literary and political meetings and befriended the future novelist Richard Wright, who would later dub Algren the "Proust of the Proletariat."[103] A year later he married (he was divorced by 1940) and began working as an editor for the Works Progress Administration. In 1942, Algren published his second novel, *Never Come Morning,* which is about first- and second-generation urban Poles and which earned critical praise. The following year, Algren began a three-year stint as a private in the U.S. Army, mostly in the Medical Corps as a litter-bearer. A poor soldier, Algren did a tour of duty in Europe during World War II. By the end of 1945, he was back in the United States. Thereafter, Algren devoted most of the rest of his life to writing and traveling. A perennial outsider and nonconformist, Algren wrote about the dispossessed, about victims of oppression. One critic maintains that Algren "is the poet of the jail and the whorehouse; he has made a close study of the cockroach, the drunkard, and the pimp, the garbage in the street and the spittle on the chin. He has a truly cloacal vision of the American experience."[104] Another critic notes: "For forty-eight years, he recorded life in the back alleys of America's cities and the problems of isolated people with no skills who are victims of hostile environments with which they are in constant combat."[105] Considering his biography and the thrust of much of his work, it is not surprising that Algren was drawn to the Black Sox scandal.

Algren's first Big Fix text, a poem entitled "The Swede Was a Hard Guy," was published in 1942 by the *Southern Review,* a well-respected literary journal.[106] A mournful, nostalgic lament laced with unmistakable sympathy for the banished ballplayers, who are described as lambs being led to a shearing (876), Algren's prose poem is comprised of more than thirty stanzas of varying lengths, few of which rhyme. The poem begins by depicting an empty, debris-strewn Comiskey Park after "the final out of the final inning / Of the final game / Of a second-division season" (874). Having established some temporal distance from the Black Sox scandal, the poem turns retrospective and offers thumbnail sketches of six of the implicated White Sox: Joe Jackson, Chick Gandil, Hap Felsch, Buck Weaver, Lefty Williams, and Eddie Cicotte. Read collectively, Algren's sketches depict the ballplayers as supremely talented, unsophisticated men from impoverished and regionally diverse backgrounds. Quietly lurking in the background are some of the involved gamblers: most notably, Arnold Rothstein, Abe Attell, and Sleepy Bill Burns. Cicotte, for instance, finds "ten Rothstein Gs. under his pillow" (875) before the first game of the series. Critical of Comiskey, whom Algren argues was penurious and "played the hero for the newspapermen" (876), the poem nonetheless notes that he "had his heart broken all the same" (877). In the end, though, rather than ascribe responsibility for the debacle, Algren encourages readers to forget the sad affair and the infamous eight: "do not be remembering the most natural man ever to wear spiked shoes," Algren writes of Joe Jackson, "the canniest fielder and the longest hitter" (878). It is, of course, an ironic admonition, for the poem itself poignantly reinscribes Jackson, Weaver, and the rest in American collective memories. Nevertheless, remembering, Algren suggests, is too painful and it is better to let the shadows fade into the past. "For Shoeless Joe is gone, long gone," Algren observes in the poem's penultimate stanza. "A long yellow grass-blade between his teeth / And the bleacher-shadows behind him" (879). More melancholy than didactic, "The Swede Was a Hard Guy" is an elegiac and certainly instructive reminder of what happened to Algren's ballplaying heroes. Republished by *Chicago* magazine in 1956, "The Swede Was a Hard Guy" anticipates Asinof's interpretation in *Eight Men Out.* For both Algren and Asinof reject the easy, simplified morality that traditionally defined the Big Fix.[107]

Algren's next Black Sox scandal text, "The Silver-Colored Yesterday," was first published as part of his famous prose poem *Chicago: City on the Make* (1951) and was anthologized five years later in *The Fireside Book of Baseball.*[108] Set in Chicago in the summer of 1919, "The Silver-Colored Yesterday" is narrated by a ten-year-old street urchin (possibly Algren himself) who proclaims the White Sox shortstop Swede Risberg to be his "fayvrut player" (35). A year later, the "Black Sox were the Reds of that October and mine was the guilt of association" (36), declares Algren's narrator, linking the Black Sox to the then-current Red Scare. Stung, he curses his fallen gods, indicting them as "Benedict Arnolds! Betrayers of American Boyhood, not to mention American Girlhood and American Womanhood and American Hoodhood" (36). Bitter and tainted by Risberg's betrayal, Algren's disillusioned narrator concludes: "I guess that was one way of learning what Hustlertown, sooner or later, teaches all its sandlot sprouts. 'Everybody's out for The Buck. Even big-leaguers.' Even Swede Risberg" (39). For many people besides Algren, this was a painful lesson, not easily forgotten. But just in case it was, Algren's narrative resurrected and reinscribed the memory of the scandal for many readers, and probably introduced the event to many others. The story vividly dramatizes the sense of betrayal and disillusionment that Algren had been experiencing and documenting for most of his life.

Certainly both works have an elegiac cast to them (as do his later Black Sox texts, which are discussed in chapter 3), but they also suggest the long-lasting impact the Black Sox scandal may have exerted across the country. In many ways Algren and his worldview were atypical for his generation, but his perception of the scandal was not unique. As one might expect, these texts illuminate some of the recurrent themes found in much of Algren's work. Like all of his novels, his Black Sox texts focus on losers, victims who have a hand in their own victimization. (Algren once wrote: "Being a loser I speak only for losers.")[109] Algren's Black Sox texts bespeak a bittersweet sense of loss and compassion, a concern for the dispossessed, his tendency to speak for the inarticulate. Tinged with sentimentality and nostalgia, yet littered with concrete historical details, they exemplify Algren's interest in acts of disillusionment and betrayal, the American Dream gone bad.

The traditional, preferred narrative about the Black Sox in these years was that the implicated ballplayers and gamblers were avaricious, immoral men who, in the words of F. Scott Fitzgerald, played "with the faith of fifty million people."[110] From this moralistic perspective, the ballplayers and the gamblers were entirely responsible for the debacle. Algren saw things differently. Despite being jilted by the Sox as a youngster, his respect and sympathy for his former heroes endured. Long before it became popular (or at least acceptable), Algren was in his own small way fighting on behalf of the Black Sox. In other words, Algren's Black Sox texts did (and do) cultural work. As the infamous event receded ever further into the past and its participants passed away, Algren's Black Sox texts helped keep the scandal alive in American collective memories. Granted, they were drops in the bucket, but they mattered: without repetition memory atrophies and dies. Clearly Algren did not tell morally neutral versions of the scandal; he always sided with the scapegoats. When asked in 1957 about the writer's role in society, Algren said "the writer's place today is with the accused, guilty or not guilty, with the accused."[111] Periodically returning to the Big Fix and reconstructing the event as a social drama in which "the ignorant were duped by the clever," and "the powerless suffered and the strong prevailed," Algren cast his lot with the outcasts and contributed to the perpetuation of their memory.[112]

Cooperstown and Selective Memory

Forgetting is a vital, inevitable, and underappreciated feature of memory. Most often frustrating, but sometimes deliberate and convenient, forgetting is as unavoidable as it is necessary. To order and make sense of the past, even the immediate past, memories "must continually be discarded and conflated," observes the historian and geographer David Lowenthal.[113] Memory without forgetting would be unbearable—perhaps just as debilitating as complete amnesia. Forgetting, in short, makes remembering possible. In addition, as Michael Schudson notes, "every memory is necessarily also a forgetting since it is a choosing of what, among a multitude of possibilities, to keep in mind."[114] Perhaps this point is best illustrated with regard to the Black Sox scandal by reflecting on why a few of the Big Fix's alleged participants (most notably, Joe Jackson, Eddie Cicotte, and Buck Weaver) were excluded (until recent exhibits) from the Baseball Hall of Fame.

Located in Cooperstown, New York, a bucolic village of twenty-five hundred residents two hundred miles northwest of New York City, the National Baseball Hall of Fame and Museum was conceived in 1934 and dedicated in June 1939. Set in the mythic (though not historical) birthplace of baseball, the Hall of Fame was intended to be a shrine for the national pastime, a place that would promote the game as an expressive and important American institution.[115] In the words of Alexander Cleland, the Scottish immigrant who gave birth to the idea of the Hall of Fame, numerous fathers "would be interested to stop at Cooperstown and show the building to their sons and perhaps throw a baseball or two on the Field."[116] An entrepreneurial and publicity venture at a time of economic deprivation, the Hall of Fame was established as a "place of memory," to use a phrase often attributed to the French historian Pierre Nora. In the same way that cemetery statuary and war memorials are established for fallen military heroes, the Baseball Hall of Fame was established to commemorate former baseball greats, their heroic deeds, and the game itself. In fact, for many Americans the very name Cooperstown was quickly recognized as a place of baseball commemoration and nostalgia. Nora argues that places of memory are like "moments of history torn away from the movement of history, then returned. No longer quite alive, not yet dead, they are like seashells on the shore from which the sea of living memory has retreated."[117] The Baseball Hall of Fame is such a place, one where artifacts and legends, preserved with great care and deliberation, can be found.

From its inception, the Baseball Hall of Fame, an architectural and archival place of memory, perhaps more alive than Nora would credit it, consciously chose not to remember the Black Sox scandal. At the Hall of Fame, the Black Sox scandal was all but deleted from history.[118] No doubt the omission was intentional—indeed, forgetting was probably the point. From the perspective of the baseball establishment, the Black Sox scandal was a moment too painful or embarrassing to recall. A repository of memory set in an idyllic American village, the Hall of Fame could not include baseball's most notorious pariahs if it was to promote a version of the national pastime that projected its virtues. For Cooperstown to serve as baseball's Valhalla or Olympus, selective remembering and forgetting was (and remains) imperative. Nonetheless, to borrow a phrase coined by the *New York Times* sports columnist Arthur Daley, the Black Sox were "Banned from Archives—But Not from Memory."[119]

Collective Counter-memories: Joe Jackson and Buck Weaver

Most remembrances and renditions of the Black Sox scandal during the years examined here simplified the affair. The characters were largely stereotypical: they included avaricious, manipulative fixers and ballplayers, rubes duped into complicity, a few innocent victims, and a lone, wrathful avenger who restored order. The setting was recognizable: the World Series. The preferred morals were plain: the wages of sin are (professional) death, so keep to the straight and narrow. In these ways one could argue that the Black Sox narrative did not evolve significantly in mainstream American collective memories and that the dominant discourse surrounding the scandal remained unchallenged.

Usually, however, when collective memories are (seemingly) stable and have been incorporated into popular consciousness—when they are institutionalized and enshrined in officially sanctioned traditions and narratives—counter-memories are not far afield. "Counter-memory," argues George Lipsitz in *Time Passages: Collective Memory and American Popular Culture* (1990), "is a way of remembering and forgetting that starts with the local, the immediate, and the personal. Unlike historical narratives that begin with the totality of human existence and then locate specific actions and events within that totality, counter-memory starts with the particular and the specific and then builds outward toward a total story. Counter-memory looks to the past for the hidden histories excluded from dominant narratives."[120] For our purposes, counter-memory refers to evocations of the Black Sox scandal that deviate from or subvert the conventional or dominant ways it was commonly conceived.[121] This is not to suggest a simple model of dominant narratives and memories versus resistant, countercultural narratives and memories; that is obviously too reductive and inaccurate, in part because dominant and competing narratives shift over time and in part because they sometimes exist simultaneously. Yet since collective memory is always linked to specific cultural contexts and places, we should examine some of the communities where unorthodox memories of the Black Sox held sway. In particular, how some local people remembered and made sense of Joe Jackson and Buck Weaver provide us with vivid examples of counter-memory—perhaps collective counter-memories—at work.

In the decades immediately after the Big Fix, Joe Jackson represented numerous, sometimes conflicting, things for most people. Clearly he was still widely recognized as a ballplayer endowed with superior natural ability.[122] The pitching great Walter Johnson of the Washington Senators put it succinctly in 1929: "The greatest natural hitter that I ever saw was Joe Jackson."[123] To his family and friends, Jackson was shy, unassuming, and considerate. To many others, Jackson was a naive busher, a fool, a dupe, a pathetic simpleton. For still others, Jackson represented the worst sort of treachery, deceit, and betrayal; he was baseball's Judas, its Benedict Arnold. One critic suggests that Jackson was a pariah, an arch villain universally "anathema to every fan."[124] Yet this was far from the case in much of Jackson's native South, where a resilient counter-memory of Jackson existed. For more than ten years after his expulsion from the Majors, Jackson played under his own name in the semiprofessional South Georgia League and in numerous promotional contests, where he was advertised in posters and treated warmly by fans.[125] In August 1932, a year before he stopped playing organized baseball, Jackson was the subject of a where-are-they-now article by Ward Morehouse in the *New York Sun*. Morehouse described Jackson as "clear-eyed, ruddy-faced, big-bellied, slow-moving, soft spoken," and he noted that in Greenville, South Carolina, Jackson's home town, "this ballplaying country boy remains something of a hero. That 1919 business is forgotten. Whatever Joe's cronies may have thought then, they now regard him as a baseball genius who got a tough break."[126] Morehouse's article was corroborated five years later by Richard McCann's "Baseball Remains Joe Jackson's First Love Seventeen Years after Ban." According to McCann, Jackson "is a respected citizen and a beloved neighbor here [in Greenville]. They just can't believe that Joe did anything wrong. Not their Shoeless Joe."[127] To express their civic pride in Jackson, the people of Brandon Mills, South Carolina, twice held "Joe Jackson Night" in the forties to celebrate their native son's birthday.[128]

Not long after one of those celebrations, in September 1942, the *Sporting News* published (much to Landis's consternation) a sensitive, sympathetic article by Carter "Scoop" Latimer entitled "Joe Jackson, Contented Carolinian at Fifty-Four, Forgets Bitter Dose in His Cup and Glories in His Twelve Hits in '19 Series."[129] Latimer, who described Jackson as an old friend, noted that the "gift-bearing delegation of well-wishers at the surprise birthday party was typical of the boys who make almost daily pilgrimages to Joe's home or gang around him in the streets and on sandlots." It is, of course, an observation that undercuts the notion that Jackson betrayed and forever disillusioned the youth of America, or at least the boys in Greenville.

To drive that point home and to redeem one of their own, the South Carolina State Senate and House of Representatives passed a resolution in February 1951 to reinstate Jackson as a member in "'good standing' in professional baseball."[130] Later that year, Jackson was inducted as a charter member of the Cleveland Indians Baseball Hall of Fame, which suggests that the counter-memory delineated here was not exclusive to the South. The prominent sports columnist Dan Daniel wrote that by "voting Joe Jackson, one of the notorious Black Sox of 1919, into their diamond shrine, the electors in Cleveland have made a daring move which will bring prolonged and heated discussion wherever fans may gather." Jackson's election, Daniel argued, "honored a man of impugned baseball integrity." However, those who elected Jackson pointed out that his "integrity never was questioned in his six years of service with the Indians, from 1910, when he was acquired from the Athletics, until his 1916 transfer to the White Sox." As for his role in the 1919 World Series, many in Cleveland believed that Jackson "was the victim of a bum rap." That sentiment was amplified in Greenville, among other places—perhaps especially those below the Mason-Dixon line.[131] After Jackson died in December 1951, Shirley Povich of the *Washington Post* remarked that Jackson "was the idol of the townfolk who ascribed the whole talk of a fixed World Series as just another dirty Yankee trick."[132]

For those who saw him as a convenient scapegoat, as a sacrificial lamb, as an icon of victimization—exploited by Comiskey, ensnared by (Jewish) city slickers, punished extralegally by Landis—Jackson evoked powerful and resilient counter-memories of the Black Sox scandal. These counter-memories resisted the hegemonic version of the Big Fix the baseball establishment and much of the media promulgated; that is, that the fix resulted solely from the dishonesty and venality of the ballplayers and gamblers. "To the local folk," writes Eliot Asinof in *Eight Men Out,* Jackson was always "a hero, well liked and highly respected. He was never without their support, and the dignity of his talent never seemed to dwindle."[133] In fact, it seems likely that Jackson was popular with and respected by some people partly due to his expatriate, outlaw status. The day before he died, Jackson apparently told an old Greenville friend: "I don't deserve this thing that's happened to me."[134] Those who embraced counter-memories of the Big Fix no doubt agreed.

Buck Weaver likewise embodied and engendered counter-memories of the Black Sox scandal, especially on Chicago's South Side, where he lived until his death in 1956. Weaver—who by all accounts did not take the offered money to participate in the conspiracy, who played extremely well in the 1919 World Series, and who made several unsuccessful attempts to return to Major League Baseball—was generally treated with respect, warmth, and sympathy by those in his community. During the years immediately after his expulsion, it was not uncommon for him to "go out to the baseball diamonds at Washington Park . . . and hit fly balls to the kids," reveals Irving M. Stein in *The Ginger Kid: The Buck Weaver Story* (1992). "They loved Buck and he returned their affection."[135] In 1927, recognizing that Weaver was still a talented ballplayer and a popular local celebrity, representatives of the Mid-West League, a semipro circuit in and around Chicago, voted unanimously to welcome Weaver as a player.[136] During the course of his first season, Weaver was cheered by thousands of Chicagoans and honored with floral tributes and gifts.[137] Stein observes that over the years the local media "sporadically focused on Weaver's situation expressing both sympathy and sorrow. Baseball fans in Chicago, in poll after poll, vouchsafed their confidence in Buck by naming him their choice as the best third baseman in either White Sox or Chicago history. While Buck was still playing semipro ball, south siders set up booths on busy street corners asking passersby to sign petitions asking for his reinstatement."[138] At one point, those petitions numbered 30,000 signatures.[139] In Chicago at least, it is reasonable to conclude, Buck Weaver was not a pariah; indeed, he was (and is) more often viewed as a victim of circumstance.[140] Like Jackson, Weaver was widely understood as a convenient scapegoat for the affair. For those who remembered Weaver as a victim of association, as an innocent entangled in a conspiracy he did not participate in, as a man who refused to be an informer, as someone who was treated unfairly by a baseball commissioner who would not recognize different degrees of culpability, the Black Sox scandal was something other than a simple morality play.[141]

Some Observations

All these Black Sox memories and stories supply us with an inkling of what personal understandings of the Big Fix may have been during the immediately succeeding decades. They do not, however, provide us with unproblematic evidence about how the Black Sox scandal was understood before it was reconstructed in more concrete cultural forms. The Black Sox scandal memories delimited here vividly demonstrate that collective memories—and meditations on those memories—are provisional and nebulous. It is difficult to reach anything but tentative conclusions about a collection of fragmentary remembrances. That may be the best conclusion to draw: where memory is concerned, conclusions are elusive. Nonetheless, it is possible to offer some observations about how Black Sox scandal memories were used and maintained during the thirty years after the scandal and about the process of collective remembering in general.

It may seem obvious, but it is worth saying: the Big Fix was remembered differently by individuals and communities in different places at different times. Always fragmentary and provisional, dynamic and ongoing, always an act or a process as opposed to an objective, static record to be recalled, memory is never monolithic. Still, since one of the most common ways both people and societies remember the recent past is through individuals, and because Landis ruled the professional game with iron-fisted panache until his death in 1944, the version of the Black Sox narrative he sought to convey remained alive (quite literally) for many Americans for most of this era. But because he occupied a prominent position, was widely respected, and had an intuitive flair for public relations (and self-aggrandizement), he exerted more influence than any other individual or institution in maintaining a particular remembrance of the affair. It seems that many Americans remembered the Black Sox scandal in the manner Landis preferred: an aberrant moral crisis (instigated by avaricious, immoral men) and a national tragedy, one that his tireless vigilance (and ruthlessness) would not permit again. Just as Landis brought order and stability to professional baseball, he did much to order and stabilize individual and collective memories of the event that brought him to power. This is not to suggest that Landis's hegemony over the deployment (and suppression) of Black Sox scandal memories was complete. For many people, especially those in places like Greenville, South Carolina, and Chicago these heroes were not easily transformed into scapegoats. Memory is not disinterested; it usually serves the interests of those doing the remembering.[142]

Memories, collective no less than private, are not recalled in sociohistorical vacuums. As always, context matters. For many Americans, the time period examined here was tremendously unsettling. "In these years," maintains the historian Michael E. Parrish, "Americans had to cope both with unprecedented economic prosperity and the worst depression in their history. Which condition produced the greater collective anxiety remains an open question."[143] Fighting World War II and living with the atomic bomb were no less anxiety-producing experiences for the next generation. The time was marked by the "uneasy coexistence of tradition and change and the relentless modifications of social institutions, habits and life-styles, linked in a complex, long-term relationship with economic change," argues the historian Ian Purchase.[144] Amidst this type of dramatic transition, tradition is usually highly valued. So perhaps it is not coincidental that these years are also considered to be professional baseball's second Golden Age, a time of larger-than-life heroes and heroics, the era that Ruth built and that Gehrig, DiMaggio, Williams, Feller, Musial, and others maintained. Unwittingly, these men induced Black Sox amnesia, for their exploits confirmed the national pastime's good health and the vigor and integrity of those who played the game. Nevertheless, the scandal was consistently (though not exclusively) reactivated to reinforce dominant memories of the affair. One of the ways preferred narratives maintain their dominance and cultural currency is through repetition.

Finally, this chapter confirms that the historian James Wilkinson is correct: there is "a powerful tension between the desire to know and the availability of materials from which to derive that knowledge."[145] A paucity of evidence is always a formidable obstacle for a historian, but adding to our burden is that few forms of knowledge are as evanescent and difficult to document as memory. While evidence is scarce and sketchy, counter-memories of the Black Sox scandal no doubt existed in numerous communities besides Greenville and Chicago. Banished ballplayers like Eddie Cicotte and Oscar "Happy" Felsch, both of whom confessed and who lived until the sixties, surely activated disparate memories of the episode. People in bars, pool halls, and barber shops all over the United States more than likely shared competing memories of the Big Fix. Only with great difficulty, effort, and luck will we ever know for sure.

3

The Novel as History, a Novel History: Bernard Malamud's *The Natural* and Eliot Asinof's *Eight Men Out*

The Black Sox scandal obviously remained active in American collective memories during the first half of the twentieth century. But by the early fifties nearly two generations of Americans had no living memory of the event. Moreover, those old enough to remember the scandal firsthand probably developed somewhat blurred and disjointed recollections of the labyrinthine plot. After all, memories usually fade and become entangled with one another rather than remain vivid and distinct. For many others, no doubt, time had effectively simplified the complicated. When these developments occur, contends the historian David Lowenthal, when events become increasingly distant from "personal recall, memory within any society gives way to history."[1] In the case of the Big Fix, as with so many other dramatic historical moments, memory also gave way to literature. At roughly midcentury, as the 1919 scandal began to fade and fragment in the consciousness of some Americans, Bernard Malamud's novel *The Natural* (1952) and Eliot Asinof's popular history *Eight Men Out: The Black Sox and the 1919 World Series* (1963) took up some of the cultural work of maintaining the affair in private and collective memories.

Malamud's and Asinof's books became important sources for new, reinvigorated understandings of the episode. They provided readers with accounts of the scandal when the event was waning in many private memories, and did so with unprecedented sophistication and complexity. Although it is not a strict analog of the affair, Malamud's novel self-consciously uses the scandal's basic outline and ethos. A mythological tale, *The Natural* brings psychological and cultural density to a story that had been traditionally told as a simple morality play. Asinof's *Eight Men Out* arguably tells the story as comprehensibly as possible and certainly set the standard by which all nonfiction accounts of the affair are still measured. Closely examining these books enables us to trace further the development of the Black Sox scandal narrative as a cultural phenomenon. To reconstruct some of the cultural work these two germinal texts originally performed, and continue to do, this chapter explores these disparate books's representations of the scandal and the aesthetic, historiographic, and ideological implications of their versions of the past. To a lesser extent, it examines the ways in which these narratives bespeak the cultural ethos of the time and considers how these singular texts relate to and reinforce one another. In short, this chapter examines how these books, both of which are essentially stories of moral crisis, simultaneously mythologize and complicate our understanding of the Big Fix.

The Natural as History

When Bernard Malamud died in 1986 at the age of seventy-one, his literary reputation was as secure as it was impressive. Born to Russian immigrant Jews and raised in Brooklyn, New York, Malamud worked as a high school English teacher for nine years. Thereafter, he taught writing at Oregon State College and Bennington College and published eight novels and three short story collections. He won two National Book Awards, the Pulitzer Prize for *The Fixer* (1966), and the respect of myriad critics, writers, and readers. Much of Malamud's work is about the plight of ordinary (often urban Jewish) men and is imbued with the theme of moral wisdom gained through suffering.[2] Both qualities are found in his first novel, *The Natural,* which, as Malamud explained, "derives from Frank Merriwell as well as the adventures of the Brooklyn Dodgers in Ebbets Field."[3]

Malamud's *The Natural* provides readers with an elaborate account of a mythical baseball world. The novel recounts the tragicomic tale of Roy Hobbs, a naturally talented but heroically flawed baseball player who, for various reasons, fails in his quest to be "the best there ever was in the game."[4] Divided into two unequal parts, the short "Pre-Game" section presents Roy as an innocent, socially inept, athletically gifted man-child. En route to his Major League tryout, Roy arouses the attention of the mysterious (and perhaps psychotic) Harriet Bird, who shoots him in the stomach, delaying his Major League debut by fifteen years. The second section, "Batter Up!" chronicles Roy's phenomenal accomplishments and failures as a thirty-four-year-old rookie outfielder for the chronically incompetent New York Knights. After a series of on-the-field heroics and two ill-fated love affairs, the novel ends with obvious allusions to the Black Sox scandal. Even though Roy changes his mind and decides not to "throw" the season-concluding playoff game, his beloved homemade bat, Wonderboy, splits in two, he strikes out, the media exposes his past and present misdeeds, and he is banished from baseball, his achievements stricken from the record. "Say it ain't true, Roy," begs a newsboy in the novel's final scene. "When Roy looked into the boy's eyes he wanted to say it wasn't but couldn't, and he lifted his hands to his face and wept many bitter tears" (217).

Often noted as an amalgamation of thinly veiled events and figures transposed from Arthurian legend and baseball lore, *The Natural* is usually discussed in terms of its mythological associations.[5] Malamud himself did much to promote this view by asserting that the "whole history of baseball has the quality of mythology."[6] In addition to the novel's mythic qualities, repeated excursions into fantasy, complex psychological nature, and overall surrealistic quality, it also evokes an equally well-documented historical past.[7] Neither historical fiction in the tradition of Sir Walter Scott nor postmodern historiographic metafiction in the tradition of E. L. Doctorow, *The Natural* is nevertheless an oblique history, one that simultaneously reconstructs and reevaluates historical events and figures.[8] This is not to suggest that *The Natural* is merely a fictionalized version of the 1919 baseball scandal, for it is obviously more ambitious and complicated than that. The argument here is that it is important not to ignore or underestimate (as most critics do) Malamud's use of the infamous fixed World Series and its most prominent participant, since the Black Sox scandal provides the narrative with its dramatic, arguably tragic, conclusion and its hero's moral crisis.

The Natural is saturated with specific characters and events drawn from baseball history, but the Big Fix is its most important historical episode. The events leading up to the fixed play-off game, as well as the game itself, occupy approximately the last fifth of the book. The night before the pennant-clinching series, Roy is hospitalized after indulging his voracious appetite. Laid up with a stomachache, he is visited by Memo Paris, the novel's femme fatale and the object of his sexual desire. Memo tries to persuade him to throw the final game (funds for the bribe are supplied by her two associates, Judge Goodwill Banner, who owns the Knights, and Gus Sands, a gambler), supposedly so that Roy can obtain the money necessary to support her in marriage. Unpersuaded, Roy is approached by the avaricious Judge Banner himself. After offering a spurious and self-righteous rationalization of his motives, Judge Banner negotiates with Roy for his betrayal. Ultimately, Roy's price is met: he is to get $35,000 for throwing the game and is promised a $45,000 contract for the following season. "The fix is on" (191), Roy tells Judge Banner through a wave of nausea.

The next day, Roy is pulled aside before the game by the Knights manager,

Pop Fisher. The paternal and luckless Fisher tries to inspire Roy to do his best and explains to his star player what winning the league pennant means to him: "Roy, I would give my whole life to win this game and take the pennant" (197). Unmoved, Roy intends to go along with the fix. He actively works to throw the game, yet as it progresses Roy begins to have some reservations about his complicity. By the seventh inning, the sun breaks through the clouds in a "golden glow" and Roy feels as though he has "regained a sense of his own well-being" (203). At this point, after intentionally hitting foul balls in the direction of a heckler, Roy accidentally blackens the eye of Iris Lemon, the novel's heroine, who is (unbeknownst to him) pregnant with his child. "What have I done," he asks, "and why did I do it?" (205). After Iris tells Roy, "Win for us, you were meant to" (206), he tries to redeem himself. It is too late. Wonderboy, his magical bat, splits in two. His efforts to dissuade Al Fowler, the Knights pitcher, from throwing the game are ineffectual. And in the bottom of the ninth inning, facing a relief pitcher who resembles himself at the beginning of the novel, Roy strikes "out with a roar" (214). Following the game, Roy buries Wonderboy in the outfield "in his stocking feet" (215) and then confronts his co-conspirators. After a brief skirmish with Judge Banner, Gus, and Memo, in which he "shower[s] the thousand dollar bills on his [Judge Banner's] wormy head" (216), Roy takes to the street, where he is unrecognized. At this point Roy realizes, "I never did learn anything out of my past life, now I have to suffer again" (217). The novel concludes with a reenactment of the apocryphal "Say it ain't so" scene.

The blending of the general premise of the fix, a few exact details from the actual affair (such as the amount of money reputedly exchanged to ensure the game's outcome), Roy Hobbs's well-noted and convincing similarities to Joe Jackson (tremendous "natural" ability, naiveté, rural origins, and farmboy candor), the apparent complicity of Al Fowler (who, as the team's best hurler, is reminiscent of Eddie Cicotte), the snooping reporter Max Mercy (whom one critic refers to as "a rough-hewn amalgamation of Hugh Fullerton and Ring Lardner"),[9] the sellout to Judge Banner and Gus Sands (often noted as an Arnold Rothstein–like gambler), and, of course, the concluding lament, "Say it ain't true, Roy," all combine to make the Black Sox echo in the novel unmistakable. The cumulative effect of these parallels and connections forces readers to (re)consider the events they are based on and to regard the narrative as something other than mere fantasy. In this way, the novel extracts from history a recognizable story and transforms it into a narrative that is, in Earl R. Wasserman's words, "both real and mythic, particular and universal, ludicrous melodrama and spiritual probing—Ring Lardner and [Carl] Jung."[10]

While the mythic elements and symbolism make Malamud's fictionalized version of the Black Sox scandal somewhat ambiguous, the narrative also seems to offer a rather traditional telling of the episode. Like so much of the novel, its final scenes are simultaneously familiar (at least to many baseball fans) and enigmatic. Roy's terrible bellyache and his intentionally hitting foul balls in the direction of an abusive fan, for instance, have relatively well-known historical referents and thus suggest a certain degree of realism.[11] Furthermore, the novel's "Casey at the Bat" ending is both formulaic and ironic in light of Iris's admonishment to Roy late in the game. And like most previous Black Sox narratives, *The Natural* surrounds its central figure with influential co-conspirators. As for Hobbs, similar to Joe Jackson at the conclusion of the Black Sox affair, the novel's indeterminate ending engenders as much pity (and perhaps sympathy) as it does contempt for the corrupted slugger. In these ways, the novel's climax and dénouement reference events and narratives that further familiarize the already familiar: they help place Roy's dramatic failure in the realm of the possible, if not the actual.

Still, there are some notable problems with Malamud's tale. When Roy is in the hospital, for example, Judge Banner urges him to consider his illicit proposition carefully, even though they both know that Roy is not fit to play. To this Roy responds, "Then what are you offering me twenty thousand smackers for—to show your gratitude for how I have built up your bank account?" (128). It is a reasonable question, and one that readers may ask themselves.[12] More substantially, Malamud's conflation of the real and the mythic in these final scenes (and in the novel in general) forces both to suffer. Malamud's novel coalesces so much into so little space that some readers are left wondering what to make of it all.

Why, for instance, does Roy Hobbs fail? As a tragic or mythic figure, he has to because it is his fate, as Pop Fisher unwittingly explains to him late in the novel: "You know, Roy, I been lately thinking that a whole lot of people are like him [an old unlucky ballplayer], and for one reason or the other their lives will go the same way all the time, without them getting what they want, no matter what" (196–97). "In baseball and in myth," write the critics Kent Cartwright and Mary McElroy, "certain things happen because they are part of a pattern that must repeat itself."[13] But as a historically based figure Hobbs must also fail. Joe Jackson's failure was not statistical—he hit .375, had a record twelve hits, and played errorless defense in the 1919 World Series—but moral; he testified before the Cook County grand jury that he received $5,000 to throw games.[14] The problem at the end of the novel is how to read Malamud's parable of failed heroism, for neither the mythical nor the historical ending is satisfying because they intrude upon and bleed into one another. This ambivalence led the literary critic Sidney Richman to call *The Natural* "one of the most baffling novels of the 1950's."[15]

Anomalous and ambiguous, ironic and indeterminate, *The Natural* is baffling from some vantage points. But *The Natural* also suggests that ambiguity, irony, and indeterminacy ruled the day; the novel refracts (not unlike a carnival fun house hall of mirrors) a complex postwar social world in which moral judgments were not absolute. Although many people continue to think of the fifties as an "innocent" era in American social history best characterized by big-finned cars, poodle skirts, and Hula Hoops, as a period when the country was lulled to sleep by prosperity, in reality the postwar years were rife with conflict and contradiction. For some it was a placid, complacent time of consumption and consensus, but it was also a time of political repression, racial segregation, and stultifying conformity. "It was not a simple time of gray flanneled respectability and not a time of tail-finned fantasy," admonishes the historian Todd Postol. "It was both, and it was neither. It was, above all, not dull, not monochromatic."[16] A great deal of scholarship suggests that the fifties was a time of significant social anxiety, conflict, and transformation.[17] An era when wartime certainties dissipated and were transformed into cold war and atomic insecurities, the fifties was a time of complexity and tension. Living and writing at a cultural moment still coming to grips with the Holocaust and Hiroshima, a moment when Senator Joe McCarthy was hunting for communists, the Korean War loomed large, and baseball was a preeminent symbol of American values and virtues, Malamud crafted a cartoonish novel in which moral judgments are difficult to make.

By presenting readers with a radically intertextual fictional world characterized by historical and mythical allusion, tragicomedy, and irony, *The Natural* offers a richly enigmatic version of the Black Sox scandal that resists a simplified moral. Instead the event is presented in all its moral complexity and opaqueness. In this way the novel resists conventional morality and implicitly argues for a version of the Black Sox scandal that adds further complexity to the already murky tale. *The Natural* culls from American collective memory a story traditionally framed in terms of deceit, betrayal, and disillusionment and retells it so that readers are left with a much less unified and coherent parable than many are comfortable with. In other words, *The Natural* is productively, and perhaps deliberately, unsettling.

Most discussions of *The Natural* focus on the mythic, universal, and spiritual elements of the novel, and thus they usually do not pay more than passing attention to its use of the Big Fix. Harley Henry's 1992 essay, "'Them Dodgers Is My Gallant Knights': Fiction as History in *The Natural* (1952)," is a notable exception. A valuable contribution to our understanding of *The Natural* as a historical text, Henry's essay documents Malamud's sources and argues that the novel is primarily "an indictment of both the vulnerability of immature American virtue as well as the corruptive tendencies of Cold War authority and power."[18] Noting that the "specter of the 1919 scandal is certainly present in *The Natural,*" Henry contends that "the novel really addresses itself much more directly to a current and immediate dilemma."[19] According to Henry, "Malamud wrote about a baseball hero who sells out because recurring sports scandals of the forties and early fifties seemed both symptoms and apt symbols of wider-spread corruption in American life."[20]

One problem with this argument is that if Malamud was so affected by the sports scandals of the early postwar era, it seems peculiar that he did not choose a subject or a style that more directly related to them. The college basketball point-shaving scandals were prominent, but this sport lacked the mythological force or cultural importance of Major League baseball in the fifties. Additionally, the language of the novel does not suggest the decade. Instead, it evokes the manner of speech employed in many of Ring Lardner's sports columns and short stories and John R. Tunis's baseball books for boys, in which ballplayers called each other "sport" and "kid" unselfconsciously. In the early fifties, when baseball's popularity and prestige were unrivaled in American sport, scandals in other athletic arenas did not necessarily debase the national pastime. Nevertheless, Henry argues that the novel "is a cry of 'foul,' a warning that 'it [corruption] can happen here.'"[21] Henry seems to have temporarily forgotten that it *did* happen here. Despite his exemplary efforts at examining the sources Malamud may have used to craft *The Natural,* Henry, like most critics, underestimates the lasting effect of the Black Sox scandal in American collective memories and underappreciates Malamud's use of and indebtedness to it.

It is worth noting that Malamud was wary of commenting on his own work. The literary critic Lawrence Lasher notes that Malamud believed authorial pronouncements were "a disservice to the work and to the reader."[22] Be that as it may, in 1984 Malamud briefly explained the process of writing *The Natural:* "During my first year at Oregon State [1949] I wrote *The Natural,* begun before leaving New York City. Baseball had interested me, especially its comic aspects, but I wasn't able to write about the game until I transformed game into myth, via Jessie Weston's Percival legend with an assist by T. S. Eliot's 'The Wasteland' plus the lives of several ballplayers

I had read, in particular Babe Ruth's and Bobby Feller's. The myth enriched the baseball lore as feats of magic transformed the game."[23] One suspects that if the college basketball point-shaving scandals of the early fifties had inspired him, Malamud would have mentioned them. To my knowledge, he never did. Then again, I have not found evidence suggesting that Malamud explicitly used the Black Sox scandal as a point of historical reference or inspiration either—with one somewhat cryptic exception. In a dialogue Malamud had with himself, he asks, "Why baseball?" Malamud answered: "The poignant Jackson story. Books are about people. Baseball is a meaningful part of the American scene."[24]

Set in an indeterminate and mythic past, *The Natural* offers Malamud's version of heroic failure and corrupted ideals. Much like Joe Jackson, Roy Hobbs cannot resist temptation and must forever bear the weight of his moral failure. A cautionary tale and a commentary on the nature of heroism and fate—for Roy is "a hero and undeniable man of destiny" (152)—*The Natural* also provides us with an oblique reconstruction of an event that, at the time of its telling, was paradoxically fragmenting and relatively secure in American collective memories. For Malamud, the Big Fix provided historical fodder and structure for his transformation of history into myth, but it also provided a site to explore the question that reputedly inspired the novel: "Why does a talented man sell out?"[25] Perhaps Henry is correct and Malamud drew some inspiration from contemporary scandals and a sense that American society was suffering from moral malaise. Perhaps the novel does, as Cartwright and McElroy put it, fall "short of (or beyond) history."[26] But I find it more compelling to speculate that Malamud created an American Adamic hero in need of redemption as an analog to Joe Jackson and the rest of the Black Sox. Regardless of his intentions, by adding layers of symbolic complexity and moral density to a generally recognizable narrative, Malamud reinvigorated and complicated the legend of Joe Jackson and the 1919 World Series. In this way *The Natural* reconstructs history and myth and explores the ways in which they are peculiarly linked. It fosters complexity and ambiguity rather than simplified, moralistic condemnation.

An Eleven-Year Interlude

During the eleven years between the publication of *The Natural* and *Eight Men Out*, Black Sox scandal memories were notably reactivated on numerous occasions. In late January 1956, Buck Weaver, who always steadfastly maintained that he was innocent of any wrongdoing, died on Chicago's

South Side. "The end actually had come to Weaver 35 years before," claimed Edward Prell of the *Chicago Tribune,* "when he and seven other members of the White Sox were banned from baseball for life as an outgrowth of the 1919 World Series scandal."[27] Not only did Chicago newspapers give Weaver's death a great deal of coverage but so did the national media.[28] A few weeks after Weaver died, the sports columnist Arthur Daley of the *New York Times* suggested that Weaver was perhaps "the most tragic figure to emerge from the infamous Black Sox scandal."[29] Later that month, the *Newsweek* columnist John Lardner penned "The Riddle of Buck Weaver." Responding to eulogizers, namely the syndicated columnist Westbrook Pegler, who maintained that "'Weaver was a martyr to circumstance,'" Lardner asked: "Who can say Weaver was guilty? Or, if he was, in what degree? On the other hand, who can say he was innocent?" Unable to determine Weaver's complicity, Lardner remarked: "It is part of the fixed general policy of baseball executives, in regard to scandals and outlaws, to leave the closet doors shut tight, and not to fiddle around with the skeletons. An innocent skeleton would deserve to have his name cleared. And to start clearing the names of skeletons would be to strike at the very foundations of the sport."[30] Ambivalent about whether Weaver should be granted posthumous amnesty, Lardner lucidly identified and rehashed the Weaver riddle without satisfactorily solving it.[31]

It seems likely that Chick Gandil never lost any sleep trying to solve such riddles. Gandil, one of the acknowledged masterminds of the fix, published an apologia of sorts in *Sports Illustrated* in September 1956. "A lot of you young readers have probably heard of the Black Sox scandal from your dads or granddads," Gandil began. "It was some mess. Eight of us Sox were accused of throwing the 1919 World Series to Cincy. We were taken into court in Chicago, tried and acquitted. But organized baseball banned us for life."[32] Not one to offer excuses, Gandil reflected: "To this day I feel that we got what we had coming." Apparently in a candid (or perhaps boastful) mood, Gandil admitted, "I have often been described as one of the ringleaders of the Black Sox scandal. There's no doubt about it. I was." By way of an explanation, Gandil maintained that he "would like to blame the trouble we got into on Comiskey's cheapness, but my conscience won't let me. We had no one to blame except ourselves. But, so help me, this fellow was tight. Many times we played in filthy uniforms because he was trying to keep down the cleaning tab." Gandil asserted that he and his teammates did in fact conspire with gamblers to fix the World Series, but (like Malamud's Roy Hobbs) in the end they could not go through with the plan, so they double-crossed the gamblers and played to win. "Our losing to Cincinnati was an upset all right, but no more than Cleveland's losing to the New York Giants by four straight in 1954. Mind you, I offer no defense for the thing we conspired to do. It was inexcusable. But I maintain that our actual losing of the Series was pure baseball fortune." Gandil claimed that he never received money from gamblers. Slithering across an admittedly difficult ethical tightrope, Gandil "had the crazy notion that my not touching any of that money would exonerate me from my guilt in the conspiracy. I give you my solemn word I don't know to this day what happened to the cash." Most historians find this claim dubious. "Inasmuch as we were legally freed, I feel Landis' ruling was unjust," Gandil concluded, "but I truthfully never resented it because even though the Series wasn't thrown, we were guilty of a serious offense, and we knew it." Coming from a man whose baseball career was tainted with gambling connections, from someone who was neither an innocent bystander nor an innocent rube, it is difficult to read Gandil's version of the story without suspicion and cynicism.[33]

The following year, the novelist James T. Farrell published *My Baseball Diary,* an eclectic, sometimes nostalgic collection of more than two dozen essays in which the author of the *Studs Lonigan* trilogy (1932–35) recalled his life as a baseball fan. In one essay, "I Remember the Black Sox," Farrell, who grew up in Chicago as a White Sox fan, recalls an incident that is reminiscent of the mythologized "Say it ain't so" courthouse exchange. After a game late in the 1920 season, as the revelations of the fix were becoming public, the fifteen-year-old Farrell

> stood near the steps leading down from the White Sox clubhouse. A small crowd always collected there to watch the players leave. But on this particular Sunday, there were about 200 to 250 boys waiting. Some of the players left. Lefty Williams, wearing a blue suit and a gray cap, was one, and some of the fans called to him. A few others came down the steps. And then Joe Jackson and Happy Felsch appeared. They were both big men. Jackson was the taller of the two and Felsch the broader. They were sportively dressed in gray silk shirts, white duck trousers and white shoes. They came down the clubhouse steps slowly, their faces masked by impassivity.
>
> A few fans called to them, but they gave no acknowledgment to these greetings. They turned and started to walk away. Spontaneously, the crowd followed in a slow, disorderly manner. I went with the crowd and trailed about five feet behind Jackson and Felsch. They walked somewhat slowly. A fan called out:
>
> "It ain't true, Joe."
>
> The two suspected players did not turn back. They walked on, slowly. The crowd took up this cry and more than once, men and boys called out and repeated:

> "It ain't true, Joe."
>
> This call followed Jackson and Felsch as they walked all the way under the stands to the Thirty-fifth Street side of the ball park. They left the park and went for their parked cars in a soccer field behind the right field bleachers. I waited by the exit of the soccer field. Many others also waited. Soon Felsch and Jackson drove out in the sportive roadsters, through a double file of silent fans.[34]

No longer silent, Farrell reveals that his interest in baseball changed dramatically after the Black Sox scandal. "For years I had no favorite team. I was growing up, and this marked the end of my days of hero-worshipping baseball players. Many fans felt betrayed. I didn't. I felt sorry. I wished it weren't true. I wished the players would have been given another chance."[35] More sympathetic toward the implicated players than embittered by the scandal, Farrell was perhaps representative of a significant minority of young White Sox fans. In another essay, "Buck Weaver's Last Interview," Farrell considers the fate of the former White Sox third baseman. "Buck Weaver was a great ball player and very likable," Farrell concludes. "He was caught in a net of circumstances as are many characters in tragic novels. For to him, baseball was a way of life, and his barring was a supreme defeat."[36] A sensitive, sympathetic chronicler, Farrell could remind readers whose memories may have been fading and mellowing that the innocent suffered along with the guilty in the Big Fix.

Late in 1959, the Black Sox scandal was revived for two reasons: in September, the White Sox finally made it back to the World Series; and in early November, the television quiz show scandal hit the country with full force. By winning the 1959 American League pennant, the White Sox—led by the infielders Nellie Fox and Luis Aparicio and called the "Go-Go Sox" due to the team's speed and aggressive play—made it back to the World Series for the first time in forty years, a fact obviously not lost on Chicago baseball fans or sportswriters. Noting that the upcoming games against the Los Angeles Dodgers would be the first post-season contests played at Comiskey Park since 1919, David Condon of the *Chicago Tribune* pondered: "One wonders just how [the White Sox's owner,] Bill Veeck, most masterful of the give-away artists, will top the generosity of the 1919 White Sox, who gave away the World Series."[37] The *Chicago Sun-Times*'s Dick Hackenberg also had history on his mind. "This is the day that Chicago has been waiting for," mused Hackenberg before the first game of the series, "for 14 years since wartime 1945 when the Cubs bowed to the Detroit Tigers, four games to three . . . for 40 years since the last White Sox World Series, in 1919, when the whole blooming business was tossed to the Cincinnati Reds, five games to three, in baseball's blackest hour." An optimist, Hackenberg hoped that the "stigma of that series will be erased now by what the 1959 Sox do to the Dodgers."[38] Unfortunately for Hackenberg and South Side baseball fans, the White Sox lost to the Dodgers, four games to two, and the stigma endured. Wandering in the wilderness for forty years did not deliver the White Sox to the promised land.[39]

Perhaps no one made as much of the connection between the two World Series as did Nelson Algren, who recorded his impressions for the *Chicago Sun-Times*. Interestingly, the first half of Algren's article from game one was entirely about "an October 40 Octobers gone." A star-struck ten-year-old baseball fan in 1919, Algren regaled his readers with memories of 1919 White Sox players before their names were besmirched. Speaking of the 1959 opener, he wrote: "I had come to the park assuming that there would be a roped-off area for Black Sox fans paroled for the series." When he finally turned his attention to the game in front of him, he "really began to enjoy being right there in the middle of first-class citizens." As the game neared its conclusion, "the big Chicago afternoon light came down like the light of no other city, and I knew I would not see the White Sox like this again," wrote Algren, referring to the White Sox's 11-0 victory. "But this day was going where Shoeless Joe went, out into the shadows of Shields Av. where Buck Weaver waited to tell his side of the story."[40] Eight days later, after the White Sox had lost the series, Algren concluded his observations by once again reminiscing about his youth, the White Sox, and his coming of age. "Nothing really had anything to do with me until I was 10-going-on-11. Then on the last afternoon of summer I saw Shoeless Joe Jackson leave his glove in left field, walk toward the darkening stands and never come back for his glove." Forty years later, after the final game of the World Series, "when the crowd was gone and I stood up at last to leave, I saw the shade of Shoeless Joe," Algren wrote. "He was walking toward the darkening stands, and he'd left his glove behind."[41] Haunted by Jackson's ghost—which W. P. Kinsella would resurrect in his novel *Shoeless Joe* (1982)—and his own past, Algren left Comiskey Park as a light drizzle fell, his body and spirit dampened.[42]

As the 1959 World Series ended, the television quiz show scandal shook the nation. A year earlier, a New York grand jury had listened to charges that some television quiz shows were rigged; there were no indictments and the grand jury results were impounded by the presiding judge. The House Subcommittee on Legislative Oversight finally subpoenaed the erudite and charming Charles Van Doren, a Columbia University instructor who had become a national hero and celebrity due to his phenomenal success as a contestant on *Twenty-One,* to testify about his alleged participation in the fixing of shows. On November 2, 1959, after more than a year of steadfastly denying he was involved in the scandal, Van Doren testified that he "was involved, deeply involved, in a deception." It was a traumatic moment. For some commentators, the quiz show scandal signaled the end of American innocence. "Not since the Black Sox scandal of 1919—to which Eisenhower compared it—had there been so widespread a sense of violation of public faith," notes the historian Stephen J. Whitfield.[43] The Eisenhower allusion is noteworthy, for the president maintained that Americans were more bewildered than angry about the quiz show scandal; according to the president, the revelations were "like an old story you know of Joe Jackson in 1919s [*sic*] when they said, 'Say it ain't so, Joe.'"[44] Perhaps following Eisenhower's lead, *Time* magazine's quiz show reportage included a photograph of Jackson batting with the caption: "Is it or ain't it so?"[45]

In retrospect, it seems plausible that at least two other Black Sox texts were partly inspired by the quiz show scandals: an article entitled "Say It Ain't So, Joe!" published in the June 1960 issue of *American Heritage* magazine and a January 1961 episode of CBS's weekly drama "The Witness," in which a simulated congressional panel investigated the 1919 World Series.[46] Unfortunately, the Black Sox episode of "The Witness," which featured the actors Biff McGuire as Joe Jackson and Royal Beal as Charles Comiskey, is probably lost to history; despite my best efforts, I have been unable to locate a copy. We do know, however, that the *New York World-Telegram* sports columnist Joe Williams did not think highly of it. He described the episode as "squalid and spurious" and suggested it was "slanderous." Williams was especially displeased with the show's portrayal of Comiskey: "If Comiskey was a tight man with a buck, he was also a man of courage and fairness. His team was still in contention when he wrecked it late in the season. And when it became known for certain that the Series had been deliberately thrown to the Reds, Comiskey rewarded the honest players on his team with the difference between winning and losing shares . . . a fact which was either unknown to CBS or ignored in its tawdry depiction of the old man."[47]

The *American Heritage* article was authored by the award-winning freelance writers Lewis Thompson and Charles Boswell. A popular magazine founded by the historian Allan Nevins, *American Heritage* was "the most influential and successful post–World War II historical publication."[48] Like many *American Heritage* articles, "Say It Ain't So, Joe!" offered readers a polished, concise, and conventional telling of the past—strictly chronological, highly descriptive, simultaneously tinged with nostalgia for a time of innocence and confidence that a similar conspiracy could not take place again. Illustrated with photographs of the principal figures and facsimiles of newspaper headlines and cartoons, "Say It Ain't So, Joe!" explored the fix's complicated machinations, but failed to examine why it had happened. Rather, Thompson and Boswell put forth a traditional, moralistic version of the affair, implying that the conspiracy was hatched and executed because a few corrupt, avaricious ballplayers and gamblers saw an opportunity to pull a fast one. In addition to reaching a vast audience (during the late fifties *American Heritage* had more than 100,000 subscribers), "Say It Ain't So, Joe!" was notable because it acknowledged, more so than any previous text, the Black Sox scandal's historical indeterminacy.[49] Throughout their essay, Thompson and Boswell concede that the case remained unsolved, that despite "the enormous publicity of the scandal, exact documentation of it is slight, and based almost entirely on circumstantial evidence."[50] They argue, for example, that the testimony of those involved in the event was necessarily limited in perspective and that many questions remained unanswered. "No one able to speak with complete authority has ever publicly named all the persons, aside from the players, who manipulated the fix, or has explained the complexities of their interrelationships. Perhaps this authoritative voice does not exist, and never did."[51] Unlike most of those who wrote (and write) about the Black Sox scandal, Thompson and Boswell, who conclude that it was "doubtful if the ultimate truth will ever be known," recognize and admit that their version of the story was limited by a variety of factors.[52] It is a rare and praiseworthy admission.

These disparate texts and moments of remembrance suggest that the Black Sox scandal remained in the consciousness of some Americans through the early sixties. More important, when read collectively they are emblematic of the ways in which the episode's meaning is fluid and contentious. The eulogies for Buck Weaver represent the lingering pathos many felt when the implicated ballplayers were banned from the game without having their degree of culpability considered. Chick Gandil's halfhearted mea culpa represents a continuation of the obfuscation practiced by some of those caught in the scandal's web. In different ways, James Farrell's and Nelson Algren's Black Sox reminiscences represent the nostalgic longings of middle-aged men for their lost youth, innocence, and heroes. The 1959 World Series and the quiz show scandal represent how the Black Sox scandal has been used as a historical touchstone and analog for contemporary events and crises. Finally, Lewis Thompson and Charles Boswell's "Say It Ain't So, Joe!" represents an uncommon admission that we may never fully grasp the Black Sox scandal, that it resists historical certainty, that the past is lost and in some ways unknowable. Taken together, these texts and moments of remembrance suggest that the terrain Eliot Asinof trod upon in 1960 when he was hired to research the scandal for a television drama was still contested.[53] They suggest that the Black Sox scandal was still a dramatic example of the struggle over how the past should be remembered and understood.

Eight Men Out: A Novel History

In contrast to most writers, including Bernard Malamud, Eliot Asinof knows baseball from the inside out. Asinof was born in New York and played baseball regularly, first on the sandlots and later on his high school varsity team, which he captained.[54] After graduating from Swarthmore College in 1940, Asinof played in an amateur league sponsored by Major League teams. He landed in the Philadelphia Phillies farm system and spent several seasons in the outfield.[55] His baseball career was cut short by World War II, during which he served in the army. When he returned from the service, Asinof worked in his family's clothing business and eventually became a writer, first for television. A few years later, the industry blacklisted him—precisely why is unclear, but the experience probably affected his attitude toward the Black Sox—and thus Asinof turned to writing magazine articles and fiction.[56] His first book, a novel entitled *Man on Spikes* (1955), is about an unsung ballplayer (based on Asinof's friend and former teammate Mickey Rutner) who struggles for sixteen years before finally appearing in a Major League game. Following the critical success of *Man on Spikes,* Asinof made it off the blacklist and found work as a Hollywood screenwriter. In 1960, the producer David Susskind approached Asinof with an idea for a live television drama about the Black Sox scandal.[57] As it turned out, the show never aired, largely because Ford Frick, the baseball commissioner, thought that it was not in the best interests of baseball and convinced its sponsor to cancel it.

Using the primary and secondary material he collected to produce the television drama, Asinof wrote *Eight Men Out: The Black Sox and the 1919 World Series,* which remains the most influential (and some say definitive) historical reconstruction of the event. In *Eight Men Out,* Asinof examines the conditions that fostered the fix, the 1919 World Series games, the exposure that led to the scandal, the subsequent trial, and the aftermath more completely and authoritatively than anyone else. As the historian Charles C. Alexander puts it, Asinof "comes as close as anybody ever will to fathoming that incredibly confused and murky episode."[58] *Eight Men Out* is still widely regarded as the most comprehensive and "objective" account of the affair and remains in print. Referred to by the writer Harry Stein as the "seminal account of the Black Sox scandal," Asinof's study has influenced everyone who has subsequently taken up the subject.[59] Yet because of its reputation and obvious importance to understandings of the 1919 World Series scandal, the dearth of critical discussion about it is surprising. Allen Guttmann, for instance, one of the few historians to approach the issue, simply maintains that *Eight Men Out* "is annoyingly undocumented."[60] Despite (or because of) this paucity of analysis, any meaningful discussion of the Black Sox scandal as a cultural phenomenon must explore how Asinof reconstructs the event.

In his preface, Asinof acknowledges that newspapers initially told the story of the Black Sox scandal and that magazines and general histories of the game later reiterated it, but he maintains that these accounts were necessarily fragmentary. "No one delved into the scandal's causes and morality, exploded its myths and distortions," writes Asinof. "The complete story, shrouded in complexity and silence, remained untold. Apparently, the real truth was lying hidden beneath the weight of all the reports and speculations."[61] To correct previous (mis)understandings of the affair, to tell the whole story, and to get at the elusive "truth," Asinof's project becomes "one of weaving together a multitude of obscure, seemingly unrelated threads" (xi). It is his intention "to recapture the turmoil" (xiii) of the participants' experience and to explain the context necessary to understand the event. To understand why the players, whom he describes as "decent, normal, talented men" (xiv), participated in the fix, Asinof offers *Eight Men Out* "as a reconstruction of the Black Sox scandal drawn from a rich variety of sources and from research into all the scattered written material concerning it" (xiii). Like most histories, *Eight Men Out* aspires to tell a more-or-less "true" story about the past.

Asinof organizes his narrative into six sections: "The Fix," "The Series," "The Exposure," "The Impact," "The Trial," and "The Aftermath." In the first, he describes the plot's genesis and establishes some context to demonstrate how and why it occurred. Asinof asserts that the betrayal was instigated by Chick Gandil when he approached a relatively small-time gambler named Joseph "Sport" Sullivan late in the 1919 season and proposed a scheme to throw the World Series (7). Asinof thus suggests that at least some of the players were not unwittingly duped by unscrupulous, aggressive gamblers or victimized. Additionally, he makes it plain that some implicated players believed they had justification for their betrayal. According to Asinof, "these were bitter men with a common enemy: Charles Albert Comiskey" (20). Asinof implies that the penurious and autocratic Comiskey was partially responsible for the game fixing by ruthlessly exploiting his employees. "No players of comparable talent on other teams were paid as little" (20), Asinof claims. "Many second-rate ballplayers on second-division ball clubs made more than the White Sox. It had been that way for years" (21). Just as important, in his opening chapter Asinof maintains that the rhetoric espousing baseball's pastoral innocence and purity, its reputed immunity from venality, was divorced from historical and social reality. Asinof emphasizes that "baseball and betting were aligned from the beginning" (10). "The official, if unspoken, policy was to let the rottenness grow rather than risk the dangers involved in exposure and cleanup," notes Asinof, thus implicating the owners and the baseball establishment in what would eventually transpire. "So all the investigations were squashed. This was business, pure and simple, for all the pious phrases about the nobility of the game and its inspirational value for American youth" (14). In Asinof's view, then, the Black Sox scandal was not an isolated incident in an otherwise unblemished history, but the culmination of numerous trends and relations that were intensified by an unfortunate confluence of personalities and events.

Turning to the games themselves, Asinof recounts how Gandil and his alleged associates purposely lost the series and the various machinations (both at the highest levels of the baseball establishment and in the media) that accompanied the games. Asinof suggests, for instance, that even without concrete evidence, Comiskey, Kid Gleason, and the sportswriters Hugh Fullerton and Ring Lardner suspected that the integrity of the games was in doubt well before the series was concluded. "It was apparent that there were no facts. Reality was a vague stink that anyone could smell, but no one knew where it came from" (89). Again evoking an olfactory metaphor, Asinof maintains: "No matter how much he [Lardner] hated to admit it—especially to himself—it was not in him to resist the logic of his cynicism. The sellout was on. He could smell it. Nothing more; just smell it" (93). To their credit, Comiskey, Gleason, Fullerton, and Lardner attempted, each in his own way, and with equal lack of success, to combat the conspiracy.[62] Yet from Asinof's perspective, their failure merely accentuates either their unwillingness to fully confront the situation and its ramifications or perhaps the reporters' subservience to the journalistic conventions of the day.

Asinof then turns to how the story came to light. Despite widespread conspiracy rumors, Asinof says little was done about the alleged malfeasance. Aside from Hugh Fullerton, whose scathing articles during the off-season attacked the games' integrity, neither the media nor the baseball establishment wanted to pursue an inquiry. Not until late in the 1920 season, when an unrelated and relatively minor betting scandal involving the Chicago Cubs surfaced, were the rumors resurrected and finally taken seriously. To "clean up" and protect baseball, the Cook County grand jury investigating the Cubs incident took it upon itself to examine "the possibility that the 1919 World Series might not have been played on its merits" (152). Even after an impressive parade of witnesses, among them assorted baseball players and officials, celebrities, and gamblers, Asinof maintains that the "hand of the law remained gentle. Nor were there any real exposures made to the public. Newspapers reported what was handed to them" (159). The grand jury investigation proved fruitless until a Philadelphia newspaper published an interview with one of the small-time gamblers associated with the fix. Within days, and "totally without the benefit of counsel" (171), three White Sox—Cicotte, Jackson, and Williams—were compelled by Comiskey, his attorney, and the state's attorney to proffer confessions and sign waivers of immunity. "The official baseball world turned a shocked face for the world to see," Asinof notes wryly. "It was as if they never dreamed that such a thing were possible" (181).

"As the impact of the confessions sank in," claims Asinof, "the American people were at first shocked, then sickened" (197). In Asinof's view, "the scandal was a betrayal of more than a set of ball games, even more than of the sport itself. It was a crushing blow at American pride" (197). Surveying the affair's fallout, Asinof contends that the "scandal touched all strata of American life. Newspapers dramatized its destructive effect on children, but adults, even intellectuals, sensed its cutting impact" (198). And though the players and gamblers were quickly condemned by the media, Asinof maintains that it "was somehow vaguely understood that the problem was bigger than" merely a few corrupt individuals (198). Just as significant, Asinof recounts the legal strategies deployed on the players' behalf by a clandestine alliance of Rothstein, Comiskey, and their respective attorneys. As if the case's legal questions were not vexing enough for the prosecution—the nature of the indictments made it extremely difficult to obtain convictions—Asinof suggests (on what evidence is not clear) that the Rothstein-Comiskey alliance made the state's task more arduous by stealing the players' original confessions and waivers of immunity.[63]

In the book's penultimate section, "The Trial," Asinof details the peculiar legal proceedings. In late June 1921, almost a year after the three White Sox had testified, the indicted players and assorted gamblers (excluding Rothstein) were tried by the Illinois state's attorney on various conspiracy charges. As Asinof puts it, "The more they [the ballplayers] were victimized by the stalling legal machinery of the State of Illinois, the more they felt purged of their guilt" (238). To some observers the trial was little more than a tempest in a teapot, but for many others "the uniqueness of major-league ballplayers standing trial excited great curiosity. The crowds came and gaped at them, asked for autographs, encouraged them, treated them more like maligned heroes than criminals. Their spirits soared at this daily show of support and public approval" (241). Over the course of the trial, the jury (which was all male) heard testimony from many of the same witnesses who had appeared before the grand jury the previous fall. This time, however, the ballplayers repudiated their confessions, and the state's attorney was forced to admit that the original copies of the signed confessions and immunity waivers had disappeared.[64] This, in conjunction with no testimony from the ballplayers, the complexity of the charges, and the judge's detailed instructions to the jury, led to full acquittals. When the jury announced its decision, a "roar went up in the courtroom" (272). Unfortunately for the players, Landis immediately banished the players from professional baseball. "So, in the end," Asinof notes, "organized baseball won its battle. They had rescued the ballplayers from the clutches of the law, only to make victims of them on their own terms" (275).

In the brief concluding section, "The Aftermath," Asinof does not examine the institutional effects of the scandal or its impact on the national psyche. Rather, he documents how the scandal affected some of its most conspicuous participants. He remarks that soon after the trial the "eight Black Sox fanned out over the vast expanse of America, but their lives ran in similar patterns. They all played semipro and outlaw baseball for a few years, then gradually settled into various occupations" (284). He also notes that while "they had almost no contact with each other over the decades that followed, they maintained a solid front of silence to the world" (284). Despite their acquittals, the ballplayers were burdened by "shame and sorrow and futility" (284) and suffered the scandal's stigma. Of the eight men out, Asinof is particularly interested in Buck Weaver and Joe Jackson, the two arguably most severely victimized who forever protested their innocence. By concluding with excerpts from Nelson Algren's poem "The Swede Was a Hard Guy," Asinof leaves readers with a sense of nostalgic loss and regret, which in the end probably best describes his view of the event.

Without question, one reason *Eight Men Out* has been consistently considered the definitive version of the Black Sox scandal is that it is remarkably detailed, coherent, and compelling in traditional historical terms. It tells a convincing story with a well-defined beginning, middle, and ending; it gives the appearance of being the complete story of the scandal; it is conventionally (i.e., chronologically) organized; it has an easily discernible plot, narrative closure, and a omniscient, morally authoritative narrator. In short, though not an academic history, *Eight Men Out* conforms to numerous (but, as we will see, not all) traditional historiographic conventions and thus satisfies the expectations of most readers of history. However, Asinof's version of the Black Sox scandal is not as seamless or as unproblematic as it appears.

In *History and Criticism* (1985), Dominick LaCapra argues that "inquiry into the past should begin at points where a document seems most opaque and alien."[65] *Eight Men Out* is "most opaque and alien" in its treatment of facts. Obviously the essential premise upon which Asinof based his work—that at least seven Chicago White Sox succeeded in their plot to lose the 1919 World Series to the Cincinnati Reds—is widely accepted. But a few writers have challenged Asinof on some specifics, and in the process they have cast doubt on his authority. In *The Great Baseball Mystery—the 1919 World Series* (1966), Victor Luhrs concurs with Asinof that the first game was tampered with; yet unlike Asinof, Luhrs contends that Cicotte "did not throw it."[66] Further, Luhrs maintains that three of the players usually associated with the fix—Cicotte, Jackson, and Felsch—did in fact "give their best efforts" throughout the series.[67] With greater specificity, Donald Gropman in *Say It Ain't So, Joe!: The True Story of Shoeless Joe Jackson and the 1919 World Series* (1979) also challenges some of Asinof's factual claims. For example, Gropman and Asinof differ on the following points: whether Jackson attended a September 21, 1919, players' meeting to discuss the fix; whether Jackson definitely joined the plot at the meeting; whether Jackson later demanded $20,000 from Gandil to participate in the conspiracy; whether Jackson told Gleason or Comiskey that he did not want to play just prior to the first game; whether Lefty Williams gave Jackson $5,000 before the fifth game or after the series; and whether Jackson accepted the money willingly.[68] If it is the historian's first duty to establish the facts, then based on these contrasting accounts Asinof seems to be derelict in his responsibilities. By briefly contrasting a few of the differences within these accounts, I want to make it clear that other writers have offered divergent versions of the Black Sox scandal and that a few of them have rejected the essential facts from which Asinof worked. The argument here is *not* that Luhrs's or Gropman's account is better or more factual than Asinof's or that its weaknesses are less problematic. It is simply that some factual aspects of Asinof's narrative have been contested.

Asinof might have avoided some of these difficulties if he had used footnotes and included a bibliography. Indeed, *Eight Men Out*'s lack of documentation is conspicuous and leaves me wondering what Asinof was referring to when he said that he "documented everything."[69] Of course, most academic historians would be disturbed by a text that failed to acknowledge its sources—a rudimentary scholarly practice. From a rigid academic point of view, no matter how plausible *Eight Men Out* may seem, no matter how honest or accurate it appears, it lacks *verifiability,* which can be frustrating for someone in pursuit of a specific detail or source.

It is worth remembering, however, that Asinof is not an academic and so is not bound by the strictures of a professional discipline. And, of course, *Eight Men Out*'s intended audience was (and remains) much broader than that of most academic texts. To appeal to the largest audience possible, Asinof no doubt eschewed footnotes because they (supposedly) impede the pleasure of reading. Omitting footnotes represents a pragmatic approach to historical writing within a consumer culture that is, at best, ambivalent about the past.

This missing documentation, however, should not be overlooked or minimized. Just as we do not know precisely what sources Asinof used when writing *Eight Men Out,* neither do we know how he used them. A wry comment by a colleague is apt in this regard: "Don't forget," he observed, "nothing is as deceptive as a document." As far as I can tell, Asinof rarely recognized the need for close, critical readings of documents such as newspapers or interviews before he used them as sources. For instance, though he occasionally acknowledges that the media's representations of the event might be construed as unreliable—he notes, for example, that some "newspapers exaggerated stories that Comiskey was close to a physical collapse" (213)—Asinof nevertheless treats newspaper reports as if they are mere "quarries for facts."[70] Similarly, Asinof often relies on participants' reminiscences and presents their stories as if their meaning is self-evident.[71] The point to be stressed here is well articulated by LaCapra: "Documents are themselves historical realities that do not simply represent but also supplement the realities to which they refer, and a critical reading of them may provide insight into cultural processes—insight of a sort that at least resists mythologizing desires."[72]

Of course, omitting footnotes is but one of the rhetorical strategies Asinof uses in *Eight Men Out.*[73] He also uses pathos and hyperbole, as well as metaphor, metonymy, synecdoche, and irony—all of the so-called master tropes. Early in the book, Asinof displays a healthy dose of hyperbole by describing the 1919 White Sox as "the all-powerful colossus from the West" (5), and he consistently invokes some of the original metaphors the media used to describe the implicated players; he often identifies them as wayward "boys" and often associates them with being "dirty." If figures of speech are, as the philosopher of history Hayden White suggests, "the very mar-row of the historian's individual style," then Asinof needs to be credited with writing a rich, vibrant history.[74] Written in accessible, lively language, *Eight Men Out* tells the story of the scandal in rhetoric reminiscent of Frederick Lewis Allen's *Only Yesterday* (1931) and William Leuchtenberg's *The Perils of Prosperity* (1958). Much like those histories, *Eight Men Out* is engaging on a rhetorical level due to its anecdotal, impressionistic, and epigrammatic quality. Still, two important points concerning Asinof's use of language need to be emphasized. First, like all historians working within the narrative tradition, Asinof was compelled to place his facts within a specific kind of structure; that he delineates the Black Sox scandal as a tragedy is significant. Second, *Eight Men Out*'s third-person omniscient perspective conceals the manner in which Asinof conflates and compresses the story, the inscrutability of some of the events, and his own position as an authoritative historian/narrator within the telling.

Though he had other options, Asinof clearly views the Black Sox scandal as a tragedy.[75] Not only does Asinof's chronological and linear approach give readers the impression that the scandal unfolded deliberately, with the measured quality of a well-paced drama, but also early on he identifies the kind of story he is telling. When reflecting on a meeting the conspiring White Sox held a week and a half before the series, Asinof writes: "With hindsight, this meeting looms as a macabre opening to a tragedy" (19). As Asinof tells the tale, the Black Sox scandal had obvious dramatic conflict, a full accompaniment of tragic heroes and villains, rising and falling action, and a well-demarcated climax and dénouement. *Eight Men Out* even offers readers the sense of catharsis that Aristotle mandated of tragedies. And if comedies end with weddings and tragedies end with funerals, it is telling that Asinof concludes *Eight Men Out* with Joe Jackson's death. Asinof, of course, was not the first (or the last) writer to tell scandal as a tragedy; we have seen, for instance, that in 1920–21 the media, particularly in Chicago, constructed the event in a similar manner. Since *Eight Men Out* is the most influential Black Sox narrative, because it is usually hailed as the definitive version of the event, and considering it helped shape the historical consciousness of two generations of readers (and writers), it is significant that Asinof crafts his story as if it were a prima facie tragedy. But it is important to note here that, as Hayden White puts it, "no historical event is intrinsically tragic; it can only be conceived as such from a particular point of view or from within the context of a structured set of events of which it is an element enjoying a privileged place. For in history what is tragic from one perspective is comic from another."[76] Leo Katcher's appraisal of the Big Fix—which he describes as a tragedy "played as a farce"—illustrates this point.[77]

Asinof's use of the dispassionate, third-person omniscient voice of history is notable for several reasons. It conceals the manner in which his narrative inescapably conflates and compresses the events it describes. Roughly one-fourth of the book is devoted to recounting the 1919 series (which lasted only nine days), whereas the myriad events that occurred between the day the scandal was first reported in the media and the end of the 1921 trial (a period of nearly a year) occupy approximately the same number of pages. By telescoping the events that occurred after the series, *Eight Men Out* suggests that the thrown baseball games are a privileged episode that should be given primacy. In this way Asinof seems to invert (or at least challenge) the convention that a scandal is corruption revealed. Given the prominence he grants the thrown games, Asinof implies that the Black Sox's alleged betrayal—rather than the conditions that fostered it or the players' subsequent treatment by the baseball establishment, the legal system, and the media—deserves the bulk of our attention. All writers necessarily condense and construct their subjects, yet the particular approach Asinof uses fosters a sense that the fixed games were the most significant link in the chain of the scandal.

Of equal or greater importance is the manner in which Asinof's omniscient and authoritative third-person narrator masks the inscrutability of some of the events it describes. An instructive moment to consider is the precise initiation of the conspiracy. Asinof maintains that three weeks before the 1919 World Series Chick Gandil met with Sport Sullivan in Boston and proposed the scheme to fix the series for $80,000 (6–8). Asinof's account appears to be objective and merely describes what (presumably) happened. Unfortunately, while this version of the conspiracy's conception is entirely plausible, Asinof does not provide any basis for it and fails to acknowledge competing claims as to who initiated the fix. And it should be noted that there are nearly as many accounts of who approached whom as there were fixers. Years later Gandil offered his own version of the fix's genesis: "I was kind of surprised when Sullivan suggested that we get a 'syndicate' together of seven or eight players to throw the Series to Cincinnati. As I say, I never figured the guy as a fixer but just one who played for the percentages."[78] Gandil's story is probably self-serving, like most versions of the past. My point is that we will never have a definitive picture of this event and that, contrary to the rhetorical assuredness Asinof offers, the truth of the matter was inevitably left behind in the hotel rooms, bars, and pool halls that the implicated White Sox and their accomplices frequented.

My final point is obvious but needs to be made: Asinof's use of an omniscient third-person voice effectively hides his own hand at work. Asinof's narrator delineates the scandal as if it were a story merely telling itself, as if it were a story that did not need someone to tell it. Asinof renders his narrative from such a distance that he seems divorced from its construction. In this way Asinof plays upon the popular notion that history means "truth" rather than an imaginative reconstruction of a particular aspect of the past by someone for a specific social group or public. Asinof thus implicitly rejects David Lowenthal's assertion that history "is persuasive because it is organized by and filtered through individual minds, not in spite of that fact" and embraces the view that it is possible for historians to establish "the real truth" (xi), to write the past as it really occurred.[79]

In some ways, then, because Asinof uses rhetorical strategies that obscure the assumptions embedded within his narrative, the burden of making sense of his reconstruction falls more heavily upon readers. Of course, texts and readers always generate meaning in relation to each other and within specific contexts, but Asinof's decision to treat the scandal as a tragedy and his comments about this work provide us with a better sense of how to understand *Eight Men Out.* For instance, by casting the eight implicated White Sox players in the role of tragic heroes, by depicting them as ordinary men with extraordinary athletic talent (and little moral sense), and by setting them within a social context that consistently exploited their talent, Asinof implies that their betrayal was probably inevitable—and perhaps just. As Asinof puts it elsewhere: "They'd been cheated and abused and exploited. They'd seen gamblers run through the baseball establishment without anyone laying a glove on them. If throwing the World Series was a heinous act, the way they saw it, they were only getting even."[80] In short, *Eight Men Out* promotes the view that the players were victimized by the baseball establishment before, during, and after the scandal; by the legal system for nearly a year after the revelations were made public; by the media throughout the affair and beyond it; and by their own ignorance. In a 1988 interview Asinof noted that when he began his project, he "came [to it] with the attitude that these eight fuckin' guys tried to ruin the game of baseball. It shocked my senses to realize that this situation was much more complicated. These players were victims—some less than others—but they were all victims."[81] This ethos of mistreatment and abuse permeates the narrative and suggests an important shift in the way the Black Sox scandal was widely understood.

Although Asinof eschews the usual hyperbolic condemnation found in other accounts of the Big Fix, he does *not* absolve the players and gamblers of their fair share of responsibility. He notes, for example, that the conspiracy was most likely Gandil's idea and that gamblers such as Sport Sullivan,

Bill Burns, and Abe Attell were most certainly blameworthy. Yet unlike most versions of the episode, *Eight Men Out* also suggests that the scandal was set in motion by a complex set of social and labor relations and that Comiskey and other powerful baseball magnates did their best to ensure that the conspiracy remained out of public view. Moreover, Asinof's appraisal of the grand jury proceedings and the behind-the-scenes machinations during the trial indicates that, much like the 1919 World Series itself, justice (or at least verdicts) could be bought. Finally, Asinof implies that the popular press unscrupulously prejudged and exploited the players through incessant sensationalistic reporting. In all these ways, *Eight Men Out* promotes the view that the baseball establishment, the judicial system, and the media were at least as culpable as the ballplayers for the Big Fix. Written by a man who considers himself a political radical at a time when the mood of the country was shifting (frequently symbolized by the election of President John F. Kennedy) and when many Americans were challenging authority in a variety of ways (perhaps best symbolized by the civil rights movement), *Eight Men Out* signified a shift in the manner in which the Black Sox scandal was conceived by countering conventional historical wisdom and by attempting to assign responsibility for the affair more equitably.[82] At the same time, because *Eight Men Out* was immediately embraced as the first well-researched, cogently argued, and comprehensive study of the scandal, it necessarily affected later historical, fictional, and cinematic versions.[83]

Conclusion

Though they deploy different discursive modes, Malamud's *The Natural* and Asinof's *Eight Men Out* are bound together by their evocations of the Black Sox scandal. Considered by many to be master narratives, they have had lasting cultural value for various reasons: because of their ability to help maintain popular memories of the 1919 World Series scandal when they were fading; because they treat their subject with previously unknown seriousness and complexity; and because they have influenced virtually every subsequent retelling of the affair. For these and other reasons, *The Natural* and *Eight Men Out* are classics in the canon of baseball literature and history, which probably contributed to their adaptations as films in the eighties. Still, despite their elevated status, if we are to examine *The Natural* and *Eight Men Out* critically in terms of their portrayals of the Black Sox scandal, we need to remember that these narratives were written at a specific historical and cultural moment and we need to take seriously Hayden White's assertion that "every representation of the past has specifiable ideological implications."[84]

Clearly, many Americans still think of the fifties and early sixties as "an age of innocence and prosperity during which traditional family values, civility, and old-fashioned patriotism flourished."[85] This is an attractive and understandable simplification. Unfortunately, it ignores the era's darker side—which includes the Korean War, McCarthyism, and racial segregation—and minimizes its contradictions and complexity. Yes, the postwar years witnessed economic prosperity, yet the economy also experienced two recessions (in 1953 and 1958) and the wealth was certainly not spread equally. Yes, millions of Americans, especially men and whites, embraced the status quo, but many challenged it—politically, aesthetically, culturally—sometimes with surprising success. It is perhaps futile to offer an accurate thumbnail history of an era, especially one as varied as the fifties and early sixties, and yet I think it is fair to describe the era in which Malamud and Asinof lived and wrote as anxious, a period wracked by uneasiness, conflict, and change, one in which ideological struggle and social discontent and dissonance were (thinly and poorly) veiled by consumerism and the appearance of consensus. In this national and cultural ethos, *The Natural* and *Eight Men Out* simultaneously represent expressions of loss and regret, pleas for compassion and understanding. When examined together, these books suggest that the country's then not-so-distant past was similarly vexed by morally complicated problems and apprehension, that one milieu had things in common with the other, and that the Big Fix still had cultural resonance and meaning. For Malamud and Asinof, New York Jews who came of age in the thirties—a commonality that may partly explain their mutual interest in outsiders and outcasts—the scandal served multiple, overlapping purposes.

The Natural imparts a mythic, indeterminate past that represents a morally bankrupt wasteland. By tracing Roy Hobbs's stunning lack of development and maturity and noting the superficiality of his values, the novel promotes a yearning for virtue and moral growth. Despite Hobbs's numerous setbacks and his chronic lack of introspection, the novel holds out hope that its protagonist may have finally learned that heroic striving without a moral or ethical imperative can only end in failure. Ultimately, the hubristic Hobbs is transformed; his arrogance is replaced with a sense of shame and "overwhelming self-hatred" (217), a transformation best symbolized by the cleansing, "bitter tears" (217) he weeps at the novel's conclusion. In the end it appears that Hobbs has finally learned the lesson Iris Lemon had tried to teach him when she said, "We have two lives, Roy, the life we learn with and the life we live with after that. Suffering is what brings us toward happiness" (143). Since Hobbs has certainly suffered, we can only hope that the novel ends with the beginning of his second life. Ideologically, then, the novel suggests that, despite our individual limitations and the social limitations imposed upon us, failure and corruption need not be our ultimate fate, that we are capable of redemption through suffering and atonement. In this way Malamud's narrative articulates a historical vision that forces us to consider the possibility that Jackson and his teammates, whatever their actual crimes may have been, are capable of moral and historical redemption.

The reclamation of the vilified Black Sox is also a significant part of Asinof's project in *Eight Men Out.* Asinof's stated intentions were to reconstruct the 1919 World Series scandal, but by reevaluating the morality traditionally associated with the affair, Asinof reinforces a position similar to Malamud's in *The Natural.* Working from the presupposition that the conspiring ballplayers had been systematically victimized, Asinof stresses that they were responding to years of dismal treatment in the only manner available to them and that they were but one of several groups of culprits enmeshed in a complex web of greed, corruption, and betrayal. In part because of the lack of critical attention given to the conditions that fostered the affair, in part because the players were the only faction to be punished for their transgressions, Asinof rejects the easy, simplified morality that had traditionally defined the scandal. Perhaps Asinof's view of the event is best expressed in his description of a prosecutor's viewpoint: "To [Hartley] Replogle, the players were victims. The owners poured out a stream of pious, pompous verbiage about how pure they were. The gamblers said nothing, kept themselves hidden, protected themselves—and when they said anything, it was strictly for cash, with immunity, no less. But the ballplayers didn't even know enough to call a lawyer. They only knew how to play baseball" (177). In place of righteous indignation, Asinof engenders sympathy for the banished players, whom he refers to as "passive participants in their own destruction" (193), and tries to redeem their battered reputations while simultaneously indicting the baseball establishment (personified by Comiskey) for its hypocrisy. As a result, *Eight Men Out* productively complicates our understanding of the fixed World Series by suggesting that moral judgments cannot be made without considering the social contexts of those being judged. It also demonstrates that traditional historiographic methods can be used to construct politically alternative historical perspectives. In effect, *The Natural* and *Eight Men Out* suggest that the Black Sox scandal is best understood as a muddled social drama in which it is considerably easier to be critical of the ballplayers than to think critically about the complicated nexus of social relations that fostered the event or to entertain the possibility that Joe Jackson and his banished teammates deserve some compassion.

1919 Chicago White Sox. (National Baseball Hall of Fame Library, Cooperstown, N.Y.)

Joe Jackson, leftfielder, 1919 Chicago White Sox. (National Baseball Hall of Fame Library, Cooperstown, N.Y.)

George "Buck" Weaver, third baseman, 1919 Chicago White Sox. (National Baseball Hall of Fame Library, Cooperstown, N.Y.)

Eddie Cicotte, pitcher, 1919 Chicago White Sox. (Library of Congress)

Eddie Collins, second baseman, 1919 Chicago White Sox. (National Baseball Hall of Fame Library, Cooperstown, N.Y.)

William "Kid" Gleason, manager, 1919 Chicago White Sox. (National Baseball Hall of Fame Library, Cooperstown, N.Y.)

Charles A. Comiskey. (University of Cincinnati Archives and Rare Books Department)

Arnold Rothstein, notorious mobster and gambler. (Library of Congress)

Judge Kenesaw Mountain Landis, baseball's first commissioner, shaking hands with Joseph Burns of the Cincinnati Reds. (Library of Congress)

Roy Hobbs (Robert Redford) in *The Natural.* (Tri-Star Pictures and the Museum of Modern Art/FilmStills Archive)

Left to right: Ray Kinsella (Kevin Costner), Annie Kinsella (Amy Madigan), their daughter, Karin Kinsella (Gaby Hoffman), and Ray's father, John Kinsella (Dwier Brown), in *Field of Dreams.* (Universal City Studios and the Museum of Modern Art/ Film Stills Archive)

The Field of Dreams in Dyersville, Iowa, 1990. (Susan E. Taylor)

Left to right: Arnold "Chick" Gandil (Michael Rooker), Fred McMullin (Perry Lang), Charles "Swede" Risberg (Don Harvey), and Oscar "Hap" Felsch (Charlie Sheen) in *Eight Men Out.* (Photo by Bob Marshak; Orion Pictures and Museum of Modern Art/Film Stills Archive)

Team members congratulate Kid Gleason (John Mahoney), second from the right, in *Eight Men Out.* (Photo by Bob Marshak; Orion Pictures and Museum of Modern Art/ Film Stills Archive)

4

Off the Bench: Historians Take a Swing at the Black Sox Scandal

Given how many people are still passionately interested in the Black Sox scandal—and the revisionist nature of writing history—it is not surprising that Eliot Asinof has not had the final word on it. Seemingly, every season produces more Black Sox narratives. The very year *Eight Men Out* hit bookstores, John Durant published a brief history of the Big Fix in *Highlights of the World Series* (1963). Much like the rendition of the scandal he tells in *The Story of Baseball in Words and Pictures* (1947), Durant characterizes the event in his later book as an unfortunate aberration and most of the men involved in it as crooks who "came very close to wrecking baseball as our national pastime."[1] In a nutshell, Durants's narrative is the traditional, moralistic version of the affair. Two years later, Bill Veeck Jr., one of the game's most innovative and colorful executives, published *The Hustler's Handbook* (1965), which has a chapter on the Black Sox scandal allegedly based on a diary kept by Charles Comiskey's secretary, Harry Grabiner. According to Veeck, Grabiner's diary reveals, "beyond any doubt, that the White Sox front office had more than some inkling what was going on from the very first game of the 1919 World Series."[2] After explicating Grabiner's diary, Veeck concludes: "Looking back at the Black Sox scandal from this comfortable distance it becomes easy to take another drag on your cigarette and sneer that everybody did their best to cover up. *Everybody.* From the Commissioner on down."[3] Veeck's iconoclastic challenge to Major League Baseball's preferred version of the scandal was not unique, but it was uncommon. The following year, in *The Great Baseball Mystery—the 1919 World Series,* Victor Luhrs made the novel but unconvincing argument that there was not enough reliable evidence to conclude that the White Sox successfully threw the series; he argues that it was possible, even probable, that they double-crossed the gamblers and played to win but that the Reds legitimately won.[4] More creative than convincing, Luhrs's book nonetheless illustrates that Asinof did not have a monopoly on the Black Sox scandal even in the years immediately after the publication of *Eight Men Out*. No one has the last word when it comes to the past.

For fifty years academically trained historians had virtually nothing to say about the Black Sox scandal.[5] Partly due to "intellectual snobbery," most historians did not consider sport to be a sufficiently scholarly subject to pursue.[6] In the early seventies, however, when the study of sport was emerging as a historical subdiscipline, two works were published that treated baseball in general, and the Black Sox scandal in particular, with academic rigor: David Q. Voigt's *American Baseball: From the Commissioners to Continental Expansion* (1970) and Harold Seymour's *Baseball: The Golden Age* (1971), both of which were the second volumes in planned baseball history trilogies.[7] An assessment of how Voigt and Seymour, baseball's most eminent and influential historians, told the Black Sox story illustrates that writing history is itself historical. It reminds us that historians, no less than other storytellers, ply their craft in specific contexts that affect how they reconstruct and interpret the past.

Contexts

Historians do not write in ivory towers, sequestered from the world. Like everyone else, they live and work in multiple contexts: cultural, economic, historical, political, and social. David Voigt and Harold Seymour researched and wrote their versions of the Black Sox scandal in the 1960s and early 1970s.

Observers tend to agree that the country John F. Kennedy bequeathed to Lyndon B. Johnson in November 1963 was undergoing significant, sometimes painful, changes. In terms of national politics, domestic reforms, social unrest, activism, and later the Vietnam war occupied center stage. According to the historian John Morton Blum, "a consciousness of politics and political issues permeated American life" during the era, which he characterizes as "a time of persisting national discord."[8] A brief catalogue corroborates this assessment. These years witnessed numerous large scale civil rights and antiwar demonstrations as well as urban race riots; the assassinations of Malcolm X, Martin Luther King Jr., and Robert F. Kennedy; the birth of the Black Power movement; the founding of Students for a Democratic Society and the National Organization for Women; the My Lai massacre; the "police riot" outside the Democratic National Convention in Chicago; and the expansion of the Vietnam war into Cambodia and Laos. Nationwide, college campuses were sites of protest, the "sexual revolution" spread, and generational conflict seemed ubiquitous. Venerable institutions and values were questioned, contested, and subsequently defended. The national mood of the late sixties and early seventies was one of disenchantment and dissent accompanied by a conservative, sometimes reactionary "backlash," perhaps best symbolized by Richard M. Nixon's presidential election victories. For some, the liberal spirit of the sixties continued into the seventies (and beyond), despite the country's overall tack to the right and despite the mentality of cold war containment and paranoia that had carried over from the fifties.

The portrait above suggests something useful and important about the period's *Zeitgeist* and the milieu in which Voigt and Seymour took up the Black Sox. The sports world endured its own politically charged turmoil. To take one example, in 1964, the charismatic Cassius Clay shocked the world not only by beating the heavily favored Sonny Liston to win the heavyweight world championship but also by renouncing his "slave name" for Muhammad Ali and by proclaiming his membership in the Nation of Islam, a Black separatist organization feared by many white Americans. When Ali refused induction in the U.S. Army on religious grounds, he was stripped of his boxing title and charged as a draft dodger. In the process, note the historians Elliott J. Gorn and Warren Goldstein, Ali "became a symbol of opposition to the Vietnam War, and of the distance America still had to travel before racial equality became a reality."[9] Reviled by much of the public, Ali inspired others. Perhaps most notable is the sociologist Harry Edwards, who urged black athletes to boycott the 1968 Summer Olympic Games in Mexico City to dramatize racial inequality and injustice in the United States. While the boycott did not occur, the black sprinters Tommie Smith and John Carlos made international headlines and were widely condemned by the media when, during the medal ceremony for the 200-meter dash, they lowered their heads and raised their fists in Black Power salutes during the playing of the national anthem.[10] The following January, "Broadway" Joe Namath, the brash, iconoclastic quarterback of the New York Jets, whom the historian Benjamin G. Rader argues "symbolized the rebelliousness of the 1960s," caused a different kind of national stir when he violated the sporting decorum of the day and "guaranteed" that the Jets would defeat the favored Baltimore Colts in the Super Bowl.[11] The flamboyant Namath further aggravated many people when he led the Jets to victory. That same year, the St. Louis Cardinals outfielder Curt Flood challenged baseball's reserve clause when he refused to be traded to the Philadelphia Phillies. With the encouragement of Marvin Miller, the executive director of the Major League Baseball Players Association, Flood took his case all the way to the Supreme

Court. The court ruled against him, but Flood's courageous act of resistance (which cost him his baseball career) contributed to the clause being overturned by an arbitrator in 1975, led to the onset of free agency and million-dollar contracts for ballplayers, and reflected and contributed to the temper of the times.

Historians were not oblivious to these events and similar social developments and currents. It is not coincidental that some historians during this period began to write what came to be called the "new social history." Proponents asked new questions of old subjects, embraced new theories and assumptions, used different types of evidence and methods, challenged numerous conventional historical conclusions, and shifted the focus of study away from national politics and social elites. They focused on people who were usually ignored or marginalized, such as women, immigrants, racial and ethnic minorities, and members of the working class.[12] As in the past, the shift in the discipline mirrored nationwide political and social changes.[13] "In the late 1960s and early 1970s," explains the historian Steven A. Riess, "a younger generation of historians—influenced by contemporary social events, left-wing scholarship, and a desire to make history more 'relevant'—became very interested in social history, particularly the history and culture of common people."[14] Sport history subsequently emerged as a subdiscipline.[15]

A handful of academically trained historians studied sport and popular recreation before the sixties, most notably Frederic L. Paxson, John Allen Krout, Jennie Holliman, Jesse Frederick Steiner, Foster Rhea Dulles, and John Rickards Betts, but their work was generally descriptive rather than analytical and it tended to posit that sport was merely a positive social practice.[16] Indebted to the aforementioned scholars yet ahead of the curve, David Voigt and Harold Seymour were among the first academics to consider *critically* how sport in general and baseball in particular were historically significant aspects of American society and culture. For this reason the historian Larry R. Gerlach describes them as the "Founding Fathers of scholarly baseball history."[17] Though pioneers, Voigt and Seymour are not quite "new historians." In many ways, their work is firmly rooted in Progressive historiography, particularly the strain that attempts to look beyond self-serving, often patriotic rhetoric and examined power relations and economic and political conflict. That is, their methods and some of their fundamental assumptions are traditional, even if their subject is not. To be taken seriously by their colleagues and readers, Voigt and Seymour had to follow the dictates of the discipline. In this way their narratives are influenced by and reflected the historical moment.[18]

Voigt's Version

Having earned his Ph.D. from Syracuse University in 1962, David Voigt was a professor of sociology at Albright College in Reading, Pennsylvania, when he wrote *American Baseball: From the Commissioners to Continental Expansion,* his second book.[19] His first was *American Baseball: From the Gentleman's Sport to the Commissioner System* (1966). Written in an accessible, fluid style, the second volume of Voigt's trilogy covers sixty years of Major League baseball history, from 1903 (when the National League and the American League reached a truce called the National Agreement) to 1920 ("Baseball's Silver Age"), 1920 to 1945 ("Baseball's Second Golden Age"), and 1945 to 1969 ("The Dawn of the Plastic Age"). He examines organized baseball's institutional structure and internal political history, its most prominent and influential ballplayers, owners, executives, teams, events, trends, and, as the historian Melvin L. Adelman puts it, "the cultural ambiance surrounding the game."[20] Given its broad scope, *American Baseball* inevitably slights or ignores some subjects, including the minor leagues, the Negro Leagues, and semipro, sandlot, and Little League baseball.[21] But Voigt does not give short shrift to the Black Sox scandal.

Voigt begins his version of the Black Sox scandal by establishing some context for the event. He notes that "war-weary fans returned in droves" for the 1919 baseball season, "bringing unprecedented profits" (124), briefly recounts Cincinnati's best-of-nine game upset of Chicago, and relates the "persistent rumors" that gamblers "corrupted some White Sox players and paid them to lose."[22] Like Eliot Asinof and many others, Voigt credits the journalist Hugh Fullerton with bringing the story to light; according to Voigt, Fullerton's "tireless digging uncovered the tangled tale of corruption that made the 1919 World Series an America tragedy" (125). Due in part to Fullerton's stories and the ongoing rumors of World Series wrongdoing, by September 1920, Voigt explains, "baseball faced a grand jury investigation into the conduct of the 1919 Series" (127). Soon thereafter, a Philadelphia newspaper published a damning interview with a small-time gambler who "supplied details of the fix and names of fixers," and subsequently a few White Sox ballplayers "confessed their part in the conspiracy" (127). At this point, Voigt maintains, "the rest of the dismal story is well known" (127). The ensuing trial "was a farce since the records of the grand jury and the confessions of Cicotte, Jackson, and Williams had mysteriously disappeared" (129). From Voigt's perspective, "the lack of evidence and a friendly jury turned the trial into a comedy" (129), and as a result the accused players were acquitted. "Even though the men were found innocent in the world of civil law," Voigt observes, "they still faced judgment in the baseball world. The final arbiter was Commissioner Landis, and he summarily barred all eight for life. For the rest of their lives they bore the stigma of "Black Sox." In spite of repeated appeals, Landis stubbornly refused to grant a single pardon" (130). Next, Voigt discusses the fate "of these baseball Ishmaels" (130) and Charles Comiskey (132), considers reasons the ballplayers "so recklessly gambled their reputations on an ill-conceived intrigue" (130), catalogues previous examples of gambling-related baseball corruption (131–32), and comments on the institutional effects of the scandal—namely, the dissolution of the national commission and the appointment of Kenesaw Mountain Landis as commissioner (132–33). In all, Voigt devotes nine pages to the Big Fix and approximately twenty pages to its aftermath. His rendition of the 1919 World Series scandal makes a long, complicated story short and intelligible. Better than most storytellers, Voigt takes a skein of facts and stories and knits it into a succinct narrative.[23]

There are many notable things about Voigt's version of the Black Sox scandal. First, despite its relative brevity, his account makes it clear that the event did not occur in a social vacuum and was not a singular transgression. After mentioning that the 1919 World Series was the first post–World War I fall classic, Voigt writes that many White Sox fans braved "late summer race riots to cheer" for their team (124), an important reference to the five days of rioting in July that left thirty-eight people dead, hundreds injured, and several million dollars in property destroyed.[24] He also notes that before the Black Sox scandal, Americans had already experienced the anxiety of alleged Bolshevik threats, the nascent Red Scare, the Boston police strike, and the rise of bootleg liquor smuggling—all of which suggest the turbulent nature of the national climate (126). Perhaps most important, Voigt documents that long before the 1919 series professional baseball was "riddled with rumors [and acts] of bribery and cheating" (131). The Black Sox scandal, Voigt suggests, may have been a "tragedy" (about which I will say more), but it was not an aberration. Voigt establishes the many precedents for game fixing. At the same time, he does not explicitly link the social conditions or relations that caused the Black Sox scandal to broader social and political trends, such as the wave of labor disputes and strikes in 1919 and organized crime's association with other sports, especially horse racing and boxing.[25]

Second, like all historians, Voigt makes a few mistakes, as Harold Seymour points out in his review: "Buck Freeman is incorrectly listed as a member of the Black Sox in the 1919 scandal and as the only one of the accused players who fought back in the courts. In reality, Freeman left baseball in 1907 and was never a member of the Black Sox; and four Black Sox players, not one, sought legal redress: Jackson, Felsch, Risberg, and Weaver. In addition it was not Weaver but Jackson who confessed to the 'fix' after Cicotte."[26] In the most recent edition of *American Baseball,* Voigt has corrected the Buck Freeman/Buck Weaver confusion. Seymour was also right about Weaver not being the only implicated ballplayer who "sought legal redress." In 1924, Joe Jackson filed suit against Comiskey for $18,000 in back pay.[27] Hap Felsch did pursue some legal action related to his banishment, but to my knowledge Swede Risberg did not. Considering his temperament and ringleader role in the fix, it seems unlikely that he would have.[28] Lastly, Seymour correctly notes that Jackson, not Weaver, was the second to confess to the conspiracy. Weaver, of course, never confessed to fixing the series, just to knowing about it, and he consistently proclaimed his innocence.[29] The point here is not that Voigt's account is more error laden than others but that the story is so convoluted that even a sure-handed scholar like Voigt will occasionally (and probably inevitably) misstate a few facts.

Third, Voigt's early use of the word *tragedy* to describe the Black Sox scandal is revealing and significant, for it "identifies the *kind of story* he is telling."[30] But for whom was the event a tragedy? Many baseball fans were deeply disillusioned and hurt by the game-fixing revelations, yet Voigt does not mention their reactions. Comiskey was surely a victim: he was denied a World Series championship, saw his powerful (and profitable) team dismantled, and had his reputation besmirched. In addition, Voigt writes, Comiskey's "colleagues avoided him after 1920, and his last years were lonely ones. His one consolation was that he kept his franchise" (132). Still, in Voigt's telling, the Black Sox are the scandal's most tragic figures; they are "scapegoats" (130) and "baseball Ishmaels," victims and outcasts. While Voigt describes the conspirators as the game's "most brazen cheaters" (132), he likewise argues that it "is not hard to understand" why they decided to throw games (130). Citing the White Sox's cliquishness, "which pitted a sophisticated element, led by captain Eddie Collins, against a more earthy, less polished group, led by 'Chick' Gandil" (130–31), Voigt comments that "none of the Gandil faction made over $6,000, this clique continually groused about Comiskey's penny-pinching, and indeed his 1919 payroll was one of baseball's lowest" (130–31). This is now a familiar explanation for the ballplayers' duplicity. When *American Baseball* was first published, however, writers rarely suggested that anything other than the ballplayers' avarice was responsible for the fix. In this regard, Voigt seems to have been influenced by Asinof's *Eight Men Out,* which he frequently cites.

A now-common corollary of this interpretation is that Comiskey and his fellow team owners exploited the ballplayers and tolerated (perhaps even promoted) the conditions that caused the game fixing. Voigt not so subtly makes these arguments. In chapter 4, for example, he maintains that Comiskey's players thought "he was a cheapskate" (112), penurious to a fault. Voigt also notes that an "old campaigner like Comiskey should have known that unpunished corruption breeds more corruption" (126), yet he chose not to act on the rumors of World Series crookedness. Only after Cicotte, Jackson, and Williams testified did Comiskey suspend the ballplayers he had suspected all along. Comiskey's "long-delayed action," Voigt writes, "revealed him as a man who put personal profits ahead of integrity and who had remained silent in the face of known corruption" (127). This was not, as we have seen, how the media had portrayed Comiskey to this point.

Voigt does not view Comiskey as an atypical baseball executive. Instead, he maintains that "by delaying the 1919 fix investigation, baseball men created a climate for more corruption in 1920" (132). This is an interesting shift in emphasis and responsibility, away from the implicated players and toward the baseball establishment, whose only redemption in this saga, as Voigt tells it, was hiring Landis as "the game's conscience" (139). Even then, Voigt points out, "if owners had kept cool under the fire of publicity and probes they might have kept their power. But they panicked" (132) and hired Landis, a patriarchal autocrat who "was to be the Moses who would lead his people back to the paths of righteousness" (143).

In general, Voigt's version of the Black Sox scandal, like most of *American Baseball,* is cogent and concise. Critically alert, it is also historically responsible. Despite a few minor mistakes, Voigt's narrative satisfies scholarly standards of history-writing; it is well-documented and balanced, though some readers may take issue with Voigt's analysis and conclusions, which probably strike some as too sympathetic toward the implicated ballplayers and overly critical of Comiskey. Yet the way he tells the story tends toward the conservative. Like most historians, Voigt uses the traditional third-person omniscient voice. In addition, Voigt adheres to historical forms by organizing his narrative chronologically. "Writing at a time when all but a handful of historians ignored sport as an area of scholarly inquiry," explains Melvin L. Adelman, "Voigt sought to overcome the prejudice of the academic community and demonstrate the worthiness of his subject."[31]

In contrast, Voigt's content, which reveals a prolabor sensibility, was uncommon in 1970. Following in Eliot Asinof's footsteps, Voigt posits that the implicated ballplayers were only one of the affair's culpable parties and that their burden of responsibility was exaggerated, primarily by baseball team owners interested in distancing themselves from the mess. This argument challenged the conventional wisdom of the day and is consistent with Adelman's trenchant observation: "In contrast to his jaundiced view of baseball owners, Voigt is a 'players' man."[32] Ideologically, then, Voigt's presuppositions and interpretations positioned him left-of-center on the spectrum of Black Sox storytellers. In short, Voigt's *form* was traditional; his *argument* was not.

No one writes outside history, and thus Voigt's rendition of the Black Sox scandal reflects some aspects of the era in which it was produced. Teaching and writing at Albright College for most of the sixties, Voigt was far from the decade's hotbeds of iconoclasm. Moreover, Voigt, who was educated during the late forties and fifties, himself says that his historical sensibility was largely shaped by earlier experiences and by his Columbia University history professors, particularly Allan Nevins and David Herbert Donald.[33] Nevertheless, even if historians (and other storytellers) do not consciously draw on the moment's *Zeitgeist,* they exist in a world of social and political relations that, consciously or not, make an impression on them and often evoke a response. So while Voigt was not necessarily from or of the sixties, his account of the scandal challenged authority in ways common to activists and reformers. It did so by reapportioning much of the responsibility for the World Series game fixing and the subsequent scandal from the implicated ballplayers to Comiskey and the baseball establishment. In addition, it challenges the widely held perspective of the Black Sox scandal as a morality tale and suggests that the event should be understood in its context, seen as something other than an avarice-driven anomaly. To what extent this interpretation drew sustenance from the era in which it was written is difficult to know, even for Voigt.

Further, while it adopts the era's standard historical narrative form, Voigt's version of the Black Sox scandal is also emblematic of the way many historians in the sixties and seventies shifted their focus from social and political elites to those marginalized people largely absent from previous histories. Some of the historians who embraced this perspective "valorized their subjects' resistance to oppression and sturdy survival," writes the historian Dorothy Ross, "or conversely, their victimization by oppressors."[34] Although there is some of the latter in *American Baseball,* for the most part Voigt merely historicizes his subjects and treats them with understanding. He does not "God them up" (to use the sports editor Stanley Woodward's famous phrase) or pardon them for their misdeeds.[35] In *American Baseball,* as befits a complicated historical moment and a sober, mature telling of a complicated story, the Black Sox are both villains and victims.

Seymour's Black Sox Scandal

Once described by *Sports Illustrated* as the "Edward Gibbon of baseball history," Harold Seymour earned his Ph.D. from Cornell University in 1957. Three years later, he published *Baseball: The Early Years,* a revised and expanded version of his dissertation—the first scholarly study devoted exclusively to the game.[36] For the next decade, Seymour taught American, European, and English history at colleges in New York City and Massachusetts.[37] "In the 1970s, when Dr. Seymour was composing his study of the Black Sox, we were living in West Newbury," explains his widow Dorothy Jane Mills, who assisted her husband on all three of his books. "I had just convinced him to leave his position as head of the history department of a small college in Beverly, Massachusetts, because he was becoming increasingly frustrated with his teaching—most of the students were not as well prepared as those he was used to teaching. Besides, as I pointed out, he just wasn't getting his writing done. He finally left and wrote full-time from then on."[38] In 1971 Seymour published *Baseball: The Golden Age,* which picked up the story of Major League Baseball where his first book had left off and continued it to 1930.[39] An impressively detailed work, *Baseball: The Golden Age* focuses on many of the same subjects as Voigt's second book: the business and politics of the Major Leagues, on-the-field trends (like the pendulum swings between defense and offense), the game's greatest players (especially Ty Cobb and Babe Ruth) and managers (most notably, Connie Mack and John McGraw), the Federal League War, the formation and demise of the the game's national commission, the development of the farm system, and the 1919 World Series scandal. At sixty-five pages, his account provides the most thorough retelling of the Black Sox scandal since Eliot Asinof's *Eight Men Out.* He tells the story of "Baseball's Darkest Hour" (294) in the same manner he treats most of his subjects, that is, as one reviewer put it, "with the raised eyebrow of the skeptic, not the open mouth of the credulous."[40]

Well before discussing the scandal, Seymour demonstrates that professional baseball was not an "innocent" endeavor. He consistently notes that as soon as professional baseball teams were formed, "players were always keenly interested in such unheroic matters as salaries and working conditions, and on two occasions even formed a union" (76). Later in the same chapter Seymour cautions that "baseball should be seen for what it is—a boy's game played by grown men for a living and run by promoters for a profit" (91). In addition, when he mentions that the White Sox won the 1917 World Series, Seymour makes clear that they did so despite the "dissension and cliques that wracked the squad" (164). A hundred pages before he takes up the Black Sox scandal in earnest, Seymour maintains that the 1920 World Series was "anti-climactic" because the "long-smoldering rumor burst into searing fact as astounded fans learned that the 1919 World Series had been 'fixed,' and a shocked public discovered that its so-called National Game and vaunted heroes were, like the politics and business of the era, susceptible to dishonesty and corruption" (165). Thus, Seymour sets the stage for his examination of the Black Sox affair, which he describes as "the most sensational scandal in the history of American professional sports" (294).

Seymour begins his history of the Big Fix by specifying why Americans were so shocked by the game-fixing revelations: "The belief that baseball was honest and upright constituted an article of secular faith" in the country (274). For most fans, Seymour suggests, baseball's integrity was a given, bordering on a moral certainty. At the same time, gambling was virtually endemic to baseball, and therefore "the shock need not have been so great or so sudden. Warning shadows were there to be seen or to be pointed out. Open betting in the ball parks was rife" (278) and more pronounced outside of them. Most team owners deplored and feared gambling, but "their vigilance in suppressing it was sporadic and lacking zeal" (278). This partly explains many of the "sordid events" (285) baseball endured before the scandal, several of which Seymour catalogues (281–93). "The evidence is abundantly clear," Seymour concludes, that "the groundwork for the crooked 1919 World Series, like most striking events in history, was long prepared. The scandal was not an aberration brought about solely by a handful of villainous players. It was a culmination of corruption and attempts at corruption that reached back nearly twenty years" (293). After fifty years, this view was finally gaining historical currency.

As for the 1919 series itself, Seymour acknowledges that, "in spite of all that has been written, precisely what happened remains uncertain or unknown" (294). He notes the shifts in the betting odds from Chicago to even money, the rumors that something was amiss, and (in one sentence) the fact that the Reds beat the White Sox. Seymour also credits Fullerton with being the "gadfly" (295) who first investigated the series and documents the criticism he received for publishing his suspicions (295–97). After clarifying that Comiskey and the baseball establishment had heard rumors of wrongdoing yet did virtually nothing, Seymour turns toward the grand jury proceedings, the testimony before it, and the confessions by Cicotte, Jackson, and Williams (309). He explains that "months would pass before the accused were arraigned and tried. But Organized Baseball dared not wait. Even as the squalid disclosures unrolled, the owners in their consternation rushed to restore public confidence in their blighted business. Basic structural changes in Organized Baseball were to result" (310)—changes that had been brewing for some time and were bitterly contested (311–19). Chief among them was the hiring of Landis as baseball's first commissioner (320). Yet Seymour shows that the Big Fix did not by itself bring "about the overthrow of the National Commission and its replacement by a new form of baseball government under Judge Kenesaw Mountain Landis"; rather, the scandal "accelerated a structural change already contemplated and which very likely would have come about in some form anyway" (311–12).

Seymour's final chapter on the scandal focuses on the trial, the banishment of the acquitted players, and the conclusions that can be drawn. According to Seymour, "The task of judging the affair is doubly difficult even half a century afterwards because of the lack of source material and because countless journalistic accounts have encrusted the event in layers of preconceived assumptions and questionable opinions" (331). Admitting that "there is no disputing that some kind of plot existed," Seymour nevertheless maintains that there is no "incontrovertible proof that the plot was carried out" (332). At several points, Seymour stresses the event's indeterminacy and suggests that many people besides the accused ballplayers were responsible. He argues, for example, that "the so-called Clean Sox were not quite so pure as some have made them out to be. Surely they had some responsibility for protecting their profession. They knew that something was wrong, and more than once they admitted as much, but they did nothing about it. In a sense they were accessories to the fact" (333). Like Asinof and Voigt, Seymour notes that Comiskey's "penny-pinching" helped create conditions that explained, but did not excuse, the game throwing (334). In addition, Seymour is critical of Comiskey's action (or inaction) during and after the series (334–36). Seymour also finds fault with other baseball executives: "For too long they had looked the other way when something shady happened, or tried to conceal it" (336). Seymour further argues that "the hearings and the trial itself are subject to skepticism. Their declared purpose was to investigate gambling in professional baseball and presumably bring crooked practitioners to justice. But none was ever punished, although there were numerous targets to aim at" (337). As for Landis, Seymour contends that he "wielded not a sword of justice but an extra-legal scythe. He recognized no degrees of guilt but cut off from their livelihood seven ball players acquitted in a court of law and two others who were not even indicted" (338). In a later chapter, Seymour describes Landis as a man with an "authoritarian personality" (368) and as someone "not bothered by any hobgoblin of consistency" (377). Seymour demonstrates that, contrary to popular opinion,

Landis did not save baseball. "Attendance picked up sharply as soon as the World War ended—before Landis entered the picture—and it continued to climb," contends Seymour. "The fans were not turning out to see Landis, colorful as he was. They were captivated by the batting exploits of Babe Ruth" (420). Ultimately, Seymour leaves his readers with the following: "The Black Sox scandal branded the nine expelled players [the eight White Sox and Joe Gedeon of the St. Louis Browns, for knowledge of the fix] as the villains who had betrayed the game; turned Comiskey into a martyr who had suffered financial loss and broken health; cast [Ban] Johnson in the role of a crusader who had worked to cleanse the game; and glorified Landis as a savior whose stern penalties had restored Organized Baseball to purity" (339). This tidy, simplified assessment belies Seymour's more complicated and critically alert appraisal.

One way of assessing Seymour's version of the Black Sox scandal is to consider the historical standards that he himself championed. In a 1986 essay, the historian Jules Tygiel wrote that Seymour, in *Baseball: The Golden Age,* "laid out three critical distinctions between popular and scholarly history." The first is that "academically trained historians [should] apply a more stringent research methodology, relying not simply on the oral folklore of the game, but on exhaustive archival and newspaper research. The historian must seek, wherever possible, new, previously untapped sources, which yield new information and/or fresh insights into timeworn tales."[41] With respect to the Black Sox scandal, Seymour follows his own advice and in fact seems to have done some original research, including interviews with a few of the men involved in the scandal, such as Joe Jackson (333). But it is hard to know with much certainty the nature of Seymour's research because he does not explicitly document his sources. Oddly enough, considering Seymour's training and the number of times he had complained that baseball lacked scholarly attention, *Baseball: The Golden Age* lacks footnotes. In his preface, Seymour explains: "The present volume, like the first one, omits footnotes, since they inhibit the general reader, for whom the book is primarily intended. The chief sources of information are indicated, however, in a bibliographical note" (vii).[42]

In his seven-page "bibliographical note" Seymour reveals that he did research at the Baseball Hall of Fame and the Chicago Historical Society, among other libraries and archives, and that he "carefully combed" periodicals like the *Sporting News* and the *New York Times* (466). As for Black Sox scandal texts, he acknowledges Asinof's *Eight Men Out,* Victor Luhrs's *The Great Baseball Mystery,* and Bill Veeck's *The Hustler's Handbook* (468). In the previous chapter, I discussed *Eight Men Out*'s lack of footnotes and some of the consequences of that decision. Seymour's failure to footnote is more conspicuous and problematic than Asinof's. Then as now, footnotes or endnotes are often omitted "for commercial reasons," writes the historian Gertrude Himmelfarb, "to make scholarly books look more accessible and thus more marketable."[43] Yet the omissions come at a high price. For as Himmelfarb observes, footnotes are about accountability: "They are meant to permit the reader to check the author's sources, facts, quotations, inferences, and generalizations."[44] Readers of *Baseball: The Golden Age* cannot easily do these things. For example, Seymour may give too much credence to Veeck's chapter on the Black Sox scandal, "Harry's Diary—1919."[45] Ever the hustler, Veeck says that Harry Grabiner's diary is sometimes "shamelessly self-serving," perhaps an indication that it is not to be taken too seriously, like Veeck himself.[46] Without more explicit documentation, we cannot know how Seymour uses Veeck. That *Baseball: The Golden Age* lacks footnotes could lead one to conclude that Seymour shirked one of his responsibilities as a historian; it certainly clouds his rendition of the Black Sox scandal.

Seymour's second criterion for writing scholarly baseball history is that "any analysis of the evolution of baseball must be placed into the context of American history. Changes in the national pastime often accompanied broader national developments."[47] Although it was not precisely an act of evolution, the Black Sox scandal did help foment significant changes in the way Major League Baseball was played on the field, run as a business, and, for some, understood as a social institution. To Seymour's credit, he goes to great lengths to put the Big Fix firmly within the context of baseball history and internal politics. Seymour notes, for instance, that "Ban Johnson finally did make a genuine effort to dig out the facts, but he did so for the wrong reasons—to destroy Comiskey and to outshine the new Commissioner" (337). Rarely, however, does *Baseball: The Golden Age* place the Black Sox scandal in the broader context of American social history. Seymour does note that the episode relegated "stories of the Red Scare that was then raging in the United States . . . to the back pages of the newspapers" and that it "created a greater stir than the charges of corruption that were leveled against members of President Harding's cabinet a few years later" (276). He also documents the prevalence of sports-related gambling at the time (278–81). Otherwise, however, he makes no attempt to understand or explain the scandal in terms of previous or contemporaneous events, relations, or trends.

Perhaps the most important of Seymour's standards is that "scholarly research deals not simply in facts and chronology, but in analysis and interpretation. The academic, building on the work of earlier scholars, identifies historically significant themes and issues, the study of which will enhance our understanding of both baseball and America."[48] Seymour certainly accomplishes this with regard to the Black Sox scandal, though he remained reluctant to admit his indebtedness to others (particularly to Asinof and to his own wife).[49] A traditional narrative history, *Baseball: The Golden Age* does more than merely tell the story of the Big Fix; in it Seymour skillfully analyzes the event and its causes and challenges some long-held assumptions, characterizations, and conclusions. Less stridently than Asinof and in more detail than Voigt, Seymour emphasizes the context of the scandal. Seymour's unacknowledged collaborator, Dorothy Jane Mills, succinctly assesses how her husband made sense of the scandal: "He did sympathize with the players who were getting such little reward that they believed it necessary to cheat, but he could not of course condone cheating, although he felt the punishment—permanent expulsion—was probably too severe."[50] In the hands of a skilled, thoughtful historian, complicated events tend to produce complex histories.

Every history has problems, contradictions, and areas of uncertainty, and one in *Baseball: The Golden Age* deserves attention. Seymour claims that when Joe Jackson testified before the Cook County grand jury he "told of moving slowly after balls hit to him, making throws that fell short, and deliberately striking out with runners in scoring position" (303). My reading of Jackson's testimony reveals no such admissions. When Assistant State's Attorney Hartley L. Replogle asked Jackson if he made any intentional errors during game four, Jackson replied: "No, sir, not during the whole series."[51] The questioning continued:

Q: Did you bat to win?
A: Yes.
Q: And run the bases to win?
A: Yes, sir.
Q: And field the balls at the outfield to win?
A: I did.[52]

Later, Replogle asked Jackson, "Did you do anything to throw those games?"

A: No, sir.
Q: Any game in the series?
A: Not a one. I didn't have an error or make no misplay.[53]

There are several versions of Jackson's testimony—none of them official since the court records long ago disappeared—and it is unclear which one Seymour used. The testimony above is from a transcript provided by Mayer, Brown, and Platt, a Chicago law firm.[54] I have quoted Jackson's testimony not to demonstrate that Seymour is wrong, but to highlight a measure of ambiguity in his telling of the scandal.

Seymour's version of the episode provides readers with a penetrating look into the scandal's internal causes, machinations, and consequences, but ignores the larger forces that contributed to the game throwing and its aftermath. While useful and illuminating, it is unclear how the representation of the Black Sox scandal in *Baseball: The Golden Age* reflects aspects of the era in which it was produced. Dorothy Jane Mills suspects that the historical moment and the surrounding culture played little role in her husband's portrayal: "I believe the era in which he wrote did not particularly affect his view of the Scandal, other 'dirty work,' or baseball history in general. By then, his views of history—and of life in general—were fully formed."[55] The sixties and seventies clearly were not Seymour's formative years. Still, it is reasonable to argue, as Paul K. Conkin and Roland N. Stromberg put it, that historians often "reflect pervasive interests and concerns when they select and group their empirically discovered facts. They readily take on the coloration of their times."[56] *Baseball: The Golden Age* reminds us that the time in which Seymour wrote was not just psychedelic but also retained more traditional hues. This comes across most vividly in Seymour's attempt to offer a balanced, even-handed assessment of the Big Fix. As one would expect of an academic historian trained at midcentury, Seymour seems to have embraced the view that the "objective historian's role is that of a neutral, or disinterested judge; it must never degenerate into that of advocate or, even worse, propagandist."[57] Thus, unlike Judge Landis, who had a different, more explicitly political job to perform and did not have fifty years of hindsight, Seymour finds many of the men involved in the scandal culpable for the 1919 World Series debacle. For Seymour, whose historical vision might best be described as morally authoritative, there was plenty of responsibility to go around. This does not mean that his account of the game fixing is apolitical or objective; rather it suggests that it embodies a different sensibility than other, more clearly partisan Black Sox stories.

Complementary History

David Voigt and Harold Seymour greatly influenced how historians understand and have written about baseball. Steven Riess, himself a respected sports historian, describes their work as "pathbreaking."[58] Voigt's and Seymour's books have certainly enriched my understanding of baseball's history and cultural significance. Read together, *American Baseball: From the Commissioners to Continental Expansion* and *Baseball: The Golden Age* complement each other and provide us with an appropriately complex history of early twentieth-century professional baseball. Their respective renditions of the Black Sox scandal epitomize this.

In most important ways, Voigt and Seymour view and represent the scandal similarly. They both explain that game fixing and other kinds of corruption were common in baseball long before 1919; they both argue that many people besides the implicated ballplayers, most notably gamblers and Comiskey, were responsible for the World Series debacle; and they both critique Landis's character and performance as baseball commissioner, specifically his decision to banish the Black Sox. While Seymour devotes more space and detail to these and other subjects, Voigt's critical edge is equally sharp. Moreover, Voigt and Seymour are both greatly indebted to Eliot Asinof's *Eight Men Out;* in addition to providing them with important information, its political sensibility seems to suffuse their histories. At the same time, Voigt and Seymour both present their versions of the Big Fix as if they are ideologically neutral, though they are not—and cannot be.

In fact, Voigt's and Seymour's narratives differ primarily in subtle ways, in the manner in which they shade their subjects. Perhaps because of its relative brevity, Voigt's account is drawn more vividly. His Comiskey, for example, is slightly more ignoble and blameworthy than Seymour's. Still, what is most striking is how similar these works are. One possible reason for this is that both men came of age and had their historical sensibilities shaped during the interwar years, when the Black Sox scandal was still alive in many memories, and both received their graduate training at roughly the same time. Seymour was older than Voigt, but they were of the same generation and shared some of its assumptions and values. In addition, they were researching, thinking about, and writing their books at approximately the same historical moment.[59] Historians, in other words, are historical products as well as producers of histories. Another explanation is that they drew on many of the same primary and secondary sources. Dependent on these texts, both historians in some ways replicated their dominant tropes and perceptions. In total, Voigt and Seymour agree about the Black Sox, and their narratives would provide the basis for the new dominant history of the scandal.

Obviously history is often contentious, with competing groups and individuals grappling over the past, its meaning, and its legacy. One result of such contests is multiple, wildly varying versions of the past. In this particular example, unlike the larger story told in this book, that is not the case.

Denny McLain, Watergate, and the Last Man Out

As important as Voigt's and Seymour's books were (and remain), most Americans in the seventies did not read them. Then as now, few people besides academic historians read histories written by academics. This, of course, did not prevent the Black Sox scandal from remaining alive in memory and occasionally figuring prominently on the American cultural landscape. In February 1970, when only two of the men involved in the Big Fix were still living, *Baseball Digest* published an aptly entitled article: "Old Men Die, but the Black Sox Scandal Lives On."[60] Soon thereafter, when another gambling controversy struck baseball, the Black Sox scandal was again newsworthy.

In late February 1970, baseball's commissioner, Bowie Kuhn, indefinitely suspended Denny McLain of the Detroit Tigers, the first pitcher since 1934 to win thirty games in a season and a two-time Cy Young Award winner, for being involved in a bookmaking operation and associating with gamblers. After Kuhn's decision, one reporter warned, "The case could become the game's most celebrated since the infamous 1919 Black Sox scandal."[61] This was not just sensationalism, but an expression of sincere concern. The McLain incident was, after all, the first time since 1924 that a baseball player had been suspended for a gambling-related offense. And as one letter writer to *Sports Illustrated* asked, "Denny McLain is only one professional athlete who has been found dealing with mobsters. How many more are there?"[62] Some had asked the same question in September 1920.

One way people made sense of the Denny McLain incident was to look to the past. Some sportswriters reminded readers that in 1963 Alex Karras and Paul Hornung of the National Football League were suspended for a year for betting on professional football games.[63] Others recalled the earlier college basketball point-shaving scandals.[64] But even more journalists referred to the 1919 World Series scandal when discussing McLain's suspension.[65] A *Chicago Daily News* article exemplifies the way many journalists used one scandal to understand another: "Denny McLain's suspension . . . for alleged 1967 bookmaking activities marks the most devastating blow to baseball since the Black Sox scandal of the 1919 World Series."[66]

More specifically, a few sportswriters used the Big Fix as a historical reference point, as a way of putting McLain's transgressions and suspension in context, to show that they had precedents. "McLain is not the first sports figure to be linked with gamblers, nor the most famous," reminded David Condon of the *Chicago Tribune*. "The most shocking sport gambling scandal was revealed in 1920, when eight members of the Chicago White Sox were accused of conspiring to lose the 1919 World Series to Cincinnati." Subtly suggesting that McLain's baseball career was in jeopardy, Condon continued, "Those eight—now remembered as the Black Sox—never drew convictions for illegal activities but were banned from organized baseball for life."[67] "Any way you look at it," wrote the *Boston Globe*'s Francis Rosa, "this is a sad time for baseball. It's the most serious loss of face the game has had since the 1919 Black Sox scandal." Rosa, however, was careful to note that there was an important distinction between the Black Sox and McLain incidents: "Unlike the 1919 scandal the McLain affair doesn't challenge the honesty of the game. It does challenge the activities of one of its name players."[68]

Predictably, the Detroit media also made connections between the McLain incident and the Black Sox scandal. In response to a fan who urged people to resist the rush to judge McLain, George Puscas, the sports editor of the *Detroit Free Press,* commented, "True, there has been no indictment, no trial, and there may not be one. But baseball does not require such steps to achieve its own form of 'justice.' Eight players involved in the Black Sox scandal of 1919 were acquitted by a grand jury—but banned for life by the commissioner."[69] The next day, the *Detroit Free Press* published an editorial on the McLain incident that concluded: "It is too late for the 'say-it-ain't-so-Joe' routine. It *is* so, at least enough of it to be embarrassing to sports."[70] This was especially so for Major League Baseball and the Detroit Tigers.

On April 1, after completing his investigation, Kuhn announced that McLain would be suspended until July 1 and placed on probation. Shirley Povich of the *Washington Post* remarked, "Kuhn tempered justice with mercy, as the book says one must, when he spanked McLain with a mere three-month sentence."[71] Many thought the suspension was too lenient. For our purposes, though, what is significant is that once again commentators drew on the Black Sox scandal to describe and make sense of the McLain incident. Joe Falls of the *Detroit Free Press,* who thought McLain's punishment was inadequate, cited the "bold stand that commissioner Kenesaw Mountain Landis took when he banned for life those eight members of the infamous Chicago Black Sox for allegedly fixing games in the 1919 World Series even though all eight were acquitted by the Cook County grand jury."[72] Others agreed that baseball needed Landis-style leadership and vigilance against gambling-related wrongdoing. *Newsweek*'s sports editor, Pete Axthelm, did not go that far, but did argue that "baseball, like all sports, is a very special segment of that society—one that depends for its very existence on the complete confidence of the public. McLain shook that confidence as badly as anyone in the last 50 years, and Kuhn's action last week compounded the error."[73] Suspended almost half a century after Joe Jackson, Eddie Cicotte, and the rest of the Black Sox were banished, McLain was never accused, officially at least, of throwing a game.[74] Nevertheless McLain's transgression was widely understood in terms of the Black Sox's misdeeds, which obviously retained their resonance and their ability to explain the present.

A few years later, the nation was rocked by a much more serious and significant scandal: Watergate, which dragged on for more than two years. It began, in White House press secretary Ron Ziegler's words, as a "third-rate burglary attempt" at the Democratic National Committee offices in June 1972 and, after many exhilarating twists and turns, led to the resignation of President Nixon on August 9, 1974.[75] It was the first time in American history that a president had resigned and was truly the scandal of the century, at least in the United States. The day after Nixon left office, the *New York Times* wrote: "Watergate has now joined Teapot Dome, Credit Mobilier and the Whisky Ring in the lexicon of political infamy."[76] Joined and surpassed them, most historians agree. Since the scandal's stakes were so high for Nixon and the country, perhaps it is not surprising that no commentators at the time (that I can document) compared Watergate with the 1919 World Series scandal. In the years since, though, numerous people have linked the two events. In 1975, for instance, the nationally syndicated columnist Mike Royko wrote a satirical editorial that indirectly criticized Nixon and his Watergate conspirators for profiting from their wrongdoing. "Shoeless Joe Jackson's biggest mistake," Royko noted, "was in being born 50 years too early":

> In his time, Jackson symbolized the betrayal of the public trust, although he never suggested that anyone commit suicide, bugged a telephone, burglarized a campaign headquarters, or plotted to assassinate somebody else's leader.
>
> But if Jackson had been born a few decades later, things might have turned out differently for him.

Royko then imagined the financial opportunities available to Jackson—TV appearances, a best-selling book, and a movie deal. Unwittingly anticipating the film version of *The Natural* (1984), Royko's fictional Jackson says, "Robert Redford is going to play me in the movie. And I've got a part in the movie, too. I play the gambler who fixes me."[77]

Eliot Asinof has connected Watergate to the 1919 World Series several times. In *Bleeding between the Lines* (1979), which tells the complicated story of the producer David Susskind's attempt to sue Asinof over the rights to make a film version of *Eight Men Out,* Asinof describes the "Black Sox Scandal, with its venality and corruption, its insidious betrayals and hypocritical cover-ups," as "a historical replica of the more recent scandal that began at Watergate."[78] He also attributes the revival of interest *Eight Men Out* enjoyed in the seventies to Watergate: "As that insidious story leaked out, I began to hear references to the Black Sox Scandal and the 1919 World Series. One scandal recapitulating another. Two portraits of hypocrisy at work, one hand swearing eternal fealty to truth and the pursuit of honor, while the other shoveled dirt to conceal its evil doings."[79] Many years later, while promoting John Sayles's film *Eight Men Out* (1988), Asinof quipped, "That a World Series should be fixed probably was more horrible then than Watergate and Contragate put together."[80] It is an exaggerated claim, but it drives the point home: acts of corruption remind people of previous acts of corruption. (Sayles, too, as we will see in the next chapter, was thinking about Watergate when he wrote the screenplay for *Eight Men Out.*)

Over the years, the political columnist George F. Will, who frequently writes about baseball, has often mentioned the two scandals in the same breath. "Who, half a century from now, will write novels and make movies about Watergate?" he asked in 1988. "As many as today are interested in the Teapot Dome scandal. But when scandal touched baseball, it touched a national nerve."[81] In 1991, Will remarked that the "Black Sox scandal of seventy-two years ago is more indelibly etched on the nation's memory than the Watergate scandal of nineteen years ago."[82] The following year Peter W. Morgan, a law professor, used the Black Sox scandal and Watergate in his study of how the "appearance of impropriety" principle had become so widespread in the United States:

> The "appearance of impropriety" rule owes its prominence today in significant measure to two of the most famous scandals of twentieth century America: the Black Sox affair and Watergate. Both involved serious crimes having little or nothing to do with the principle that we should try to avoid creating improper appearances, even when our behavior is quite honorable. Yet both episodes undermined public confidence in existing institutions, thereby prompting professionals and public officials to regulate ethics more vigorously.[83]

One could argue that baseball executives have been more successful at "cleaning up" their game than have politicians.

Soon after Richard Nixon died in 1994, the *New York Times* sports columnist Robert Lipsyte suggested: "If Watergate was the political equivalent of the Black Sox scandal, the loss of innocence in a national pastime, then perhaps Richard M. Nixon was our President Shoeless Joe Jackson, a great hitter whose passion for the arena should earn him the peace of forgiveness. Joe played in New Jersey sandlots under assumed names into middle age. Former President Nixon also never stopped coming back after he was banned from the game."[84] No one ever suggested that Nixon was an innocent hayseed or a rube, but there are those who believe that Nixon, like Jackson, was scapegoated, unfairly driven from his rightful place in American politics and history. Additionally, campaigns to redeem Jackson's and Nixon's reputations are ongoing.

Collectively, these references illustrate how two watershed events have become intertwined. They demonstrate that the Black Sox scandal and Watergate sometimes serve as mutually reinforcing historical reference points and as a kind of cultural shorthand for corruption, betrayal, and disillusionment. They represent the myriad ways meaning is made (and remade) and memory is preserved.

One final Black Sox moment from the seventies: The media historian Michael Schudson writes that "everyone involved in Watergate is publicly marked by its shadow."[85] The same is true of the Black Sox scandal. By 1975, Swede Risberg was the sole surviving member of the Black Sox. His eighty-first birthday that year was his last; he died the same day, making him the last man out. The sports columnist Bob Broeg put the news succinctly: "And then there was none."[86] Twenty-six years old when he was expelled, Risberg quickly dropped out of public sight. "For a while he worked a dairy farm in Minnesota, then he wandered to Northern California," wrote Red Smith in the *New York Times*. "He played a little semipro ball. He ran a tavern, and he died." Despite living for more than half a century after his banishment from baseball, Risberg never shook the ignominy of the Black Sox scandal. This was partly due to his unrepentant stance, of course. "Unlike Jackson and Weaver," Smith reported, "the Swede never claimed innocence or sought to clear his name."[87] But Risberg also lived with his Black Sox infamy because the scandal stubbornly persisted in many memories. With Risberg's death, explained the *Sporting News*, "only the Black Sox memory remains, almost 56 years to the day it all started."[88] That memory was stoked for many years by different people for different reasons long before Risberg's death. It continues to be.

Post-Seymour Histories

The writing of history, like history itself, is an ongoing process. Thus it is unsurprising that many historians have told the Black Sox scandal story since David Voigt and Harold Seymour. Some of these historians were academically trained, some were not. This is important to note because popular or nonacademic historians have continued to write versions of the Big Fix, generally for wider audiences than academic historians intend to reach. The work of these historians—both academic and popular—illustrates how (and perhaps why) common themes often emerge from the past, how the past can be rendered differently, and a few of the differences and similarities among historians.

Other than *Eight Men Out*, probably the most widely read account of the Black Sox scandal is Donald Gropman's *Say It Ain't So, Joe!: The True Story of Shoeless Joe Jackson and the 1919 World Series* (1979), the first biography of a Black Sox ballplayer. A freelance writer, Gropman offers an impressively detailed reconstruction of Jackson's life—from his childhood in Brandon Mill, South Carolina, through his remarkable ten-year Major League career to his death in 1951. A well-researched and sensitive portrait, it depicts Jackson as a shy, soft-spoken, unassuming, easy-going, and considerate man who possessed extraordinary natural athletic ability. He was a man of pride and dignity who was close to his family, popular and respected by virtually everyone in his local community. Though Jackson was frequently teased, insulted, and verbally abused by ballplayers, writers, and spectators during his baseball career, Gropman contends that he was almost peerless as a hitter and as an outfielder. "As a player there is no doubt he belongs in the Hall of Fame," Gropman concludes. "But it might be a disservice to the memory of the man to take his name out of banishment, for it was in his banishment that he achieved his greatest feat: under the weight of a great slander he played baseball as long as he was able and he carried himself with dignity."[89] Described by critics as "persuasively loving,"[90] "honest and credible,"[91] and "sympathetic but impartial,"[92] *Say It Ain't So, Joe!* is reminiscent of the hagiographic ballplayer biographies of yesteryear, but with a twist. It is an impassioned apologia that simultaneously demythologizes Jackson as a pariah and remythologizes him as a scapegoat. In this latter way it anticipates, and contributes to, one of the dominant ways in which Jackson and the Black Sox scandal were appraised in the eighties

Gropman explains that the "trail that led me to Shoeless Joe Jackson began when my father arrived in America in 1909" (xi). Similar to many immigrants, including Eric Rolfe Greenberg's fictional Jackie Kapp in *The Celebrant* (1983), the senior Gropman was acculturated and assimilated in large part by sport, particularly baseball. Often described as a link between generations, baseball was a conduit for the Gropmans:

> As it had been for so many fathers and sons, baseball was a way of sharing experience between my father and me. It was not the only way, but at times

> it proved to be one of the easiest: a game of catch between the two of us or, later when I was bigger, a Sunday morning game of ball, the fathers against the boys. Other times he took me to see the Boston Braves or Red Sox. But most frequent were the stories he told me, the anecdotes or bits and pieces about players he'd seen, or particular plays that had become fixed in his memory. That was how I heard about the first big-league game he ever saw. It was an important event in my father's life and his memory of it focused on the image of Joe Jackson. (xiii)

In some ways, then, Gropman's attempt to rehabilitate Jackson's historical reputation is enmeshed in his family history and private memories. It can be read, in part, as an attempt to validate the "beauty" his father saw in Jackson's play (xiii).

Gropman leaves little doubt that he is a true believer in Jackson's innocence, dignity, and heroism. Like virtually all of Jackson's defenders, Gropman points out that Jackson played stellar baseball in the 1919 World Series: he stroked twelve hits (more than any player on either team), had a .375 batting average, hit the lone home run, and played errorless defense. "On the face of it," Gropman maintains, "any relationship between his record and the accusation that he had played to lose seemed farfetched. It seemed so absurd to Robert Ripley, himself a former sports cartoonist, that he once featured it in *Believe It or Not*" (169). For Gropman, Jackson's performance alone suggests his integrity and greatness. Moreover, Gropman uses the indeterminacy that obfuscates the conspiracy to his advantage: "Despite the gaps in our knowledge and the contradictions that still cloud the whole affair, we know enough about Joe and the scandal to make assumptions that have at least the weight of probability behind them" (162). Over the course of *Say It Ain't So, Joe!* probability and indeterminacy are transformed into faith and, later, apparent certainty. Acknowledging that Jackson "has become a symbol of failure and corruption," Gropman concludes: "In truth, Joe Jackson's greatest crime was his innocence" (229). With that, Gropman delivers the promise of his subtitle: the "truth" of the matter (for him) is that Jackson was literally innocent of any wrongdoing in the Big Fix.

Even for those sympathetic to Jackson, in Gropman's portrait he comes across as overly flattering and unbalanced, completely devoid of warts or any sense of culpability for his situation. Similar to the Joe Jackson found in W. P. Kinsella's *Shoeless Joe* (1982) and Phil Alden Robinson's *Field of Dreams* (1989), Gropman's Jackson is a blameless scapegoat and victim, a hero denied justice. Indeed, one critic, Ray Merlock, argues that *Say It Ain't So, Joe!* "is essentially a tall tale with tragic overtones, a glorification of Jackson's abilities and a defense of a player whose illiteracy and Southern background led to shabby treatment from the press even before the Scandal. Gropman is unwavering in his belief that Jackson's claim (supposedly spoken the day before he died in 1951) 'I don't deserve this thing that's happened to me' was valid."[93] Gropman employs the rhetoric of historical "truth" and veracity, but in its own way *Say It Ain't So, Joe!* is nearly as mythic as the famous exchange from which its title is derived. This is not to suggest that Gropman's biography is an utter fabrication. Rather, *Say It Ain't So, Joe!* is a multilayered narrative that rehabilitates and exalts Jackson's legacy and serves a specific sociopolitical interest: the reclamation of disgraced heroes and (what Gropman perceives to be) lapsed ideals, such as truth and justice. Ironically, *Say It Ain't So, Joe!* lacks historical credibility with some historians, at least with regard to Jackson's participation in the Black Sox scandal. *Say It Ain't So, Joe!* is mythic in the same way that many popular biographies of figures such as George Washington, Daniel Boone, and John F. Kennedy are: it tells the truth it wants to believe.[94]

The title of Gropman's book provides us with a useful starting point to examine how other historians represent the Black Sox scandal. A handful of historians recount the alleged "Say it ain't so, Joe," incident as a matter of fact. In *Baseball as I Have Known It* (1977), the Baseball Hall of Fame journalist and popular historian Fred Lieb writes that a "young boy who worshipped the White Sox confronted Jackson with words that rang throughout the country: 'Say it ain't so, Joe!'"[95] Dean Smith, a university administrator (not the former University of North Carolina basketball coach), likewise writes in a piece for *American History Illustrated* that the incident did take place, but adds, "Historians may note with some amusement that the original Associated Press quote of the remark was a more grammatical 'It isn't true, is it, Joe?'"[96] Most historians, however, treat the scene with more circumspection. In *The American Dream and the National Game* (1975), which should be required reading for anyone interested in the Black Sox scandal, Leverett T. Smith Jr. notes that the famous saying was "apparently actually a cry of small boys," not of a single distraught youth.[97] Richard C. Crepeau, in *Baseball: America's Diamond Mind, 1919–1941* (1980), cites the account and remarks that the line "became part of the folk language."[98] Another academic historian, Benjamin G. Rader, carefully prefaces his telling with "according to baseball legend," thereby acknowledging the incident's mythological quality.[99] Some popular historians also regard the story with wariness. In *Baseball America: The Heroes of the Game and the Times of Their Glory* (1985), for example, Donald Honig offers a relatively melodramatic version of what "supposedly" occurred outside the Chicago courthouse. "Apocryphal or not," he writes, "it was a plea that rang from the hearts of the nation's baseball fans."[100] It may have done so, but when historians put pen to paper the alleged incident is most often ignored; several historians considered here do not mention the episode at all in their versions of the scandal.[101] The omission of the plea, one pregnant with indeterminacy and symbolic possibilities, in some histories demonstrates how differently the past can be rendered.

This is less evident when we note how historians represent Charles Comiskey. Some historians, but fewer than one might expect, are critical of Comiskey's treatment of his players. Historians generally agree that Comiskey—because of a penurious disposition, the reserve clause, and a nonunionized labor force—paid most of the White Sox poorly compared with their peers.[102] Thus some ballplayers, Richard Crepeau notes, rationalized the game fixing as justified.[103] Other historians regard Comiskey and "his pinch-penny handling of his players" as largely responsible for the game-fixing and the subsequent scandal.[104] According to Leo Lowenfish and Tony Lupien in *The Imperfect Diamond: The Story of Baseball's Reserve System and the Men Who Fought to Change It* (1980), a book with an explicitly political agenda, Comiskey was "tight-fisted" and the White Sox implicated in the scandal were victims of his "stinginess."[105] Still, most historians do not examine Comiskey's complicated relationship with the men who devastated his franchise and seemingly shattered his world.[106]

In the same vein, few historians consider *why* the White Sox players may have done what they were accused of doing. For the most part, historians writing after Voigt and Seymour do not attempt to explain its causes. Richard Crepeau, like Voigt and Seymour, explains that betting on baseball and game fixing were not aberrations, that the fixed series "was the culmination of at least twenty years of unattended corruption."[107] Crepeau is correct, but it is an explanation short on specifics. Donald Honig is one of the few who considers the event's causes: "Their motives were probably multilayered, but chief among them was that old reliable: money. When White Sox owner Charles Comiskey heard what had taken place, he was shocked; he no doubt thought that his boys were adequately paid. Anyone as self-righteously parsimonious as Comiskey was *had* to think his employees were well paid."[108] Honig also comments that Comiskey was not atypical of his time: "Comiskey was no different from most employers of the day. Meager pay checks, execrable working conditions, endless workdays, management tyranny—they were the standard lot for labor then."[109] No matter what one thinks of Comiskey, he was certainly representative of many of his contemporaries.

Honig's trenchant observation underscores how lacking these histories are in context, especially contexts beyond baseball history. Most ignore or minimize the larger socioeconomic structure in which the 1919 World Series took place, the ways in which the implicated ballplayers were related to other working-class people at the time, and how their situation was similar to that of laborers in many other industries.[110] To his credit, Crepeau puts the scandal within a postwar context in which, as the writer Henry Adams suggests and others dispute, "the standards and values of the nineteenth century were irrelevant to the realities of the new industrial America."[111] Similarly, Steven Riess notes that the Big Fix occurred

> when many old-stock Americans were worried about the future of their country. Although the United States had won World War I, it seemed we were losing the peace. The Republic was in danger of being drawn into foreign entanglements through the League of Nations. Growing fears of Bolshevik successes in Europe and radicalism at home led to a Red Scare and the suppression of civil liberties. Strikes occurred in the steel industry, the railroads, and even the Boston Police Department. It appeared that the country was coming apart at the seams. Now baseball, that great American institution which represented our finest traditional values, was revealed to be corrupt, done in by Jewish criminals who had masterminded and bankrolled the plot. If baseball was no good, what hope was there for the rest of our culture and society?[112]

Crepeau and Riess are rare exceptions. Most historians have their eye on the game so intently that they fail to see much else. Historical myopia has consequences. It hinders historians and their readers from seeing broader social vistas and society-wide patterns. It diminishes one's ability to make meaningful connections between previous and contemporaneous relations and events. In short, the failure of most historians to put the Black Sox scandal in a broader historical context promotes an underhistoricized understanding of the event. Furthermore, it makes it more difficult for readers to grapple with the complicated issue of determining responsibility for the scandal.

For many writers and fans, it is important to know who or what was chiefly responsible for the 1919 World Series debacle. This book demonstrates that people have always attributed responsibility for the scandal differently, according to their own perspectives and politics. Most journalists and those employed by organized baseball at the time of the scandal viewed the implicated ballplayers and gamblers as the event's primary culprits. Many baseball fans, especially in South Carolina, perceived Joe Jackson to be an innocent victim duped by gamblers and corrupt teammates and scapegoated by the media, the legal system, and baseball commissioner Landis. As for historians writing after Voigt and Seymour, they generally avoid the issue of ascribing responsibility for the Black Sox scandal. It is, of course, hard to make such a determination if one has not carefully examined the event's causes. There are several ways to make sense of the conspicuous omission of causation in these histories. It might suggest that many historians implicitly endorse the traditional, moralistic version of the story originally told by the media and the Landis-led baseball establishment. It might suggest an unwillingness to take sides or to judge degrees of culpability; in this way, historians' failure to assess responsibility may strike some as a dereliction of their duty. At the same time, failing to pinpoint blame for the scandal might be a historically mature, practical way of avoiding the false binary of pitting the Black Sox ballplayers against Comiskey and organized baseball. Whatever the reasons, when it comes to the Black Sox scandal, the historians examined here are disinterested in pointing fingers of blame.

Conversely, most historians suggest that Babe Ruth and Kenesaw Mountain Landis deserve a great deal of credit for reenergizing and relegitimating baseball. This is one of the most common themes in historical accounts of the scandal. (It is also found in Ruth's and Landis's obituaries.) In *America's Sporting Heritage* (1974), for example, an important, posthumously published scholarly study, John Rickards Betts notes that baseball enjoyed an attendance boom in the twenties and thirties. Sportswriters generally attributed it either to "the mighty popularity of Babe Ruth" or to "the crusading spirit of Commissioner Judge Kenesaw Mountain Landis."[113] Betts himself seems to lean toward the latter explanation. His fellow academic historians John A. Lucas and Ronald A. Smith put the matter more judiciously: they argue that after the Black Sox affair "Landis gave baseball integrity; Ruth gave it flare. Baseball needed both."[114] Fred Lieb also notes the roles Landis and Ruth played in providing closure to the World Series scandal. "The Judge ran the curtain down on a sleazy scene," Lieb remarks. "Babe Ruth, already sticking his head out from the wings, would in the next scene make sports fans forget almost overnight what had just happened."[115] Lieb obviously overstates, but no historian doubts that Ruth was instrumental in sustaining popular interest in baseball after the scandal. Nevertheless, a few do call into question Landis's role as "an ethical hero who 'redeemed' baseball from the sins of the Black Sox."[116] In his 1977 essay, Dean Smith explains: "Part of the Black Sox legend is that Landis' stiff punishments saved baseball in its darkest hour. A glance at the soaring major league gate receipts in 1920 and 1921, however, seems to show that the sporting public would have supported the game whether or not the Black Sox had been punished." Still, Smith acknowledges that Landis's "decision undoubtedly discouraged future cozy dealings between players and gamblers."[117] To argue otherwise would stray too far from historical conventional wisdom.

Conclusion

Although it is difficult to make generalizations about these historical accounts of the Black Sox scandal, my reading suggests that they are more alike than dissimilar, regardless of the author's credentials. Clearly, professional training and a Ph.D. do not guarantee a great degree of insight into the past or the ability to represent it intelligibly, though academics do a better job than nonacademics of documenting their sources. In addition, academic and popular histories are virtually indistinguishable ontologically. They are both, after all, linguistic (some argue literary) representations of the past. Obviously one reason for some of the commonalities found in these histories is that they are constructed from basically the same sources, most often newspaper accounts and earlier histories, especially *Eight Men Out.* Another important reason for their similarity is that something approaching a historical consensus on the scandal—one shaped in large part by Eliot Asinof, David Voigt, and Harold Seymour and by then-current cultural, social, and political sensibilities—apparently coalesced by the midseventies. This is not, of course, to suggest that historians agree about the Big Fix; it means that they generally see the broad outlines of the World Series scandal similarly and share presuppositions. If there is a notable difference among the histories examined here, it is that academic and popular historians often have different intended audiences: for many years now, most academic historians have been content to write for their colleagues, whereas most popular historians hope to reach a broader readership.[118] One might reasonably assume that work directed to a general reading public would be less critical, didactic, and rigorous than texts intended for academics and would certainly be more accessible. In general, this is not the case with the texts considered here. At least with regard to the Black Sox scandal, the differences between academic and popular histories are relatively minor. Collectively, historians writing about the Black Sox scandal after Voigt and Seymour proffer a version of the past that emphasizes what happened at the 1919 World Series and immediately thereafter but does not address the complex issue of causation, neglects to put events and social relations in larger contexts, and avoids ascribing responsibility for the debacle.

By the late 1970s, after all the eight men out had finally met the One Great Scorer who marks against our names, the Black Sox scandal was still alive for some Americans. This situation existed for many reasons. First, while memory is notoriously fickle and malleable, it also can be extremely resilient; despite our best efforts, we do not easily forget painful events or moments of disillusionment. For some baseball writers and fans, this appears to have been the case with the Black Sox scandal. Second, journalists have often used the Black Sox scandal as an analog to understand similarly disturbing incidents, like the Denny McLain gambling affair. These rearticulations sustain the scandal's presence in the consciousness of some people and introduce it to others. "Of all the dark moments in sports, the throwing of the 1919 World Series by the Chicago White Sox to the Cincinnati Reds remains the darkest," asserted the sportswriter Charles Chamberlain in 1970. "And it never dies. The aura of mystery and myth—conjured by truths and untruths—still lingers."[119] Chamberlain was (and remains) correct. The Black Sox scandal narrative is going strong, partly because it retains its narrative utility to explain the present. Perhaps this phenomenon is responsible for how the scandal narratives examined in this chapter—none of them was a best-seller, although several were critical successes and remain in print—have, nevertheless, become widely accepted by fans, journalists, and historians.

Historians, especially academics, often feel marginalized and underappreciated. Yet in many ways they are and have long been privileged storytellers. The stories historians tell are widely respected and sometimes influential, even if their audiences are small compared to those reached by even moderately successful novelists and filmmakers. Despite reaching relatively few readers, historians' stories matter. They regularly "trickle down" into the mainstream, helping to shape public opinion about the past and the present. In part because they are based on documents carefully scrutinized by critical men and women, histories often have more credibility than other narratives about the past. The anthropologist Michel-Rolph Trouillot is correct: "Every historian delivers a narrative with a certificate of authenticity, however qualified."[120] When historians have diplomas testifying to their professional training, their authority is further enhanced; such is the case with David Voigt, Harold Seymour, and some of the historians who later wrote about the Black Sox scandal.

5

Idyll and Iconoclasm: Retelling the Black Sox Scandal in the Eighties

"Much as they may deplore the fact," observes the historian C. Vann Woodward, "historians have no monopoly on the past and no franchise as its privileged interpreters to the public."[1] Woodward's observation is particularly germane when we consider how the Black Sox scandal was rendered in the post-Watergate United States, especially during the eighties. For many reasons, the Black Sox scandal became a popular subject (and commodity) during the "decade of money fever," to use Tom Wolfe's apt phrase.[2] In addition to several novels—W. P. Kinsella's *Shoeless Joe* (1982), Eric Rolfe Greenberg's *The Celebrant* (1983), and Harry Stein's *Hoopla* (1983)—the scandal appeared on a few stages and thousands of movie screens during the eighties. In 1981, Rusty Magee and Rob Barron wrote and produced *1919: A Baseball Opera.*[3] Later, Richard Pioreck's *Say It Ain't So, Joe!* (1983) and Lawrence Kelly's *Out!* (1986) were staged.[4] Toward the end of the decade, John Sayles's *Eight Men Out* (1988) and Phil Alden Robinson's *Field of Dreams* (1989) brought the Black Sox scandal and Joe Jackson to millions of moviegoers. And from October 1988 to the following June, the Chicago Historical Society curated a popular exhibit on the affair.[5] If the episode had ever been out of popular consciousness, it would seem as though the eighties was a renaissance period for the Black Sox scandal.[6]

This chapter reflects on this outpouring of interest. How did storytellers perceive the scandal with nearly seventy years of hindsight, and how did they portray it for audiences who had virtually no living memory of the event? It also notes how historical developments and social relations during the era—such as the decade's resurgent nationalism, myriad scandals, and baseball's acrimonious labor conflicts—affected the way the scandal was rewritten and remembered. It explores the ways in which the Black Sox scandal can be read as a narrative emblematic of the eighties and its reputed profligacy and argues that the scandal—from one perspective, a story of greed, betrayal, and moralistic hypocrisy—was a vivid cultural metaphor for the decade. Though only a handful of the Black Sox scandal narratives examined here were popular, critical, or financial successes, they all participated in a dialogue that reconfigured understandings of the past. Narrating from disparate ideological positions, the storytellers examined here bridged their own private concerns and interests with the same moment of public crisis. In the process each offered a decidedly different interpretation of its cultural significance.

The Eighties

Although it may be too soon to render historical judgment on the eighties, some observations and generalizations are possible. Viewed by many as a rapacious, superficial time, and by many others as a period of national virility and abundance, these years are often constructed and understood as an era in which the political activism of the sixties and the early seventies gave way to more socially conservative worldviews. The decade was marked by cultural flux that conservatives (and some fundamentalists) were able to use to their political advantage. In American politics, notes the columnist George F. Will, the name of the game is "capture the flag. The party that identifies with American nationalism wins."[7] That game was fiercely contested, but political conservatives were undoubtedly the American flag bearers during the decade.

There were many milestones in the conservative ascension in America, the most obvious and significant among them the 1980 election of President Ronald Reagan. Many Americans were seeking to reverse what they perceived to be the pessimism and despair that had enveloped the country in the wake of the Vietnam war, sometimes violent civil rights struggles, the Watergate debacle, the disintegration of the economy, and the Iranian hostage crisis. "Self-assurance reassures others," writes the historian Garry Wills, and that was not "the least of Reagan's gifts to us, at a time when the nation needed some reassuring."[8] To his credit, Reagan had the ability to represent various things to his many supporters. Religious conservatives and fundamentalists seized upon his rhetorical invocation of piety.[9] Millions looked upon him as a champion of "traditional family values" (though he was the first divorced president in American history) and populism (though his closest associates were millionaires), as a strong leader at home (though the Iran-Contra affair cast doubt on his competence and ethics) and abroad (though the marine deployment and withdrawal from Lebanon occurred on his watch). In other words, many Americans saw in Reagan what they wanted to see and glossed over the rest. By pursuing right-wing initiatives (such as the drive for a constitutional amendment requiring school prayer, supply-side economic policies, the deregulation of big business, and heavy investments in military spending), Reagan sought "to restore a golden past, a version of an America that never actually existed," argues the film and cultural critic Frank Ardolino. "He offered himself as the embodiment of this mythic past, which he would install as the country's future."[10] In the process of restoring the country's battered self-esteem, Reagan reintroduced comfortable nationalism and encouraged nostalgia for an invented time when families were stable, men were self-reliant patriots and providers, and women aspired to be happy homemakers.

In spite of these ideals and aspirations, the Reagan years were fraught with excess and greed. During this period of "new inequality," the chasm between rich and poor widened and the middle class shrank.[11] For many well-off people, it was a boom time. Partly due to the restructuring of the tax code in 1981, wealthy Americans had more disposable income. For them, acquisitiveness and conspicuous consumption ruled the day. In what have become cultural clichés, names like Ivan Boesky, Michael Milken, and Donald Trump and television programs like "Dynasty," "Dallas," and "Lifestyles of the Rich and Famous" represent the era's rampant materialism and cupidity. At the same time, official statistical evidence indicates that during the decade one out of four children lived in poverty and the work force was diminished by the loss of 1.6 million manufacturing jobs.[12] According to one source, "less than 1 percent of wage earners were doing fantastically well. For much of the rest of America the 1980s revealed new depths of poverty and despair with levels of misery approaching that of the developing countries."[13] A popular film like Michael Moore's *Roger and Me* (1989), which traces the precipitous decline of Flint, Michigan, as General Motors shut down automobile plants while the automobile executives who closed them commanded exorbitant salaries, poignantly bespeaks the socioeconomic duality of the eighties. It was, in short, a time of polarization.

It is also fair to say that the Reagan years were plagued by widespread corruption, particularly in the federal government. The House Subcommittee on Civil Service reported that over 225 Reagan appointees had faced allegations of ethical or criminal wrongdoing. Although not all of these charges were serious and many no doubt were politically motivated, as one historian puts it, "the sheer number of scandals in the Reagan administration is unprecedented in American history."[14] From Wedtech to HUD, from Iran-Contra to S&L, the United States in the eighties was awash in political scandal. Of course, controversy and scandalous activity were not limited to the political sphere. Due in part to the possibility of tremendous financial rewards, and in part to a more permissive ethical climate, scandals came in all shapes, sizes, and locations: Washington, Wall Street, the Chicago futures markets, savings and loans across the country, evangelical empires, and collegiate and professional athletic teams. While some scandals were probably the result of distaste for practices and behavior that were previously accepted or ignored, the sheer quantity of scandals in the eighties pointed to the troubled nature of the decade.

The sports world in general, and Major League Baseball in particular, reflected the historical moment. Sports enjoyed financial prosperity and mass popularity, perhaps even surpassing that of the so-called Golden Age of the twenties when, according to the historian Roderick Nash, "the nation went sports crazy."[15] Yet Americans' views on sports figures in the eighties were contradictory. On the one hand, athletes like the gymnast Mary Lou Retton, the quarterback Joe Montana, and the basketball players Earvin "Magic" Johnson, Larry Bird, and Michael Jordan were hailed as celebrities and heroes. They enjoyed tremendous wealth and status, were praised lavishly by critics and fans alike, and were often treated as secular deities. Athletic superstars became personifications of values many Americans wanted to believe they too possessed. On the other hand, for many of those same celebrants, professional athletes were notable for their "obscene salaries, grandiose life-styles, out-for-number-one philosophies, and lack of commitment to the teams that employed them or the cities in which they performed."[16] Despite their on-the-field heroics, many athletes were castigated for their arrogance and braggadocio.

These years witnessed superb individual and team performances in the Major Leagues, but the period was just as notable for its labor disputes, strikes, threats of strikes, owner collusion scandals, substance abuse revelations, the Al Campanis "necessities" incident, the Pete Rose betting affair, and, in general, shortsightedness on the part of those who ran the game. Somehow, in spite of these and other serious problems, Major League Baseball remained vibrant and popular. In 1980, a record 43 million people paid to see Major League games, income from television and radio contracts was booming, and television ratings for the World Series had never been higher.[17] Over the course of the decade, all of these leading indicators would improve. In addition, rotisserie leagues (in which members own imaginary big league teams) became increasingly popular, the membership rolls of the Society for American Baseball Research grew, baseball card and memorabilia collecting became a big business, and scores of baseball nostalgia books were published.[18] During this decade, "profits, salaries, attendance, and general excitement over things baseball would be greater than ever, but it would be an unprecedentedly strife-filled period," observes the historian Charles C. Alexander. "Baseball's best of times, the 1980s, in some ways, would also be its worst."[19]

There was obviously more to American life during the decade than nationalism, materialism, corruption, and ambivalent athletic hero worshipping. From the restoration of the Statue of Liberty to the construction of the Vietnam Veterans Memorial, from Earth Day celebrations to the Exxon Valdez oil spill, from Steven Bochco's "Hill St. Blues" (1981–87) to Jay McInerney's *Bright Lights, Big City* (1984), from the *Return of the Jedi* (1983) to the Strategic Defense Initiative, the social, moral, and political climate—which was in some ways reminiscent of the era in which the Black Sox scandal occurred—was extraordinarily conducive for those who created narrative versions of the Black Sox scandal.[20]

Black Sox Fictions

By the early 1950s, F. Scott Fitzgerald, Nelson Algren, and Bernard Malamud had used the Black Sox scandal prominently in their work. They did so differently and for different reasons. The same was true of W. P. Kinsella, Eric Rolfe Greenberg, Harry Stein, and Brendan Boyd, all of whom wrote or published Black Sox–related novels during the eighties. Though Kinsella's book was the only one to achieve popular success, every novel examined here did significant cultural work.[21] Besides providing entertainment and escape, dramatizing and interpreting experience, they played an active role in the production of the Black Sox scandal's cultural and historical meaning and memory.

They did (and still do) so for several reasons. First, novels usually reach larger and wider audiences than histories, especially those written by academics. As the historian Richard N. Current puts it, "Even the author of a widely adopted textbook is unlikely to reach as large a readership as does a leading writer of fiction—a Gore Vidal, an Alex Haley, or a William Styron."[22] Novels that are *not* best-sellers probably are more widely read than most histories. Second, for many readers the pasts that novels construct are more vibrant, compelling, and influential than those found in histories. In this way novels frequently wield considerable power in shaping popular understandings of the past—whether factual or not. Obviously none of the novels discussed here achieved the level of success or influence of, say, James Fenimore Cooper's *The Last of the Mohicans* (1826) or Margaret Mitchell's *Gone with the Wind* (1936); however, on a smaller scale they do the same kind of work.[23] Finally, it needs to be acknowledged that contemporary fiction does not make the same kinds of "truth" claims that history does and thus requires no documentation, no qualifying. Nonetheless, novels must be taken seriously as texts that animate the past. Certainly the novels examined here inform, enrich, and (in some cases) complicate historical understandings of the Black Sox scandal.

Paradise Regained

Of the novels considered here, W. P. Kinsella's *Shoeless Joe* (1982) has earned by far the most critical attention and acclaim.[24] Since its initial publication, critics have consistently noted the novel's use of "magical realism," transcendent qualities, and lyrical evocation of nature, the pastoral ideal, and the past. In terms of the amount of critical attention it has received, *Shoeless Joe*'s only rival as far as baseball fiction goes is Bernard Malamud's *The Natural* (1952). Similar to Malamud's book, Kinsella's novel is a lively amalgamation of historical fact and fantasy that draws upon the Black Sox scandal and its most famous participant to render a surreal, mythical world. Yet unlike Malamud, Kinsella—a graduate of the University of Iowa Writers' Workshop and an incredibly prolific Canadian short story writer and novelist—has created a realm of perpetual innocence and possibility, rather than one of disappointment and disgrace.[25] In this way, among others, Kinsella's novel (and the 1989 film *Field of Dreams,* which was adapted from *Shoeless Joe*) represents Joe Jackson and the Black Sox scandal remarkably differently than other narratives of this period. Even the sense of innocence and hero worship expressed in Donald Gropman's biography *Say It Ain't So, Joe!* pales in comparison. Often noted as a romantic excursion and a religious allegory, *Shoeless Joe* promotes an explicitly mythic vision of the United States, its past, and its national pastime that millions of Americans—many of them aging baby boomers who feel a kinship with the quest Kinsella describes—have embraced enthusiastically.

Shoeless Joe is narrated by Ray Kinsella, a floundering thirtysomething Iowa farmer. One spring evening, after having been told by a phantom ballpark announcer, "If you build it, he will come," Ray intuitively knows "it" is a baseball field and "he" is "Shoeless" Joe Jackson.[26] With his wife's consent, Ray lovingly carves his corn field into a left field, complete with an outfield wall, luxurious grass, and a bleacher "for an audience of one" (8). One night three years later Ray finds Joe Jackson's ghost playing ball against a nameless, faceless team. After speaking with the ballplayer, Ray agrees to complete his field so that the rest of the banned-for-life 1919 White Sox can return to the game. In exchange, Jackson promises to have a look at a minor league catcher, who is in fact Ray's deceased father. Some readers will surely disagree, but at this point the novel becomes convoluted with the introduction of J. D. Salinger, Eddie "Kid" Scissons (who fraudulently poses as "the oldest living Chicago Cub"), Archie "Moonlight" Graham, and Ray's identical twin brother, Richard, all of whom represent a mixture of fact and fiction.[27] In fact, by streamlining and simplifying the narrative, the rendition of the story told in *Field of Dreams* is an improvement over the novel, though the critic C. Kenneth Pellow maintains that the film "eliminates the important socio-political dimension" of the book.[28]

In contrast to most versions of the Black Sox affair, Kinsella's novel—which is set just outside of Iowa City sometime during the early eighties—is far removed in space and time from the scandal. As a result, Ray's narrative is necessarily mediated through his father's memories and often-repeated stories. For instance, Ray reminisces: "Dad told the story of the Black Sox Scandal for the last time. Told of seeing two of those World Series games, told of the way Shoeless Joe Jackson hit, told the dimensions of Comiskey Park, and how, during the series, the mobsters in striped suits sat in the box seats with their colorful women, watching the game" (13). Because his portrayal and defense of Jackson and the Black Sox are derived from his father's crystallized memories, Ray's narrative is imbued with his father's spirit. Like his father, Ray is first and foremost a reverent fan, someone for whom baseball "is the most perfect of games, solid, true, pure and precious as diamonds" (78). Ray narrates: "When he [Jackson] comes, I won't put him on the spot by asking. The less said the better. It is likely that he did accept money from gamblers. But throw the Series? Never! Shoeless Joe Jackson led both teams in hitting in that 1919 Series. It was the circumstances. The circumstances. The players were paid peasant salaries while the owners became rich. The infamous Ten Day Clause, which voided contracts, could end any player's career without compensation, pension, or even a ticket home" (8). Though many historians take issue with Jackson's innocence—he did, after all, admit to taking money from gamblers—what is important here is Ray's portrait of Jackson and by implication Kinsella's conception of the Black Sox scandal. According to the novel, Jackson was a man of incomparable natural talent, simplicity, and naiveté. Far from the rube that most historians portray, Kinsella's Jackson is articulate and heroic, "a symbol of the tyranny of the powerful over the powerless" (7). Perceived to be unjustly punished, Kinsella's Jackson ascends to mythic status. In this way Kinsella plays to the American populist myth and portrays the players as the victims of the owners and of an unjust system, implicating the owners and the gamblers as abettors, if not instigators. By creating a magical Edenic ballfield in Iowa, Kinsella establishes Paradise Regained where the fallen heroes of the past are resurrected Lazarus-like, a ballfield where Joe Jackson is absolved of his sin, where ghosts from the past can mingle with mortals of the present. "Not only has Eden been recreated," writes the literary critic August J. Fry, "but Eden before the Fall where those excluded, many believe unjustly, can continue in their first innocence."[29] Ray's ballfield is virtually prelapsarian, a cultural space devoid of stain, unsoiled soil.

Yet because it is not earned, this redemption is a notable flaw in the novel. Because he is deemed blameless, Kinsella's Jackson is automatically absolved, without penance, without having matured, and without having learned anything from his banishment. For instance, Ray asks Jackson and the rest of the resurrected players what becomes of them when they leave his magical field:

> "We sleep," says Chick Gandil finally.
> "And wait," says Happy Felsch.
> "And dream," says Shoeless Joe Jackson. "Oh, how we dream . . ." (186)

But they do not feel remorse or shame because they have nothing to be sorry about in this telling. And thus their dreams are destined to be fulfilled, their spirits restored to a state of grace. Kinsella's Joe Jackson has gained nothing from his fall and remains the Joe Jackson of 1919, minus his Southern drawl and human imperfections. In *The Use and Abuse of History* (1971), M. I. Finley notes that at the end of Homer's *Odyssey* "neither Odysseus nor Penelope has changed one bit; they have neither developed nor deteriorated, nor does anyone else in the epic. Such men and women cannot be figures in history; they are too simple, too self-enclosed, too rigid and stable, too detached from their backgrounds. They are as timeless as the story itself."[30] The same can be said of Kinsella's Joe Jackson, who is stripped of his historicity, sanitized, and transformed into a friendly ghost. Kinsella arguably abuses one past to right another, for ultimately Ray and his deceased father are the beneficiaries of Jackson's fall and resurrection. Jackson's misfortune allows the Kinsellas to reconcile their strained relationship and gives the elder Kinsella the opportunity to realize his Major League dreams.

Kinsella uses magic and nostalgia to recreate a mythic world of integrity, simplicity, and innocence.Unlike Washington Irving's Rip Van Winkle—who awakens from his twenty-year slumber to find his formerly tranquil, pre–Revolutionary War community transformed into a contentious, bustling village—Kinsella's unlucky eight are transported to their version of paradise. The literary critic Richard Alan Schwartz points out that "Kinsella uses

Shoeless Joe and the other Black Sox players to celebrate dreams, private aspirations, and appreciation for the land, and to attack corporate indifference to these human necessities."[31] In the process, however, Kinsella fosters a wholly romantic and mythological conception of the implicated players and of the American past, one in which troubling racial and gender biases are reconstituted. After all, the Eden Kinsella creates is not encumbered with racial minorities or mature, autonomous women. In the first place, the perfect world Kinsella has created is located in a region that is relatively racially homogenous; moreover, the era he romanticizes was a time when African Americans were not permitted to play Major League Baseball. As for gender, in Kinsella's perfect world, writes the critic Bryan K. Garman, "good women remain confined to the home where both their domestic and child-bearing labour can be concealed, de-valued, and controlled. Such an arrangement prevents and discourages them from participating in the fraternity of baseball."[32] Far from a fountainhead of democracy or equity, Kinsella's utopia fosters exclusivity and white male privilege.

Much like the sentiment expressed in the baseball writings of A. Bartlett Giamatti, a former baseball commissioner, and George F. Will, Kinsella's conception of baseball radiates conservative romanticism.[33] Near the end of the novel, Kinsella's J. D. Salinger lectures:

> I don't have to tell you that the one constant through all the years has been baseball. America has been erased like a blackboard, only to be rebuilt and then erased again. But baseball has marked time with America [as it] has rolled by like a procession of steamrollers. It is the same game that Moonlight Graham played in 1905. It is a living part of history, like calico dresses, stone crockery, and threshing crews eating at outdoor tables. It continually reminds us of what once was, like an Indian-head penny in a handful of new coins. (213)

In Kinsella's universe—as on Ray's ballfield—the mythic past and the magical present converge beyond the point of recognition. The novel represents a contemporary yearning for an unrecoverable and illusory past. Ray's miraculous ballfield brings the era of the "1950s small town back to life. This resurrection simultaneously fills the reader with hope for the future and nostalgia for the past."[34] Of course, the version of the past the novel evokes is not historically verifiable; it exists only in the collective fantasies of some Americans.

Reality over Romance

Eric Rolfe Greenberg's *The Celebrant* (1983) also uses historical and fictional characters to tell the story of the Black Sox scandal, though it is a much different kind of book. Greenberg's second novel, *The Celebrant* is narrated by Jackie Kapp (formerly Yakov Kapinski), a Jewish immigrant jewelry designer from New York City, who, when he first sees the baseball great Christy Mathewson of the New York Giants pitch a no-hitter in St. Louis in 1901, is captivated. As a token of his admiration, Jackie designs a ring to commemorate the occasion for Mathewson and thus begins Jackie's twenty-year-long relationship, mostly from afar, with Mathewson. Through Jackie's first-person narrative, Greenberg chronicles the fortunes of the growing Kapp family and their expanding jewelry business, the successes and failures of the New York Giants, the role of baseball in the social integration of immigrants, and Jackie's own relationships, most notably with his older brother, Eli, and his hero, Mathewson. The literary critic Deeanne Westbrook correctly notes that "*The Celebrant* is an extraordinary exploration of fan psychology belonging to the literary tradition of the confession," but it is also important to note that the novel culminates with the 1919 World Series, which the historical Mathewson covered for the *New York World*.[35]

Greenberg's novel begins with a "Historical Note" that serves as a disclaimer. It alerts readers that the novel, while based on the facts of Mathewson's life and career, is ultimately an invention. Yet it is one of the novel's purely imaginative moments that best illustrates Greenberg's perception of the Black Sox scandal. Near the end of the novel Jackie meets with the dying Mathewson, who was exposed to poison gas while serving in World War I.[36] Despite his weakened condition, Mathewson sat with and advised the journalist Hugh Fullerton about questionable plays during the 1919 World Series. Jackie, whose brother Eli had bet heavily on the White Sox to win the series, seeks Mathewson's insight into the integrity of the games. No longer the dominant figure of his playing days (and thus perhaps a heroic prefigurement of the Black Sox's and baseball's fate), Mathewson angrily responds that Jackie does not need his "wisdom to see the truth of the matter in this World Series. It takes no profound knowledge of the game" to recognize that the White Sox were not playing to win.[37] Mathewson then bitterly curses the conspirers: "With a mark I damn them. I damn Cicotte. I damn Jackson. I damn Risberg and Gandil and Williams. And if there be others I will damn them as well, I will root them out and damn them for eternity. And I damn the filth that corrupted them, the dicers and the high rollers. They will pay. They will pay in time. I shall not rouse them now, for I will allow them their full portion of loss, and when the corrupters are counting their gains I shall spring upon them and drive them from the temple!" (262). Mathewson's vitriolic damnation of the Black Sox, in the voice of the Old Testament's angry and unforgiving God, undermines the novel's often-noted Christ/Christy analogies.[38] At the same time, Mathewson's rant reveals a much different perspective on the scandal than that offered by any other eighties narrative. In *Shoeless Joe* (and later in *Field of Dreams*), the scandal's participants are guileless, unfortunate, but ultimately redeemable men. And as we will see, Harry Stein's *Hoopla* and John Sayles's *Eight Men Out* view the scandal more broadly, put it in context, and are subsequently sympathetic toward the players. In contrast, *The Celebrant* looks at the scandal relatively myopically and unsympathetically. Mathewson's scathing denunciation suggests an overtly moral vision of the Big Fix, which is seen as a moment of supreme betrayal and sin. Greenberg's Hugh Fullerton observes, "Heroes are never forgiven their success, still less their failure" (196); still less, of course, when their failures are purposeful and morally reprehensible.

Nonetheless, that Greenberg relates the story of the besmirched national pastime from the perspective of an immigrant Jew—one loosely based on his grandfather, to whom the book is dedicated—poses a challenge to those who have idealized baseball as a nativist institution.[39] In Jackie Kapp, Greenberg has created a narrator who lives on the margins of Major League Baseball and, at least initially, of American society. In large part due to his ethnic and religious heritage, Jackie is distanced from an activity that claims to contribute to and reflect the identity of American boys and men.[40] However, because he tells the tale, because his voice is heard, Jackie is not completely marginalized or silenced out of existence. His narrative is confessional and certainly glorifies Mathewson and celebrates his accomplishments, but it does not whitewash the past. In fact, the critic Tim Morris describes *The Celebrant* as a "historically sensitive" and "hyper-realistic" novel.[41] If anything, Jackie's narrative bristles with the fervor and righteousness of the newly converted and assimilated.

Employing an immigrant Jew as a narrator also affirms the vital place that baseball maintained for newcomers at the beginning of the twentieth century. "No single New World institution has provided as viable a symbol of Americanization for second-generation European immigrants as did baseball during the first decades of the present century," remarks the historian Peter C. Bjarkman. "For waves of East European Jews, in particular, baseball became the first and most obvious badge of newfound American citizenship."[42] Jackie is acculturated, for instance, primarily on ballfields, not in school rooms: "First by imitation, then by practice, we learned the game and the ways of the boys who played it, the angle of their caps, the intonations of their curses and encouragements. Our accents disappeared, our strides became quick and confident" (12). Jackie becomes an American by investing ardently and substantially in the game. His own ball-playing dreams have faded and his innocence was disabused long ago, but his admiration (and faith) in the game and its players persist. Before the 1919 World Series, Jackie espies the White Sox players in their hotel lobby on the eve of the first game:

> Such a collection of citified dandies, such a display of white cuff extending two inches below the sleeve, such an array of pearl stickpins and diamond rings! Our trophies would merely gild these glorious lilies. They moved with grace and restless energy as they jousted and joked with one another; they moved with confidence and delight in themselves and the occasion; they moved as champions, who shared a sacred mystery denied to those of us who stared at them from our high remove. We would witness the event; they would shape it to their will. (232)

It is, of course, an ironic commentary considering how some of the White Sox chose to play. The commingling of the players' deceit and Mathewson's decline contributes to Jackie's disillusionment.

In some respects, Greenberg's portrayal of the series represents the traditional one that Malamud's *The Natural* problematizes and that (as we will soon see) Stein's *Hoopla* and Sayles's *Eight Men Out* challenge and seek to displace. Indeed, Greenberg's ailing Mathewson serves as a voice of moral outrage and condemnation and personifies the country's shaken faith in baseball and perhaps in itself.

For Greenberg, history is shaped by the actions of individuals, rather than the complicated interplay of individuals, institutions, and social relations. Thus, disillusionment is rooted in the fall of heroic individuals. In 1919, the clean-cut, college-educated Christy Mathewson came back from Europe and World War I a dying man, the victim of gassing, his own moral sensibility, and sweeping historical forces. Baseball lost a virtuous hero. A little over a year later, the fallen Black Sox revealed that baseball was not an innocent pastime, that it was big business, a money game. Many similarly jarring events occurred before Greenberg finished his novel, but he points in particular to the assassination of John F. Kennedy. Greenberg notes that if there is a "parallel to be drawn between that event and the Black Sox scandal, it is the imposition of the victory of hard and cruel reality over romance. The cruel reality of the Black Sox scandal was that these heroes were greedy men of no moral worth. The cruel reality of the Kennedy assassination was that Kennedy was a mortal man who could be snuffed out like that, never to rise again."[43] In Greenberg's novel, the imposition of "reality over romance" devastates Jackie. It leads to an acute sense of loss—mostly personal, but also cultural. As a result, Jackie looks to the future with disdain and despair. *The Celebrant* concludes with Eli Kapp's suicide after he loses everything on the 1919 World Series. The novel's final image is of Eli's brand-new Chalmers automobile "shattered and burning, against the black walls of the Polo Grounds" (264). *The Celebrant* thus concludes that betrayal cannot be forgiven, that redemption is virtually impossible, and that the past is marred by shattered heroes. In contrast to *Shoeless Joe,* which remythologizes and romanticizes the American past via verdant cornfields, *The Celebrant* leaves readers with grief and smoldering debris.

Counterhistory

A compelling, vivid novel, Harry Stein's *Hoopla* (1983) provides a historically nuanced, revisionist rendition of the Black Sox scandal, which might explain its more limited popular appeal compared with that of Kinsella's *Shoeless Joe* and Greenberg's *The Celebrant.* Stein, a former *Esquire* columnist and the author of six other books, including *Ethics (and Other Liabilities)* (1982) and *How I Accidentally Joined the Vast Right-Wing Conspiracy (and Found Inner Peace)* (2000), makes it clear that who speaks matters, that authority is often linked to integrity.

Hoopla is told by two alternating first-person narrators: Luther Pond, a fictional Walter Winchell–like newspaper reporter, whose narrative is dated 1974, and George "Buck" Weaver, whose narrative is dated 1944. From the outset, the novel's dual narration forces readers to confront reified assumptions about the Black Sox scandal as well as the role of the historian in understanding the past. Skillfully using two divergent perspectives and narrative voices, Stein accentuates Pond's claim "that popular history is written in the sand," that our understanding of the past is forever mutable.[44] In this way *Hoopla* presents a less tidy picture of the past and encourages readers to take more responsibility for puzzling it all out.

Weaver's narrative begins on November 25, 1944, the day Judge Kenesaw Mountain Landis died, with a phone call from his former teammate, Joe Jackson. Both Weaver and Jackson have been futilely trying for years to be reinstated to the game and to clear their names. Eventually, after years of petitioning the intractable Landis, Weaver had finally accepted his fate and given up his quest. However, upon Landis's death Jackson calls Weaver to convince him to make one more "appeal together . . . [to] clear up [our] names" (45), never really understanding his transgression or the Black Sox's role in baseball history and mythology. Stein's Weaver, on the other hand, seems to now understand the significance of his banishment:

> Nineteen nineteen. There is that word, and I already know what is going on in your skull. I suppose I cannot blame you, for it is the same with everyone. It is almost like saying 1776 or some year like that. But just one time I would like to hear someone say "Nineteen nineteen, wasn't that the year all them nabobs got together in Versailles?" Or "Nineteen nineteen, wasn't that when old man Ford started up with the Model-T?" Or "Nineteen nineteen, wasn't that the year Babe got dealt to New York?"
>
> But I am no sucker, and I gave up waiting for such events a long time ago. (257)

By comparing 1919 with 1776, not only does Weaver link baseball history with national history but he also places baseball within that broader historical context, and thus enables his narrative to draw upon the mythology of baseball as the country's cultural common denominator. Furthermore, Weaver the memoirist writing from experience separates himself from Buck the ballplayer who was a sucker for taking the fall, despite not participating in the fix. In fact, Stein initially identifies Weaver as George D. Weaver, who contrasts sharply with the Lardnerian Buck Weaver that is recalled throughout the narrative. George Weaver is no longer the innocent, arrogant young man of his playing days, vainly seeking to have his name cleared. Writing from 1944, he is a man who has moved from innocence to experience, incurring painful disillusionment in the process. As a result, a more mature and cautious Weaver emerges. Unlike Kinsella's Joe Jackson, Weaver has learned from his experience and has gained self-awareness. He has come to understand both his own complicity and the injustice of his punishment, which he ultimately accepts heroically. Weaver has learned that, from the perspective of the baseball establishment and the media, his silence was tantamount to guilt, and he has therefore left the confines of the ballfield—leaving behind Buck, but not his love for the game.

Luther Pond's competing narrative conflicts with Weaver's, if not in points of fact, then in spirit. Unsympathetic to the players, Pond's rendition of the scandal implicitly argues that the fixed series was a singular event orchestrated by foolish men and not "the culmination of a long string of injustices."[45] Since Pond is a member of the media, and therefore might be considered more objective, his account might understandably be given primacy over that of the implicated Weaver. Yet just like Weaver, Pond is shown to have a vested interest in promoting a specific version of the scandal. He candidly recounts that as a journalist his sensational and unscrupulous reportage—which in large measure launched his meteoric career—was intended to help sell newspapers. Ultimately, though, Pond's crass, self-serving account lacks the integrity of Weaver's narrative. The literary critic Peter

Carino suggests that "unlike the false eloquence that indicts Pond unawares, the style of Weaver's narration characterizes him as a common man offering straight talk. Though he lacks Pond's intelligence, like Huck Finn, he commands a vernacular that endears him to the reader and lends credibility to his point of view."[46] David McGimpsey, the author of *Imagining Baseball: America's Pastime and Popular Culture* (2000), similarly observes, "Stein uses Weaver's voice to challenge the class authority of literate cynics who create the fictions which will deny him his livelihood."[47] Unfortunately, Weaver's account cannot overcome these authoritative cynics.

Despite the self-serving quality of Pond's account—it is "the memoir of a scoundrel," writes Carino—Pond still commands authority as a narrator.[48] As a successful and influential reporter and columnist for over fifty years, he was close to history-makers and was one himself and as such his perspectives on the past have a certain degree of legitimacy. "Never before in my long experience has this nation been in such a sorry condition as it is today," he narrates from his porch on Long Island in September 1974. "Never before have the values upon which I was nurtured been in such desperate need of affirmation" (5). Perhaps writing in response to the Watergate scandal, Pond suggests that what he has to say now about the past "is of considerable moment" (5). No stranger to political intrigue, Pond had covered the 1920 Republican Convention in Chicago for the *New York Daily News* and eventually came to see that convention "as much as the fixed World Series itself, as a harbinger of the approaching age" of contempt and greed (291). Being of their ilk, Pond has long since recognized that "the world is full of quietly unscrupulous men and, more important, that their shortcomings rarely lead to their ruination" (4). However, it is in those infrequent moments when they are revealed that journalists like Pond and novelists like Stein are thrust into the role of popular historians, tellers of the past.

Both in terms of content and form, *Hoopla* offers a revisionist appraisal of the Black Sox scandal that resists conventional historical wisdom and morality. Even though he has created disparate narrators who have different perspectives, agendas, and styles of storytelling, Stein ultimately portrays the fixed World Series as the result "of a long history of unfair labor practices by stingy industrialist/owners [rather than] the result of the greed of a few players," argues the literary critic Richard Alan Schwartz.[49] Within the structure of his fictional world, Stein makes the case that the institutionalized abuse of the White Sox and the media's sensationalistic reportage left a deep scar on baseball and the national psyche, but most especially on the players themselves, personified by the resilient Buck Weaver. In this way *Hoopla* resists the master narrative of the scandal promoted by Major

League Baseball. For readers dissatisfied with "official" explanations or for those enamored with the idea of reapportioning responsibility for the Black Sox scandal, Stein offers a counterhistory that puts the infamous event in context and gives an earnest voice to one of its victims.

Nothing Is the Way It Seems

Since it was published in the twilight of the Reagan-Bush years, Brendan Boyd's *Blue Ruin: A Novel of the 1919 World Series* (1991) deserves attention here.[50] Boyd's first (and so far only) novel, *Blue Ruin* is narrated by Joseph "Sport" Sullivan, one of the gamblers involved in the fix. Over the course of the novel, Boyd's unrepentant and not-so-trustworthy narrator coolly delineates his part in the machinations and offers an irreverent, worm's-eye view of American history. Like Harry Stein's Luther Pond and Buck Weaver, Boyd's Sullivan writes retrospectively, many decades after the conspiracy. Divided into three long sections and a brief conclusion, *Blue Ruin* is organized more or less chronologically. Populated by a cast of historical characters—some of whom only make cameos, such as Ring Lardner, Babe Ruth, George M. Cohan, Warren G. Harding, and John Reed, some of whom are vitally important to the narrative, such as Arnold Rothstein, Abe Attell, Bill Burns, Chick Gandil, and Swede Risberg—*Blue Ruin* is written in a hard-boiled, terse style that evokes the fiction of both Raymond Chandler and Raymond Carver. Self-consciously stylized, more comic than tragic, *Blue Ruin* does for the gamblers involved in the Big Fix what John Gardner's *Grendel* (1971) does for the renowned beast in *Beowulf:* it tells the tale from the perspective of one of the monsters.

Blue Ruin is almost completely bereft of any sense of disillusionment, remorse, or moral outrage. Boyd's Sport Sullivan is not burdened by guilt, except for one brief moment. While boarding the train to Cincinnati for the series opener, Sullivan confesses: "I'd felt no guilt at past manipulations, but this one made me queasy. Here were thousands of innocents nursing one common delusion. I alone knew how delusory, for I alone had ordained it. It was a brief twinge, but a genuine one. I'm nothing if not human" (120). That twinge of morality does not deter him, however: after all, he is chasing a version of the American Dream. (This passage is also illustrative of the way in which Sullivan occasionally exaggerates his role.) Far from an apologia or a mea culpa, Sullivan's rendition radiates self-pride and a sense of accomplishment. For Sullivan, participating in the Black Sox scandal is a badge of honor that signifies his status as a "sport," as an iconoclast. For Sullivan, the Big Fix first appeared to be a life-long dream come true.

Blue Ruin is also notable because it suggests that at the time of the scandal a universally pervasive culture of gambling existed and, as Diane Cole of the *New York Times* puts it, "that the baseball owners in particular and American moneyed interests in general were in their way perhaps as crooked—and certainly more hypocritical—than the men behind the scam."[51] Cole is correct; however, *Blue Ruin* is more than revisionist history: it is virtually antihistory. It emphasizes the impossibility of writing traditional narrative history in a postmodern era. Although it is playful, *Blue Ruin* is also profoundly skeptical about telling and knowing the past. Similar to the postmodern historiographic metafiction (that is, intensely self-conscious postmodern novels that contest and blur the boundaries between fiction and history) of E. L. Doctorow, *Blue Ruin* forces readers to reevaluate how they know what they know (in general and with regard to the Black Sox scandal) and to reexamine the fixing of the 1919 World Series as something other than a debacle.

An overtly controlling narrator, Sport Sullivan embodies *Blue Ruin*'s vision of the past. Thirty-six years old in 1919, Sullivan, a former numbers runner in Boston whom one critic describes as "a small-timer and a born loser," is essentially a nobody.[52] He is a loner: furtive, aloof, and alienated. Peter Carino argues that Boyd's Sport Sullivan is "a rogue hero in the mode of F. Scott Fitzgerald's Jay Gatsby, a man whose capacity to dream mitigates his corruption but whose attempts to make dreams reality destroy him."[53] Occasionally, Sullivan appears to be brash and confident, but he (candidly? ironically?) admits to being less shrewd than he seems. He is moody and insecure, a sour, ambivalent, nihilistic con man, a bit player in a cast full of bit players. Like many protagonists in historiographic metafictional narratives, Boyd's Sullivan is an eccentric, peripheral figure.[54] Keenly aware of the vagaries of knowing the past and his own marginal status, Sullivan acknowledges his status as an untrustworthy narrator. From the very beginning, he warns readers:

> So much is lost in shadow now, though parts remain resolutely visible. In those days every detail seemed so plain to me that I never dreamed any would require illumination. Volumes have been written about the fix. Those who didn't squeal confided in those who did. I've read it all—the memoirs, the depositions, the speculations—hoping to learn what occurred beyond my sight. It's amazing what people will admit to, in what detail, to justify themselves. No one will ever know the whole story, I suppose. There will always be gaps, to be filled in, as I have tried to do, over the years. There is no truth, only versions. This is mine. (7)

This passage explains how Sullivan can describe events he obviously did not participate in or witness and serves as Sullivan's own justification. But perhaps most important, it attests that narrating the past is anything but objective and impartial, that history is always constructed to serve particular interests. Versions of the past, Sullivan reminds readers, are always by someone for someone, always contingent and incomplete.

Accordingly, the past *Blue Ruin* articulates is rife with ambiguity. As Sullivan tells it, the fixed World Series was a poorly planned and executed labyrinthine episode of deceit and double-cross whose driving forces were opportunity, greed, and happenstance. "Only fixers know how random fixes are," confides Sullivan, "how resistant even the simplest events are to rigging" (52). The conspiracy was more amorphous than commonly believed, Sullivan explains, for none of its participants was fully aware of who knew what and when. After he tells his lover about the upcoming fix, Sullivan admits that he can only tell her "everything I knew about it, which seems pitifully little now" (113). Ensconced in an extremely complicated affair, which the historical Abe Attell described as "a game of cheaters cheating cheaters," Sullivan conveys a sense of its chaos.[55] The ballplayers and gamblers communicated with one another infrequently and ineffectively; moreover, subterfuge ruled their relations. With the World Series in full swing, Sullivan admits: "I was stunned by the shifts my scam was experiencing, day to day, hour to hour. One moment triumph seemed assured, the next instant ruin appeared inevitable. It was disorientating, yet stimulating" (164). The novel (especially its first two-thirds) simulates that same sense of commotion and excitement.

Sullivan (and by extension his version of the past) is also beset with acute anxiety, even before Chick Gandil proposes that they conspire to throw the series. One reason for this is that the novel opens with a moment of crisis and transition: the death of Sullivan's father. An undistinguished and overly cautious man of limited ambition, the senior Sullivan once warned his son "never to dream," Sport remarks, "because if my dreams didn't come true, I'd be disappointed, and if they did, I'd be even more disappointed" (3). Fearful that he has unwittingly heeded his father's advice, that he has in effect become his father, Sullivan is anxious to stop living a life of quiet desperation; he is anxious for an opportunity to enact his dream of "the perfect scam" (30), his dream of triumph and accomplishment. (For those who value authorial insight, Boyd contends that *Blue Ruin* is about "the point in almost every man's life that he's been dreading or trying not to think about for a long time where he realizes he's become, if not precisely his father, partly his father.")[56] Once his scheme is in motion, Sullivan finds that more than anything else his anxiety drives him on. Unconcerned about the ethics, legality, or logistics of the fix, Sullivan is anxious about the discovery of his scam for more pragmatic financial reasons: disclosure would further depress the odds, reduce his return, and diminish his achievement.[57]

Not coincidentally, *Blue Ruin* marginalizes those men whose achievements are regularly lauded and obsessively recorded: the ballplayers. From Sullivan's perspective, Gandil and his conspiring teammates are pawns—which is not to suggest that the conspiring ballplayers are innocents led to slaughter. In *Blue Ruin,* it is worth repeating, Gandil initiates the fix by approaching Sullivan. At one point during the series, Sullivan observes that the ballplayers "looked less like victims than victimizers" (167). *Blue Ruin* thus undercuts the version of the Black Sox scandal that it is arguably most dependent upon—Eliot Asinof's *Eight Men Out* (1963)—and it upgrades the status of an obscure underworld figure, though perhaps not as much as Sullivan imagines. For example, after game four, when Sullivan refers to himself as a well-known gambler, Gandil responds: "Well-known, Sport? By who?" (167). Even after participating in and profiting from the fixed games, Sullivan remains relatively anonymous and obscure. While visiting the rich and famous in California after the series, Sullivan is approached by a young man who inquires whether he is "the famous gambler Sport Solomon" (218). A hustler who enjoyed fifteen minutes of fame among a small circle of fellow sports, Sullivan never duplicates his antiheroics, loses most of his series loot, and fades into oblivion.

The same cannot be said of the infamous gambler Arnold Rothstein. From some perspectives, Rothstein was the Judas-in-chief of the plot. For Sullivan, however, Rothstein is an incomparable underworld genius, an antihero of mythic proportions. More than anything else, Rothstein's domineering and invincible presence gives *Blue Ruin* the imprimatur of antiheroism. Similar to the Rothstein portrayed in Leo Katcher's *The Big Bankroll: The Life and Times of Arnold Rothstein* (1974), Boyd's Rothstein is brilliantly analytical, imperious, ruthless, charming when it is convenient, seemingly omniscient. Clearly Sullivan is enthralled by Rothstein and quixotically dreams of emulating him. To Sullivan, Rothstein represents an unattainable ideal: he is the apotheosis of the successful American of ethnic origins, "a man who makes things work, a man who knows" (328). "I'd been following his career clandestinely for years," Sullivan confesses. "He was what I would have been, if I could have been anything" (29). Sullivan goes so far as to muse that God is probably "the spitting image of Arnold Rothstein" (24). For his part, Rothstein does nothing to discourage such hyperbole: "'With one black telephone, and a pot of heavy java,' Rothstein would tell dinner guests, 'I could make a running start at taking over the universe'" (89). To realize his dream, Sullivan solicits Rothstein for financial backing.

After some deliberation, Rothstein assents. "If you pull this off your life will be over," Rothstein forewarns Sullivan, much as Sullivan's father did. "You'll have gotten exactly what you wanted" (74). As usual, the Big Bankroll is correct; the year after the series, Sullivan drifts all over the country, is separated from three-fourths of his winnings, and pathetically plans his ever-elusive next great success. Temporarily dropping the facade (perhaps the delusion) that he was the driving force behind the fix, Sullivan notes that Rothstein "was manipulating an event the whole country cared about, queering it without precedent or sponsorship, from one tiny room in a tiny town in the Adirondacks" (89). Despite this admission, it (apparently) comes as a shock to Sullivan when Rothstein disabuses him of the notion that he had fixed the series: "You didn't fix anything, Sport. I was one step in your size nines all the way. I did it. That's why it worked. You never could have done it. Not alone. I kept you in it to smooth the edges. You were useful. I liked you. It was amusing. But you botched it. Now it's unraveling" (327). To ensure they remain unscathed by the scandal, Rothstein dispatches Sullivan to Mexico, where he will be beyond the reach of the grand jury. Rothstein admonishes Sullivan: "Stuff your dreams back inside your head now, enjoy Mexico, and keep your mouth shut" (332). For a variety of reasons—an acute sense of self-preservation, respect for Rothstein, and the prospect of beginning a new life—Sullivan complies, aware that he will never be a man of will and substance, of wealth and power. His acquiescence signifies the death of one of his impossible dreams.

Blue Ruin, contends one reviewer, is a novel that has "found its age—an age that suffers from too much history, too many names dropped."[58] Whether the novel suffers from too many historical cameos is unimportant to me; moreover, it is difficult to imagine that the Reagan-Bush era was a time of too much history. Nonetheless, *Blue Ruin* is of its age, a moment characterized by contingent, partial truths and indeterminate narratives, by amoral (or immoral) fixers, libertines, and leaders, by corruption and cupidity. Self-reflexive and subversive, *Blue Ruin* presents readers with a radically intertextual fictive world distinguished by historical appropriation, ambiguity, and anti-heroism; it offers a unique version of the Black Sox scandal that inverts conventional historicity and morality. Ultimately, *Blue Ruin* challenges readers to reexamine the past from nontraditional and sometimes unsavory perspectives, it insists on the unreliability of narrative history to convey the past impartially, and it encourages readers to remember that sometimes historical facts can play "havoc with the truth" (117). These lessons aside, *Blue Ruin* leaves some with a nagging sense that they have been duped or conned. "Was I the meticulous enigma who'd fixed last October's Series?" Sullivan asks. "Or the pathetic shlub who'd botched every shakedown since?" (295). At first glance, the answer seems clear: the latter, of course. But Boyd's fictionalized Arnold Rothstein provides readers with another alternative. "Nothing is the way it seems, is it, Sport?" Rothstein observes. "Most things are the opposite. That's how you know" (332). In *Blue Ruin,* irony rules.

The Black Sox on the Silver Screen

Often formulaic and insipid, most of the scores of baseball films produced in Hollywood are forgettable.[59] That is not the case with the three examined here: Barry Levinson's *The Natural* (1984), Phil Alden Robinson's *Field of Dreams* (1989), and John Sayles's *Eight Men Out* (1988). In dramatically different ways, these films engage and imaginatively reanimate the books on which they are based and the past itself. As ours is an increasingly visual culture—some have gone so far as to describe the contemporary United States as a postliterate society, in which most people can read but do not—it is important to acknowledge that films can powerfully influence the ways in which we understand the past.[60] Working from the presupposition that filmic representations need to be taken seriously, the historian Robert A. Rosenstone argues that films should be considered "another way of understanding our relationship to the past, another way of pursuing that conversation about where we came from, where we are going, and who we are."[61] The conversations that films like *The Natural, Field of Dreams,* and *Eight Men Out* participate in and the stories they tell certainly deserve our attention, especially considering the size of their audiences. Even compared with a best-selling novel, an unremarkable Hollywood film reaches a staggering number of people. A film, of course, is not a visual novel. "There are no ways to film thought process or narrative voice; film cannot get the tone, the style, or the inward size of a novel and shouldn't even try," observes the film critic David Thomson. "If I proposed to you that we might try to make sculpture of a sonnet, say, you would see the nonsense immediately. Such forms do not translate any more than you can turn an anchovy into an orange. We have both. Yet an attitude has developed—in the picture business and in academia—that one can film novels and then study the process."[62] Although Thomson overstates some of the differences between films and novels, his larger point has merit: a film is not a book, and thus it requires a different kind of critical analysis. At the same time, like most novels, most feature films do not make bold "truth" claims about their subjects. Rather, they are usually content to remain loosely—sometimes very loosely—connected to their historical referents.

Hollywood Hokum

In 1984, Bernard Malamud's *The Natural* was finally made into a movie—albeit one retaining only the most tenuous connections to the heart of the novel. It was adapted for the screen by Roger Towne and Phil Dusenberry and directed by Barry Levinson, now well known for his semi-autobiographical Baltimore films and *Rain Man* (1988), which won him the Academy Award for best director. Yet before *The Natural,* Levinson had only directed *Diner* (1982), the first of his "Baltimore stories."[63] A character-driven film, *Diner* is about a group of close-knit young men on the brink of full adulthood and their ambivalence about the choices they are making and who they are becoming. Part of its charm resides in its nostalgic yet gritty portrayal of Baltimore in the late fifties. *The Natural* is similarly nostalgic, but it is also cartoonish and lacks the authenticity and poignancy Levinson achieved in *Diner.*

Primarily set in 1939, *The Natural* traces the abbreviated baseball career of thirty-six-year-old rookie outfielder Roy Hobbs (played by Robert Redford), the resurgence of his team (the New York Knights), and his various love interests. A beautifully filmed movie, it garnered Academy Award nominations for best cinematography and best art direction. With a superb cast, which includes Kim Basinger, Wilford Brimley, Glenn Close, Robert Duvall, and Barbara Hershey, *The Natural* is a fairy tale–like movie that self-consciously evokes the values and strategies of baseball films of an earlier era. According to Gary E. Dickerson in *The Cinema of Baseball* (1991), *The Natural* "is reflective of a nostalgic yearning for a period of our personal histories when issues seemed to be less complex, a period when good and evil, and black and white, were clearly distinguishable."[64] It romantically evokes a quietly heroic ballplayer who overcomes tremendous setbacks and experiences phenomenal success. For those unfamiliar with Malamud's novel, the movie is engaging; steeped in sentimentality, *The Natural* glows. However, as is often the case when a well-regarded novel is adapted for the screen, many objected to how the film modified and streamlined the novel. While the changes are numerous and significant, only one merits attention here.[65] The cultural critic Gerald Early puts it succinctly: "In the film version, Roy Hobbs ultimately becomes the golden boy who hits the homerun to win the championship instead of the jerk who both sold out and struck out."[66] It is a remarkably jarring change, one that constitutes a conspicuous artistic and historical erasure, for the Black Sox scandal is whitewashed out of existence. Betrayal has been transformed into righteousness, defeat into victory.

In the novel, Hobbs accepts a bribe from his corrupt team owner and a gambling accomplice to throw the season finale.[67] He changes his mind during the course of the game, but it is too late. At his moment of reckoning, Hobbs strikes "out with a roar."[68] In the film, he refuses the lucrative bribe and hits a dramatic home run into the stadium lights to win the game. As he circles the bases (in slow motion, no less), the music swells, and he is bathed by exploding light. It is an inversion of the novel's "Casey at the Bat" conclusion and a moment that borders on parody. The film critic David Denby speaks for many when he argues that *The Natural* has "an overinsistent happy ending, complete with fireworks. This golden-hued kitsch is so wildly unreal that it's supposed to make you laugh even as the lump rises in your throat."[69] Despite all the pyrotechnics and manipulative special effects, Hobbs's home run is a spectacularly hollow, false victory. It is completely underwhelming—the ultimate sports movie cliché. "In the end," the critic James Griffith argues, "although the climactic homerun may feel wonderful to the audience, nothing important has been accomplished. Roy's triumph comes over weak, even silly adversaries. His character is too good to be seriously tempted by the venal blandishments they offer, or seriously intimidated by the slight threats they hold."[70] Unlike Malamud's protagonist and the historical Black Sox, Roy Hobbs is an untouchable. It is as if the filmmakers forgot that in order to sustain dramatic tension heroes need to triumph over legitimate rivals, that they are more heroic when their victories are in doubt.[71]

The way the film's makers reworked—in effect, reversed—Malamud's bitter conclusion of moral failure is disconcerting, even when one acknowledges that films adapted from books often deviate considerably from the original, that films infrequently claim to present historical truth, and that, as the cultural critic George Lipsitz puts it, "filmmakers have our permission to tell fanciful lies."[72] Although I am not censuring the filmmakers for modifying Malamud's novel, a more cynical critic might suggest that the filmmakers' betrayal is rooted in the desire for financial gain.[73] Reflecting on the way in which *The Natural* was adapted, John Sayles notes: "I think the filmmaker said he wanted to be more in tune with the Eighties. Or he may have meant, 'I want to make more money, and that's what we're doing.'"[74] These are not necessarily contradictory statements or mutually exclusive aims. Nonetheless Sayles seems to imply that Levinson and his associates cynically "fixed" the movie, that, like the Black Sox, they "sold out." The *New Yorker*'s Pauline Kael offers slightly more temperate criticism: "This picture looks to be a case of intelligent people putting enormous care into a project that they have emasculated to the point of idiocy."[75]

Anticipating these objections, Robert Redford and Barry Levinson defended their project and its lack of fidelity to Malamud's novel. Before the film was released, Redford conceded that Malamud was able to be far more inclusive than the filmmakers could be. The novel, Redford noted, is "richly allegorical. There's Babe Ruth in there, Shoeless Joe Jackson, the Miracle Braves of 1914 and Casey at the Bat. There's the Arthur legend with Hobbs's bat as Excalibur. And, of course, there's Eddie Waitkus. Remember him? It's extremely difficult to combine all of these elements into a picture, so, yes, we dared alter Malamud. Film is just not a literary medium, I'm afraid."[76] Unlike the novel, Redford added, "this picture will have less to do with the darker side of life."[77] Precisely why is unclear. Less apologetic than Redford, Levinson acknowledged that it "was extremely difficult getting a hold on this film stylistically and holding it in line. It's heroic, romantic. It's fable material, and that's a fine line to have to walk. You don't want to make it a cartoon and on the other hand, you're not doing hardcore reality either." Therein lies part of the problem. Malamud wrote a tragicomic, cartoonish novel that added layers of symbolic complexity and moral density to a generally recognizable narrative and series of events—that is, a complex and ambiguous narrative about betrayal and failure. Levinson's objective was to make "a baseball movie that conjures up all the American dreams. This movie is once upon a time, and if we can pull that off without making it fake it'll be exciting. And we can all root and cheer and be upset and laugh and cry and finally go, 'Oh, my God, I had a helluva time! I had a helluva time watching that movie.' If we can accomplish that, then it'll be worthwhile."[78] Not only did the filmmakers fail to capture the spirit of Malamud's novel—indeed, they inverted it—they did not accomplish their own objective, which is why the film version of *The Natural* is sentimental, unsatisfying, and irksome.[79]

Produced at a time when Major League Baseball was plagued by acrimonious labor disputes and numerous substance abuse revelations, when unemployment and conspicuous consumption were on the rise and "traditional" values and fiscal restraint appeared to be in decline, when President Reagan would joke about his inability to discuss important issues without cue cards, and when the U.S. Marine presence in Lebanon was proving to be ineffectual, *The Natural* reaffirmed the value of heroes. By the mideighties, argues Gary Dickerson, "American audiences seemed to have tired of their heroes, dreams, and myths being destroyed by stories of reality. They needed something to be happy about. Roy Hobbs could not make them forget the realities of heroic figures, but he could help them remember the value of having heroes. Baseball fans, especially, needed the filmic Roy Hobbs to restore their faith in one of the greatest traditions of America."[80] Whether Dickerson is correct is not the point. What matters here is the degree to which storytellers like Levinson seem to have believed this to be the case and reworked their materials so as to appeal to (and thus reproduce) "the prevailing box-office values of the era."[81] No matter how chimerical, far-fetched, or absurd, the children of light subdue those of darkness. Temptation is resisted, integrity sustained. In the end, ballplayers do not accept bribes. Heroes never fail when they are most needed. Fathers still play catch with their sons in amber fields of grain. Morally unambiguous, drenched in nostalgia, devoid of annoying complexity, the film version of *The Natural* reshapes the substance of the American past nearly as dramatically as it modifies Malamud's novel.

Nostalgia Pays

Released in April 1989, *Field of Dreams* was written and directed by Phil Alden Robinson and featured Kevin Costner as Ray Kinsella. At the time, Robinson, who began his career making industrial and educational films, had only directed *In the Mood* (1987), a moderately successful forties period comedy. Costner had starred in hits like *The Untouchables* (1987), *No Way Out* (1987), and *Bull Durham* (1988). Described by David Thomson as "reasonably handsome, passably virile, [and] unequivocally ordinary," Costner was well cast as a nondescript Iowa farmer.[82] For both men, *Field of Dreams*—which was nominated for three Academy Awards, including best film and best screenplay adaptation—was a professional turning point. Robinson went on to co-write and direct the comedy-thriller *Sneakers* (1992) and co-write *Dances with Wolves* (1990), which won seven Academy Awards, including best director for Costner, and which transformed the actor into a major Hollywood player.

A streamlined version of W. P. Kinsella's *Shoeless Joe, Field of Dreams* is essentially faithful to the book, partially because Robinson and Kinsella share a similar worldview. Responding to a society overrun by disappointment, greed, and cynicism, Robinson and Kinsella create fictional universes in which perfection is possible. Kinsella asserts that his "novel is about a perfect world. It's about a man who has a perfect wife, a perfect daughter and wants to keep it that way. In a perfect world you would be able to resurrect the dead. In a perfect world, you could play ball at midnight on the grass of your favorite ballpark."[83] They create realms where dreams come true for the faithful. "I don't believe in UFOs or ESP or any of those things," said Robinson after the film's debut. "But I would like to believe that good triumphs over evil, and that you can reach into the past and right an old wrong. It's not as important whether it happens as it is that you take the risk. It's the act of daring that's important."[84] (For Ray, who is a skeptic transformed into a selfless believer, the risk is both emotional and financial.) In both the novel and the movie, daring faith—and the lengths one will go ("Go the distance," says the disembodied voice) in the name of that faith—is a preeminent theme. According to the film critic James M. Wall, for skeptics and nonbelievers the film "is either a hokey longing for values that modernity mocks or a magical treatment of impossible dreams. But from the perspective of anyone willing to take a radical leap of faith, *Field of Dreams* recalls James Joyce's reminder that we are related to 'all the living and all the dead.'"[85] In *Field of Dreams,* there is little distinction between the two.

Like the novel from which it was adapted, *Field of Dreams* depicts a mythic—that is, ahistorical and sanitized—Joe Jackson, played by Ray Liotta. By extension, the narrative renders a gentler and more attractive country, one in which a coarse, illiterate Southerner is resurrected as an articulate, "diffident hunk of vaguely Italianate appearance, Rousseau's Noble Savage as painted by Raphael."[86] For these and other reasons, *Field of Dreams* was a huge popular and financial success. The phrase "If you build it, he will come" quickly became part of the American lexicon and the film reportedly made at least $62 million.[87] Movie reviewers and critics, however, were far from unanimous in their appraisal. Often noted as a Capraesque production, *Field of Dreams,* observes the film critic Hal Erickson, "comes as close to an ideal grown-up fantasy as one could ask for."[88] Millions of moviegoers and numerous critics agreed and were enamored by the film's romantic and nostalgic evocations of nature, family, baseball, and the past. "Full of wit, whimsy and honest sentiment," writes the reviewer Brian D. Johnson, "*Field of Dreams* slides home—and into the heart—in fine style."[89] Harlan Jacobson, among other critics, however, disparages the film's saccharine qualities and notes that "Capra's movies didn't reflect reality, they wished it away. They wished for an America that never was, but that they were taught, nonetheless, had been." Much like Pauline Kael, who refers to *Field of Dreams* as an eighties version of *It's a Wonderful Life* (1946), Jacobson is wary of the film's political implications. He argues that the film "weeps for what is not now and never was. It remembers America before it lost control. It touches an anger that runs so deep, the time may soon come when America will not wait to fire till it sees the whites of your eyes."[90] Resplendent in pastoral imagery, *Field of Dreams* conceals its cultural politics, which are just below the topsoil and seething with muted resentment.

Due to an excellent cast, beautiful cinematography (the Iowa countryside is luminous in its simplicity and grandeur), a haunting musical score, and what seems to be sincere affection for its subject, *Field of Dreams* is a seductive film. No less than Kinsella's novel, Robinson's movie draws viewers into Ray's quest. For many, *Field of Dreams* is a disarming fantasy that transcends the sports film genre. Even (perhaps especially) for literal-minded and cynical moviegoers and those hit hardest by the socioeconomic realities of the eighties, it can be an inspiring and emotionally moving film. Anecdotal evidence suggests that many people, especially middle-aged white men, "sat with reddened, runny eyes" at the film's conclusion.[91] The journalist Ron Rosenbaum argues that *Field of Dreams* goes

> straight to the heart of all the thirtysomething guys in America who still have a romantic, quixotic streak in them, but like Costner in the movie, they're settling in, settling down, they see all their romantic dreams of themselves being shut off, and this is a film about someone like them who suddenly gets a chance—one last shot—at a quest, a meaningful adventure. That's what the father-son thing at the end of the film is about, that feeling of wanting one last shot at getting it right with your dad, which is something practically every guy in America suffers from.[92]

In this way *Field of Dreams* is a continuation of the Black Sox scandal narrative as a masculine touchstone, a site where men can commune and commiserate. But in addition to lamenting lost opportunities for fathers to play catch with sons, the film also implicitly decries other losses. As Jacobson puts it, *Field of Dreams* "wishes aloud that America could return to the innocent days of white baseball. When there were no stains on American honor, no scandals, no dirty tricks, no surprises. When everything was white, pure and clean and simple and, well, white."[93] The film yearns for a bygone era when baseball (and by extension the nation) was not burdened by complexity, to say nothing of visible and vocal racial minorities.

Several critics have noted this and other troubling aspects of the film. Robinson has been taken to task most notably for the incongruous soliloquy delivered by Terence Mann, the reclusive African American writer who was an inspirational counterculture leader in the sixties and whose pain Ray is presumably easing, near the end of the film. Looking out on Ray's magical field, Mann, played by James Earl Jones, implores Ray not to sell his farm, even though he is in jeopardy of losing it to foreclosure, because baseball "reminds us of all that once was good and can be good again." C. Kenneth Pellow offers an excellent critique of the moment:

> The illogic of the situation undermines everything positive about the scene. "People will come," Terence Mann says, "as innocent as children, searching

> for the past. . . ." He stands with the field as backdrop and proclaims, "the one constant through all the years has been baseball." With all those exclusively white ballplayers' faces behind him, he can say this? "It reminds us of all that's good. . . ." This from a Black radical novelist, an activist in the sixties? The character is middle-aged. He must remember Jackie Robinson. He must know that Josh Gibson and Cool Papa Bell never got to play in the Bigs at all, and Satchel Paige not until he was—who knows what?—fifty maybe? And that even then *The Sporting News* said Bill Veeck had "demeaned the standards" of major league baseball in signing him. He must know all of this. Yet he stands there celebrating baseball for its maintaining of innocence and "purity" (in this context, one of the most consistently racist terms).[94]

For knowledgeable, critical viewers, it is more difficult to suspend disbelief here than at any other moment in the film. If the point of the field is to provide opportunity and redemption for those who need it, then Mann's speech borders on the absurd, if not the incomprehensible.

Nearly as disturbing is the manner in which Ray takes advantage of his own faith and commodifies his magical baseball field. In keeping with the spirit of the eighties, when televangelists "flourished because they combined all the elements that most characterized the Reagan era: money, morality, conservatism, entertainment, and religious and patriotic symbolism," *Field of Dreams* offers visitors and viewers alike a type of religious experience, for a price.[95] As Terence Mann preaches, "They'll pass over the money without even thinking about it, for it is money they have and peace they lack." Ray's personal and spiritual quest not only resurrects Joe Jackson, the rest of the implicated White Sox, and Ray's father, but it also produces a shrine with a bright fiscal future. In this way, argues the critic Bill Brown, the field "has become a capitalist dream, a fast way to save the farm (as the young girl and the Black activist are the first to sense), indeed a way for the radical students of the '60s to become entrepreneurs, a way for former radicals to re-emerge as Americans."[96] Ultimately, *Field of Dreams* sows faith and harvests cash. With such a miraculous formula for regeneration, which presumably saves the financially troubled farm and is completely in step with the quick-fix ethos of the eighties, this fantasy must have been particularly attractive for those caught in the farm crisis that ravaged the Midwest during the decade.

By the late spring of 1988, when *Field of Dreams* was being filmed in and around Dubuque, Iowa, the value of farmland in Iowa (and its neighboring states) had already bottomed out, and more than 150,000 farms had gone bankrupt nationwide since the beginning of the decade.[97] "Simultaneous industrial and agricultural decline wrought severe hardship throughout the Middle West," writes the journalist Haynes Johnson. "In factory and farm communities, cases of human suffering multiplied, and the Middle West's unemployment rate was twice that of the national average."[98] Although in 1988 farmland prices were beginning to increase, thanks in large part to the federal government's intervention, the long-term trend was not encouraging. To make matters worse, the drought that spring and summer substantially reduced crop yields.

In this context, Universal Pictures's decision to film *Field of Dreams* in Iowa was seen by many, including Governor Terry Branstad, as a major boon for the state. According to the Iowa Film Office, the four months of filming pumped an estimated $5 million into the Dubuque economy. Described by an official from the Iowa Film Office as a "love letter to the state of Iowa,"[99] *Field of Dreams* was seen by many locals as priceless advertising for a state with an ailing economy.[100] (This was an uncommonly prescient observation, as we will see in the next chapter.) Since the filmmakers built it, people have come—from all over the world, in droves, sometimes "for reasons they cannot exactly articulate, except that the movie touched something inside them, something about the romance of baseball, childhood and their memories," comments the journalist William E. Schmidt.[101] Few films have done as much to transform a simple geographical space into a "place" that people travel to, mythologize, and consume.[102]

Whimsically romantic and (despite a veneer of liberalism) politically conservative, *Shoeless Joe* and *Field of Dreams* vividly reflect and effectively reproduce eighties culture. They are charming escapist fantasies that sentimentalize rural (white), nuclear (patriarchal) families and the land they farm, to say nothing of the national pastime they play and supposedly revere. For all their seemingly universal appeal, *Shoeless Joe* and *Field of Dreams* promote a specific set of values. Neither narrative, for example, is interested in seriously exploring the guilt of Joe Jackson and the rest of the White Sox—perhaps to do so would allow too much history to bleed into and ruin the fantasy. Even though they go "from charming to preposterous to preachy,"[103] *Shoeless Joe* and *Field of Dreams* have not disappointed the millions of Americans yearning for golden yesterdays and brighter tomorrows. They are narratives—particularly *Field of Dreams*—well on their way to becoming cultural touchstones for a generation of Americans.

Multiple Perspectives on the Big Fix

Adapted from Eliot Asinof's 1963 historical account of the same title, John Sayles's *Eight Men Out* (1988)—which Sayles wrote, directed, and acted in—

offers a version of the Black Sox scandal that is as unsentimental and antiheroic as *Field of Dreams* is romantic and worshipful. A graduate of Williams College, a well-known progressive, and one of the country's most successful and respected independent filmmakers—to date he has made thirteen films since 1980, in addition to working on many others—Sayles often tackles sensitive, complicated subjects and insists on complete artistic control over his films, which frequently have morally ambiguous conclusions.[104] Such is the case with *Eight Men Out,* which Sayles had been trying to make for years.

In many ways, *Eight Men Out* resists providing a unified vision of the Black Sox scandal. The film begins, for instance, by offering multiple perspectives on the narrative's principal actors: we are introduced to the cliquish and quarrelsome White Sox by Charles A. Comiskey (played by Clifton James), who is wining and dining journalists covering the team, and two gamblers (played by Christopher Lloyd and Richard Edson) musing about whom to approach for the fix. Moreover, the film early on introduces its alternating Greek choruses who comment on the characters and events: two cynical sportswriters (Hugh Fullerton and Ring Lardner, played by Studs Terkel and Sayles, respectively) and two earnest, baseball-loving boys. David Scobey, who reviewed the film for the *American Historical Review,* correctly points out that these two factions personify the "producers and the consumers of the heroic myth Shoeless Joe Jackson and the others betrayed."[105] This approach to narration is reminiscent of the one Asinof used. And like Asinof—who briefly appears in the film as John Heydler, president of the National League—Sayles does not view the implicated players in terms of their heroic accomplishments (and failures) or in terms of moral absolutes.[106]

Rather, Sayles presents the players as victims of circumstance (which is linked to their social class and status as exploited workers), gullibility, ignorance, inertia, and, to a lesser extent, their own avarice and lack of courage. Ben Henkey of the *Sporting News,* who maintains that *Eight Men Out* is "arguably the best baseball movie ever," also notes that Sayles's "sympathies obviously lie with the players. He portrays them as grossly underpaid hirelings of a miserly owner, more or less victims of their own financial insecurity, unscrupulous gamblers, and a baseball establishment which might have looked the other way had it not been for the dislike of one man for another."[107] (Henkey is referring to American League president Ban Johnson, who recognized that pressing the matter would ruin his nemesis, Comiskey.) Though Sayles may view the players as casualties of labor and class relations and conflicts—the subject of his previous film, *Matewan* (1987), which was also set in the early twenties—he does not romanticize or celebrate their victimization. They are for the most part portrayed as crude, immature, bitter men. But Sayles does not treat the players condescendingly. Instead, *Eight Men Out* offers a rich mosaic in which there are no heroes and a variety of villains.

Eight Men Out is frequently lauded by critics and moviegoers for its stark realism and historical veracity. Filmed in what Scobey describes as a "flat, uninviting light"—which effectively combats the glow of nostalgia—*Eight Men Out* pays meticulous attention to details.[108] The sets, costumes, and props, some of which "was original stuff from 50, 60, 70 years ago," all lend the appearance of historical authenticity.[109] The actors seem able to approximate the ball playing of the original White Sox, with David Strathairn particularly good as Eddie Cicotte. Cumulatively, Sayles creates an accessible and alluring world that seems palpably real. For these reasons, and because Sayles's screenplay is essentially faithful to Asinof's original narrative, the film *Eight Men Out* is widely thought to be "without unnecessary embellishment," according to the *Journal of American History*.[110] One reviewer describes *Eight Men Out* as "objective, honest and historically accurate."[111] Charles Alexander suggests that the film is "considerably closer to historical verisimilitude than most movies ever made."[112] In fact, no less an authority than Ring Lardner Jr. maintains that *Eight Men Out* "is an admirable, objective account of historical events that leaves it up to the moviegoer to assign blame and credit."[113] These appraisals suggest that the idea and ideal of historical objectivity is alive and well, despite postmodernist critiques to the contrary. But they also suggest that some critics believe feature films are capable of rendering historical truth—or at least, in this case, Asinof's version of it. For some of these critics, it seems that Sayles's *Eight Men Out* is a kind of historical docudrama, a type of documentary that is able to convey "historical truth" in ways that magically realistic novels and feature films apparently cannot. Docudramas and documentaries, of course, are but other, not necessarily more "truthful" or less-biased or more effective ways of telling. All filmmakers are confronted with myriad possibilities and decisions in terms of rendering the past. As Sayles says, "The minute someone sits down in an editing room, even for a documentary, choices are made. Some footage is kept; other footage is not."[114]

Sayles is keenly aware that choices (and films) are not made in social or historical vacuums. For Sayles, contexts matter. Thus from his perspective, *Eight Men Out* is about "how people are corrupted by each other and their environment. How they fall into it is a gradual, not an immediate process. There's a different reason for everybody. Some of it was greed, some of it was peer pressure, just wanting to get along."[115] Like a few of the other storytellers examined in this book, Sayles's interest in and understanding of the Black Sox scandal can be traced to a similarly complex but more contemporaneous moment of deceit:

> One of the things I was thinking about [in 1977] when I wrote it [the *Eight Men Out* screenplay] was the Watergate conspiracy. As that conspiracy became public, it always reminded me of the Black Sox. Just like those guys, they got into trouble in different depths for different reasons—sometimes because they're weak; sometimes because they're greedy, evil motherfuckers; sometimes because they really don't know it's wrong, it just seems like everybody else is doing it: "I guess it's fine—we work for the President." But what was unique about this conspiracy is that everybody was selling everybody else out.[116]

Despite his empathy for the conspiring ballplayers, Sayles does not absolve them of their duplicity. If anything, *Eight Men Out* criticizes them for "selling out" their own teammates.

Not surprisingly, *Eight Men Out* was not an unqualified popular or critical success. "Of the four major-studio baseball pictures released in 1988 and 1989," writes Hal Erickson, alluding to *Bull Durham* (1988), *Field of Dreams,* and *Major League* (1989), "*Eight Men Out* was the least successful financially."[117] Of course, Sayles's box office appeal has always been limited, in part because he eschews portraying his subjects in an idyllic manner, in part because, as an independent filmmaker, his ambitions for audience are modest. Of more importance here, however, is the critical response the film engendered. To usefully simplify, most critics commended the film for its richly detailed evocation of the past but were less enamored with it as a work of drama. Sayles's ensemble approach, in which no single character receives much more attention than any other, feeds directly into this line of criticism. David Denby maintains that "*Eight Men Out* is a beautifully made movie without a dramatic center" and faults Sayles for failing to shape his "material dramatically and intellectually, so that all the little pieces of observation add up to something. *Eight Men Out* is all texture."[118] Likewise, *Commonweal*'s Tom O'Brien contends that the film's fundamental "problem lies with trying to tell too many stories at once; other ballplayers [than Weaver and Jackson], their wives, the gamblers—are all given idiosyncrasies that demand more space and time than the unmerciful frame of a two-hour film allows." The root of this problem, O'Brien argues, is that "Sayles cares so much about the real that he tries to fit too much in."[119] This common critique bespeaks the risks that storytellers take when they deviate from conventional narrative strategies.

It could be argued that *Eight Men Out* confuses complexity with ambiguity and victimization for tragedy, but to do so would be a mistake. Though the film moves fluidly from character to character, lacks a morally authoritative narrator, and has no overarching vision of the affair, all are purposeful choices made in an attempt to present a fragmented story in a fragmented manner and to destabilize audience expectations. If the film is sometimes difficult to follow and vague, it is because the Black Sox scandal was (and still is) often difficult to follow and vague. Sayles explains: "I was committed always to telling the big story, rather than saying this is from Buck Weaver's point of view, or an overview from the reporter's eyes, or through flashbacks. We decided to plunge in and try to make sense out of all the characters with all their cross-purposes and different stories. But it has to be an ensemble piece. I kept telling people, 'This is called Eight Men Out—not Three Men Out.' It is a complex story that will raise questions rather than satisfy expectations."[120] By failing to provide viewers with a single story to follow or an explanation of the complicated machinations at the 1921 conspiracy trial or any definitive closure, Sayles risked confusing and alienating his audience. Many viewers probably feel unfulfilled at the end of the film. But this is part of the price of depicting the scandal in the broadest possible terms, as opposed to sentimentalizing the affair by focusing exclusively on Jackson or Weaver. David Scobey puts it well when he argues that Sayles's film "seeks to unpack the contending interests and motives that produced the scandal and determined its trajectory; to recover sympathetically the experiences of the anti-heroes at its center; to explore the desires, grievances, and inequities that formed and deformed their choices."[121] Thus, regardless of its faults, Sayles's film, like Harry Stein's *Hoopla,* adeptly historicizes the past and provides us with a text to counterbalance more popular and romantic versions of the Black Sox scandal. Far from interest-free, *Eight Men Out* clearly has an agenda: it does not aspire to vindicate or absolve the players but instead seeks to redistribute responsibility more equitably. Viewers are left to determine whether Sayles has created an aesthetically and historically satisfying film.

Unflattering in their portraits of the baseball establishment and formally unconventional (compared to most best-selling novels and commercially successful movies), Stein's *Hoopla* and Sayles's *Eight Men Out* effectively redistribute and complicate responsibility for the Black Sox scandal and suggest that to convey the complexity of the past, nontraditional (but far from avant-garde) narrative strategies are useful. Over the course of both narratives it becomes apparent that baseball's corruption went much deeper than the fixing of the 1919 World Series and that the past was just as complex and sordid as the present from which Stein and Sayles were producing their accounts. By focusing on the relations among unscrupulous management, exploited ballplaying laborers, and cynical (yet aggrieved) members of the media and by rendering those relations in an unsentimental manner with multiple narrators and within multilayered contexts, *Hoopla* and *Eight Men Out* expose the national pastime as big business. Such a strategy suggests possibilities for rendering the past to popular audiences in ways besides conventional, commercially established storytelling; it suggests that to provide alternative, counterhistories which deviate from commonly accepted master narratives, storytellers must sometimes employ techniques that upset or challenge commonly accepted narrative forms.

Conclusion

John Sayles suggests that the Black Sox scandal "was really the kickoff of the Roaring Twenties. A lot of the cynicism that followed was certainly helped along by the idea that even America's game, which was supposed to be pure and good—white ballplayers, green grass, and blue skies—could be corrupted."[122] Journalists and historians sometimes maintain that the Big Fix launched one of the most uproarious, corrupt, and irresponsible eras in American history—one with which numerous storytellers in the eighties could identify.Considering their disparate agendas, it is not surprising that these writers and filmmakers create narratives that reveal widely divergent aesthetic and ideological possibilities while engaging similar subject matter at the same historical moment. Indeed, it is difficult to imagine narratives about the Black Sox scandal more dissimilar in their cultural politics than *Shoeless Joe* and *Hoopla.* Still, each narrative responds to social tensions that existed at the time of their creation. They also enter into an already ongoing dialogue. As some of the storytellers examined here suggest, during the eighties many people rejected the traditional version of the Black Sox scandal, that is, the simple fix tale of greedy men. With more than a half a century of hindsight and nearly twenty years to digest Eliot Asinof's *Eight Men Out,* the scandal was increasingly perceived as the culmination of an unfortunate nexus of personalities, circumstances, and social relations. Hackneyed though it may seem, for some in the eighties the Black Sox scandal appeared to mark the end of American innocence. "Popular perception ultimately becomes a reality," says Eric Rolfe Greenberg, "and if enough people say that the 1919 World Series was the end of American innocence, then it of course becomes the end of American innocence."[123] Yet that "popular perception" or popular memory was constructed in no small part by storytellers like Kinsella, Greenberg, Stein, Boyd, Levinson, Robinson, and Sayles. In a sense, their stories have become our remembered past. If this is so, we can be assured that the scandal will be remembered—for a while at least—as something more complicated than a morality tale.

The views one gets of the Black Sox scandal, American history, and the eighties from these novels and films are fragmentary and often contradictory. At one extreme, we find idyllic, pastoral worlds where dreams come true if only one believes in magic; at the other extreme, we find worlds where corruption and exploitation are nothing new, the exploited have no legitimate recourse to do anything about it, and irony is the last recourse; in between, disappointment and disillusionment remain fresh. Working from the presupposition that the narratives examined in this chapter were not acts of antiquarianism divorced from their own historical-social contexts, I think that they express the crises of their times. At the end of the decade the essayist Roger Angell noted that many people had "grown more, instead of less, oppressed by the Black Sox scandal as it recede[d] in history." In the process of surveying their own historical moment, a few storytellers tried, in Angell's words, to get the scandal "back and re-write it, to see if it won't come out better."[124] Meanwhile others saw the fixing of the World Series as a metaphor for their own age of hypocrisy at work. All of the themes commonly expressed in literature about the eighties—greed, corruption, duplicity, divisiveness, betrayal, moralistic hypocrisy, and a loss of faith in traditional American institutions and values—can be found in these narratives. Individually and collectively, these novels and films provide ways of comprehending a tumultuous, confusing historical moment: they give order to both the past and the present.

Far from isomorphic, the narratives examined here represent different mediums and points of view. Moreover, their purposes differ dramatically and their intended audiences differ as well. A film by an independent artist like John Sayles, for instance, has much more modest ambitions for audience than most commercial motion pictures—as a result, it arguably has more freedom to explore nontraditional viewpoints and themes.[125] Despite their notable differences, these texts illuminate some of the roles contemporary American artists frequently perform. Sometimes viewed as gadflies who question conventional wisdom and prevailing assumptions, artists often see it as their responsibility to oppose cultural consensus, to disrupt and to debunk. Concurrently, artists (usually those who are commercially successful) are also regularly noted for contributing to clichéd, simplified understandings of complicated subjects, perhaps especially historical subjects. "It is likely that from the time artists began to use, portray, or celebrate historical subjects," observes C. Vann Woodward, "their freedom to invent, to imagine, and to alter as against their obligations to accuracy, to fact, and to 'truth' has been debated. Were artists makers of myth, or were they seekers of truth? Were they to tell it like it should have been or like it really had been?"[126] These Black Sox scandal narratives obviously engage such questions.

Perhaps the most gadfly-like, Brendan Boyd takes pleasure from inverting traditional perspectives on the Black Sox scandal. In *Blue Ruin,* it is the gamblers, not the players, who are on center stage, and the Big Fix is an antiheroic accomplishment as opposed to a collective tragedy. In this way Boyd reconstructs the past against the grain of popular memory. Not quite gadflies, Harry Stein and John Sayles nevertheless demythologize and historicize the Black Sox scandal and eschew nostalgia for a sentimentalized past that never was. Although I doubt they intended to seek the "truth" of the matter, they do counterbalance more traditionally popular and romantic versions of the Black Sox scandal. Eric Rolfe Greenberg, by way of transforming Christy Mathewson of the New York Giants into a tragic Christ-like figure, represents that Black Sox scandal more conventionally than either Stein or Sayles and couches his interpretation of the scandal in moral terms. *The Celebrant* uses history to martyr Mathewson and it occupies the narrow space between iconoclasm and idyll. Finally, W. P. Kinsella, Barry Levinson, and Phil Alden Robinson all effectively further mythologize and sanitize Joe Jackson and come close to whitewashing the Black Sox scandal out of existence. They all reclaim the past and make it new and improved.

"If baseball is a Narrative," comments the baseball commissioner A. Bartlett Giamatti, "it is like others—a work of imagination whose deeper structures and patterns of repetition force a tale, oft-told, to fresh and hitherto-unforeseen meaning."[127] That is what is at stake in the Black Sox scandal narratives examined here: hitherto-unforeseen cultural meaning. Though the narratives discussed here more or less share the view that the implicated ballplayers were pawns of the powerful and sacrificed for the benefit of the game (and by implication the nation), they also provide vastly different understandings of the American past. Read within the context of baseball in the eighties—specifically, the bitter fifty-day Major League Baseball strike of 1981 (which led to the cancellation of 713 games) and the owner collusion scandals later in the decade—it would be difficult for readers to ignore the reappraisal of baseball's labor relations that *Shoeless Joe* and *Hoopla* suggest.[128] Just as important, however, is that these versions of the past accentuate and perhaps invert the didactic quality of the traditional morality play associated with the scandal, which *The Celebrant* plays upon to a fevered pitch. By contrasting these apparently conflicting versions of the past we occupy the troubling position of taking sides, of ascribing responsibility for the scandal. We fall into the trap of viewing the scandal in terms of moral extremes rather than acknowledging the complicity, guilt, and responsibility of the team magnates, the judicial system that acquitted the implicated players, the media that sensationalized the story, and the conspirators. If nothing else, these narratives complicate simplistic black-and-white conceptions of history, social relations, and their own moment of creation.

Coda: Say It Ain't So, Pete

Perhaps every generation has its own Black Sox scandal. During the eighties (and into the nineties), no sports scandal received as much attention or caused as much debate and historical reflection as the Pete Rose betting affair. A traumatic episode in baseball history, it further refreshed Black Sox scandal memories; and like the Black Sox scandal, it has doggedly endured.

Born and raised in Cincinnati and an integral cog in the famous Cincinnati Big Red Machine, which won four National League pennants and two World Series during the seventies, Pete Rose played baseball with passion and intensity. He ran to first base on walks and slid into bases head first. He stretched singles into doubles and by example challenged his teammates to do likewise. His nickname, Charlie Hustle, was intended to be derisive, but Rose embraced it. According to *Sports Illustrated*'s Ron Fimrite, "He seemed to have come from an earlier time when professionals always played hard, and out of joy, not greed."[129] Appearances, however, can be deceptive. George Will describes Rose as "a man utterly defined by his vocation—perhaps too much so. The melancholy example of Rose shows that people with particularly narrow tunnel vision have no peripheral vision for adult responsibilities."[130] Portrayed by the media as the quintessential self-made man, Rose was named Player of the Decade in the seventies, when he collected more hits and scored more runs than anyone else in the Major Leagues. Despite his numerous accomplishments and records, his single most impressive deed still lay in front of him.

In 1984, Rose returned to the Reds as a player-manager after stints with the Philadelphia Phillies and the Montreal Expos. The following season, on September 11, before a hometown crowd at Riverfront Stadium, Rose stroked a first-inning single to left center. It was his 4,192 Major League career hit and it broke Ty Cobb's record that had stood since 1928. It was a monumental feat and a testament to his consistency, endurance, and desire. Reds fans cheered him for seven minutes. Rose cried on first base. Following the game Rose said, "I'm not smart enough to really have the words to describe my feelings."[131] When he finished his playing career the next year, he had collected more hits, played in more games, been to bat more times, and had more two-hundred-hit seasons than anyone in Major League history. In all, he set thirty-four Major League and National League records. "But it wasn't so much the record-busting that made Rose such an appealing national icon," remarks Fimrite, "it was the sheer gusto with which he played the game, the belly-sliding, glove-banging intensity he brought to the ballpark every day."[132]

Having retired as a player, Rose continued to manage the Reds. Early in 1988, in a game against the New York Mets, Rose twice shoved Dave Pallone, the home plate umpire, during an argument over a close play. Pallone tossed Rose from the game and Reds fans bombarded the field with debris for fifteen minutes. For his own safety, Pallone was forced to leave the game. The next day A. Bartlett Giamatti, then president of the National League, suspended Rose for thirty days and fined him $10,000. It was the most severe penalty for an on-field transgression in baseball history.

When gambling allegations hounded Rose in the winter and spring of 1989, he quickly became an object of national ridicule. For many, the name Charlie Hustle took on new meaning. The sports columnist Thomas Boswell asked, "Whoever dreamed that Pete Rose, who's given us such childish pleasure, would now give us such deeply adult pain?"[133] After a lengthy—and, some have said, inconclusive and flawed—investigation, first-year baseball commissioner Giamatti was convinced that Rose had bet on baseball and thus had damaged the integrity of the game.[134] "Certainly Rose may have bet on baseball. His lawyers are slick and his denial skill is most ornate," notes Roger Kahn, one of Rose's biographers. "It is impossible, of course, to prove the negative, that Rose did not bet [on] baseball, but it seems important here for both sides to go beyond assurances and pleas of 'trust me.'"[135] (An indication of things to come occurred on August 11 when Giamatti turned down a request to reinstate Joe Jackson, explaining that he did not "wish to play God with history.")[136]

Late in the season Rose accepted Giamatti's lifetime suspension from baseball—though the investigation did not formally find that Rose had bet on the game—with the right to apply for reinstatement in a year. Said Giamatti:

> The banishment for life of Pete Rose from baseball is the sad end of a sorry episode. One of the game's greatest players has engaged in a variety of acts which have stained the game and he must now live with the consequences of

> those acts. It will come as no surprise that like any institution composed of human beings, this institution will not always fulfill its highest aspirations. I know of no earthly institution that does. But this one, because it is so much a part of our history as a people, and because it has such a purchase on our national soul, has an obligation to the people for whom it's played.[137]

If Rose had always been considered coarse by some standards, his respect for the game had never before been doubted. Now he was revealed to be something less than honorable. Eight days later the fifty-one-year-old Giamatti died of a heart attack, which many argued was partially the result of the strain from the Rose controversy. Rose's fate was sealed. "Pete Rose hardly seemed the stuff of Aristotelian poetics," Ron Fimrite observes. "Ordinary in appearance and demeanor, sometimes crude, occasionally even vulgar, he certainly didn't reflect the Greek ideal of the Great Man. But through a combination of unabashed enthusiasm, sly intelligence and unshakable self-confidence, he did, in fact, achieve a form of greatness. And he had within him the Aristotelian 'fatal flaw' that led inevitably to his tragic fall."[138]

Looking back, it is difficult to ignore the ways in which the past was being repeated during this episode. Predictably, some commentators noted connections between the Rose scandal and the Black Sox scandal. "Rose was the 14th player, coach, or team owner suspended for gambling-related offenses in the history of the big leagues," reported Charles Leerhsen of *Newsweek*, "but this was the most significant infraction since the Black Sox scandal of 1919."[139] *Newsweek* also featured a photograph of Rose next to one of Joe Jackson, which had the caption: "Say it ain't so (again)."[140]

More so than any of the books or films examined in this chapter, the Rose affair rekindled Black Sox scandal memories and reminded people (as if they needed it) that baseball was far from an idyllic, escapist diversion from reality. "Seventy years ago," observed Thomas Boswell, "fans echoed the child who begged Shoeless Joe to 'Say it ain't so, Joe.' Now, Charlie Hustle says it ain't so; says he never bet on baseball or his Reds."[141] The sports columnist Mike Lupica put it succinctly: "He spent his whole life trying to be Ty Cobb and ended up as 'Shoeless' Joe Jackson."[142] Much like Jackson, with whom he probably will be forever linked, Rose is notable for his lack of refinement, on-the-field excellence, and lack of judgment away from the diamond. Yet in important ways, as national heroes and icons, Jackson and Rose signify fundamentally different values. Jackson is supposed to have been the naive, rustic, supremely talented rube: The Natural. Conventional wisdom has it that Rose was less talented, but remarkably hard working and tenacious, the personification of the self-made man: The Unnatural. No matter, both were confronted by a powerful establishment intent on defending its integrity. And thus despite a lack of evidence that conclusively revealed wrongdoing, Rose's fate was predictable.

In the years since Pete Rose's banishment, many sportswriters and fans have debated whether Rose deserves to be inducted into the Baseball Hall of Fame.[143] It is an issue that does not interest me. As the historian Elliott J. Gorn puts it, the "question is silly. It assumes that baseball was once pure, that Rose sullied it, that he must be made an example to others."[144] What does interest me, however, are the ways the Rose affair further reactivated cultural and personal memories of Joe Jackson and the Black Sox scandal.[145] A few examples illuminate the power of the Rose case to evoke the past.

The day after Rose's banishment, *USA Today* carried an editorial cartoon of Rose cleaning out a locker in which his baseball spikes are beside Joe Jackson's.[146] Four months later, in late December, the Associated Press selected the Pete Rose betting episode, which Hal Bock described as "the sport's most sordid affair since the 1919 Black Sox scandal," as the top sports story of the decade.[147] In August 1990, Wilfrid Sheed wrote an essay entitled "One Man Out . . . Too Long." In it, he contended that after seventy years the time had come to admit Joe Jackson to the Baseball Hall of Fame. Sheed argued that "it must have come as just one more vexation for this sorely tried man to find himself blackballed from an institution that didn't even exist when he was playing. Unlike Pete Rose, who is currently down on his knees trying to wriggle into the Hall, Jackson didn't even know that there was any such place to qualify for." For Sheed, it was unimportant that Jackson probably accepted money to throw the series: "Leaving him out of the Hall of Fame is a bit like omitting the brontosaurus from the Museum of Natural History—it hurts us more than it hurts him by now, and it leaves an awful hole in the historical record."[148] In response to Sheed's plea, Ira Berkow of the *New York Times* penned a column entitled "The Hall, Rose, and Shoeless Joe." Berkow argued that Rose's transgressions did not affect his play and thus should have no bearing on his Hall of Fame status. As for Jackson, "despite Sheed's engaging argument and the sentimental movie 'Field of Dreams,' relating to Jackson's ghost returning from that clubhouse in the sky," Berkow insisted that he does not belong in Cooperstown. "The argument here is that the Hall of Fame should be reserved for those who never fixed or attempted to fix a game. Any of the other business about role models off the field is just so much junk and banality."[149]

As one might expect, those representing Major League Baseball management and labor view the Rose matter differently, yet both have linked it to the Black Sox scandal. Since becoming baseball commissioner in 1992, Allan "Bud" Selig has made it clear that he has no intention of reinstating Pete Rose to the game's good graces. At the same time, Selig notes: "In Shoeless Joe's case, there's so much history that needs to be looked at, and that's what we're trying to do, to understand why Judge Landis did what he did. He deserves a look."[150] Marvin Miller, the former executive director of the Major League Baseball Players Association, writes, "Giamatti's action against Rose was a classic case of the punishment not fitting the crime. The Black Sox players who allegedly threw games for money in 1919—considered baseball's worst offense—received the stiffest penalty possible, banishment from the game for life. Rose, of course, was not even charged with such an offense or anything resembling it."[151] As always, perspective and politics contribute to the way in which meaning is made.

Regardless of whether Rose and Jackson were guilty of the offenses they were accused of, whether they were treated unfairly, whether they are seen as martyrs or pariahs, they have come to signify one another.[152] Separated by more than half a century, Rose and Jackson form a link between one era of profligacy and disappointment and another. Eight months after Pete Rose's banishment, Thomas Boswell remarked: "Shoeless Joe Jackson refused to rat on his Black Sox buddies seventy years ago. And they're still writing books and making movies with him as a central character. If Rose has the misfortune to go to jail [he eventually served five months after pleading guilty to federal tax evasion charges], even if it's only for a fraction of the maximum six-year term that he might face, the story of Charlie Hustle will make 'Say it ain't so, Joe' seem like small potatoes in the gallery of American pop-culture pathos."[153] Perhaps, but I doubt it. Time and future storytellers will tell. More important, Boswell's point demonstrates that the issues Jackson and Rose vividly represented in the eighties—the integrity of American sport, labor-management relations, and relations between heroes and their fans—are ongoing, culturally illuminating concerns.

6

Dreaming and Scheming: The Black Sox Scandal at the End of the Twentieth Century

When Katie Jackson, Joe Jackson's widow, died in 1959 she left her estate to the American Heart Association and the American Cancer Society. Years later, after the two charities discovered the value of Joe Jackson's signature—one autograph was sold in 1991 for over $23,000 and some sports memorabilia collectors thought it was worth more—they argued that Joe's will was Katie's personal property and now it belonged to them.[1] In 1993, frustrated by their inability to procure the document, the two charities sued Judge Diane Smock of the Greenville County Probate Court and the county itself to obtain it. The case was in litigation for four years. This was but one of the many Black Sox references to appear on the American cultural landscape since the Pete Rose affair. If anything, interest in the scandal and its participants, especially Joe Jackson, was renewed by Rose's suspension and the novels and films examined in the previous chapter. Even a partial list of the ways in which the Black Sox scandal has been retold and has resurfaced in recent years is impressive.

During the decade, three books about Joe Jackson were published, as were biographies of Buck Weaver and Kenesaw Mountain Landis.[2] Several baseball histories and encyclopedias devoted significant attention to the scandal.[3] Three dramas about the 1919 World Series scandal were staged: Thomas Perry's one-man play *Shoeless Joe,* Brian Cimmet's musical *Black Sox,* and Louis R. Hegeman's *The Trial of Buck Weaver and Shoeless Joe Jackson.*[4] Since 1992, a few hundred Jackson aficionados have been receiving the *Shoeless Joe Jackson Times,* a newsletter about the ballplayer.[5] In 1993, San Francisco's Court of Historical Review ruled that Joe Jackson ought to be reinstated by Major League Baseball and thus should be eligible for the Baseball Hall of Fame.[6] Late that summer, after Bo Jackson hit a home run to clinch the American League Western Division title for the White Sox, Joey Reaves of the *Chicago Tribune* wrote: "For now, the '93 Sox are more than division champions. They are absolution. They are vindication for baseball's greatest sin—the infamous Black Sox scandal."[7] Soon thereafter, a statistician used a complex analysis to argue that Joe Jackson did not throw the 1919 World Series.[8]

The nineties also witnessed momentum in amnesty movements for some Black Sox players: one such movement collected nearly sixty thousand petition signatures on behalf of Joe Jackson.[9] More recently, the baseball legends Ted Williams and Bob Feller have lobbied for Jackson's admission to the Baseball Hall of Fame.[10] Their efforts have inspired others to reconsider the issue. In January 1998, National Public Radio's "All Things Considered" aired a segment on Jackson that featured Eliot Asinof and former baseball commissioner Bowie Kuhn. Despite efforts to end Jackson's ban, in July 1999 a Gallop poll found that "only 38 percent of Americans—and 44 percent of baseball fans—say Jackson merits induction into the Hall of Fame."[11] That such a poll was even taken indicates the scandal's persistence.

One reason is that the Big Fix is financially profitable. Black Sox scandal products are common. A few years ago, one of the best-selling items in the Chicago Historical Society's souvenir shop was a T-shirt with the inscription "Say it ain't so, Joe."[12] One of many Black Sox Web sites, Shoeless Joe Jackson's Virtual Hall of Fame (http://www.blackbesty.com) includes collectibles such as a Jackson statue, a Jackson prepaid phone card, and a CD that features the song "Shoeless Joe Jackson."[13] Amazon.com recently listed the comic book *Shoeless Joe and the Black Sox Scandal* and a set of Black Sox baseball cards. At the other end of the spectrum is a remarkable collection of baseball memorabilia Sotheby's sold in September 1999; it included baseballs autographed by the unlucky eight that sold for almost $53,000.[14] Jackson's name has even been used prominently in a Nike TV commercial. Aired during the 1995 All-Star Game, the ad concluded with Don Mattingly of the New York Yankees saying, "If Shoeless Joe Jackson were playing today, he'd have a shoe commercial."[15] Undoubtedly.

The catalogue above confirms that the Black Sox scandal, a seemingly indefatigable cultural narrative, continues to be remembered, retold, and resold. This final chapter examines three ways the Big Fix was put to use and represented at the end of the twentieth century. It scrutinizes the ongoing phenomenon of mass pilgrimage to Dyersville, Iowa, where thousands of tourists from all over the world visit the ballfield depicted in the movie *Field of Dreams* (1989); locates ways in which the Black Sox scandal was evoked over the course of the disastrous 1994–95 Major League Baseball strike; and critiques Ken Burns's treatment of the World Series scandal in his acclaimed television documentary *Baseball* (1994).

Since It Was Built, People Have Come

In Dyersville, Iowa, a generally nondescript farm community of 3,800 residents near Dubuque, the Black Sox scandal is alive like nowhere else. This is not to suggest that other communities do not have some purchase on the scandal. They do. In Chicago, the game-fixing scandal is well known, partly because the White Sox have not won the World Series since, and partly because memories of Buck Weaver persist. In Cooperstown, although Joe Jackson is persona non grata within the Hall of Fame, it is difficult to walk along Main Street without encountering Black Sox photographs, postcards, replica trading cards, caps, and jerseys. Even a Cooperstown restaurant—Shoeless Joe's Ballpark Cafe—pays homage. In Greenville, South Carolina, Jackson's hometown and final resting place, people have long since forgiven but not forgotten their native son.[16] The town dedicated Shoeless Joe Jackson Memorial Park in 1995, and part of a highway in Greenville has been designated the "Shoeless Joe" Jackson Memorial Parkway.[17] The state is also home to the Shoeless Joe Jackson Society.[18] No doubt responding to the will of the people, South Carolina politicians Sen. Strom Thurmond and Rep. Jim DeMint have actively campaigned to make Jackson eligible for the Baseball Hall of Fame.[19]

Yet it is in Dyersville—where an estimated fifty thousand tourists a year visit the ballfield where *Field of Dreams* was filmed—that the Black Sox scandal arguably takes its most vivid and palpable contemporary form.[20] For some, the ballfield is a fitting monument to the Black Sox.There is no denying that historical imaginations sometimes work in mysterious ways. Since few people are old enough to remember the scandal, all of its participants are dead, and the ballpark where the Black Sox played has been razed, perhaps there is no good reason why an improbable ballfield in Iowa should not powerfully evoke the Black Sox scandal and help maintain its memory. Before that could happen, however, the Field of Dreams needed to be built and preserved.[21]

The Field of Dreams story begins with the director Phil Alden Robinson's criteria for locations: "The place couldn't be a dairy farm, the farmhouse had to be isolated from a highway and it had to be surrounded on three sides by corn."[22] Universal Studios worked with the Iowa Film Office and commissioned Sue Reidel, a member of the Dubuque Chamber of Commerce Film Bureau, to research possible movie sites.[23] Eventually, the filmmakers decided to shoot their motion picture on land that straddles two properties, one owned by Don Lansing and the other by Al Ameskamp and Rita Ameskamp. Lansing owns the farmhouse depicted in the movie and most of the land used for the ballfield. The Ameskamps' own the land used for left and center field. The filmmakers apparently liked "that a small stream ran through the property, that the farmhouse was set on a rise and would photograph well and that the layout of the land enabled a diamond to be built so that the sun would set over the outfield."[24] In the summer of 1988, the studio made some minor modifications to Lansing's house (such as adding some windows and a porch swing and extending the front porch) and, in just three days, built an impressive baseball diamond. The *Des Moines Register* reported that its construction "was an awesome undertaking. Four feet of dirt was moved from right field to left field to level it. Seven semi-truck-loads of sod were laid by baseball players from three Dubuque high schools."[25] Furthermore, because of a terrible drought that summer, the filmmakers dammed a nearby creek and irrigated the fields so that the corn could grow. At the time, one of the film's producers said, "My corn is only 2 feet tall. I need it to be 4 feet tall or America won't believe it is corn."[26] After sixteen weeks of filming, the production crew departed in August and left behind its handiwork.

The following spring, the Ameskamps plowed under their portion of the ballfield to plant corn. "I'm a farmer," Al Ameskamp said. "A cornfield is a cornfield."[27] Lansing, on the other hand, decided to maintain his portion: "I enjoyed having the movie made here," Lansing explained. "It seemed a shame to destroy all that hard work. Then people started coming, and I could see what it meant to them. One fellow said that it should be made a national park for dreamers. I decided to leave it alone."[28] At the same time, by registering the ballfield as "unused" land in the federal Conservation Reserve Program, Lansing's decision was (initially) modestly remunerative.[29] Still, it is unlikely that Lansing, the Ameskamps, or anyone else could have imagined the kinds of responses the ballfield would elicit.

Not long after the movie was released in May 1989, W. P. Kinsella's often-quoted refrain, "If you build it, he will come," was realized. People began visiting the field, many with what seemed like stardust in their eyes. As early as mid-June, hundreds of tourists had already been to the site. Some came because they were deeply moved by the film's message that redemption and reconciliation are possible, others due to a vague sense of pastoral nostalgia. Others were Kevin Costner fans who wanted to see one of his movie locations. But more than a few could not explain why they had made the journey to Dyersville.[30] Asked why he thought people were attracted to the ballfield, Lansing replied, "They think the scenery is beautiful, and they liked the story too."[31] According to one estimate, by the end of the year ten thousand visitors had been to the Field of Dreams. The following spring, the

Ameskamps decided "to replant grass seed and to restore left [and center] field to its movie condition with a fresh planting of corn beyond it."[32] Within the year, Lansing and the Ameskamps had rival concession/souvenir stands at the site, though admission to the field remained (and remains) free. In the years since, hundreds of thousands of people from all over the world have visited the Field of Dreams in what is frequently described as a life-imitating-art phenomenon.

"The significance of Don Lansing's actions to preserve the baseball diamond cannot be overstated," writes the anthropologist Charles Fruehling Springwood in *Cooperstown to Dyersville: A Geography of Baseball Nostalgia* (1996), a superb ethnography of the Baseball Hall of Fame and the Field of Dreams.[33] As Springwood and others have pointed out, trips to Dyersville "have largely been cast in terms of pilgrimages; and, in fact, this baseball field has been transformed in the imagination of many of the game's fans into a baseball mecca."[34] Moreover, Springwood is correct that there "is a veritable polyphony of experiences and representations of experience surrounding the Field of Dreams that cannot be fully captured in prose" and that the ballfield is "a site of myth, fantasy, religion, enchantment, magic, redemption, and dream-seeking."[35] But like the ballfield in the movie, it has also become (what some critics have decried as) a capitalist utopia.[36] Although Lansing and the Ameskamps "do not talk about their finances, others in town believe that the donation boxes more than cover the estimated $2,000 a year in revenue the farmers lost by taking five acres of land out of production." In addition, the long-term economic impact of the Field of Dreams is much greater than the $5 million Universal Studios spent in Dyersville to make the movie, for tourists pump an estimated $1.6 million per year into the local economy.[37]

Used in the novel *Shoeless Joe* and in *Field of Dreams* as a vehicle to reunite and reconcile Ray Kinsella with his deceased father, the Black Sox scandal has a complex and, to many visitors, obscure relationship with the Field of Dreams. On one level, the ballfield obviously lacks historical depth and "authenticity." Joe Jackson never came to Iowa, except in Kinsella's imagination. In fact, Kinsella himself has said, "I always wonder about these people [who visit Dyersville]. There are no gods. There is no magic."[38] He might have added that there is a dearth of history at the site, too. For the Field of Dreams is, quite literally, a Hollywood creation, one that provides visitors with "a utopian space in which to dream, reminisce, and wax nostalgic."[39] One need not be aware of the Hollywood-spun connection between the ballfield and the game-fixing scandal to enjoy the site. When asked, however, most Field of Dreams visitors sympathize with Jackson and the rest of the banished White Sox. Springwood notes that most tourists concede that "the players may actually have been involved in some attempt to throw the series," but they also believe that the implicated men "were generally naive and at the mercy of the gamblers' corporate financial interests. Therefore, most people feel that they were truly innocent heroes, perhaps too harshly condemned by history, and that Shoeless Joe, in particular, deserves to be inducted into the Hall of Fame."[40] In other words, as far as the Black Sox scandal is concerned, most visitors endorse the viewpoint expressed in *Shoeless Joe* and *Field of Dreams:* namely, that the time has come to extend the ballplayers compassion, forgiveness, and redemption.[41] Possibly mesmerized by the ballfield's beauty, perhaps culturally predisposed to be sensitive to the plight of fallen baseball heroes in the wake of the Pete Rose betting affair, most people who visit the Field of Dreams are willing to pardon the Black Sox. Contributing to the atmosphere are the Ghost Players, a local group comprised of semiprofessional and former college ballplayers who regularly don 1919 woolen White Sox–style uniforms and entertain tourists by playing catch and jockeying with one another.[42] Nicknamed the Harlem Globetrotters of Baseball, the Ghost Players enliven the Field of Dreams experience for visitors. Like Civil War reenactors who try to recapture the immediacy of long-ago fought battles, the Ghost Players help constitute the Field of Dreams as a three-dimensional, interactive, living monument to Joe Jackson and his Black Sox teammates.

The Great Strike of 1994

In a seemingly different social universe, far from the serenity of Dyersville, Major League Baseball was on the verge of a disaster in the early nineties, even though (and to some extent because) it was an extraordinarily lucrative industry. Despite the self-destructive shortsightedness of those who ran the game, the eighties had been tremendously profitable. By the end of the decade over fifty million fans annually attended Major League games, baseball's gross revenues were more than $1 billion a year, and the average player's salary had risen to almost $600,000 a season.[43] The historian Benjamin G. Rader notes that when Peter Ueberroth became baseball's commissioner in 1984, "twenty-one of the twenty-six teams claimed to be losing money; four years later, when he left, all were making money."[44] Nevertheless, in February 1991, Commissioner Fay Vincent presciently observed: "Baseball is poised for a catastrophe and it might not be far off."[45] Forced by the owners to resign his post less than two years later, in large part, writes the essayist Roger Angell, because he exhibited "some sense of obligation to the fans and to the game itself," Vincent was powerless to stave off the debacle he envisioned.[46] Some described the strike of 1994–95 as the lowest moment in professional baseball's long history. Less than a week after the 1994 season had been canceled, the *Washington Post*'s Mark Maske offered the following analysis:

> An industry that had been projecting $1.8 billion in revenues in an uninterrupted season this year—and in which the average player's salary has soared to nearly $1.2 million per season—will not stage its crown jewel event, the World Series, for the first time in 90 years because management and labor cannot agree to a compensation system. Such squabbles are nothing new to baseball. This is the game's eighth work stoppage in 23 years, and labor-relations spats as far back as the 1800s have been chronicled. But never before did a shutdown do this kind of damage. The great strike of 1994 wiped out the final 52 days and 669 games of what had been shaping up as one of the most invigorating seasons in memory. Above all, it claimed the World Series as one of its victims. If the game hasn't reached its nadir, most people agree that it's at its lowest point since the "Black Sox" game-fixing scandal of 1919.[47]

A tumultuous event that cast a pall over the remainder of the summer (and much of the ensuing spring) for many fans, the baseball strike of 1994 is an ugly chapter in the game's history. As such, commentators at the time frequently used the Black Sox scandal as a point of historical reference and comparison. Although my focus here is on the ways in which the baseball strike reactivated and reinvigorated memories of the Black Sox scandal, it is important to review briefly the strike itself.

Like the Big Fix, the 1994 baseball strike illustrates the complexity of causation. Perhaps the economist Paul D. Staudohar is right and the "first shot leading to the 1994–95 strike was the decision of the owners in December 1992, a year before the four-year collective bargaining agreement expired, to reopen negotiations on salaries and the free agency system."[48] Or perhaps the strike seeds were sown three months before its start when Vincent was forced to resign. Maybe the strike can be traced back to when the owners hired Richard Ravitch, the former New York City transit chief who admitted to having "been characterized as a union buster," to direct the Player Relations Committee, which negotiates with representatives from the Major League Baseball Players Association.[49] It is possible, of course, to locate the strike's origins in earlier management-labor conflicts. By 1994, a baseball work stoppage was nothing new: since 1972, there had been seven of them (either player strikes or owner lockouts)—each one after a collective bargaining agreement had expired. Likewise, the issues that led to the

1994 strike were familiar. Months before the impasse, the owners unanimously had decided to implement a revenue-sharing plan—that is, the super-wealthy, big-market teams in cities like New York, Chicago, and Los Angeles would share a portion of their revenue with small-market teams such as Seattle, Pittsburgh, and Milwaukee—but only if the players would accept a salary cap. Not surprisingly, the players were not interested. The players consistently maintained that they had been dragged into a debate the owners should have been having among themselves. In the face of an expired agreement and intractable owners, the players set their strike date for August 12.

Just over a month later, after several rounds of ineffective and bitter negotiations with union representatives, the owners voted (26-2) to cancel the remainder of the season, the playoffs, and the World Series.[50] "Now baseball's longest unbroken streak has ended," Shirley Povich of the *Washington Post* reflected after the decision was announced. "It is reckoned not in terms of hits or homers or games, but in years. It can be accurately described in baseball's jargon as 89–for-89." A sportswriter who had begun his career in the twenties, Povich continued: "For those 89 years the continuity of the World Series was a given in the American character, rooted in the love of the game from generation to generation. But it's a wipeout now that the club owners and the athletes refused to terminate their choke hold on the game."[51] The cancellation of the 1994 World Series signified a dramatic rupture, a breach that, in the words of the sportswriter Murray Chass, sent "the game staggering into the great unknown."[52] The World Series—a national ritual that had survived world wars, a gambling scandal, the depression, and a natural disaster (the earthquake of 1989)—was canceled because of an inability to negotiate and compromise. Blinded by bitter enmity and deep-seated distrust, the owners and players brought baseball to a standstill.

A similar sense of antipathy and suspicion plagued the Chicago White Sox in 1919 and contributed to the Black Sox scandal, but commentators did not mention that particular similarity between the baseball strike and the Big Fix. Instead, they made other connections. For the columnist Walter Shapiro, the strike simultaneously evoked baseball's (apocryphal) moment of lost innocence and accentuated the long-standing commercial character of the game: "Ever since that mythic street urchin wailed, 'Say it ain't so, Joe' to Shoeless Joe Jackson after he confessed that he was involved in fixing the 1919 World Series, generations of sad-eyed children have been forced to learn that baseball can be a cruel business."[53] The baseball strike revivified that lesson for many adults, too. A week and a half into the strike, while considering the possibility that the season and the World Series could be canceled, the sportswriter Mike Lupica argued that if that scenario occurred, "it will be the worst scandal in baseball since the Black Sox. This time, it will look as if they all dumped the whole sport."[54] Roughly three weeks later, as the work stoppage continued and the cancellation of the World Series seemed imminent, Thomas Boswell laid responsibility for the strike squarely on the owners' shoulders. "Lord, what fools these owners be," lamented the *Washington Post* columnist. "It was all for nothing. In the end, this was the work stoppage that had nothing to do with the players! What an incredible, comical, disgusting debacle the game's numbskull bosses have put us through this time." Noting that the ballplayers were basically bystanders during the conflict, Boswell further editorialized:

> A month ago, at the start of this foolishness, union leader Don Fehr said it all: "It strikes me as a terrible shame that, because the large-market and the small-market owners can't agree on how to sort out baseball's $1.8 billion in revenue among themselves, that they have to force the players to strike. . . . Make no mistake. This is primarily a dispute between the owners."
>
> At least the nine Black Sox who fixed the 1919 World Series had excuses. As a group, they were poor, exploited and about as educated as a heap of rocks. What about the nine multimillionaire owners who ruined the 1994 season? And may ruin the 1994 World Series. What excuse do you guys have?[55]

Despite his uncharacteristic historical gaffe—there were eight Black Sox—Boswell, more so than anyone else, made explicit the association between the Black Sox scandal and the 1994 baseball strike. Sensitive to the plight of the disgraced Black Sox, Boswell was obviously contemptuous of the owners, whose intramural conflict was forced on the ballplayers (and the public). Six days later, on September 14, after Allan "Bud" Selig, the acting baseball commissioner and owner of the Milwaukee Brewers, announced that the owners had voted to cancel the World Series, Boswell, always a keen baseball moralist, wrote: "Now, 1919 and 1994 will always be linked in baseball infamy. In '19, nine poor men fixed the World Series for a few thousand dollars. In '94, 700 rich players and 28 multi-millionaire owners killed the World Series—a kind of innocent bystander—in their barroom brawl over a billion-dollar pot. What may prove doubly tragic, in due time, is that the men of '94 have not yet grasped that they sold out baseball—and their country's good faith—every bit as much as the banished and disgraced Black Sox. Perhaps more."[56] Surveying the damage the baseball strike wreaked, Boswell argued that all of its principals—Selig, Ravitch, Jerry Reinsdorf (owner of the Chicago White Sox and one of the most hawkish owners), and Fehr—would likely "be seen as American traitors" for many years to come and he recommended that they "ask old-timers what it was like to be one of the Black Sox." Taking no prisoners, Boswell declared that everyone involved in the affair was guilty:

> Everybody in baseball has welched on the implicit social contract between pro sports and its fans. Oh, you didn't know about that contract? It says: "We pay you 10 times too much. We cheer you. We repeat your legend for generations. In return, you don't do basic damage to the game itself. Or else."
>
> That's the contract Pete Rose broke. And it's the contract that every player and owner has now violated. They deserve everything they're gonna get.[57]

Despite his obvious disappointment, frustration, and anger with the strike and the men who brought it about, Boswell did not endow baseball with more social significance than it warranted. His rant was spiced with some perspective:

> Baseball itself is not important. A country can do without a game. However, this strike is important because it represents so much that's ugly in our society. The public knows this. People are not trivially, heatedly mad. They're deeply, coldly angry at baseball. Rich, vain men with special interests have bickered away the tradition of the World Series. That's unconscionable.
>
> Intoxicated by their wealth and fame, owners and players believe the rich landscape they have inherited from their forebears belongs entirely to them. They act like they're entitled to despoil it if they wish.[58]

For Boswell, the 1994 strike, like the Black Sox scandal seventy-five years before it, was a social drama in which some particularly objectionable contemporary cultural values—arrogance, ignorance, narcissism, greed, pomposity, and an appalling disregard for others—were on public display. Like the Black Sox scandal, the strike was an occasion for Americans to reevaluate and think out loud about themselves and their values as well as about baseball's status as a privileged and venerable social institution. If it had not done so already, baseball was on the verge of abdicating its mantle as the national pastime. Badly battered, baseball in the summer of 1994 appeared to be plummeting toward the abyss of irrelevance. And like the Black Sox scandal—which lasted for almost a year—the strike dragged on, its end nowhere in sight.

Infotainment: Ken Burns's *Baseball*

By mid-September 1994, when the Major League pennant races should have been taking place, many fans turned their attention to *Baseball,* a nine-episode, 18.5-hour documentary history by Ken Burns. An expansive, self-consciously comprehensive narrative, *Baseball* took over four years and $7 million to make and was eagerly anticipated.[59] As it turned out, the timing of its broadcast was both fortuitous and incongruous. For many, *Baseball* was an agreeable substitute for the real game. A few commentators noted that Burns was probably the only beneficiary of the strike because his film was the only game in town. Yet its epic grandeur—or what some described as grandiloquence and pretentiousness—struck some critics as nostalgic and remarkably hollow (even laughable), especially considering the cancellation of the series. As one reviewer quipped, "It's hard to enjoy a love song after you've been jilted."[60] Still, since baseball fans had been jilted many times since 1972, *Baseball* no doubt provided some viewers with a bittersweet sense of comfort.

Burns came to the project as unquestionably the most successful documentary filmmaker in the United States. The son of a cultural anthropologist, Burns grew up in Ann Arbor, Michigan, and attended Hampshire College, where he studied with the photographers Jerome Liebling and Elaine Mayes. In 1975, Burns and two friends formed a film company, Florentine Films.[61] His first major documentary, *The Brooklyn Bridge* (1982), was based on David McCullough's book *The Great Bridge* (1972) and took four years to produce. Nominated for an Academy Award, *The Brooklyn Bridge,* Burns says, was an attempt to create "a new kind of visual history": "I was trying to forge a new history, to show that the visual form was developing a grammar and syntax that could express information as complex as that expressed by literature."[62] During the eighties, Burns honed his distinctive style (which combines numerous techniques, such as narration, quotation, "rephotographing," and interviews) and produced wide-ranging, critically acclaimed documentaries: *The Shakers: Hands to Work, Hearts to God* (1985), *The Statue of Liberty* (1985), *Huey Long* (1986), *Thomas Hart Benton* (1989), *The Congress* (1989), and, most notably, *The Civil War* (1990). An eleven-hour, five-episode series, *The Civil War* was first broadcast on PBS in September 1990 and became the highest-rated show in the history of public television, drawing an audience of thirty-nine million people.[63] Remarkably popular with the public and critics, it earned Burns widespread respect and thrust him into the national limelight. "More than anyone before him," argues the critic Gary Edgerton, "Burns has made the historical documentary a popular and gripping form for large segments of the American viewing public. He has successfully seized the attention of the mass audience through the topics he chooses, as well as created a stylistic approach that is well suited to his subjects and his ideological outlook."[64]

Despite the conservative quality of his approach, which is almost exclusively linear and biographical, and his choice of subject matter, which seems to be drawn from a fifties American history primer, Burns is frequently described as a liberal and his perspective is considered pluralistic.

In a 1993 interview, Burns defined himself: "I'm primarily a filmmaker. That's my job. I'm an amateur historian at best, but more than anything if you wanted to find a hybridization of those two professions, then I find myself an emotional archeologist. That is to say, there is something in the process of filmmaking that I do in the excavation of these events in the past that provoke a kind of emotion and a sympathy that reminds us, for example, of why we agree against all odds as a people to cohere."[65] Reminiscent of the so-called consensus historians, Burns subscribes to a vision of the past that emphasizes the ties that bind Americans to one another.[66] "As a historian," observes David W. Blight, "Burns is a thoroughly American brand of the Whiggish persuasion. He wants to be some combination of Homer and Macaulay, perhaps Carl Sandburg with a camera."[67] Unlike Oliver Stone, a different kind of "cinematic historian" but one who also addresses important historical subjects and contributes to public thinking about the past, Burns is no conspiracy monger. On the contrary, most of his films accentuate and celebrate American exceptionalism.

An enthusiastic baseball fan, Burns decided to do a documentary on the game in 1985, the same year he began working on *The Civil War*.[68] Burns explains that he conceived of *Baseball* as a sequel to *The Civil War* and argues that the film "is an attempt to go to the emotional heart of the histories of the people that we became once that war was done."[69] Producing *Baseball* was a monumental and expensive undertaking. Burns and his colleagues "shot 32,000 feet of footage, screened 6.4 million feet of archival film, examined thousands of still photos, interviewed more than 65 subjects."[70] Burns also recruited a team of distinguished baseball historians to serve as consultants, though not all of their suggestions and corrections made it into the film.[71] Since sources of funding sometimes suggest ideological underpinnings, it is worth mentioning that *Baseball* was financed in large part by the National Endowment for the Humanities, PBS and the Corporation for Public Broadcasting, and General Motors.[72]

Baseball examines the Black Sox scandal and its immediate outcome in discrete segments at the end of its third episode. The first of these is entitled "An Awful Thing to Do," which is what Katie Jackson reportedly said when she learned that her husband had taken money from gamblers to throw the series; the second is "The Law," a reference to Kenesaw Mountain Landis. Burns explains that the first draft of the *Baseball* script "had a great deal of setup for the Black Sox scandal and a great deal of the aftermath of that scandal, but it had three or four lines pertaining to the actual World Series itself. We then found some footage, we came across some interesting stories, and we ended up writing—in the editing room—another five or six pages detailing precisely what was occurring in each of the games. We essentially quadrupled the length of the original scene by opening it up."[73] Considering the scope and stated intentions of his project—one of which was to employ baseball's history as a sociocultural mirror for the United States—Burns gives the Black Sox scandal its fair share of attention. All told, the documentary devotes approximately thirty-five minutes to the Big Fix. Yet the result of including more of the 1919 World Series itself is twofold: it minimizes the conditions that fostered the fix and it shortchanges the scandal's institutional and social significance. It is important to note that the film's representation of the scandal immediately follows a brief discussion of the ways in which World War I affected the Major Leagues and immediately precedes an examination of how Babe Ruth and his power-hitting exploits revived the game. Like the rest of the series, the Black Sox scandal segment is organized within a rigid chronological structure.

"An Awful Thing to Do" begins with a photograph of Arnold Rothstein. As the camera slowly pans the image, the often-cited passage from *The Great Gatsby* in which Nick Carraway first encounters the gambler Meyer Wolfsheim is read. Clearly unoriginal, the lead suggests how Burns envisions the scandal: one clever, opportunistic man fostered the Big Fix. Viewers are then introduced to some of the 1919 White Sox players and are made aware of the team's internal fractiousness and cliques. In addition, Charles Comiskey is portrayed as a miserly tyrant. According to Daniel Okrent, a writer and editor who appears in the segment four times,the players "were abused horribly by Charles Comiskey, who was a man of a small-mind, tight fist, and a nasty temperament. The climate was too good for it not to happen." John Sayles agrees on camera and relates an anecdote about how the White Sox players were known as the Black Sox even before the fixed World Series because Comiskey had for a time apparently refused to launder their dirty uniforms. Although Chick Gandil is charged with organizing the game-fixing and Abe Attell and "Sleepy" Bill Burns with involvement in the conspiracy, the film nonetheless demonstrates that Rothstein was behind it all.

After introducing the eight ballplayers allegedly involved in the scheme—paying special attention to Joe Jackson—the film offers a relatively detailed game-by-game account of the series. Actual game clips are accompanied by Okrent's commentary, by quotations from Hugh Fullerton (read by Studs Terkel) and Kid Gleason (read by Gregory Peck), by newspaper headlines, and by three renditions of "Take Me out to the Ball Game." The segment is further enlivened by the testimony of Gardner Stern, who was a fifteen-year-old eyewitness: "I was the most disappointed kid in the city of Chicago," says Stern, reflecting on the White Sox's final loss to the Cincinnati Reds. "I couldn't understand it, you know, this was just a terrible thing to happen. I didn't know about gambling or anything else of that kind. I was just heartbroken." Burns then notes how Comiskey conveniently ignored the game-fixing rumors and he very briefly chronicles how the scandal was exposed. The documentary credits Fullerton's investigative reporting and Ban Johnson's enmity toward Comiskey as the primary reasons the scandal finally came to light in September 1920. In a few deft sentences and scenes, Burns suggests that, despite the confessions proffered by Eddie Cicotte and Joe Jackson and the subsequent indictments issued by the Cook County grand jury, the ballplayers and gamblers evaded justice. "In the end," intones *Baseball*'s narrator, John Chancellor, "no one went to jail." Finally, "An Awful Thing to Do" concludes with Gardner Stern's appraisal of the trial. His voiced tinged with sadness, Stern reflects: "They were tried, and found innocent. A travesty, really. But it came out that Arnie Rothstein and the rest of them were crooked gamblers, and were able to persuade the boys to throw the games, even though some of them, I guess, never got a dime. And they weren't—most of the Black Sox were not crooks, they were dumb farm boys, who didn't know anything about finance or anything else."

The episode concludes with "The Law," a seven-minute segment devoted to Kenesaw Mountain Landis, "a federal judge with a reputation for willful independence equaled only by his flair for self-promotion," narrates Chancellor. Landis, whom Sayles describes on-camera as a "showboat judge," is said to have been hired by the owners to lend the game the appearance of integrity. *Baseball* accentuates this by having Landis, whose part is performed by the actor Jason Robards, proffer his famous "Regardless of the verdict of juries . . ." decree. Thus in addition to profiling baseball's first commissioner, the documentary brings closure to the Black Sox scandal. The film notes that none of the Black Sox ever played in the Majors again, and that while Joe Jackson lived another thirty years, he did not do so happily. "Had he any sense of the consequences," remarks Daniel Okrent, near the end of the segment, "there is no way he would have taken part in it. But I don't think anyone could guess that a man as basically simple as Jackson could have known, really, what it meant what he was doing." Burns then segues to Babe Ruth and the twenties.

Baseball's portrayal of the Black Sox scandal is certainly engaging. It skillfully synthesizes photographs, film clips, interviews, dramatic readings, music, and sound effects into a satisfying viewing experience. While the documentary probably places too much emphasis on the World Series games themselves, three aspects of its treatment of the game-fixing scandal are noteworthy. First, Burns does an excellent job of dramatizing Joe Jackson's testimony before the grand jury. The viewer is presented with a photograph of what one presumes to be the courthouse where Jackson was questioned. A gavel hammers. Jackson (whose part is read by Keith Carradine) answers the questions put to him with quiet dignity, his voice subtly echoing. In the background is the sound of muffled whispers and shuffling feet. Lastly, Jackson's interrogator sighs (with sadness? annoyance?) before asking, "Does Mrs. Jackson know that you got $5,000 for helping throw these games?" Taken together, these details produce a moment that conveys the solemnity of the bond that had apparently been broken. Second, Burns prudently chose not to reproduce the apocryphal and hackneyed "Say it ain't so, Joe," scene, although a similar one is narrated.[74] Finally, Burns found a gem in Gardner Stern, the octogenarian White Sox fan. His remarks do not shed light on the Big Fix, but Stern lends the segment humanity by putting a face on the disappointment of it all.

Many baseball historians tend to focus on this segment's errors—of commission and omission—and misrepresentations. For example, Burns has reversed a photograph of the Black Sox and their attorneys in court, and several clips allegedly from the eighth game of the World Series in Chicago appear to show different ballparks. Moreover, Jerome Holtzman of the *Chicago Tribune* has pointed out some more substantial distortions. Holtzman, who describes Burns as "a master of overkill" and *Baseball* as "pretentious and repetitious," argues that "several of the [film's] talking heads, who have some knowledge of the game and should know better, insist Arnold Rothstein, the notorious New York gambler, fixed the 1919 World Series."[75] The historian Steven A. Riess follows a similar line of inquiry:

> Burns suggests that the entire fix was orchestrated by Arnold Rothstein. However, his major source, Eliot Asinof's *Eight Men Out,* points out that Rothstein was too smart and never was directly involved, largely working through intermediaries like Abe Attell, who is just mentioned in passing. Was the scandal inevitable as Okrent points out? Did Arnold Rothstein run this all? How does John Sayles, producer of *Eight Men Out,* know what Rothstein was thinking when the Black Sox scandal unfolded? Neither he nor his confederates left any diaries or memoirs. Literary license is fine for fiction, but not a documentary.[76]

These are important, unanswered questions. A baseball historian would want to know: where is Eliot Asinof? Why is *Eight Men Out* (the book) ignored? Why overrely on Daniel Okrent, whose commentary is often hyperbolic? A cultural critic and historian, however, might ask other equally important questions: how is *Baseball*'s treatment of the Black Sox scandal constructed? What does that construction mean to us? And what does the film's portrayal of the past suggest about its moment of creation?

Seemingly uncomfortable with ambiguity and difficult questions, Ken Burns and his collaborators constructed a rendition of the Black Sox scandal that eschews complexity and depth. As one might expect of the medium, the version of the Big Fix that *Baseball* offers viewers is dramatically simplified and superficial, and Burns himself admits as much: "You have to shorten, you have to take shortcuts, you have to abbreviate, you have to sort of make do with, you have to sometimes go with something that's less critically truthful imagery-wise because it does an ultimately better job of telling the larger truth, but who is deciding and under what system becomes the operative question."[77] Burns takes full responsibility for his work and, if prodded, might admit that his portrayal of the Black Sox scandal is less nuanced than he would have liked, yet given the many constraints he labored under, it was the best he could do.

Still, Burns's documentary does not move far beyond—indeed, it contributes to—the historical orthodoxy of its day. In *Baseball,* Arnold Rothstein is, as is so often the case despite a lack of evidence, the principal villain. To a lesser extent, the documentary holds Charles Comiskey and Chick Gandil accountable, but their culpability is minimized. The implicated players are generally portrayed as ignorant, exploited dupes who deserve more pity than contempt. Burns apparently wants viewers to feel their pain. In other words, *Baseball* does not challenge viewers to think very hard about the causes or consequences of the scandal. As an "emotional archeologist," Burns is more interested in excavating and exhibiting the ways in which ordinary Americans felt about the scandal than he is in trying to figure out what brought it about or what it meant and means.

To his credit, Burns does a good job of communicating that emotional experience, thanks largely to Gardner Stern. In this way *Baseball,* an acutely visceral documentary, bespeaks the manner in which the late-twentieth-century United States placed a premium on sentiment and style, on feeling and form. In *Baseball,* image is almost everything. If Burns is correct in maintaining that the "story of baseball is the story of America" and that the game is "a startling mirror of American life," his rendition of the Black Sox scandal casts a somewhat troubling reflection on his era.[78] For rather than closely reexamining and interrogating the most common ways the infamous event has been told and understood, Burns recycles them. With few exceptions,

Burns fails to make it new. Reflecting the cultural climate of the nineties, which has been described as postliberal and politically moderate, *Baseball*'s portrayal of the Black Sox scandal is, despite its visual pleasures, tepid and tame.

In some ways, a documentary filmmaker like Ken Burns occupies the middle ground between Hollywood "historians" and professionally trained historians. Usually committed to telling reality-based or nonfiction stories, a documentarian works under a much different set of constraints—creative, epistemological, and financial—than does a feature filmmaker or an academic historian. In addition, though often textually similar to feature films, documentaries usually make different kinds of truth claims about their subjects and are met with different kinds of audience expectations. But like a feature film—and more traditional works of history, for that matter—a documentary "is a careful construction, an intervention in the politics and the semiotics of representation."[79] John Sayles puts it well: "The minute someone sits down in an editing room, even for a documentary, choices are made. Some footage is kept; other footage is not. I've seen some extremely biased documentaries—some well made, some not—so making a film a documentary doesn't really solve the problem" of portraying the past with veracity or integrity.[80] Obviously, a nonfiction film is as constructed as any other text.

By skillfully weaving together visual fragments and sounds, *Baseball* provides viewers with a rich sensory experience. But because it is largely driven by nostalgic images, dramatizations, and sound bites rather than analysis, it implicitly argues that feeling is first, that the best way to know the past is emotionally. Perhaps sometimes it is. In *Baseball*'s case, the result is essentially superb infotainment and mediocre social history—at least in terms of its portrayal of the Black Sox scandal. My use of the word *infotainment* is only partly pejorative. Over the course of his career, Burns has demonstrated time and time again that a well-crafted documentary can teach as well as entertain. What *Baseball* teaches, however, what lessons it imparts, what vision of the past it offers is of consequence, perhaps more than any written history, considering the size of the audience it continues to reach. In *Baseball,* Burns provides viewers with a relatively prosaic version of the game fixing that does not disrupt historical conventions or challenge its audience. As the documentary filmmaker Jill Godmilow says of Burns in a different context: "He uses documentary as a kind of national therapy, producing a kind of mourning moment, a nostalgia for the past, in which one can find no useful questions or analyses that we could employ in today's realities."[81] While it may strike some as overly harsh, Godmilow's critique certainly applies to Burns's version of the Black Sox scandal, which is saturated with nostalgia and suffers from a paucity of analysis, precisely the inverse of what baseball history needs most.

And the Strike Went On

That fall, with no end to the baseball strike in sight, a few observers, unsurprisingly, continued to make connections between it and the Black Sox scandal. The *Wall Street Journal* ran an editorial entitled "Say It Ain't So."[82] A week before the World Series should have been played, the *Sporting News* published an article about the Black Sox scandal written from the perspective of 1922. While it did not explicitly mention the strike, the story concluded by foreshadowing it: "Players may think twice before looking to gamblers to supplement their incomes, but maybe they will turn to more acceptable modes of rebellion for their right to make the dollars they are worth. For even if the Black Sox are never allowed to return to the game, I fear the legacy of why they threw games in the first place will keep coming up 25, 50, even 75 years after the fact, when baseball turns toward the 21st Century and the 1919 World Series is merely remembered as the ugliest chapter in the epic that is baseball."[83] Soon thereafter, Harry Stein, the author of *Hoopla,* argued that "the strike is a compelling metaphor for what most ails America: the impulse to put self above all else, including community or the greater good." Stein claimed that "the revulsion this strike has provoked shows how millions of us feel about the drift of the entire culture. Though the players are less wrong than the owners, our impulse is to say: To hell with them all."[84] After several more months of ineffectual negotiations and posturing, a letter writer to the *Sporting News* declared: "Baseball's image is at its lowest point since the 1919 Black Sox scandal. If the owners were smart, they would do now what they did then: give a fair and respectable person the strong authority necessary to restore baseball's goodwill. It worked with Kenesaw Mountain Landis."[85] (Instead, three years after the strike, Bud Selig officially became baseball commissioner.) A few weeks later, with opening day around the corner, Donald Kaul of the *Des Moines Register* asserted that no matter where one laid responsibility for the strike, using "replacement" players, as the owners proposed, instead of actual Major Leaguers would be a grave mistake: "It will put a scar on the game like nothing since the Black Sox scandal of 1919. Like that gambling scandal, replacement baseball goes to the very heart of the integrity of the game."[86] As it turned out, the replacement players, who were pawns in the clash, never realized their Major League dreams.

The baseball strike finally ended on April 2, 1995, thanks to a federal court injunction that basically restored the expired collective bargaining agreement.[87] It was by far the longest, most bitterly contested, and costliest work stoppage in sports history: "the 232–day strike cost the owners an estimated $700 million, the players $250 million and the fans 921 regular-season games, not counting the World Series and other postseason games."[88] Accentuating the pointlessness of the conflict, the strike concluded without a new labor agreement. "In the end," argues Paul D. Staudohar in *Playing for Dollars: Labor Relations and the Sports Business* (1996), "everything had happened yet nothing really changed. Despite all the monetary losses by both sides, all the maneuvering, all the damage to the game, the collective bargaining agreement remained as is."[89] To make matters worse, an ABC News poll revealed that baseball's popularity was at a thirty-five-year low.[90] As Major Leaguers finally geared up to play for the first time in eight months, 79 percent of the people surveyed said labor disputes between the owners and the players had "taken the fun out of baseball" and 53 percent said they were "disgusted" with the game. Of course, numbers rarely tell the whole story. Many fans were willing to let bygones be bygones. "It was disappointing what happened," said one New York Yankees fan in Florida during spring training, "but as far as any hard feelings, I don't think so. As soon as the players came back, the excitement came back."[91] Another fan noted that, despite their enormous salaries and celebrity status, the ballplayers are laborers: "They did what they had to do. Sure, they make a lot of money, but they're still workers."[92] Like some 1919 fans, many baseball fans after the strike could (or would) not divorce themselves from their partisan loyalty to their team and favorite ballplayers and recognized the owners' culpability for the strike.

For those who cared and who felt betrayed, however, bitterness ruled the day. "The players and owners can both go to hell," said one former fan. "I'll find other outlets for my time and money."[93] Others were less concise and more melodramatic. "This most recent stalemate between players and owners suddenly feels as grim and tragic as Verdun—irrational as that seems," wrote the journalist Bill Gallo, two months before the strike ended. "Never again will baseball occupy the cherished place in the American imagination that it once held. Never again will we believe. No matter what the loudmouths in Washington proclaim, or how the owners backpedal, or what concessions the players now make, the essential joy of the game is gone."[94] Admittedly hyperbolic, Gallo nonetheless articulated the way numerous fans felt about the labor dispute. Public opinion surveys, lagging ticket sales, and depressed television ratings—not to mention a few acts of protest and civil disobedience—indicated deep resentment and misgivings about reinvesting—financially and emotionally—in the game.[95] One letter to *Sports Illustrated* explained: "Baseball's back. So what! As a fan who was cheated out of last year's postseason play, I'm not ready to come back."[96] Clearly, many fans saw the cancellation of the playoffs and the World Series as going too far. "For a lot of people," said Bill Giles, owner of the Philadelphia Phillies, "taking away the World Series was like taking away the American flag."[97] Many Americans simply found it inconceivable that the owners and the players would despoil baseball's most revered event.

The 1995 shortened season did conclude with the World Series, but that alone did not ennoble the year's play. Many observers noted that the imprimatur of integrity came instead when Cal Ripken Jr. broke Lou Gehrig's record for consecutive games played. More than anything else, said some commentators, the streak gave the 1995 season meaning and helped restore the game's battered image and its broken link to the past. As the columnist Charles Krauthammer observed in May, many in baseball were "counting on Cal Ripken's consecutive games streak to revive the game, some say, as Babe Ruth did after the Black Sox scandal."[98] The analogy is compelling and deserves attention.

2,131

According to conventional wisdom, George Herman "Babe" Ruth, with his brilliant power hitting and exuberant and flamboyant lifestyle, rejuvenated—indeed, transformed—baseball after the Black Sox scandal.[99] It is commonly held that, having slugged a record-shattering fifty-four home runs the year that the game fixing was revealed, Ruth galvanized popular interest in the game. To the delight of the baseball establishment, argues the writer Ken Sobol, most fans "were more interested in speculating about what the Babe would do for an encore in 1921 than they were in rehashing the delinquencies of the White Sox."[100] To put it mildly, the public loved Ruth, in part because he represented the realization of the American Dream and in part due to his rambunctiousness. Even more so than Judge Kenesaw Mountain Landis, Ruth revitalized professional baseball. "If Landis was the image of its new purity," argues Eliot Asinof, "it was Babe Ruth who gave it excitement."[101] Historians and critics have identified Ruth as a vibrant cultural symbol for his era.[102] According to the historian Warren I. Susman, Ruth "was the perfect creation for an increasingly mechanized world that still hungered for the extraordinary personality, that tired of the Model T automobiles and yet was also appreciative of their virtues—wanting only something more, something bigger than life."[103] Ruth was certainly that. Yet in terms of baseball history and mythology, he was (and remains) the game's savior.

By the spring of 1995, Major League Baseball once again desperately needed redemption. "Yes, there was a certain amount of joy over the return of the game," wrote Tom Verducci of *Sports Illustrated,* after the first week of the season. "But in ballparks all across the country people spit on the flag of baseball. The return of the game was greeted with anger, derision, mockery and—the worst insult of all—indifference."[104] Considering baseball's public relations problem, as early as spring training some observers were positioning Cal Ripken Jr., the thirty-five-year-old Baltimore Orioles shortstop, and his endurance record as the focal point of the upcoming season. Mark Maske of the *Washington Post,* for example, wrote that Ripken's "pursuit of Gehrig is *the* story to which baseball people can point these days as a positive while their ravaged sport tries to put the pieces back together following the strike."[105]

A quiet, confident man with a strong work ethic, Ripken did not exactly eschew media attention, but he was clearly uncomfortable with it. "In some ways, I wish I wouldn't receive so much attention for this," Ripken remarked. "But I guess I understand what the importance is, and I accept it."[106] As one writer put it, Ripken was "Baseball's Reluctant Messiah."[107] Ripken was cast in the role because he had been in the Orioles' lineup every day since May 30, 1982. Since then Ripken had been the AL's Rookie of the Year (1982), was named the AL's Most Valuable Player twice (1983 and 1991), was on thirteen straight All-Star teams, and set numerous Major League records for his power hitting and fielding, accomplishments which were (and remain) often overshadowed by his playing streak. Unassuming and seemingly unflappable, Ripken appeared to be a throwback to an earlier era when baseball players seemed more dignified and humble and less motivated to perform for financial rewards. The veteran observer Heywood Hale Broun mused, "Ripken seems like some figure emerging from a time machine. You half expect him to be wearing a baggy flannel uniform and using a skimpy glove."[108] Of course, the post-strike timing of his final assault on Gehrig's record probably contributed to the sense that Ripken was a living relic from a more innocent, less contentious age. "At a time when the game is in serious rehab," wrote Curry Kirkpatrick of *Newsweek,* "Ripken stands out as the ideal role model—an anti–[Mickey] Mantle who, rather than abuse his family and body over the span of a distinguished career, has held them aloft as the twin citadels of his success."[109] Unlike so many of his colleagues, Kirkpatrick continued, Ripken is "a quiet, serene hero so gracious that he actually respects the integrity of the sport. He also signs autographs for hours for no charge, and drives and drinks what he endorses (Chevy Suburban, milk)."[110] Hailed by the media nationwide as a paragon of steadiness, hard work, determination, and decency, Ripken was transformed from an All-Star ballplayer into an icon of All-American homespun masculine virtues.

Ripkenmania reached a crescendo on September 6, 1995, in Baltimore when the shortstop officially broke Gehrig's record in the fifth inning of a game against the California Angels.[111] To commemorate the historic moment, play was interrupted, fireworks exploded, and balloons were released. Major League games all over the country stopped so that fans and players could watch the celebration.[112] Millions more watched on television in what turned out to be the highest-rated baseball game ever broadcast by ESPN.[113] Back in Baltimore, after more than ten minutes of cheering by over 46,000 fans, Ripken was pushed out of the dugout by his teammates for an impromptu goodwill lap around the ballpark. All told, the game was suspended for twenty-two minutes. "If there was a more joyful 22 minutes in baseball," wrote the sportswriter Tim Kurkjian, "no one could remember it."[114] The indefatigable Ripken retained his composure despite the hoopla and later hit a home run. At the conclusion of the game, the Orioles held an hour-long ceremony to honor Ripken and his achievement. The most notable dignitary who offered congratulations was the legendary Hall of Fame outfielder Joe DiMaggio, who said, "Wherever my former teammate Lou Gehrig is today, I'm sure he's tipping his cap to you, Cal Ripken."[115]

Finally, after midnight, Ripken spoke. He expressed his gratitude to Baltimore's baseball fans and to fans all over the country for their kindness and support. He honored his parents for their guidance and love. He thanked his former teammate Eddie Murray for his example and friendship. And he acknowledged his wife, Kelly, for her advice, support, and for enriching his life. Ripken concluded:

> Tonight I stand here, overwhelmed, as my name is linked with the great and courageous Lou Gehrig. I'm truly humbled to have our names mentioned in the same breath.
>
> Some may think our strongest connection is because we both played many consecutive games. Yet I believe in my heart that our true link is a common motivation—a love of the game of baseball, a passion for our team, and a desire to compete on the very highest level.
>
> I know that if Lou Gehrig is looking down on tonight's activities, he isn't concerned about someone playing one more consecutive game than he did. Instead, he's viewing tonight as just another example of what is good and right

> about the great American game. Whether your name is Gehrig or Ripken; DiMaggio or Robinson; or that of some youngster who picks up his bat or puts on his glove: You are challenged by the game of baseball to do your very best, day in and day out. And that's all that I've ever tried to do.[116]

Like the man, remarked many observers, Ripken's speech was respectful and gracious; it lent dignity to the streak and to the game itself, which was still suffering from the post-strike doldrums. At the same time, by evoking names like Gehrig, DiMaggio, Robinson, he explicitly tapped into the nostalgia upon which the game thrives.

Immediately after game 2,131, the streak was hailed as a vehicle to restore interest, respect, and faith in Major League Baseball. At the conclusion of the record-breaking game, for example, one fan held a sign that read: "CAL, THANK YOU FOR SAVING BASEBALL."[117] Even President Bill Clinton, who was at Camden Yards, remarked: "I think the games last night and tonight are going to do a lot to help America fall back in love with baseball."[118] Some of Ripken's colleagues concurred. According to Buster Olney in the *Baltimore Sun,* "Fans were angered by the strike, and they've taken out some of their frustration on the players. But, some players say, Ripken and his streak have served as a salve. 'With everything that baseball went through last year with the strike, the loss of fans and some of the loss of popularity for the sport, things like this are nice to see,' [the Orioles catcher Chris] Hoiles said." The pitcher Mike Mussina observed that, if one were to chose a year to break a major record, "you couldn't have picked a better year, under better circumstances, in a better period of time for baseball."[119] When asked about the streak and its possible salutary effects on the game, the first baseman Rafael Palmeiro noted: "We—baseball—really needed this, and Cal came through."[120] Sportswriters (especially in Baltimore) lauded Ripken. More than a few saw connections between the streak and the strike. The longtime *Baltimore Sun* sports columnist John Steadman argued that Ripken, "whether he knows it or not, stands as an animated monument to all that's good about America's most revered but too often beleaguered pastime."[121] Murray Chass, a columnist for the *New York Times,* described Ripken's feat as "the brightest, most dramatic development of a season damaged by an unresolved labor dispute."[122] Bob Verdi of the *Chicago Tribune* opined: "The Streak was years of hard labor. The Lap was a spontaneous love-in. Cal Ripken did everything Wednesday night but restore peace to his embattled industry. He took a run at it, though. Maybe baseball will take the hint."[123] Unfortunately, the players and owners took another fourteen months to reach a collective bargaining agreement.[124]

To Ripken's apparent discomfort, some journalists viewed the streak as a remedy for baseball's strike-induced blues. "If the owners and the players had wanted to invent an antidote to their image problems," the columnist E. J. Dionne Jr. quipped, "they would have invented Cal Ripken."[125] For some, the streak seemed to be a baseball tonic or a healer. As Tony Kornheiser of the *Washington Post* put it: "Baseball was ailing, and Cal became its Florence Nightingale." Thanks to his relentless, self-effacing pursuit of excellence, Ripken somehow made a great many people care about baseball again. Still, Kornheiser reflected, Ripken "couldn't rescue baseball by himself; not even Babe Ruth could after what Bud Selig and Donald Fehr did to the game. But Cal saved it from disappearing down a rat hole. Baseball has become passé lately. Football has surpassed it as the national pastime, and basketball has all the younger demographics. But baseball is still the sport of fathers and sons and myth in this country, and it is no small cultural accomplishment that Ripken was its life preserver."[126]

In recognition of Ripken's achievement, *Sports Illustrated* named him Sportsman of the Year for 1995, and the Associated Press selected his streak as the sports story of the year.[127] Six months later, the streak still going strong, Thomas Boswell maintained in his column that Ripken broke baseball's endurance record "with such humility and generosity of spirit that he restored half the good name of his tarnished sport."[128] All of which suggests that, to many people, especially journalists, Ripken revived, perhaps even re-ennobled, baseball after the strike, somewhat like Babe Ruth did after the Black Sox scandal. As Buster Olney of the *Baltimore Sun* put it: Ripken may have done "more for baseball than any player since Babe Ruth in 1920 and 1921, when the Bambino's awesome power overwhelmed the cynicism created by the 1919 Black Sox scandal."[129]

The analogy is not precise, of course. The two men clearly embody radically different (even antithetical) versions of baseball heroism: one appears to be the quintessential self-made man, disciplined and modest, while the other seems to be the ultimate natural man, hedonistic and brash. In this way Ruth and Ripken illustrate the truism that different historical moments demand and produce different types of heroes. But Ruth and Ripken both provided the baseball crises of their day with (the appearance) of narrative closure that they so desperately needed. Both ballplayers refocused popular and media attention on the game and projected cultural values that many Americans esteemed and apparently yearned for in themselves. Like Ruth, a fellow Baltimorean, Ripken seemed to provide baseball with redemption when it needed it most.

My argument is not that Ripken actually redeemed baseball, though obviously some people think he did. I am not arguing that the streak—a genuinely impressive accomplishment rather than a pseudo-event—was somehow innocent or pure. Among other things, the streak was a media-created cultural commodity eagerly consumed by hungry fans. One way of illustrating this is to note the myriad products—T-shirts, hats, bumper stickers, posters, videos, "limited edition" collector plates, newspaper and magazine articles, and books, including Ripken's autobiography, *The Only Way I Know* (1997)—sold to commemorate Ripken's feat before, during, and after the record-setting game. My point is that many fans and journalists made interesting connections between the Black Sox scandal and baseball's most recent labor debacle, between Ruth and Ripken. For many, the streak was an occasion that promoted dialogue between the present and the past, one in which the past could be used to make sense of the present.

Dyersville, Where Baseball Has Never Struck Out

Meanwhile, in Dyersville people continue to visit the Field of Dreams. If anything, the baseball strike enhanced the ballfield's allure. According to one estimate, a record two hundred thousand people visited Dyersville in 1994.[130] Perhaps more than before, the Field of Dreams was perceived to be a baseball haven, a utopic space unencumbered by failed labor negotiations, greedy ballplayers, and equally avaricious team owners. Or as Becky Lansing, Don Lansing's wife, described it in 1999: "This is a vortex for all that is good."[131] For fans still afflicted with the baseball strike blues, visiting the Field of Dreams may have become a salutary breath of fresh air. "In a year when legions of fans have turned their backs on baseball as big business," observed the journalist Michael Hirsley in October 1995, "this rural ballfield, where rough-hewn posts hold the backstop and lights in place, has thrived. It courses with the affection of those who want the game's simple innocence and purity preserved."[132] Although professional baseball has never been as innocent as some of its celebrants like to imagine, nostalgia for a mythic time before it was a cutthroat business is resilient, especially in the face of baseball's distressing and distasteful recent past.

Predictably, some visitors express these yearnings. "Baseball is just so sickening right now with all the fighting over money," said a woman from Montana. "This reminds me of when it was just a game." A man from Oklahoma agreed: "People don't dislike baseball any more than they did in the 1920s. They just hate all the money. If you take the money out of baseball, this is what you get."[133] That is, one gets a beautiful baseball field where the admission is free and there is no audible carping about revenue sharing. (Actually, there is some. From the beginning there has been tension between Lansing and the Ameskamps about the Field of Dreams, but apparently it remains imperceptible to visitors.)[134]

The irony is that the Field of Dreams is intimately linked to—actually, it owes its existence to—business decisions and acts of commercialism. If Joe Jackson had not been expelled from baseball for his alleged participation in the fix, there would be no reason to conjure his ghost. If *Field of Dreams* had not grossed over $62 million—and, in the process, garnered thousands of fans—the field likely would have been plowed under.[135] If Don Lansing had not registered the field as "unused" land in the federal Conservation Reserve Program—and thereby gained a one-time monetary compensation—he would have had to plow it under.[136] In addition, it should be remembered that the Ameskamps rebuilt their portion of the Field of Dreams well after its surprising popularity was established. Certainly other factors were involved in all these decisions and actions: the Black Sox no doubt wanted to stick it to their parsimonious employer; Phil Alden Robinson surely chose the Dyersville filming location for aesthetic reasons; and Lansing kept the ballfield in part due to sentimentality. However, the dominant discourse about the Field of Dreams elides the financial interests of the site. Surveying the Field of Dreams and how most visitors respond to it, Michael Hirsley concludes that, despite widespread disenchantment with Major League Baseball, "there is still joy in Dyersville, where baseball has never struck out."[137]

Maybe so, but the Field of Dreams is not simply an innocent, joyous place where vague middle-class dreams for the way we never were come true, nor is it devoid of cultural meaning or historical significance. On the contrary, it is a cultural space that, in Charles Fruehling Springwood's words, offers "an inverted, glossy aesthetization of race, politics, and the democratization of everyday life in the United States."[138] In many ways a remarkable and seductive place, the Field of Dreams celebrates and promotes a sanitized, mythic version of Joe Jackson, and by extension the Black Sox scandal, one that simultaneously obfuscates, erases, and sugarcoats the past.

Conclusion

Popular culture greatly influences the ways in which the public views historical subjects. Certainly the disparate texts scrutinized in this chapter have provided millions of people with different, sometimes competing visions of the Black Sox scandal. The numbers alone are startling: approximately fifty thousand tourists have visited the Field of Dreams annually for the last ten years; an average of five million households tuned into *Baseball* for at least part of every episode when it was first aired; and untold millions more were reminded or advised of the Black Sox scandal by media references during the strike of 1994–95.[139] Obviously the game-fixing affair still speaks to many people, at the very least those who produce and frame much of our public discourse. Although Americans seem to prefer to dwell on the present, the texts examined here suggest that the past is ever with us and is manifested in distinct yet intertwined ways. During the strike, it was not uncommon for the media to evoke *Field of Dreams* to describe the impasse. Anticipating the work stoppage, *Time* entitled an article on the labor conflict "An Empty Field of Dreams?"[140] A week later an editorial in the *New Republic* was entitled "Field of Schemes."[141] Aired in the midst of the strike, *Baseball*—which almost never missed an opportunity to align itself with the pastoral serenity associated with the Field of Dreams—could not help but be compared and contrasted with the labor strife. These three texts offer lucid examples of the interplay among popular culture, history, and cultural politics. They illustrate a few of the myriad ways baseball continues to stimulate American imaginations, and they suggest that retelling and remembering the Black Sox scandal remain important ways of linking the past to the present.

Postscript: A Final Testament

In February 1997, having lost their suit to obtain Joe Jackson's will from Greenville County, the American Heart Association and the American Cancer Society appealed their case to the South Carolina Supreme Court. Referring to the legal proceedings, one journalist declared: "Because he signed it, they will come."[142] Another reported that, while the charities claim Jackson's will belongs to them, the "state of South Carolina says it ain't so."[143] The court subsequently ruled that Jackson's will is a public document and thus belongs to the state.[144] The case speaks to the value, both historical and financial, that many people—most obviously the case's plaintiffs and defendants, but also journalists, editors, sports memorabilia collectors, and baseball fans—place on Joe Jackson. Despite fading ever further into the past, the Black Sox scandal remains a presence in American culture. Its fascination has not yet waned; its cultural work is not yet done.

Conclusion

The eightieth anniversary of the Black Sox trial was commemorated with an Internet auction on eBay for Joe Jackson's famous bat, Black Betsy. Hyping the sale, one baseball memorabilia expert described the forty-ounce hickory bat as "the Holy Grail of sports collectibles."[1] Black Betsy eventually sold for over $577,000, believed to be the highest price ever paid for a single bat.[2] In American culture, infamy sells well, especially when a miscarriage of justice may have taken place. But that in and of itself does not explain why the Black Sox scandal has been retold so many times, in so many different mediums.

Few Black Sox scandal storytellers were inspired to tell the tale for the same reasons. Harry Stein's *Hoopla,* with its dueling narrators, encapsulates this idea. However, one reason the Black Sox scandal gets retold so frequently is due to narrative physics: an untold story tends to stay untold, whereas an often-told story tends to be repeated. The historian Steven Biel argues that one reason the *Titanic* disaster, for example, remains part of our collective memory and cultural vocabulary is momentum: "In the marketplace this translates into the notion that with the right amount of modification and repackaging, what has sold before will continue to sell. The *Titanic* generates interest because it generates interest. It is an icon because it is an icon. In this way a good story can prolong itself indefinitely."[3] This is certainly the case with the Black Sox scandal, too. In other words, the 1919 World Series scandal retains its cultural currency partly because it retains its cultural currency.

For the less tautologically inclined, there are at least two more reasons the Black Sox scandal narrative endures: the indeterminacy of the event and the social utility of the story. The former no doubt contributes to the latter. Despite the best efforts of historians, in many ways the Black Sox scandal remains an unsolved mystery. It has stubbornly resisted historical verifiability and certainty. This apparently makes the scandal attractive to storytellers at least in part because it can be put to various (sometimes conflicting) uses: as a fable of lost innocence, as a masculine cautionary tale, as a historical reference point for contemporary crises, as a narrative that critiques the past and the present. In the hands of popular (and a few academic) storytellers, the Black Sox scandal has become an occasion to consider the fragile mortality of heroes, changing conceptions of middle-class manhood, temptation, corruption, justice, and the vagaries of history and historical knowledge. Because it is such a malleable cultural moment, the Big Fix has provided journalists, novelists, filmmakers, historians, and others with an episode that can be used to address their own contemporary issues.

In spite of this narrative plasticity, the dominant or preferred constructions of the story have proven remarkably resilient. In addition, they have had an influential and lasting effect on how the Black Sox scandal has been retold, rewritten, and remembered. From the very beginning, and for at least three decades, the media (with the generous help of Kenesaw Mountain Landis and others in the baseball establishment) commonly constructed the scandal as an aberrant case of a few immoral, greedy men betraying their teammates, employer, profession, and nation. Widely reviled, the implicated ballplayers were usually depicted as dupes and "dumb farm boys." The professional gamblers (read: Jewish gamblers) allegedly involved were repeatedly portrayed as a nefarious menace to the national pastime. Even by the fifties—when baseball had entered its so-called second Golden Age and after the nation had experienced unknown prosperity and depression and was emerging as a super power—simplifying the tale was more convenient and palatable than examining it critically. Neither time nor baseball's designated saviors (Landis and Babe Ruth) had sufficiently healed the game's wounds. More complex, richly described, and nuanced renditions of the Black Sox scandal would have to wait. Just as important, the earliest views of the scandal are deeply embedded in the narrative building blocks all subsequent storytellers rely upon, which suggests that the earliest versions of the Black Sox scandal continue to wield power. Thus, while the writing of history is an inherently revisionist enterprise and while meaning is perpetually renegotiated, it appears that once an event has been transformed into a specific kind of news story, it is very difficult (though not impossible) to imagine it differently. Like other social structures and institutions, dominant versions of cultural narratives appear to be endowed with a certain degree of permanence.

But like most (all?) master narratives, the dominant constructions of the game fixing have been contested and resisted, especially since the 1963 publication of Eliot Asinof's *Eight Men Out,* which represented the affair as something other than a simple morality play and the Black Sox as three-dimensional men. Thanks to Asinof, to fissures in the master narratives caused by the passage of time, and to subtly changing attitudes, the story could be imagined less monolithically and moralistically. (It should be noted, however, that "alternative" renditions and understandings have always been present in nontextual, and thus difficult to document, forms.) In addition to the empathy and commiseration that Joe Jackson and Buck Weaver elicited from their local communities during (and after) their lifetimes, a lingering sense of injustice has been associated with the Big Fix. If anything, this attitude has grown, due to nostalgia and the assumption that the past must be set straight for there to be progress. So, while contemporary athletes are infrequently thought of as laborers (perhaps because of their substantially higher salaries compared with 1919 pay), the notion that the banished Black Sox ballplayers were exploited workers has gained currency. One historian expresses this idea by arguing that the Big Fix "was part counterculture revolt and part class struggle."[4] The Black-Sox-as-victims construct finds its apotheosis in W. P. Kinsella's *Shoeless Joe* and Phil Alden Robinson's *Field of Dreams,* works that have done a great deal to redeem and remythologize the players, particularly Joe Jackson. They reconstitute baseball as a privileged cultural practice and the United States as a land where dreams can come true. Of course, all versions of the past have ideological implications. Some, like the version of the scandal Landis embodied for twenty-four years, contribute to the status quo and conventional wisdom, and others, like Stein's *Hoopla,* John Sayles's *Eight Men Out,* and Brendan Boyd's *Blue Ruin,* complicate historical simplifications and resist traditional power relations. In constant dialogue and competition with one another, eighty years' worth of Black Sox scandal narratives vividly illustrate the combative and political nature of representing the past.

The narratives critiqued here also exemplify that cultural meaning is not fixed. Perhaps inevitably, as storytellers come to understand and represent the past differently, meaning changes to reflect new social realities, needs, and desires. This is not to suggest that cultural meaning is so fluid that it can take any form. Yes, narratives can be twisted into many shapes, used in various ways, made to serve a wide range of purposes. But in practice, there are limits. There appears to be a range of possible meanings. Although the Black Sox scandal narrative could not be reshaped to support any purpose or historical interpretation, neither has it been emptied of specific meanings and become just a generic name for sports-related scandals, something like "-gate" in political discourse (Iran-gate, Travel-gate, Monica-gate). For many writers and fans, the Big Fix still signifies betrayal, corruption, and disillusionment, even if its causes and facts are uncertain. This shared sensibility is expressed in the title of a story about a Japanese wrestling scandal: "Say It Ain't Sumo!" It also encouraged ESPN's Rich Eisen to write: "Do we call this the Black Knickers Scandal? Hansie Cronje, the Babe Ruth of South African cricket, is accused of taking at least $10,000 to throw a match in India. Say it ain't so, Hansie!!!"[5]

The Black Sox scandal has long been a site of disappointment and intrigue, one that throws into relief questions about memory and historical representation. When read collectively, the narratives examined here suggest that the tension between social reality and representation is unresolvable and that remembrances and retellings of the Big Fix have always been selective, partial, and contentious. Furthermore, they suggest that when we have something invested in a historical moment and a particular version of it, we tend to see what we want to see, believe what we need to believe. We can give reasons in support of an interpretation or a position and can cite evidence and authorities, but at the end of the day different—sometimes competing, sometimes complementary, sometimes equally plausible and legitimate—versions of the moment in question persist. This situation is not unique to the Black Sox scandal, obviously.[6] Still, thinking about the Big Fix and the stories that have kept it a vibrant presence in American culture forces us to confront how people remember the past and write history; also, it reminds us that storytellers have always seen and understood the past from specific historical and political perspectives and that, in addition to providing entertainment, popular narratives do important cultural work.

While working on this book, I was frequently asked two questions. Many people—not all of whom are baseball fans or history students—wanted to know if I thought Joe Jackson participated in the plot to fix the 1919 World Series. I have always been uncomfortable answering this question in part because the evidence is inconclusive and in part because the question does not interest me—at least not in the way that it concerns people who think Jackson should be in the Baseball Hall of Fame. In response I usually explain that my project is less about the Black Sox scandal itself and more about how the event has been represented and remembered and what those things says about our culture and the process of making meaning. Nonetheless, it is interesting that so many people care about Jackson's guilt or innocence. After all, the Black Sox scandal took place over eighty years ago and Jackson died in 1951. One might reasonably ask, What difference does it make if he helped fix the 1919 World Series? And yet many people want to know, or at least to consider the possibilities, and as a result the question retains its resonance. This continued interest bespeaks the desire to know the past with certainty, the belief that the "truth" is accessible, the idea that justice delayed is justice denied, and the notion that Joe Jackson is somehow linked to baseball's integrity.

Second, I was often asked—usually by puzzled though well-meaning colleagues—about the "significance" of my study. Why spend so much time researching and thinking about a long-ago sports scandal? (Especially, said one friend, when there are so many contemporary scandals to write about.) The simple answer is that this project is significant because its subject is singular and because it demonstrates popular culture's capacity to function as public history and the ways in which memory and meaning are contested and revised. Unlike some observers, I do not think the Black Sox scandal marked the end of American innocence, whatever that may mean. Moreover, the cultural importance of the Big Fix can be (and often is) exaggerated. Statements about the sociopolitical effects of the scandal often result in facile generalizations and hyperbolic claims. But I also firmly believe that close, contextualized readings of Black Sox scandal narratives necessarily engage the politics of rewriting and remembering the past and the production of cultural meaning and that these are vital endeavors that fundamentally shape who we are and can become. Every time a Black Sox storyteller says it's so provides us with an opportunity to better understand and critique the past *and* the present, to participate in ongoing conversations about myriad subjects: crime and punishment, myth and memory, labor-management relations, and the fate of a long gone ballplayer with a lyrical name.

Notes

Introduction

1. Lawrence S. Ritter, *The Glory of Their Times* (New York: William Morrow, [1966] 1992), 222.

2. Stephen Jay Gould, introduction to *Eight Men Out: The Black Sox and the 1919 World Series* by Eliot Asinof (New York: Henry Holt, [1963] 1987), xv.

3. The first World Series was in 1903 when the Pittsburgh Pirates, who won the National League pennant, invited the American League pennant winners, the Boston Red Sox, to compete in a best-of-nine game series. With the exception of 1904, the series between the champions of the two leagues was an annual event. It is also worth noting that in the late nineteenth century a relatively informal postseason series was played by teams from the National League and the American Association of Base Ball Clubs. Lee Allen, *The World Series: The Story of Baseball's Annual Championship* (New York: G. P. Putnam's Sons, 1969).

4. John Thorn and Pete Palmer with Michael Gershman, eds., *Total Baseball: The Official Encyclopedia of Major League Baseball,* 4th ed. (New York: Viking, [1989] 1995), 311.

5. Daniel E. Ginsburg, *The Fix Is In: A History of Baseball Gambling and Game Fixing Scandals* (Jefferson, N.C.: McFarland, 1995), 128–29.

6. Richard C. Lindberg, *Who's on Third?: The Chicago White Sox Story* (South Bend, Ind.: Icarus Press, 1983), 43; *Chicago Tribune,* Oct. 11, 1919, 15; Asinof, *Eight Men Out,* 129.

7. *Philadelphia North American,* Sept. 28, 1920, 1.

8. For Jackson's grand jury testimony, see Harvey Frommer, *Shoeless Joe and Ragtime Baseball* (Dallas: Taylor, 1992), 191–215.

9. *Chicago Herald and Examiner,* Sept. 29, 1920, 2.

10. Shoeless Joe Jackson (as told to Furman Bisher), "This Is the Truth!" *Sport,* Oct. 1949, 14.

11. *Chicago Herald and Examiner,* Sept. 30, 1920, 2.

12. *Chicago Tribune,* Oct. 28, 1920, 19.

13. J. G. Taylor Spink, *Judge Landis and Twenty-Five Years of Baseball* (New York: Thomas Y. Crowell, [1947] 1953), 72.

14. *Chicago Herald and Examiner,* July 21, 1921, 1.

15. *Chicago Tribune,* Aug. 3, 1921, 1.

16. *Chicago Herald and Examiner,* Aug. 4, 1921, 1.

17. George Grella, "Baseball and the American Dream," *Massachusetts Review* 16:3 (Summer 1975): 560.

18. Cordelia Candelaria, *Seeking the Perfect Game: Baseball in American Literature* (Westport, Conn.: Greenwood Press, 1989), 70.

19. Donald Honig, *The American League: An Illustrated History* (New York: Crown, 1983), 50.

20. Barry Abrams, letter to author, Aug. 1, 2001.

21. Jacques Barzun, *God's Country and Mine: A Declaration of Love Spiced with a Few Harsh Words* (Boston: Little, Brown, 1954), 159.

22. Stephen Jay Gould, "The Creation Myths of Cooperstown: Or Why the Cardiff Giants Are an Unbeatable and Appropriately Named Team," in *Writing Baseball,* ed. Jerry Klinkowitz (Urbana: University of Illinois Press, 1991), 26.

23. Frommer, *Shoeless Joe and Ragtime Baseball,* 188.

24. David Q. Voigt, "The Chicago Black Sox and the Myth of Baseball's Single Sin," in *America through Baseball* (Chicago: Nelson-Hall, 1976), 65, 73.

25. Christian K. Messenger, "Expansion Draft: Baseball Fiction of the 1980s," in *The Achievement of American Sport Literature: A Critical Appraisal,* ed. Wiley Lee Umphlett (Cranbury, N.J.: Associated University Presses, 1991), 63.

26. George F. Will, "Black October: The Year the Series Was Fixed," *Washington Post,* Oct. 6, 1988, A25.

27. Evan Connell, *Son of the Morning Star: Custer and the Little Big Horn* (New York: HarperCollins, [1984] 1991), 106.

28. Michael Schudson, *Watergate in American Memory: How We Remember, Forget, and Reconstruct the Past* (New York: Basic Books, 1992), 3.

29. Keith Jenkins, *Re-Thinking History* (New York: Routledge, 1991), 5.

30. Ibid., 3.

31. Schudson, *Watergate in American Memory,* 218.

32. Albert E. Stone, *The Return of Nat Turner: History, Literature, and Cultural Politics in Sixties America* (Athens: University of Georgia Press, 1992), 25.

33. Ibid., 29.

34. Ibid., 30.

35. Robert Darnton, *The Kiss of Lamourette: Reflections in Cultural History* (New York: W. W. Norton, 1990), 181.

36. Hayden White, *The Content of the Form: Narrative Discourse and Historical Representation* (Baltimore: Johns Hopkins University Press, [1987] 1990), ix.

Chapter 1: History's First Draft

1. Robert Darnton, *The Kiss of Lamourette: Reflections in Cultural History* (New York: W. W. Norton, 1990), xvi.

2. William K. Klingaman, *1919: The Year Our World Began* (New York: St. Martin's Press, 1987), 564.

3. Darnton, *The Kiss of Lamourette,* xx.

4. Carey quoted in Robert Karl Manoff and Michael Schudson, introduction to *Reading the News,* ed. Manoff and Schudson (New York: Pantheon Books, 1986), 6.

5. There were ways of knowing about the Black Sox scandal besides newspapers. News magazines like the *Literary Digest,* the *North American Review,* the *Nation,* and the *New Republic* occasionally discussed the scandal. Specialty magazines like the *Sporting News* and *Baseball Magazine* also paid attention to it, but not as much as one might expect. Baseball almanacs, like the *Reach Baseball Guide* and *Spalding's Baseball Guide,* offered cursory but noteworthy discussions of the affair. Where it is appropriate, I have incorporated information from these sources into my narrative. Finally, of the many secondary texts I have drawn upon here, one deserves special acknowledgment: Leverett T. Smith Jr.'s *The American Dream and the National Game* (Bowling Green, Ohio: Popular Press, 1975), which paved the way to much of my research. But it should be noted that my aims are different than Smith's. Whereas Smith refers to the Black Sox news stories as an expression of the "public image" and the "public response" the scandal engendered, I view the same material as an expression of how the press imagined, made sense of, and responded to the affair (6). It seems to me that the "public response" to the Black Sox scandal—or any event, for that matter—is harder to locate and more complicated than what newspapers print.

6. Daniel H. Borus, "The Unexplored Twenties: 'These United States' and the Quest for Diversity," in *These United States: Portraits of America from the 1920s,* ed. Daniel H. Borus (Ithaca: Cornell University Press, 1992), 1.

7. Michael E. Parrish, *Anxious Decades: America in Prosperity and Depression, 1920–1941* (New York: W. W. Norton, 1992), ix.

8. William E. Leuchtenberg, *The Perils of Prosperity, 1914–32* (Chicago: University of Chicago Press, 1958), 141–43.

9. See Edwin Emery and Michael Emery, *The Press and America: An Interpretative History of the Mass Media,* 7th ed. (Englewood Cliffs, N.J.: Prentice-Hall, [1954] 1992); Jean Folkerts and Dwight Teeter, *Voices of a Nation: A History of the Mass Media in the United States* (New York: Macmillan, 1989); Frank Luther Mott, *American Journalism, a History: 1690–1960,* 3d ed. (New York: Macmillan, [1962] 1972); Michael Schudson, *Discovering the News: A Social History of American Newspapers* (New York: Basic Books, 1978).

10. Emery and Emery, *The Press and America,* 172–74.

11. Andie Tucher, *Froth and Scum: Truth, Beauty, Goodness, and the Ax Murder in America's First Mass Medium* (Chapel Hill: University of North Carolina Press, 1994), 199.

12. Frederick Lewis Allen, "Newspapers and the Truth," *Atlantic Monthly,* Jan. 1922, 45.

13. Frederick Lewis Allen, *Only Yesterday: An Informal History of the 1920s* (New York: Harper and Row, [1931] 1964), 157.

14. See John Rickards Betts, "Sporting Journalism in Nineteenth-Century America," *American Quarterly* 5:1 (Spring 1953): 39–56; John Stevens, "The Rise of the

Sports Page," *Gannett Center Journal* 1:2 (Fall 1987): 1–11; and Robert W. McChesney, "Media Made Sport: A History of Sports Coverage in the United States," in *Media, Sports, and Society,* ed. Lawrence A. Wenner (Newbury Park, Calif.: Sage Publications, 1989), 49–69.

15. McChesney, "Media Made Sport," 57.

16. Harold Seymour, *Baseball: The Golden Age* (New York: Oxford University Press, [1971] 1989), vii.

17. Morris R. Cohen, "Baseball," *Dial,* July 26, 1919, 57.

18. Steven A. Riess, *Touching Base: Professional Baseball and American Culture in the Progressive Era* (Westport, Conn.: Greenwood Press, 1980), 13–14.

19. Ibid., 233.

20. For a useful discussion of the reserve clause, see Robert F. Burke, *Never Just a Game: Players, Owners, and American Baseball to 1920* (Chapel Hill: University of North Carolina Press, 1994), 62–63.

21. Daniel E. Ginsburg, *The Fix Is In: A History of Baseball Gambling and Game Fixing Scandals* (Jefferson, N.C.: McFarland, 1995), 5.

22. Melvin L. Adelman, *A Sporting Time: New York City and the Rise of Modern Athletics, 1820–1870* (Urbana: University of Illinois Press, 1986), 162.

23. Ginsburg, *The Fix Is In,* 48.

24. Riess, *Touching Base,* 221.

25. Eliot Asinof, *Eight Men Out: The Black Sox and the 1919 World Series* (New York: Henry Holt, [1963] 1987), 123.

26. Ibid., 47.

27. Hugh Fullerton, "Fullerton Says Seven Members of the White Sox Will Be Missing Next Spring," *Chicago Herald and Examiner,* Oct. 10, 1919, 9.

28. Asinof casts Fullerton in the role of the muckraking, ethical hero: "His love for the game permitted no whitewashing. He insisted on a cleanup. With a sense of outrage, he began a series of articles to jolt the executive world of baseball into action. He would expose, finally, what every decent baseball writer knew, but never had the courage to write. He would break down the hypocritical wall of silence behind which baseball pretended to be holy. He would quote gamblers he had spoken with, recount experiences that indicated dirty work, and above all, name names, lots of names." Asinof, *Eight Men Out,* 132.

29. Hugh Fullerton, "Is Big League Baseball Being Run for Gamblers, with the Players in the Deal?" *New York Evening World,* Dec. 15, 1919, "sporting page."

30. Seymour, *Baseball: The Golden Age,* 288–90.

31. Fullerton, "Is Big League Baseball Being Run for Gamblers."

32. David Q. Voigt, *American Baseball: From the Commissioners to Continental Expansion* (University Park: Pennsylvania State University Press, [1970] 1983), 126.

33. For instance, an editorial in the November 1919 issue of *Baseball Magazine* ripped Fullerton: "If a man really knows so little about baseball that he believes the game is or can be fixed, he should keep his mouth shut when in the presence of intelligent people." Immediately after the series, editors of the *Sporting News,* with-

out mentioning Fullerton by name, ridiculed any thought that the games were fixed and disparaged those who suspected corruption. Later, after Fullerton's articles appeared in the *New York Evening World,* a writer at *Baseball Magazine* noted that the "sport world was recently greeted with a giddy screed from the facile pen of Hugh Fullerton," who was described as a "visionary and erratic writer." Even after the game-fixing charges were confirmed—by ballplayer confessions—late in the 1920 season, the editors at *Baseball Magazine* were unrelenting in their criticism of Fullerton: "Mr. Fullerton picked up an ugly story that was kicking around the gutter, a story that most reputable writers refused to handle. His articles were constructed out of gamblers' rumors and bar-room conversation. His attack was vicious, premature, unfounded. Under the circumstances the *Baseball Magazine* could do nothing but defend the game from such a tirade of abuse. At that time it could not know whether the investigation of baseball would disclose crooked work. No one knew. The fact that events have proved those ugly rumors true is beside the point. Mere empty suspicion offers no just ground for wholesale mudslinging. Mr. Fullerton merely made a wild, hazardous guess and for once in his life he guessed right." "Editorial Comment," *Baseball Magazine,* Nov. 1919, 458; "Editorial Comment," *Baseball Magazine,* Feb. 1920, 519; "Editorial Comment," *Baseball Magazine,* Dec. 1920, 316.

34. Peter Williams, "When Chipmunks Became Wolves: The Scapegoating of Sportswriter Joe Williams by His Peers," *Nine: A Journal of Baseball History and Social Policy Perspectives* 4:1 (Fall 1995): 51.

35. For more on Fullerton, see Steve Klein, "The Lone Horseman of Baseball's Apocalypse," *Blue Ear,* <http://www.blueear.com/features/apocalypse.html> (Nov. 1, 1999).

36. Peter Andrews, "The Press," *American Heritage,* Oct. 1994, 60.

37. Kevin Barnhurst, *Seeing the Newspaper* (New York: St. Martin's Press, 1994), 196.

38. Bruce J. Evensen, *When Dempsey Fought Tunney: Heroes, Hokum, and Storytelling in the Jazz Age* (Knoxville: University of Tennessee Press, 1996), 65.

39. *Des Moines Register,* Sept. 29, 1920, 1.

40. *Chicago Tribune,* Sept. 19, 1920, pt. 2, p. 1, Sept. 23, 1920, 3, Sept. 24, 1920, 3.

41. *New York Tribune,* Sept. 29, 1920, 2.

42. *Chicago Tribune,* Sept. 24, 1920, 1, 8.

43. *Chicago Herald and Examiner,* Sept. 27, 1920, 6.

44. *New York Tribune,* Sept. 30, 1920, 10.

45. *St. Louis Star* quoted in *Literary Digest,* Oct. 9, 1920, 12.

46. Charles Dryden, "Here's Hope for Black Sox," *Chicago Herald and Examiner,* Oct. 1, 1920, 9.

47. *Chicago Tribune,* Sept. 24, 1920, 2, Sept. 29, 1920, 15.

48. *Chicago Tribune,* Sept. 26, 1920, 10.

49. *Chicago Daily News,* Sept. 30, 1921, 1.

50. For a cultural history of the color black, see John Harvey, *Men in Black* (Chicago: University of Chicago Press, 1995).

51. Suellen Hoy, *Chasing Dirt: The American Pursuit of Cleanliness* (New York: Oxford University Press, 1995), 88.

52. Ibid., 86.

53. *Chicago Tribune,* Sept. 19, 1920, pt. 2, p. 1. The Loomis letter is also notable because Loomis probably did not write it. In his history of the *Chicago Tribune,* Lloyd Wendt writes: "In July, 1920, [James] Crusinberry [a *Chicago Tribune* sportswriter] prepared a story about an impending baseball scandal, based in part upon a conversation he had overheard between two gamblers about the fix of the 1919 Series, but [Harvey] Woodruff [the *Tribune*'s sports editor] held the story, feeling there were not enough facts available. By late August, although no new information had surfaced, there was talk of initiating a grand jury investigation. In early September, Crusinberry, convinced that matters were moving too slowly, persuaded Fred M. Loomis, a Chicago businessman and baseball fan, to sign a letter to the *Tribune* that he, Crusinberry, had written." Since Loomis was willing to put his name to the letter, it is fair to assume that he shared its sentiments. Lloyd Wendt, *Chicago Tribune: The Rise of a Great American Newspaper* (Chicago: Rand McNally, 1979), 452.

54. *Chicago Tribune,* Sept. 19, 1920, pt. 2, p. 1.

55. Mary Douglas, *Purity and Danger: An Analysis of the Concepts of Pollution and Taboo* (New York: Routledge, [1966] 1991), 2.

56. *Chicago Tribune,* Sept. 26, 1920, pt. 2, p. 1.

57. *New York Times,* Sept. 27, 1920, 11.

58. *New York Tribune,* Sept. 27, 1920, 11.

59. *New York World,* Sept. 29, 1920, 14.

60. *Chicago Tribune,* Sept. 29, 1920, 3.

61. *New York World,* Sept. 29, 1920, 2.

62. *Cincinnati Enquirer,* Sept. 29, 1920, 2.

63. Ibid.

64. *Cincinnati Enquirer,* Sept. 30, 1920, 7.

65. Damon Runyon, "The Grand Jury Resume," *Chicago Herald and Examiner,* Oct. 21, 1920, 9.

66. *Chicago Tribune,* Sept. 29, 1920, 2.

67. *Chicago Herald and Examiner,* Oct. 3, 1920, 3.

68. *Chicago Tribune,* Sept. 29, 1920, 1.

69. *Washington Post,* Sept. 29, 1920, 6.

70. *Cincinnati Enquirer,* Oct. 3, 1920, 38.

71. *Cleveland Plain Dealer,* Sept. 30, 1920, 14.

72. I. E. Sanborn, "Johnson Hints New Baseball Scandal Coming," *Chicago Tribune,* Oct. 15, 1920, 22.

73. Voigt, *American Baseball,* 133.

74. *Chicago Herald and Examiner,* June 22, 1921, 10.

75. *Chicago Tribune,* Aug. 3, 1921, 2.

76. *Chicago Herald and Examiner,* Aug. 3, 1921, 1.

77. *New York Daily News,* Aug. 3, 1921, 1.

78. *New York Daily News* quoted in *Literary Digest,* Aug. 20, 1921, 13.

79. Morgan Blake, "Dirty Sox Only Dry Cleaned," *Atlanta Journal,* Aug. 3, 1921, 17.

80. *Chicago Daily News,* Aug. 4, 1921, 1.

81. *New York Times,* Aug. 4, 1921, 14.

82. John B. Sheridan, "Back of the Home Plate," *Sporting News,* Oct. 23, 1919, 6.

83. *Sporting News,* June 17, 1920, 4.

84. *Brooklyn Eagle* quoted in *Literary Digest,* Oct. 9, 1920, 12.

85. *New York Times,* Sept. 27, 1920, 11.

86. *Chicago Tribune,* Sept. 23, 1920, 2.

87. *Chicago Herald and Examiner,* Nov. 12, 1920, 6.

88. *Chicago Herald and Examiner,* Mar. 31, 1921, 8.

89. *Detroit Free Press,* Sept. 30, 1920, 6.

90. *Literary Digest,* Aug. 20, 1921, 14. Other writers used different metaphors to convey the same message. For example: "Whitewash alone will not remedy a bad smell. The public does not distrust the players, but it distrusts the management; and as sure as God made little apples the owners must provide a management above suspicion of carelessness and inefficiency, or professional baseball will go over Niagara in a broken barrel." *Chicago Herald and Examiner,* Oct. 18, 1920, 6.

91. Tucher, *Froth and Scum,* 9–11.

92. Ibid., 11.

93. Harper Leech and John C. Carroll, *What's the News?* (Chicago: Pascal, 1926), 13.

94. *New York Tribune,* Sept. 28, 1920, 1.

95. *Chicago Tribune,* Sept. 28, 1920, 1.

96. Cliff Abbo, "The Gambling Mess," *New Orleans Times-Picayune,* Sept. 29, 1920, 14.

97. Grantland Rice, "The Sportlight," *New York Tribune,* Sept. 30, 1920, 12.

98. Abbo, "The Gambling Mess," 14.

99. *New York Times,* Oct. 1, 1920, 2.

100. Morgan Blake, "Baseball Traitors and Crooks Are Uncovered," *Atlanta Journal,* Sept. 29, 1920, 11.

101. Charles Dryden, "Benedict Arnold's Team," *Chicago Herald and Examiner,* Sept. 30, 1920, 9; Alexander F. Jones, "'Benedict Arnolds' of Baseball Slink from View of Oldtimers, Who Can't Believe Disclosures," *Pittsburgh Post,* Sept. 30, 1920, 8.

102. *Chicago Herald and Examiner,* July 21, 1921, 4.

103. *Pittsburgh Post,* Sept. 30, 1920, 8.

104. The jury was all male, all but two jurors were married, and their ages ranged from thirty to forty-seven. The *Washington Post* reported that "none is a student of the game or of the un-fan type." *Washington Post,* July 16, 1921, 8.

105. George Phair, "Breakfast Food," *Chicago Herald and Examiner,* Feb. 8, 1921, 8.

106. The mysterious disappearance of the original confessions and waivers of immunity is often noted to suggest that corruption was widespread. It was. But as a purely legal matter, it was not significant, for Judge Hugo M. Friend ruled that in place of the original confessions, the state could have the court stenographers from the grand jury inquiry read from their shorthand notes the testimony of the three players. The judge also granted permission for Judge Charles McDonald (who presided over the grand jury investigation) and others to whom the players told their stories before appearing before the grand jury to testify about these conversations. According to the *Washington Post:* "The actual transcripts of the confessions varied but little from the frequently published reports of them." *Washington Post,* July 27, 1921, 10.

107. *Chicago Herald and Examiner,* Aug. 1, 1921, 5.

108. *Chicago Tribune,* Aug. 3, 1921, 1.

109. *Chicago Herald and Examiner,* Aug. 4, 1921, 1.

110. *Chicago Tribune,* Aug. 4, 1921, 8.

111. *Cleveland Plain Dealer,* Aug. 4, 1921, 8.

112. *Cincinnati Enquirer,* Aug. 4, 1921, 8.

113. Peter Hühm, "The Detective as Reader: Narrativity and Reading Concepts in Detective Fiction," *Modern Fiction Studies* 33:3 (Autumn 1987): 452.

114. Ibid.

115. *Chicago Tribune,* July 21, 1921, 1.

116. See Leonard Dinnerstein, *Uneasy at Home: Antisemitism and the American Experience* (New York: Columbia University Press, 1987); David A. Gerber, ed., *Anti-Semitism in American History* (Urbana: University of Illinois Press, 1986); John Higham, "American Anti-Semitism Historically Reconsidered," in *Jews in the Mind of America,* ed. George Salomon (New York: Basic Books, 1966); Harold E. Quinley and Charles Y. Glock, *Anti-Semitism in America* (New York: Free Press, 1979); and Frederic Cople Jaher, *A Scapegoat in the Wilderness: The Origins and Rise of Anti-Semitism in America* (Cambridge, Mass.: Harvard University Press, 1994).

117. Although Peter Levine observes that the Black Sox scandal "did not include any Jewish athletes," he notes that "Erskine Mayer, a Jewish boy of German descent born in Atlanta, and the first Jewish hurler to win 20 games in two consecutive seasons, appeared in one inning of the fifth game of the series for Chicago. Mayer, however, was not involved in the conspiracy. His name does not appear in the *Baseball Encyclopedia*'s White Sox team roster for the 1919 season nor was he mentioned in contemporary accounts of the 'fix' or in studies of" the scandal. Peter Levine, *Ellis Island to Ebbets Field: Sport and the American Jewish Experience* (New York: Oxford University Press, 1992), 84, 103.

118. *Sporting News,* Oct. 9, 1919, 4.

119. *Sporting News,* Oct. 16, 1919, 4.

120. *Sporting News* quoted in Richard C. Crepeau, *Baseball: America's Diamond Mind, 1919–1941* (Gainesville: University Presses of Florida, 1980), 14.

121. Leo Katcher, *The Big Bankroll: The Life and Times of Arnold Rothstein* (New York: Harper and Brothers, 1974), 139.

122. Ibid., 148.

123. F. Scott Fitzgerald, *The Great Gatsby* (New York: Collier Books, [1925] 1986), 74.

124. Asinof, *Eight Men Out,* 218–19.

125. *New York World,* Oct. 1, 1920, 1.

126. Katcher, *The Big Bankroll,* 148.

127. *Chicago Tribune,* Oct. 1, 1920, 1.

128. George Barton, "Weaver's Role in Fixed World Series," *Baseball Digest,* Apr. 1956, 49.

129. Asinof, *Eight Men Out,* 231–33.

130. Eliot Asinof, *Bleeding between the Lines* (New York: Holt, Rinehart, and Winston, 1979), 105.

131. Levine, *Ellis Island to Ebbets Field,* 106.

132. Deborah Lipstadt, *Denying the Holocaust: The Growing Assault on Truth and Memory* (New York: Free Press, 1993), 37.

133. See "Jewish Gamblers Corrupt American Baseball" and "The Jewish Degradation of American Baseball," in *Jewish Influences in American Life,* volume 3 of *The International Jew: The World's Foremost Problem* (Dearborn, Mich.: *Dearborn Independent,* 1921).

134. "Jewish Gamblers Corrupt American Baseball," 49 (first quote), 37 (second quote), 50 (sixth quote); "Jewish Degradation of American Baseball," 53 (third and fifth quotes), 54 (fourth quote).

135. Levine, *Ellis Island to Ebbets Field,* 107.

136. "Jewish Gamblers Corrupt American Baseball," 43 (first and second quotes), 44 (third quote), 46 (fourth and fifth quotes), 47 (sixth quote).

137. Levine, *Ellis Island to Ebbets Field,* 108.

138. The idea of beset manhood is borrowed from Nina Baym, "Melodramas of Beset Manhood: How Theories of American Fiction Exclude Women Authors," *American Quarterly* 33:1 (Spring 1981): 123–39.

139. This crisis of masculinity affected men from different socioeconomic classes differently. Michael S. Kimmell observes that the "perceived crisis of masculinity was not a generic crisis, experienced by all men in similar ways. It was essentially a crisis of middle-class white masculinity, a crisis in the dominant paradigm of masculinity that was perceived as threatened by the simultaneous erosion of traditional foundations (e.g., economic autonomy and the frontier), new gains for women, and the tremendous infusion of nonwhite immigrants into the major industrial cities." Michael S. Kimmell, "Baseball and the Reconstitution of American Masculinity, 1880–1920," in *Sport, Men, and the Gender Order: Critical Feminist Perspectives,* ed. Michael A. Messner and Donald F. Sabo (Champaign, Ill.: Human Kinetics, 1990), 57.

140. Michael A. Messner, *Power at Play: Sports and the Problem of Masculinity* (Boston: Beacon Press, 1992), 14.

141. Adelman, *A Sporting Time,* 174.

142. William McKeever, *Training the Boy* (New York: Macmillan, 1913), 91, quoted in Charles Fruehling Springwood, *Cooperstown to Dyersville: A Geography of Baseball Nostalgia* (Boulder: Westview Press, 1996), 47.

143. *Chicago Tribune,* Sept. 24, 1920, 8.

144. Henry H. Brigham, "Indictments for Guilty Players, Foreman Says," *Chicago Herald and Examiner,* Sept. 25, 1920, 2.

145. *Chicago Tribune,* July 30, 1921, 5.

146. Bill Starr, *Clearing the Bases: Baseball Then and Now* (New York: Michael Kensend, 1989), 1.

147. Warren Goldstein, *Playing for Keeps: A History of Early Baseball* (Ithaca: Cornell University Press, [1989] 1991), 43.

148. Ibid., 45.

149. Many Major League ballplayers at the time came from working-class and rural backgrounds. However, the rhetoric the media used to discuss the game and the ideology baseball promoted about itself are best characterized as middle class. Moreover, although the White Sox players implicated in the scandal were not paid well in comparison to some of their peers, they did earn considerably more money than most working-class men at the time, and, once they established themselves in the Majors, they seem to have embraced some traditional middle-class values.

150. Babe Ruth, "Greatest Sport in World on Brink of Ruin, Declares Babe Ruth," *Baltimore Sun,* Sept. 29, 1920, 2.

151. *Chicago Tribune,* Sept. 29, 1920, 2.

152. Robert Edgren, "Edgren's Column," *New York Evening World,* Oct. 1, 1920, 30.

153. *Chicago Herald and Examiner,* Aug. 3, 1921, 1.

154. *New York Times,* Oct. 1, 1920, 10.

155. Billy Sunday, "Billy Sunday Says Average Boy Hates Crooks," *New York Daily News,* Oct. 1, 1920, 21.

156. *Chicago Herald and Examiner,* July 21, 1921, 6.

157. *Cincinnati Enquirer,* Oct. 1, 1920, 8.

158. *Chicago Herald and Examiner,* Sept. 29, 1920, 2.

159. Shoeless Joe Jackson (as told to Furman Bisher), "This Is the Truth!" *Sport,* Oct. 1949, 14.

160. Hugh Fullerton, "Joe Jackson, Idol of the Kids, Fell from His Throne when He Told 'Em 'It's True,'" *New York Evening World,* Sept. 30, 1920, 2.

161. Blake, "Baseball Traitors and Crooks Are Uncovered," 11.

162. *Philadelphia Bulletin* quoted in *Literary Digest,* Oct. 9, 1920, 13.

163. *Chicago Tribune,* Dec. 10, 1920, 21.

164. *Cincinnati Enquirer,* Oct. 3, 1920, 38.

165. Dryden, "Benedict Arnold's Team," 9.

166. *Chicago Tribune,* Sept. 30, 1920, 8.

167. *Chicago Tribune,* Nov. 11, 1920, 8.

168. *Chicago Herald and Examiner,* Oct. 2, 1920, 9.

169. *Washington Post,* Sept. 29, 1920, 6.

170. *Chicago Tribune,* Sept. 29, 1920, 1.

171. *New York Tribune,* Sept. 29, 1920, 2.

172. *Cincinnati Enquirer,* Sept. 29, 1920, 2.

173. Regis M. Walsh, "Verdict Is Shock to Clean Element in Ball Circles," *Pittsburgh Post,* Aug. 3, 1921, 8.

174. *Chicago Herald and Examiner,* July 20, 1920, 6.

175. Charles C. Alexander, *Our Game: An American Baseball History* (New York: Henry Holt, 1991), 109.

176. As one of the few White Sox who earned a salary commensurate with his skills and market value—he negotiated an annual salary of $15,000 with Comiskey before agreeing to join the White Sox—Collins incurred the enmity of many teammates. It did not help matters that, as Gerry Hern tells it, "a rough play at second base when Collins was with the Athletics had made Gandil a bitter enemy." Gerry Hern, "The Tipoff on the Black Sox," *Baseball Digest,* June 1949, 12.

177. James T. Farrell, *My Baseball Diary* (New York: A. S. Barnes, 1957), 189.

178. Ibid., 193.

179. Ibid., 189.

180. Seymour, *Baseball: The Golden Age,* 333.

181. *Chicago Tribune,* Sept. 29, 1920, 3.

182. *Chicago Daily News,* Sept. 29, 1920, 21.

183. Blake, "Baseball Traitors and Crooks Are Uncovered," 11.

184. *Chicago Herald and Examiner,* Oct. 2, 1920, 9.

185. *New Republic* quoted in Alexander, *Our Game,* 133.

186. Two years before he died, and almost thirty years after the Big Fix, Eddie Collins observed: "All the things you think are vital to the success of any athletic organization were missing from it [the 1919 White Sox], and yet it was the greatest collection of players ever assembled, I would say. The wonderful [Philadelphia] Athletics teams I played for believed in teamwork and cooperation. I always thought you couldn't win without those virtues until I joined the White Sox." Hern, "The Tipoff on the Black Sox," 12.

187. Jules Tygiel, *Past Time: Baseball as History* (New York: Oxford University Press, 2000), 36.

188. Asinof, *Eight Men Out,* 49.

189. Donald Honig, *Baseball America: The Heroes of the Game and the Times of Their Glory* (New York: Galahad Books, 1993), 103.

190. G. W. Axelson, *"Commy": The Life Story of Charles A. Comiskey* (Chicago: Reilly and Lee, 1919), 315.

191. Ibid., 318.

192. Charles A. Comiskey, "Comiskey Assails Johnson in Bribe Case," *Chicago Herald and Examiner,* Sept. 25, 1920, 2.

193. "Comiskey Hard Hit by Perfidy of His Players," *Chicago Tribune,* Sept. 29, 1920, 3.

194. *Chicago Daily News,* Sept. 29, 1920, 3.

195. *Chicago Tribune,* Sept. 30, 1920, 15.

196. *Chicago Herald and Examiner,* Oct. 2, 1920, 9.

197. James O'Leary, "Men's Confessions Shock Boston Fans," *Boston Evening Globe,* Sept. 29, 1920, 9.

198. *Cincinnati Enquirer,* Sept. 30, 1920, 4.

199. *Los Angeles Times,* Sept. 30, 1920, 4.

200. *Cleveland Plain Dealer,* Sept. 30, 1920, 14.

201. *Chicago Herald and Examiner,* Oct. 1, 1920, 9.

202. *Pittsburgh Post,* Oct. 1, 1920, 8.

203. *Cincinnati Enquirer,* Oct. 3, 1920, 38.

204. *Kansas City Star,* Sept. 30, 1920, 26.

205. Hugh Fullerton, "Baseball on Trial," *New Republic,* Oct. 20, 1920, 184.

206. Asinof, *Eight Men Out,* 147.

207. Burke, *Never Just a Game,* 233.

208. Fullerton, "Baseball on Trial," 184.

209. Before Landis accepted the position of baseball commissioner, the *Chicago Tribune* editorialized: "Landis is a synonym for a square deal, and nothing could rehabilitate a scandal shot enterprise so quickly as the guaranty of Landis' name. It's worth a mint of money to baseball, which has to win back public confidence." *Chicago Tribune,* Nov. 10, 1920, 8.

210. Most famously, Landis gained national attention in 1907 due to an unprecedented $29,240,000 ruling against John D. Rockefeller's Standard Oil Company that was later overturned by the Supreme Court. J. G. Taylor Spink, *Judge Landis and Twenty-Five Years of Baseball* (New York: Thomas Y. Crowell, [1947] 1953), 20.

211. Seymour, *Baseball: The Golden Age,* 368.

212. Harvey Frommer, *Shoeless Joe and Ragtime Baseball* (Dallas: Taylor, 1992), 156.

213. Norman L. Rosenberg, "Here Comes the Judge!: The Origins of Baseball's Commissioner System and American Legal Culture," *Journal of Popular Culture* 20:4 (Spring 1987): 140.

214. Ron Fimrite, "His Own Biggest Fan," *Sports Illustrated,* July 19, 1993, 76.

215. Honig, *Baseball America,* 115.

216. Lee Lowenfish and Tony Lupien, *The Imperfect Diamond: The Story of Baseball's Reserve System and the Men Who Fought to Change It* (New York: Stein and Day, 1980), 104.

217. Larry Woltz, "General Baseball Public Indorses Judge Landis," *Chicago Herald and Examiner,* Nov. 14, 1920, 15.

218. Asinof, *Eight Men Out,* 275.

219. *Chicago Herald and Examiner,* June 22, 1921, 10.

220. W. J. Macbeth, "In All Fairness," *New York Tribune,* Aug. 1, 1921, 9.

221. "All Agree with Landis," *Kansas City Star,* Aug. 4, 1921, 10.

222. Rosenberg, "Here Comes the Judge!" 142.

223. Honig, *Baseball America*, 115.

224. *Chicago Herald and Examiner*, Aug. 4, 1921, 6.

225. Darnton adds: "Information must be sifted, sorted, and interpreted. Interpretive schemes belong to cultural configurations, which have varied enormously over time. As our ancestors lived in different mental worlds, they must have read differently, and the history of reading could be as complex as the history of thinking." Darnton, *The Kiss of Lamourette*, 187.

226. Cathy N. Davidson, ed., *Reading in America: Literature and Social History* (Baltimore: Johns Hopkins University Press, 1989), 19.

227. Crepeau, *Baseball*, 10.

228. Farrell, *My Baseball Diary*, 105.

229. Grantland Rice, "The Sportlight," *New York Tribune*, Sept. 30, 1920, 12.

230. Harvey Woodruff, *Chicago Tribune*, Sept. 26, 1920, pt. 2, p. 1.

231. The game-fixing revelations, Woodruff continued, "almost destroys one's faith in human nature. That men who have been hailed as heroes, who have been idolized as no other ball players ever have been idolized, who have been supported in victory and defeat as no other team ever has been supported, should sell their honor and their souls, their obligations to their supporters, their obligations to their teammates, must rock almost to its foundations our confidence in everything." Harvey Woodruff, *Chicago Tribune*, Sept. 30, 1920, 15.

232. Harvey Woodruff, *Chicago Tribune*, Oct. 1, 1920, 19.

233. Harvey Woodruff, *Chicago Tribune*, Dec. 17, 1920, 22.

234. *New York Daily News*, Sept. 30, 1920, 21.

235. *Chicago Tribune*, Oct. 3, 1920, pt. 2, p. 1.

236. *Chicago Tribune*, Oct. 3, 1920, 8.

237. *Chicago Tribune*, Nov. 13, 1920, 8.

238. *Chicago Tribune*, Dec. 14, 1920, 19.

239. *Chicago Tribune*, Dec. 11, 1920, 19.

240. *Chicago Tribune*, Dec. 16, 1920, 19.

241. *Chicago Tribune*, Dec. 17, 1920, 22.

242. *Chicago Tribune*, Dec. 15, 1920, 19.

243. *Chicago Tribune*, Dec. 18, 1920, 19.

244. *Chicago Tribune*, Nov. 18, 1920, 8.

245. *Chicago Herald and Examiner*, Mar. 17, 1921, 8.

246. *Chicago Herald and Examiner*, June 11, 1921, 6.

247. *Chicago Herald and Examiner*, June 29, 1921, 6.

248. Robert Scholes, *Protocols of Reading* (New Haven: Yale University Press, 1989), 10.

249. Asinof, *Eight Men Out*, 198.

250. Grantland Rice, *The Tumult and the Shouting: My Life in Sport* (New York: A. S. Barnes, 1954), 351.

251. Westbrook Pegler, *Chicago Tribune*, Nov. 13, 1932, pt. 2, p. 3.

Chapter 2: "Fix These Faces in Your Memory"

1. *Sporting News,* Oct. 7, 1920, 2.

2. C. Vann Woodward, *The Strange Career of Jim Crow,* 3d rev. ed. (New York: Oxford University Press, [1955] 1974), xvi.

3. Jim Collins, *Uncommon Cultures: Popular Culture and Post-Modernism* (New York: Routledge, 1989), 2.

4. Meg Greenfield, "Chronic Political Amnesia," *Newsweek,* Sept. 22, 1980, 96.

5. David Thelen, ed., *Memory and American History* (Bloomington: Indiana University Press, [1989] 1990), ix–x.

6. The wide-ranging influence of Maurice Halbwachs's *La Mémoire collective* has led me to choose the term *collective memory* over *social memory.* Halbwachs's text was translated by Francis J. Ditter Jr. and Vida Yazdi Ditter and published as *The Collective Memory* (New York: Harper and Row, [1950] 1980). See also Maurice Halbwachs, *On Collective Memory,* ed. and trans. Lewis A. Coser (Chicago: University of Chicago Press, 1992). For Halbwachs's intellectual indebtedness to Bergson and Durkheim, see Mary Douglas, introduction to *The Collective Memory,* 1–10.

7. Halbwachs, *The Collective Memory,* 69.

8. Patrick H. Hutton, *History as an Art of Memory* (Hanover, N.H.: University Press of New England, 1993), 76.

9. Halbwachs, *The Collective Memory,* 84.

10. Ibid., 23.

11. Halbwachs, *On Collective Memory,* 52.

12. Although the Halbwachsian perspective on collective memory is useful, his approach poses at least two problems. First, it is insistently, perhaps overly, presentist in orientation. Second, the Halbwachsian formulation probably does not credit individuals with the necessary agency to produce or maintain counter-memories that resist the traditions and narratives promulgated by the social groups to which those individuals belong. This is problematic because, no matter how uncommon it may be, individuals are certainly capable of remembering against the grain. Halbwachs, *The Collective Memory,* 48.

13. According to Douglas, Bergson, for example, "supposed that the whole of past experience is always present to us, like the printed pages of a book, complete and entire in subterranean galleries of the mind." Douglas, introduction, 5.

14. Iwona Irwin-Zarecka, *Frames of Remembrance: The Dynamics of Collective Memory* (New Brunswick, N.J.: Transaction, 1994), 18.

15. James Wilkinson, "A Choice of Fictions: Historians, Memory, and Evidence," *Publications of the Modern Language Association* 111:1 (Jan. 1996): 86.

16. Ibid., 81.

17. Harold Seymour, *Baseball: The Golden Age* (New York: Oxford University Press, [1971] 1989), 318–20.

18. Tristram P. Coffin, *The Old Ball Game: Baseball in Folklore and Fiction* (New York: Herder and Herder, 1971), 95–96.

19. Ibid., 100.

20. J. G. Taylor Spink, *Judge Landis and Twenty-Five Years of Baseball* (New York: Thomas Y. Crowell, [1947] 1953), 80. For a more recent (and complete) biography of Landis, see David Pietrusza, *Judge and Jury: The Life and Times of Judge Kenesaw Mountain Landis* (South Bend, Ind.: Diamond Communications, 1998).

21. Eliot Asinof, *Eight Men Out: The Black Sox and the 1919 World Series* (New York: Henry Holt, [1963] 1987), 230.

22. Ibid., 179.

23. Ibid., 272.

24. Ibid., 273.

25. Associated Press quoted in Harvey Frommer, *Shoeless Joe and Ragtime Baseball* (Dallas: Taylor, 1992), 169.

26. Spink, *Judge Landis and Twenty-Five Years of Baseball,* 84.

27. Asinof, *Eight Men Out,* 275.

28. Charles C. Alexander, *Our Game: An American Baseball History* (New York: Henry Holt, 1991), 143.

29. Spink, *Judge Landis and Twenty-Five Years of Baseball,* 96.

30. Ibid., 91.

31. "Why was Kauff deprived of his livelihood and the New York club of his services, even though the court had acquitted him?" asks Harold Seymour. "Evidently because the outcome of his trial did not suit Landis." Seymour, *Baseball: The Golden Age,* 375.

32. *New York Times,* Aug. 17, 1922, 9.

33. Seymour, *Baseball: The Golden Age,* 38.

34. Spink, *Judge Landis and Twenty-Five Years of Baseball,* 133.

35. The *Sporting News* editorialized "that starting an inquiry into the Dolan-O'Connell case would [not necessarily] develop into such a tremendous scandal [as the Black Sox affair]—and yet no one ever knows when a stone starts to roll what sort of an avalanche may be the finale." *Sporting News,* Jan. 22, 1925, 4.

36. Daniel E. Ginsburg, *The Fix Is In: A History of Baseball Gambling and Game Fixing Scandals* (Jefferson, N.C.: McFarland, 1995), 204.

37. The economist Clark Nardinelli maintains that "the real battle during the Cobb-Speaker case was between Landis and [Ban] Johnson [who was president of the American League]. Johnson had announced that Cobb and Speaker would never again play baseball in the American League. When he reinstated them, Landis insisted that the two play in the American League. Cobb signed with the Philadelphia Athletics, Speaker with the Washington Senators. A humiliated Ban Johnson retired shortly thereafter and Landis' position as the exclusive guardian of the baseball cartel was secure." Clark Nardinelli, "Judge Kenesaw Mountain Landis and the

Art of Cartel Enforcement," in *Baseball History: An Annual of Original Baseball Research,* ed. Peter Levine (Westport, Conn.: Meckler Books, 1989), 110.

38. According to Harold Seymour, "Eddie Collins, former captain of the Clean Sox, explained that the fund was raised more than a month after the series at issue—an implication that time converted a bribe into a gift. 'In those days,' Collins pointed out, 'it was nothing out of the ordinary to give a player on another team some sort of gift if he went out of the way to turn in a good performance against one of a team's leading rivals in the [pennant] race. Frank admission of this custom was somewhat disillusioning. It ran counter to the article of faith that the heroes were straining their hardest to win at all times." Seymour, *Baseball: The Golden Age,* 385.

39. Dan Gutman, *Baseball Babylon: From the Black Sox to Pete Rose, the Real Stories behind the Scandals that Rocked the Game* (New York: Penguin Books, 1992), 222.

40. Ibid., 223.

41. Spink, *Judge Landis and Twenty-Five Years of Baseball,* 184.

42. Jules Tygiel, *Baseball's Great Experiment: Jackie Robinson and His Legacy* (New York: Oxford University Press, [1983] 1993), 31.

43. *Chicago Herald-American,* Nov. 27, 1944, 10.

44. Spink, *Judge Landis and Twenty-Five Years of Baseball,* 294.

45. Nardinelli convincingly argues that early in his tenure Landis "established a harsh and arbitrary enforcement policy that effectively kept" Major League Baseball's "cartel in place. The key was the fear he inspired in players. No player dared risk his career in order to challenge the monopsony. With players unwilling to jump to a new league, no league could hope to compete with organized baseball. None tried. The seeming arbitrariness of Landis' rulings probably enhanced his effectiveness, as uncertainty raised the expected costs of defiance." Nardinelli, "Judge Kenesaw Mountain Landis," 111.

46. Bill Rabinowitz, "Baseball and the Great Depression," in *Baseball History,* 49–59.

47. Even a partial list of the writers who allude to the Black Sox scandal moment in *The Great Gatsby* is long and impressive. See, e.g., Asinof, *Eight Men Out,* xix; Coffin, *The Old Ball Game,* 98–99; Lawrence S. Ritter, *The Glory of Their Times* (New York: William Morrow, [1966] 1992), 218; Seymour, *Baseball: The Golden Age,* 337; and Joel Zoss and John Bowman, *Diamonds in the Rough: The Untold Story of Baseball* (New York: Macmillan, 1989), 270.

48. F. Scott Fitzgerald, *The Great Gatsby* (New York: Collier Books, [1925] 1986), 74.

49. John A. Lauricella, "The Black Sox Signature Baseball in *The Great Gatsby,*" *Aethlon: The Journal of Sport Literature* 10:1 (Fall 1992): 86.

50. Ibid., 93.

51. Rothstein's biographer, Leo Katcher, notes: "Fitzgerald, in Nick Carraway's interior monologue, came closer to the truth of the 1919 World Series than most. The fix did happen as the end of an inevitable chain of events." Leo Katcher, *The*

Big Bankroll: The Life and Times of Arnold Rothstein (New York: Harper and Brothers, 1974), 138.

52. Josephine Z. Kopf, "Meyer Wolfsheim and Robert Cohn: A Study of a Jewish Type and Stereotype," *Tradition: A Journal of Orthodox Jewish Thought* 10:3 (Spring 1969): 98.

53. Ibid., 99.

54. Allan Boyer, "*The Great Gatsby,* the Black Sox, High Finance, and American Law," *Michigan Law Review* 88:2 (Nov. 1989): 332.

55. Michael Schudson, "When?: Deadlines, Datelines, and History," in *Reading the News,* ed. Robert Karl Manoff and Michael Schudson (New York: Pantheon Books, 1986), 87.

56. *Chicago American,* Oct. 27, 1931, 21.

57. Comiskey's son, Louis, received this message of condolence from President Hoover: "Every one interested in clean and honest sportsmanship will grieve with you in the death of your father, Charles A. Comiskey. His career coincided with the evolution of baseball into our national sport. His rugged character was reflected in the ideals and standards which he valiantly championed in his responsible connection with the sport." *Chicago American,* Oct. 27, 1931, 21.

58. John Kieran, *New York Times,* Oct. 27, 1931, 32.

59. Edward Geiger, *Chicago American,* Oct. 27, 1931, 21.

60. *Chicago Herald and Examiner,* Oct. 27, 1931, 1.

61. Harry Neily, *Chicago American,* Oct. 26, 1931, 11.

62. *Washington Post,* Oct. 27, 1931, 16.

63. Irwin M. Howe, "Death Summons Charles A. Comiskey," *Sporting News,* Oct. 26, 1931, 3.

64. Warren Brown, *Chicago Herald and Examiner,* Oct. 27, 1931, 17.

65. *New York Times,* Jan. 3, 1933, 18. The *Chicago Tribune* reported his death in almost precisely the same manner. See "Heart Attack Fatal; Chicago Boss Five Years," *Chicago Tribune,* Jan. 3, 1933, 17; see also *Sporting News,* Jan. 5, 1933, 1.

66. Asinof, *Eight Men Out,* 283.

67. For another example of this phenomenon, see Pete Dexter's "Black Sox Blues," which profiles an old ballplayer, Darby Rathman, who was barred from baseball by Judge Landis for playing on a semipro team that included White Sox players implicated in the scandal. According to Rathman: "I'm not afraid to die, but I am afraid of life. I am afraid of the way things get thrown out of whack. All it takes is a nudge. That's why I never talked much about what happened. I didn't want my name associated with it again. But that doesn't mean it ever left me alone. After sixty-four years I still wake up some mornings and there it is." Pete Dexter, "Black Sox Blues," *Esquire,* Oct. 1984, 265.

68. Donald Gropman, *Say It Ain't So, Joe!: The True Story of Shoeless Joe Jackson and the 1919 World Series* (New York: Lynx Books, [1979] 1988), 215.

69. "Reinstate Shoeless Joe!" *New York World-Telegram,* Dec. 21, 1933, 26.

70. Gropman, *Say It Ain't So, Joe!* 217.

71. Edwin Emery and Michael Emery, *The Press and America: An Interpretative History of the Mass Media,* 7th ed. (Englewood Cliffs, N.J.: Prentice-Hall, [1954] 1992), 318.

72. Westbrook Pegler, *New York World-Telegram,* Dec. 23, 1933, 15.

73. Halbwachs, *The Collective Memory,* 48.

74. Richard Schickel, "Brave Cuts at a Knuckle Ball," *Time,* Sept. 5, 1988, 63.

75. Alf H. Walle, "'I'm Afraid It Is, Kid': The Social Dynamics of a Baseball Story," *New York Folklore* 3–4 (Winter 1979): 197–202.

76. Ibid., 197, 202.

77. Ibid., 198.

78. Ibid.

79. Ibid.

80. Ibid., 199.

81. Ibid., 200. Evidence is scant, but for others it may have dramatized the ethos expressed in the maxim It ain't cheatin' if you don't get caught. No matter how often it was repeated, the Black Sox story must have strained the credulity of many youthful audiences around the barber shop, in the fields, or at bedtime. It was simply too fantastic to be credible. "How could we possibly believe those yarns?" asks Bill Starr. "We were ball players, too. We knew from our own experiences in our schoolyard games the burning intensities in each of us to get a hit, to catch a ball, to score a run—to win. There was no other way to play the game, not for us and certainly not for our heroes, the gods of baseball, the American League Champions—the Chicago White Sox." Bill Starr, *Clearing the Bases: Baseball Then and Now* (New York: Michael Kensend, 1989), 1.

82. David Cataneo, *Hornsby Hit One over My Head: A Fans' Oral History of Baseball* (New York: Harcourt Brace, 1997).

83. Carl Becker, "Everyman His Own Historian," *American Historical Review* 37:2 (Jan. 1932): 221–36.

84. Interview with Ben Bruhn, July 11, 1998.

85. Telephone interview with Bill Gleason, Aug. 25, 1998.

86. Telephone interview with Dave Fitzsimmons, Aug. 6, 1998. See also Warren Brown, *The Chicago White Sox* (New York: G. P. Putnam's Sons, 1952).

87. Phil Bergen, "Black Sox Memories," Sept. 24, 1998, personal e-mail message. See Algren, "The Silver-Colored Yesterday," in *The Fireside Book of Baseball,* ed. Charles Einstein (New York: Simon and Schuster, 1956), 2–5. Algren's "The Silver-Colored Yesterday" was first published in his prose poem *Chicago: City on the Make* (New York: McGraw-Hill, [1951] 1983).

88. Telephone interview with Albert E. Stone, Sept. 25, 1998; Allen Guttmann, "Re: Do You Remember Learning about the Black Sox Scandal?" Sept. 24, 1998, personal e-mail message.

89. Interview with Melvin L. Adelman, June 25, 1998.

90. Gleason interview.

91. Interview with Bill Jauss, June 17, 1998.

92. John Lardner, "Remember the Black Sox?" *Saturday Evening Post,* Apr. 30, 1938, 14–15, 82–85. Lardner's article was later anthologized in Thomas L. Stix's *Say It Ain't So, Joe* (New York: Boni and Gaer, 1947), 2–21.

93. Jonathan Yardley, *Ring: A Biography of Ring Lardner* (New York: Athenum, 1984), 5. Ring Lardner Jr. adds that his father's "disenchantment with baseball had clearly begun with the 'Black Sox' Series of 1919, but I feel the extent of it has been exaggerated, along with the idea that he came to hate the whole human race." He further notes: "I was only four at the time and can't testify directly to my father's reaction, but I don't think a deeply disillusioned man could dash off that lyric [the parody "I'm Forever Blowing Ball Games"], and the way he spoke about the event later gave me the feeling he was at least as concerned about losing a substantial bet . . . as he was about the moral turpitude of the players." Ring Lardner Jr., *The Lardners: My Family Remembered* (New York: Harper and Row, 1976), 146–47.

94. Asinof, *Eight Men Out,* 198. Lardner did allude to the Black Sox scandal in some of his stories about the 1920 World Series between Cleveland and Brooklyn. See "Ring Approached by 'Fixers,'" *Chicago Herald and Examiner,* Oct. 6, 1920, 9.

95. A phrase used by the literary critic Harold Bloom, *anxiety of influence* refers to how literary influence inescapably involves a distortion of a predecessor's work. Harold Bloom, *The Anxiety of Influence: A Theory of Poetry* (New York: Oxford University Press, 1973).

96. Lardner, *The Lardners,* 286.

97. Red Smith, *To Absent Friends* (New York: Atheneum, 1982), 366.

98. Malcolm Cowley, "Chicago Poem," *New Republic,* May 4, 1942, 614; Leslie Fiedler, "The Noble Savages of Skid Row," *Reporter,* July 12, 1956, 43.

99. Martha Heasley Cox and Wayne Chatterton, *Nelson Algren* (New York: Twayne, 1975), 9.

100. My biographical sketch is culled from a variety of sources, most notably Bettina Drew's *Nelson Algren: A Life on the Wild Side* (New York: G. P. Putnam's Sons, 1989), Cox and Chatterton's *Nelson Algren,* and H. E. F. Donohue's *Conversations with Nelson Algren* (New York: Hill and Wang, 1964).

101. Drew also notes that dropping his surname allowed him "to separate from both his family and his Jewish origins." Drew, *Nelson Algren,* 34–35.

102. Kenneth G. McCollum, "Nelson Algren," in *Dictionary of Literary Biography,* vol. 9, ed. James J. Martine (Detroit: Gale Research, 1981), 10.

103. Drew, *Nelson Algren,* 129.

104. Chester E. Eisinger, *Fiction of the Forties* (Chicago: University of Chicago Press, 1963), 76.

105. McCollum, "Nelson Algren," 10.

106. Nelson Algren, "The Swede Was a Hard Guy," *Southern Review* 7:4 (1942): 873–79.

107. Asinof uses excerpts from Algren's poem four times in *Eight Men Out,* including a lengthy passage on the final page.

108. Nelson Algren, *Chicago: City on the Make* (New York: McGraw-Hill, [1951] 1983). Quotations of "The Silver-Colored Yesterday" are from this edition.

109. Nelson Algren, "Being a Loser," ms., Ohio State University Division of Rare Books and Manuscripts, quoted in Drew, *Nelson Algren,* 112.

110. Fitzgerald, *The Great Gatsby,* 74.

111. Quoted in Cox and Chatterton, *Nelson Algren,* 132.

112. Frommer, *Shoeless Joe and Ragtime Baseball,* 188.

113. David Lowenthal, *The Past Is a Foreign Country* (New York: Cambridge University Press, [1985] 1990), 205.

114. Michael Schudson, *Watergate in American Memory: How We Remember, Forget, and Reconstruct the Past* (New York: Basic Books, 1992), 220.

115. James A. Vlasich, *A Legend for the Legendary: The Origin of the Baseball Hall of Fame* (Bowling Green, Ohio: Bowling Green State University Popular Press, 1990), 30, 175.

116. Memo from Alexander Cleland to Stephen C. Clark, May 8, 1934, quoted in ibid., 31.

117. Pierre Nora, *Les lieux de mémoire* (Paris: Gallimard, 1984), 1:xxiv, quoted in Hutton, *History as an Art of Memory,* 152.

118. It would return many years later as a small exhibit in the museum. In June 1996, the following text accompanied a small glass-enclosed case containing the shoes and glove used by the pitcher Urban "Red" Faber:

> One year after finishing on top, the White Sox slipped to sixth place in 1918 because of injuries and callups by the military service. But with all of their stars back in action, they regained the heights the following season and were favored to beat the Cincinnati Reds in the World Series. The Series, then a best-of-nine affair, saw the Reds win instead, five games to three. Subsequent investigation revealed that several Chicago players accepted bribes to throw games, and eventually eight White Sox players were banned from baseball for life.
>
> The scandal had its impact. That potentially great team was broken up and the White Sox did not contend again for many years. Because the investigation did not develop until close to the end of the 1920 season, the so-called "Black Sox" remained with the team that year as it finished second. Rising above the shame were a number of distinguished players—including Ray Schalk and Urban "Red" Faber—who never had knowledge of the "fix" until it was revealed.

119. Arthur Daley, "Finest Natural Hitter of Them All," *Baseball Digest,* Feb. 1949, 8.

120. George Lipsitz, *Time Passages: Collective Memory and American Popular Culture* (Minneapolis: University of Minnesota Press, [1990] 1991), 213.

121. Lipsitz posits that "counter-memory forces revision of existing histories by supplying new perspectives about the past" and argues that "counter-memory is not a rejection of history, but a reconstitution of it." While Lipsitz asserts that his notion "of counter-memory differs sharply from that used by Michel Foucault," it should be noted that Foucault himself does not use the phrase, though it is often used to describe some of his work. Nonetheless, like Foucault, Lipsitz offers a crit-

ical perspective that challenges dominant ideologies and conceptions of history. In this way, both critics probe (and celebrate) the subversive and fissures in the conventional wisdom about the past. Ibid., 213, 227. See also Michel Foucault, *Language, Counter-Memory, Practice: Selected Essays and Interviews* (Ithaca: Cornell University Press, 1980).

122. Daley, "Finest Natural Hitter of Them All," 8–10.

123. Walter Johnson, "The Greatest Players I Ever Saw," *Baseball Magazine,* Oct. 1929, 488.

124. Peter Williams, "You Can Blame the Media: The Role of the Press in Creating Baseball Villains," in *Cooperstown Symposium on Baseball and the American Culture (1989),* ed. Alvin L. Hall (Westport, Conn.: Meckler, 1991), 345.

125. Gropman, *Say It Ain't So, Joe!* 203–8.

126. Ward Morehouse, "Joe Jackson at Forty-Four Weighs 220, but He Still Can Slug the Ball," *New York Sun,* Aug. 1932, Joe Jackson Folder, National Baseball Library and Archive, Cooperstown, N.Y.

127. Richard McCann, "Baseball Remains Joe Jackson's First Love Seventeen Years after Ban," Joe Jackson Folder, National Baseball Library and Archive.

128. Frommer, *Shoeless Joe and Ragtime Baseball,* 178. When Jackson died, Carter "Scoop" Latimer of the *Greenville News* reminisced: "Several years ago a huge crowd turned out in the rain to shower Jackson with gifts and to attend an 'appreciation night' game staged in his honor at Brandon field near the spot where he played his first baseball as a towsle-headed kid." See the obituary written by Carter "Scoop" Latimer in the Joe Jackson Folder, National Baseball Library and Archive.

129. Carter "Scoop" Latimer, "Joe Jackson, Contented Carolinian at Fifty-Four, Forgets Bitter Dose in His Cup and Glories in His Twelve Hits in '19 Series," *Sporting News,* Sept. 24, 1942, 1.

130. James Walker, "House Makes Strong Appeal for Jackson," *Greenville News,* Feb. 22, 1951.

131. Also according to Dan Daniel, "Jackson's plight as one of the officially blacklisted players has excited the sympathy of many influential citizens. But the stigma attached to him through connection with the Black Sox never will be erased by a baseball commissioner." Dan Daniel, "Cleveland Honors Joe Jackson," Joe Jackson Folder, National Baseball Library and Archive.

132. Shirley Povich, "This Morning," *Washington Post,* Dec. 7, 1951, B5.

133. Asinof, *Eight Men Out,* 292.

134. Gropman, *Say It Ain't So, Joe!* 229.

135. Irving M. Stein, *The Ginger Kid: The Buck Weaver Story* (Dubuque, Ia.: Elysian Fields Press, 1992), 300.

136. "Buck Weaver Given Welcome to Diamond," Buck Weaver Folder, National Baseball Library and Archive.

137. *Chicago Tribune,* May 9, 1927, 22.

138. Stein, *The Ginger Kid,* 308–9.

139. Edgar Munzel, "Weaver, Former Sox Star, Dies at Sixty-Four," *Chicago Sun-Times,* Feb. 1, 1956, 66.

140. Similar sentiment has been expressed by some people in Pottstown, Pennsylvania, where Weaver was born and raised. According to one octogenarian who remembered Weaver: "You know he was one of us. We have a closed mouth but we stand behind him and defend him." That sense of loyalty contributed to Weaver's election into the Pottstown Area Chapter of the Pennsylvania Sports Hall of Fame in 1981. Stein, *The Ginger Kid,* 324–25. See also Greg Couch, "The Wrong Man Out," *Chicago Sun-Times,* June 28, 2000, 146.

141. Bob Broeg, "Buck Weaver's Case Lesson to Remember," Buck Weaver Folder, National Baseball Library and Archive.

142. The historian Michael Kammen argues: "We arouse and arrange our memories to suit our psychic needs. Historians on the left are surely correct in referring to 'the social production of memory,' and in positing the existence of dominant memories (or a mainstream collective consciousness) along with alternative (usually subordinate) memories. Such historians are equally sensible to differentiate between official and more spontaneous or populistic memories." Michael Kammen, *Mystic Chords of Memory: The Transformation of Tradition in American Culture* (New York: Vintage Books, [1991] 1993), 9.

143. Michael E. Parrish, *Anxious Decades: America in Prosperity and Depression, 1920–1941* (New York: W. W. Norton, 1992), x.

144. Ian Purchase, "Normalcy, Prosperity, and Depression, 1919–1933," in *America's Century: Perspectives on U.S. History since 1900,* ed. Iwan W. Morgan and Neil A. Wynn (New York: Holmes and Meier, 1993), 47.

145. Wilkinson, "A Choice of Fictions," 81.

Chapter 3: The Novel as History, a Novel History

1. David Lowenthal, *The Past Is a Foreign Country* (New York: Cambridge University Press, [1985] 1990), 256. History in this sense of the word refers not to past events themselves, but to a particular type of discourse about the past.

2. Peter S. Prescott, "Malamud: 'A Universal Writer,'" *Newsweek,* Mar. 31, 1986, 78.

3. Bernard Malamud, "The Art of Fiction LII," *Paris Review* 61 (1975): 43.

4. Bernard Malamud, *The Natural* (New York: Avon Books, [1952] 1980), 26.

5. See Norman Podhoretz, "Achilles in Left Field," *Commentary,* Mar. 1953, 321–26; Earl R. Wasserman, "*The Natural:* Malamud's World Ceres," *Centennial Review* 9:4 (Fall 1965): 438–60; Frederick W. Turner, "Myth inside and Out: Malamud's *The Natural,*" *Novel* 1:2 (Winter 1968): 133–39; Michael Oriard, *Dreaming of Heroes: American Sports Fiction, 1868–1980* (Chicago: Nelson-Hall, 1982), 211–20; Kent Cartwright and Mary McElroy, "Malamud's '*The Natural*' and the Appeal of Baseball in American Culture," *Journal of American Culture* 8:2 (Summer 1985): 47–55; and Cordelia Candelaria, *Seeking the Perfect Game: Baseball in American Literature* (Westport, Conn.: Greenwood Press, 1989), 63–74.

6. Malamud quoted in Hal Erickson, *Baseball in the Movies: A Comprehensive Reference, 1915–1991* (Jefferson, N.C.: McFarland, 1992), 217.

7. Of the many essays that explore Malamud's historical references and allusions, the following are particularly good: Eric Solomon, "Jews, Baseball, and the American Novel," *Arete: The Journal of Sport Literature* 2:1 (Spring 1984): 43–66; and Harley Henry, "'Them Dodgers Is My Gallant Knights': Fiction as History in *The Natural* (1952)," *Journal of Sport History* 19:2 (Summer 1992): 110–29.

8. To suggest that there are notable parallels between the characters and the action in *The Natural* and baseball history is not a particularly novel or acute observation. Virtually every critic has noted them. Besides the obvious allusions to Eddie Waitkus, Babe Ruth, Bob Feller, and Joe Jackson, among others, Malamud's novel includes versions of Chuck Hostetler's fall between third base and home in the sixth game of the 1945 World Series, Pete Reiser's ruined career from a crash against an outfield wall, and Ruth's timely home run for a sick child in the hospital. Usually, however, after these obligatory historical allusions are acknowledged, critics quickly move on to examine the ancient epics and medieval romances that inform the novel or to discuss what the book is *really* about.

9. Erickson, *Baseball in the Movies,* 218.

10. Wasserman, "*The Natural:* Malamud's World Ceres," 440.

11. Richard Scheinin notes that Babe Ruth's notorious spring 1925 "bellyache," which forced him to miss almost half the season and cost him a $5,000 fine for failure to manage his personal life, was most likely the result of something more serious than too much beer and hot dogs: "Most of the people who knew him assumed the Babe was suffering from syphilis." Moreover, Harley Henry argues that the intentional hitting episode is derived from a moment during a 1942 game when the Boston Red Sox outfielder Ted Williams "purposely hit foul balls into the stands at a heckler. The incident, frequently offered as an example of Williams's hubristic hostility toward fans, was later authenticated by Williams himself." Richard Scheinin, *Field of Screams: The Dark Underside of America's National Pastime* (New York: W. W. Norton, 1994), 179; Henry, "'Them Dodgers Is My Gallant Knights,'" 126.

12. For other inconsistencies in the novel, see Gerry O'Connor, "Bernard Malamud's *The Natural:* 'The Worst There Ever Was in the Game,'" *Arete: The Journal of Sport Literature* 3:2 (Spring 1986): 37–42.

13. Cartwright and McElroy, "Malamud's '*The Natural,*'" 51.

14. *Chicago Tribune,* Sept. 29, 1920, 2.

15. Sidney Richman, *Bernard Malamud* (New York: Twayne, 1966), 28.

16. Todd Postol, "Reinterpreting the Fifties: Changing Views of a 'Dull' Decade," *Journal of American Culture* 8:2 (1985): 39.

17. See, for example, Joel Foreman, ed., *The Other Fifties: Interrogating Midcentury American Icons* (Urbana: University of Illinois Press, 1997).

18. Henry, "'Them Dodgers Is My Gallant Knights,'" 128–29.

19. Ibid., 128.

20. Ibid., 110.

21. Ibid., 128–29.

22. Lawrence Lasher, ed., *Conversations with Bernard Malamud* (Jackson: University Press of Mississippi, 1991), x, xiv.

23. Bernard Malamud, "Long Work, Short Life," *Michigan Quarterly Review* 26 (Fall 1987): 606.

24. Bernard Malamud, "*The Natural:* Raison d'etre and Meaning," in *Talking Horse: Bernard Malamud on Life and Work,* ed. Alan Cheuse and Nicholas Delbanco (New York: Columbia University Press, 1996), 41.

25. Marcus Klein, *After Alienation: American Novels in Mid-Century* (New York: World, 1962), 256.

26. Cartwright and McElroy, "Malamud's '*The Natural,*'" 48.

27. Edward Prell, "Third Baseman of 1919 Team Passes at Sixty-Four," *Chicago Tribune,* Feb. 1, 1956, pt. 3, p. 1.

28. See "End for an Old Pro," *Newsweek,* Feb. 13, 1956, 87; *Time,* Feb. 13, 1956, 88; *New York Times,* Feb. 1, 1956, 31; and *Washington Post,* Feb. 1, 1956, 27.

29. Arthur Daley, "Dusting Off an Old Scandal," *New York Times,* Feb. 19, 1956, sec. 5, p. 2.

30. John Lardner, "The Riddle of Buck Weaver," *Newsweek,* Feb. 27, 1956, 64.

31. Weaver's association with the Big Fix continued to elicit interest in the months immediately after his death. See George Barton, "Weaver's Role in Fixed World Series," *Baseball Digest,* Apr. 1956, 49–50; and James T. Farrell, "Did Buck Weaver Get a Raw Deal?" *Baseball Digest,* Aug. 1957, 69–78.

32. Arnold "Chick" Gandil (as told to Melvin Durslag), "This Is My Story of the Black Sox Scandal," *Sports Illustrated,* Sept. 17, 1956, 62.

33. Ibid., 62 (first quote), 64 (third quote), 68 (fourth, fifth, and sixth quotes). Thirteen years later, Gandil once again defended himself: "I have taken an awful beating in this thing. But it's all on record. My hits won two of the games against the Reds. If I'd been trying to throw the Series, would I have tried to win those games?" Gandil asked. "I'll tell you this. I'm going to my grave with a clear conscience." Paul Walsh notes: "Gandil died in Dec. 1970 in virtual obscurity in California's Napa Valley at age 82. His four-paragraph obituary in the St. Helena (Calif.) Star made no mention of his baseball past." Dwight Chapin, "Gandil: 'I'll Go to My Grave with a Clear Conscience,'" *Sporting News,* Sept. 6, 1969, 4; Paul Walsh, "Breaking the Fix: Gandil and Risberg: Last of the Black Sox," *Minneapolis Star Tribune,* Sept. 25, 1994, C6.

34. James T. Farrell, *My Baseball Diary* (New York: A. S. Barnes, 1957), 105–6.

35. Ibid., 108.

36. Ibid., 186.

37. David Condon, *Chicago Tribune,* Sept. 22, 1959, pt. 4, p. 1.

38. Dick Hackenberg, "Time Ripe for Sox to Square Stigma of '19," *Chicago Sun-Times,* Oct. 1, 1959, 64.

39. Perhaps trying to capitalize on memories reactivated by the recent World Series, *Baseball Digest* and *Sport* magazine both published articles about the Black Sox in the fall of 1959. See James C. Isaminger, "My Part in the 1919 World Series Fix—Bill Maharg," *Baseball Digest,* Oct.–Nov. 1959, 9–12; Herbert Simons, "How the 1919 Series Was Thrown," *Baseball Digest,* Oct.–Nov. 1959; and Harold Rosenthal, "The Scandalous Black Sox," *Sport,* Oct. 1959, 42–43, 98–102.

40. Nelson Algren, "Nelson Algren Writes Impressions of Series," *Chicago Sun-Times,* Oct. 2, 1959, 5.

41. Nelson Algren, "Nelson Algren's Reflections: Hep-Ghosts of the Rain," *Chicago Sun-Times,* Oct. 10, 1959, 12.

42. Years later, Algren consolidated and rewrote his *Chicago Sun-Times* articles on the 1959 World Series. See "Go! Go! Go! Forty Years Ago," in *The Last Carousel* (New York: G. P. Putnam's Sons, 1973).

43. Stephen J. Whitfield, *The Culture of the Cold War* (Baltimore: Johns Hopkins University Press, 1991), 176.

44. *Washington Post,* Nov. 5, 1959, A16.

45. *Time,* Nov. 16, 1959, 27.

46. Lewis Thompson and Charles Boswell, "Say It Ain't So, Joe!" *American Heritage,* June 1960, 24–27, 88–93; *New York Times,* Jan. 26, 1961, 59.

47. Joe Williams, *New York World-Telegram,* "Should Baseball Demand Equal Time on TV?" Black Sox Scandal Folder, National Baseball Library and Archive, Cooperstown, N.Y.

48. Roy Rosenzweig, "*American Heritage* and Popular History in the United States," in *Presenting the Past: Essays on History and the Public,* ed. Susan Porter Benson, Stephen Brier, and Roy Rosenzweig (Philadelphia: Temple University Press, 1986), 22.

49. Ibid., 28.

50. Thompson and Boswell, "Say It Ain't So, Joe!" 24.

51. Ibid., 88.

52. Ibid., 93.

53. Eliot Asinof, *Bleeding between the Lines* (New York: Holt, Rinehart, and Winston, 1979), 12.

54. Ibid., 58–60.

55. Ibid., 60–62; see also Eliot Asinof, *Man on Spikes* (Carbondale: Southern Illinois University Press [1955] 1998), xv.

56. Asinof, *Bleeding between the Lines,* 137.

57. Joe Goldman, "Writer of the Storm," *Village Voice,* Sept. 6, 1988, 62.

58. Charles C. Alexander, *Our Game: An American Baseball History* (New York: Henry Holt, 1991), 367.

59. Harry Stein, *Hoopla* (New York: St. Martin's Press, 1983), 367.

60. Allen Guttmann, *A Whole New Ball Game: An Interpretation of American Sport* (Chapel Hill: University of North Carolina Press, 1988), 212.

61. Eliot Asinof, *Eight Men Out: The Black Sox and the 1919 World Series* (New York: Henry Holt, [1963] 1987), xi.

62. For instance, Asinof notes that after the first game Kid Gleason "tried several times to see Charles Comiskey. He wanted desperately to talk to him. But Comiskey, as usual, was not available." Asinof adds that when Comiskey first heard the rumors that the series was fixed, he brought his concerns to National League president John Heydler and American League president Ban Johnson, neither of whom took him seriously. Asinof also points out that Hugh Fullerton (with the legendary former pitcher

Christy Mathewson sitting by his side offering advice) recorded plays on his scorecard that "looked suspicious" and later wrote what he knew but his newspaper refused to publish it. As for Ring Lardner, like Fullerton, he could not print what he knew about the World Series, so Asinof recounts the often-noted incident when a slightly inebriated Lardner sang a parody of "I'm Forever Blowing Bubbles" (called "I'm Forever Blowing Ball Games") for the benefit of the White Sox on the train ride back to Chicago after the games in Cincinnati. Ibid., 71, 76–77, 62, 93–94.

63. Without citing a source, Asinof suggests that in November 1920 Illinois state's attorney Maclay Hoyne, who was being replaced by the newly elected Robert Crowe, "lifted the confessions of Cicotte, Jackson, and Williams along with the waivers of immunity they had signed before giving testimony." Asinof also notes that several members of the outvoted prosecution, needing jobs, joined the players' team of defense lawyers. Ibid., 226.

64. Much has been made of this revelation, but Asinof points out that the presiding judge, Hugo M. Friend, ruled "that the confessions had been made voluntarily. They would be admissible as part of the State's case. The confessions, however, were to implicate the confessors only." Ibid., 260.

65. Dominick LaCapra, *History and Criticism* (Ithaca: Cornell University Press, [1985] 1992), 139.

66. "Only God knows what went through Cicotte's mind as he took the mound [for the first game], but he had taken $10,000 and was expected to give the sign. To throw or not to throw? He gave no sign on his first pitch, but he hit [Morrie] Rath on his second. He was uncertain; it must have been hell." Victor Luhrs, *The Great Baseball Mystery—the 1919 World Series* (South Brunswick, N.Y.: A. S. Barnes, 1966), 245–46. Cicotte's own testimony to the Cook County grand jury would seem to contradict Luhrs. See *Chicago Tribune,* Sept. 29, 1920, 2.

67. Luhrs adds that the "Reds would have won anyhow, simply because the uninitiated [White Sox] players made an even worse showing than did the allegedly tainted players." Luhrs, *The Great Baseball Mystery,* 248.

68. Mike Shannon, *Diamond Classics: Essays on One Hundred of the Best Baseball Books Ever Published* (Jefferson, N.C.: McFarland, 1989), 325.

69. Asinof, *Bleeding between the Lines,* 163.

70. LaCapra, *History and Criticism,* 62.

71. See, e.g., Asinof, *Eight Men Out,* 188–93, 285; and Asinof, *Bleeding between the Lines,* 103–9, 113–17.

72. LaCapra, *History and Criticism,* 62. That *Eight Men Out* lacks a bibliography seems far less defensible to me than Asinof's failure to footnote because a historical narrative without a bibliography is inappropriate (bordering on the irresponsible), even for nonacademic writing. For a discussion of the importance of documentation, see Gertrude Himmelfarb's "Where Have All the Footnotes Gone?" in *On Looking into the Abyss: Untimely Thoughts on Culture and Society* (New York: Alfred A. Knopf, 1994).

73. It is important to remember that since historical reconstructions are represented in language, they are justifiably subject to rhetorical analyses. In fact, Hayden White

asserts that "the clue to the 'meaning' of a given historical discourse is contained as much in the rhetoric of the description of the field as it is in the logic of whatever argument may be offered as its explanation." Hayden White, "Historicism, History, and the Figurative Imagination," *Tropics of Discourse: Essays in Cultural Criticism* (Baltimore: Johns Hopkins University Press, [1978] 1992), 106.

74. Ibid., 105.

75. The process of writing about the past necessarily forces a historian to make difficult decisions. "Confronted with a chaos of 'facts,' the historian must 'choose, sever and carve them up' for narrative purposes," writes Hayden White. But, as White notes, the choices confronting someone working in the narrative tradition are not simply limited to deciding what to include and what to foreground (and thus what to exclude and marginalize) within his or her story. A historian must also decide, among other things, what form the narrative will take; that is, he or she must encode the facts within a specific kind of plot structure. As White puts it, "What one historian may emplot as a tragedy, another may emplot as a comedy or romance." Hayden White, "Interpretation in History," in *Tropics of Discourse,* 55, 58.

76. Hayden White, "The Historical Text as Literary Artifact," in *Tropics of Discourse,* 84.

77. Leo Katcher, *The Big Bankroll: The Life and Times of Arnold Rothstein* (New York: Harper and Brothers, 1974), 139.

78. Gandil, "This Is My Story of the Black Sox Scandal," 64.

79. Lowenthal, *The Past Is a Foreign Country,* 218.

80. Asinof, *Bleeding between the Lines,* 192.

81. Goldman, "Writer of the Storm," 62.

82. Interview with Eliot Asinof, June 20, 1994.

83. Asinof remains steadfast in his reconstruction of the Black Sox scandal. Over the years, he has retold his version of the affair at least twice: in *Bleeding between the Lines,* an autobiographical narrative in which he recounts being sued by David Susskind in 1976 over the production of a television drama, and in *1919: America's Loss of Innocence* (New York: Donald I. Fine, 1990), which examines the four major events that exemplify his subtitle: President Woodrow Wilson's defeats at the Paris Peace Conference, the Red Scare, the enactment of the Eighteenth Amendment, and the Black Sox scandal. In both narratives, Asinof rearticulates the version of the 1919 World Series scandal that he offers in *Eight Men Out.*

84. White, "Interpretation in History," 69.

85. Philip J. Landon, "*The History Channel* Presents *The Fifties* (1997)," *Film and History: An Interdisciplinary Journal of Film and Television Studies* 28:1–2 (1998): 57.

Chapter 4: Off the Bench

1. John Durant, *Highlights of the World Series* (New York: Hastings House, [1963] 1971), 49.

2. Bill Veeck (with Ed Linn), *The Hustler's Handbook* (New York: G. P. Putnam's Sons, 1965), 255.

3. Ibid., 298.

4. Victor Luhrs, *The Great Baseball Mystery—the 1919 World Series* (South Brunswick, N.Y.: A. S. Barnes, 1966).

5. A few academically trained historians briefly mentioned the Black Sox scandal in their work before Voigt and Seymour. See John Allen Krout, *Annals of American Sport* (New Haven, Conn.: Yale University Press, 1929), 136; and Foster Rhea Dulles, *America Learns to Play: A History of Popular Recreation, 1607–1940* (New York: D. Appleton-Century, 1940), 356.

6. Steven A. Riess, "The Historiography of American Sport," *OAH Magazine of History* 7:1 (Summer 1992): 10.

7. Seymour published a third baseball history, *Baseball: The People's Game* (New York: Oxford University Press 1990), before he died in 1992, but strictly speaking it was not the third volume in his planned trilogy. David Q. Voigt, *American Baseball: From the Commissioners to Continental Expansion,* vol. 2 (Norman: University of Oklahoma Press, 1970); Harold Seymour, *Baseball: The Golden Age* (New York: Oxford University Press, 1971).

8. John Morton Blum, *Years of Discord: American Politics and Society, 1961–1974* (New York: W. W. Norton, [1991] 1992), x. For general works on the sixties and seventies, see Todd Gitlin, *The Sixties: Years of Hope, Days of Rage* (New York: Bantam Books, 1987); James Miller, *"Democracy Is in the Streets": From Port Huron to the Siege of Chicago* (New York: Simon and Schuster, 1987); David Chalmers, *And the Crooked Places Made Straight: The Struggle for Social Change in the 1960s* (Baltimore: Johns Hopkins University Press, 1991); David Farber, *The Age of Great Dreams: America in the 1960s* (New York: Hill and Wang, 1994); David Steigerwald, *The Sixties and the End of Modern America* (New York: St. Martin's Press, 1995); David Burner, *Making Peace with the Sixties* (Princeton: Princeton University Press, 1996); James J. Farrell, *The Spirit of the Sixties: The Making of Postwar Radicalism* (New York: Routledge, 1997); and Maurice Isserman and Michael Kazin, *America Divided: The Civil War of the 1960s* (New York: Oxford University Press, 2000).

9. Elliott J. Gorn and Warren Goldstein, *A Brief History of American Sports* (New York: Hill and Wang, 1993), 219–20.

10. Harry Edwards, *The Revolt of the Black Athlete* (New York: Free Press, [1969] 1970), 91–114.

11. Benjamin G. Rader, *American Sports: From the Age of Folk Games to the Age of Televised Sport,* 2d ed. (Englewood Cliffs, N.J.: Prentice Hall, [1983] 1990), 330.

12. Michael Kammen, "Introduction: The Historian's Vocation and the State of the Discipline in the United States," in *The Past before Us: Contemporary Historical Writing in the United States,* ed. Michael Kammen (Ithaca: Cornell University Press, 1980), 19–46.

13. Lawrence W. Levine, *The Opening of the American Mind: Canons, Culture, and History* (Boston: Beacon Press, 1996), 26, 67, 99.

14. Steven A. Riess, "Sports and the American Jew: An Introduction," in *Sports*

and the American Jew, ed. Steven A. Riess (Syracuse: Syracuse University Press, 1998), 2–3.

15. For more on the rise of sport history, see Melvin L. Adelman, "Academicians and American Athletics: A Decade of Progress," *Journal of Sport History* 10:1 (Spring 1983): 80–106; S. W. Pope, "American Sport History—toward a New Paradigm," in *The New American Sport History: Recent Approaches and Perspectives,* ed. S. W. Pope (Urbana: University of Illinois Press, 1997); and Nancy L. Struna, "Sport History," in *The History of Exercise and Sport Science,* ed. John D. Massengale and Richard A. Swanson (Champaign, Ill.: Human Kinetics, 1997), 143–79.

16. Frederic L. Paxson, "The Rise of Sport," *Mississippi Valley Historical Review* 4:2 (Sept. 1917): 143–68; Krout, *Annals of American Sport;* Jennie Holliman, *American Sports, 1785–1835* (Philadelphia: Porcupine Press, [1931] 1975); Jesse Frederick Steiner, *Americans at Play: Recent Trends in Recreation and Leisure Time Activities* (New York: McGraw-Hill, 1933); Dulles, *America Learns to Play;* John Rickards Betts, *America's Sporting Heritage, 1850–1950* (Reading, Mass.: Addison-Wesley, 1974).

17. Larry R. Gerlach, "Not Quite Ready for Prime Time: Baseball History, 1983–1993," *Journal of Sport History* 21:2 (Summer 1994): 104.

18. A few popular histories of baseball chronicled the Black Sox scandal before Voigt and Seymour published the books considered here. I have already mentioned Durant's *Highlights of the World Series.* See also Robert Smith, *World Series: The Games and the Players* (Garden City, N.Y.: Doubleday, 1967), 74–77; and Lee Allen, *The World Series: The Story of Baseball's Annual Championship* (New York: G. P. Putnam's Sons, 1969), 91–100. The most interesting popular history is *Baseball: An Informal History* (New York: W. W. Norton, 1969), 168–79, by Douglass Wallop, author of the best-selling novel *The Year the Yankees Lost the Pennant* (1954), which was adapted into the musical (1955) and film *Damn Yankees* (1958).

19. Melvin L. Adelman, "Captain Voigt and American Baseball History," *Canadian Journal of History of Sport* 20:1 (1989): 69.

20. Ibid., 72.

21. Ibid., 70; John Rickards Betts, rev. of *American Baseball: From the Commissioners to Continental Expansion, American Historical Review* 77:1 (Feb. 1972): 218.

22. Voigt, *American Baseball,* 124, 125.

23. Voigt's section on the Black Sox scandal in *American Baseball* was originally published in 1969 in the *Journal of the Illinois State Historical Society* and later revised for publication in *America through Baseball* (Chicago: Nelson-Hall, 1976). The essay is basically the same as the account of the scandal in *American Baseball,* with a few exceptions. David Q. Voigt, "The Chicago Black Sox and the Myth of Baseball's Single Sin," *Journal of the Illinois State Historical Society* 62:3 (Autumn 1969): 302.

24. William M. Tuttle Jr., *Race Riot: Chicago in the Red Summer of 1919* (Urbana: University of Illinois Press, [1970] 1996).

25. John Milton Cooper Jr., *Pivotal Decades: The United States, 1900–1920* (New York: W. W. Norton, 1990), 322–24; Stephen Fox, *Blood and Power: Organized Crime in Twentieth-Century America* (New York: William Morrow, 1989), 99–111.

26. Harold Seymour, rev. of *American Baseball: From the Commissioners to Continental Expansion, Journal of American History* 69:1 (June 1972): 193–94.

27. The jury ruled in Jackson's favor, but the presiding judge set the verdict aside and dismissed the case. Eliot Asinof, *Eight Men Out: The Black Sox and the 1919 World Series* (New York: Henry Holt, [1963] 1987), 289.

28. In *Baseball: The Golden Age,* 331, Seymour contends that Felsch and Risberg sued the White Sox in 1923. However, the White Sox historian Richard C. Lindberg writes: "Toughened by a life that included little formal education, fistfights with Ty Cobb, the humility of banishment from professional baseball following the Black Sox scandal, and the loss of his life savings in the stock market crash of 1929, 'Swede' Risberg remained unrepentant and a 'hard guy' to the very end." Richard C. Lindberg, *The White Sox Encyclopedia* (Philadelphia: Temple University Press, 1997), 209.

29. Irving M. Stein, *The Ginger Kid: The Buck Weaver Story* (Dubuque, Ia.: Elysian Fields Press, 1992), 1–2, 315–16.

30. Hayden White, "Interpretation in History," in *Tropics of Discourse: Essays in Cultural Criticism* (Baltimore: Johns Hopkins University Press, [1978] 1992), 59.

31. Adelman, "Captain Voigt," 70.

32. Ibid., 71.

33. Telephone interview with David Q. Voigt, July 10, 2000.

34. Dorothy Ross, "The New and Newer Histories: Social Theory and Historiography in an American Key," in *Imagined Histories: American Historians Interpret the Past,* ed. Anthony Molho and Gordon S. Wood (Princeton: Princeton University Press, 1998), 95.

35. Quoted in Jerome Holtzman, ed., *No Cheering in the Press Box: Recollections—Personal and Professional—by Eighteen Veteran American Sportswriters* (New York: Holt, Rinehart, and Winston, 1973), 259.

36. Harold Seymour, *Baseball: The Early Years* (New York: Oxford University Press, [1960] 1989), ix.

37. Dorothy Jane Mills, "Sport Historian," Feb. 10, 2000, *Sport History Listserv.* sporthist@pdomain.uwindsor.ca.

38. Dorothy Jane Mills, "Re: Questions about Baseball: The Golden Age," Sept. 2, 1999, personal e-mail message.

39. Other aspects of baseball history, Seymour explains in his preface, like the Negro Leagues and sandlot ball, "are dealt with incidentally" in *Baseball: The Golden Age* and "will be treated more fully" in a later volume (v; all quotations in this chapter are from the 1971 edition); they were, in *Baseball: The People's Game* (New York: Oxford University Press, 1990), a unique look at how the game was played by those not associated with organized baseball.

40. Robert L. Beisner, rev. of *Baseball: The Golden Age, American Historical Review* 77:5 (Dec. 1972): 1519.

41. Jules Tygiel, "Playing by the Book: Baseball History in the 1980s," *Baseball History* 1:4 (Winter 1986): 7.

42. In *Baseball: The Early Years,* Seymour writes: "All statements in this book are supported by documentary evidence. Since this is not a work addressed to specialists, I have not attempted formal documentation of every point. Thus, I have included only a general bibliographical note describing the nature and location of the materials used. However, all my notes showing sources of information are available to any readers who wish to consult them" (viii).

43. Gertrude Himmelfarb, *On Looking into the Abyss: Untimely Thoughts on Culture and Society* (New York: Alfred A. Knopf, 1994), 124.

44. Ibid., 127.

45. Seymour, *Baseball: The Golden Age,* 314, 317, 384, 468.

46. Veeck, *The Hustler's Handbook,* 254.

47. Tygiel, "Playing by the Book," 7.

48. Ibid.

49. According to Dorothy Jane Mills, "For nearly fifty stimulating years I worked closely with my late husband, Harold Seymour, on his chosen subject, the history of American baseball. Seymour, as he preferred even me to call him, felt it necessary to let the public believe he had produced the entire three-volume project himself, with only secretarial and other minor assistance from me and others. For many years I went along with this, because I knew whatever kudos these unique books received were important to Seymour. But the falsity of this stance grated on me so much that toward the end I began requesting an adjustment in crediting that would more closely reflect reality. He could not agree to this. To receive the recognition I felt was due me, I had to wait until his life was over." Dorothy Jane Mills, "A Woman's Work," *Blue Ear,* Apr. 17, 2000, <http://www.blueear.com/articles/womans 170400html> (May 15, 2000).

50. Mills, "Re: Questions about Baseball: The Golden Age."

51. "In the Matter of the Investigation of Alleged Baseball Scandal," transcript of Cook County grand jury testimony, Sept. 28, 1920, 10. This transcript was provided by the law firm Mayer, Brown, and Platt to the Chicago Historical Society for its 1988 exhibit on the Black Sox scandal.

52. Ibid.

53. Ibid., 12.

54. The version of Joe Jackson's grand jury testimony cited here has also been published as an appendix to Harvey Frommer's *Shoeless Joe and Ragtime Baseball* (Dallas: Taylor, 1992), 200, 202.

55. Mills, "Re: Questions about Baseball: The Golden Age."

56. Paul K. Conkin and Roland N. Stromberg, *Heritage and Challenge: The History and Theory of History* (Wheeling, Ill.: Forum Press, [1971] 1989), 86.

57. Peter Novick, *That Noble Dream: The "Objectivity Question" and the American Historical Profession* (New York: Cambridge University Press, [1988] 1993), 2.

58. Steven A. Riess, *Touching Base: Professional Baseball and American Culture in the Progressive Era* (Westport, Conn.: Greenwood Press, 1980), xiii.

59. Place, too, may account for their shared sensibilities. Both Voigt and Seymour were born, raised, and educated in the East.

60. Charles Chamberlain, "Old Men Die, but the Black Sox Scandal Lives On," *Baseball Digest,* Feb. 1970, 60–62.

61. "Kuhn Suspends McLain from Baseball," *Washington Post,* Feb. 20, 1970, D1.

62. *Sports Illustrated,* Mar. 9, 1970, 72.

63. Pete Axthelm, "Slap on the Wrist," *Newsweek,* Apr. 13, 1970, 48.

64. Murray Chass, "Scandals in Past Rocked Baseball," *New York Times,* Apr. 2, 1970, 48.

65. See, for example, Harold Kaese, "Kuhn Action Unavoidable," *Boston Globe,* Feb. 20, 1970, 25; Hal Lebovitz, "McLain, a Dupe Stupe?" *Cleveland Plain Dealer,* Feb. 2, 1970, sec. C, p. 1; Curt Sylvester, "Baseball Suspends McLain," *Detroit Free Press,* Feb. 20, 1970, 2A; George Vecsey, "Baseball Suspends McLain for Ties to Gambling," *New York Times,* Feb. 20, 1970, 50; Arthur Daley, "Downfall of Denny," *New York Times,* Feb. 22, 1970, sec. 5, p. 2.

66. "Remember Black Sox?" *Chicago Daily News,* Feb. 20, 1970, 42.

67. David Condon, "Kuhn Suspends Denny McLain Indefinitely," *Chicago Tribune,* Feb. 20, 1970, sec. 3, p. 1.

68. Francis Rosa, "McLain Squirming as Kuhn Fumbles," *Boston Evening Globe,* Feb. 20, 1970, 24.

69. George Puscas, "Justice, Baseball Style," *Detroit Free Press,* Feb. 20, 1970, 4D.

70. "A Long Fall for Denny," *Detroit Free Press,* Feb. 21, 1970, 6A.

71. Shirley Povich, "McLain Victim of Bookies' Curve, Kuhn Says," *Washington Post,* Apr. 2, 1970, E1.

72. Joe Falls, "Kuhn Took Easy Way Out," *Detroit Free Press,* Apr. 2, 1970, 1D.

73. Axthelm, "Slap on the Wrist," 48.

74. Some wondered, however, about an odd injury McLain suffered late in the 1967 season that may have cost Detroit the American League pennant. According to Tom Callahan, McLain "had a delightful alibi for two mashed toes that cost the 1967 pennant. He said he hurt himself shooing a raccoon away from a garbage can. Whether the raccoon had a Mob connection was a matter of speculation, but McLain was definitely the garbage can. When his bookmaking sideline was uncovered, he blurted, 'My biggest crime is stupidity.' Actually, it was just the thing at which he was most accomplished." Tom Callahan, "Did Pete Do It?: What Are the Odds?" *Time,* June 26, 1989, 92.

75. James T. Patterson, *Grand Expectations: The United States, 1945–1974* (New York: Oxford University Press, 1996), 773.

76. Clifton Daniel, "Gains of Watergate," *New York Times,* Aug. 10, 1974, 1.

77. Mike Royko, "Shoeless Joe Likes the Fit," *Chicago Daily News,* Nov. 24, 1975, 3.

78. Eliot Asinof, *Bleeding between the Lines* (New York: Holt, Rinehart, and Winston, 1979), 13.

79. Ibid., 169.

80. Ed Sherman, "Chicago Strikes Out," *Chicago Tribune,* Aug. 21, 1988, sec. 13, p. 4.

81. George F. Will, "Black October: The Year the Series Was Fixed," *Washington Post,* Oct. 6, 1988, A25.

82. George F. Will, *Bunts: Curt Flood, Camden Yards, Pete Rose, and Other Reflections on Baseball* (New York: Scribner, 1998), 202.

83. Peter W. Morgan, "The Appearance of Propriety: Ethics Reform and the Blifil Paradoxes," *Stanford Law Review* 44:3 (Feb. 1992): 595–96.

84. Robert Lipsyte, "Of Sports, Comebacks, and Nixon," *New York Times,* May 1, 1994, sec. 8, p. 11.

85. Michael Schudson, *Watergate in American Memory: How We Remember, Forget, and Reconstruct the Past* (New York: Basic Books, 1992), 128.

86. Bob Broeg, "Black Sox Weren't Solid Black," Black Sox Scandal Folder, National Baseball Library and Archive, Cooperstown, N.Y.

87. Red Smith, "Last of the Black Sox," *New York Times,* Nov. 2, 1975, sec. 5, p. 3.

88. *Sporting News,* Nov. 1, 1975, 26.

89. Donald Gropman, *Say It Ain't So, Joe!: The True Story of Shoeless Joe Jackson and the 1919 World Series* (New York: Lynx Books, [1979] 1988), 229.

90. Ronald Story, "The Greening of Sport: Jackson, Dempsey, and Industrial America," *Reviews in American History* 8:3 (Sept. 1980): 387.

91. James T. Farrell, "Replaying the Black Sox Scandal," *Chicago Tribune,* Sept. 2, 1979, sec. 7, p. 1.

92. Mike Shannon, *Diamond Classics: Essays on One Hundred of the Best Baseball Books Ever Published* (Jefferson, N.C.: McFarland, 1989), 322.

93. Ray Merlock, "Shoeless Joe: From the Rural South to the Field of Dreams," *Southern Partisan* 10 (Fall 1990): 20.

94. With its compassionate, charitable portrait of a good man wronged, *Say It Ain't So, Joe!* struck a chord with many readers in the eighties, so much so that it was republished in 1988. Four years later, *Say It Ain't So, Joe!* was revised and reissued—with a new preface, an introduction by the Harvard Law School professor Alan Dershowitz, a new concluding chapter, and sixty pages worth of appendixes that support Gropman's claim that Jackson was and continues to be ill-treated by the baseball establishment. A second revised edition of *Say It Ain't So, Joe!* was issued in 1999.

95. Fred Lieb, *Baseball as I Have Known It* (New York: Coward, McCann, and Geohegan, 1977), 111–12.

96. Dean Smith, "The Black Sox Scandal," *American History Illustrated,* Jan. 1977, 22.

97. Leverett T. Smith Jr., *The American Dream and the National Game* (Bowling Green, Ohio: Popular Press, 1975), 141.

98. Richard C. Crepeau, *Baseball: America's Diamond Mind, 1919–1941* (Gainesville: University Presses of Florida, 1980), 14–16.

99. Benjamin G. Rader, *American Sports: From the Age of Folk Games to the Age of Spectators* (Englewood Cliffs, N.J.: Prentice Hall, 1983), 200.

100. Donald Honig, *Baseball America: The Heroes of the Game and the Times of Their Glory* (New York: Galahad Books, 1993), 112.

101. See Betts, *America's Sporting Heritage;* John A. Lucas and Ronald A. Smith, *Saga of American Sport* (Philadelphia: Lea and Febiger, 1978); Riess, *Touching Base;* and Richard C. Lindberg, *Who's on Third?: The Chicago White Sox Story* (South Bend, Ind.: Icarus Press, 1983).

102. See Asinof, *Eight Men Out,* 15; Wallop, *Baseball,* 170; Stein, *The Ginger Kid,* 157; and Daniel E. Ginsburg, *The Fix Is In: A History of Baseball Gambling and Game Fixing Scandals* (Jefferson, N.C.: McFarland, 1995), 103. The historian Richard C. Lindberg argues: "The Old Roman paid his players what the market would bear. His salaries were in line with what other owners were paying, less in some cases, more in others. At times Comiskey could be surprisingly generous; bench-warming substitutes and slump-ridden ballplayers were occasionally rewarded with extra coin as an inducement to play harder." Richard C. Lindberg, *Stealing First in a Two-Team Town: The White Sox from Comiskey to Reinsdorf* (Champaign, Ill.: Sagamore, 1994), 103.

103. Crepeau, *Baseball,* 19.

104. Lieb, *Baseball as I Have Known It,* 111.

105. Leo Lowenfish and Tony Lupien, *The Imperfect Diamond: The Story of Baseball's Reserve System and the Men Who Fought to Change It* (New York: Stein and Day, 1980), 98, 103.

106. Lindberg, *Who's on Third?* 45.

107. Crepeau, *Baseball,* 16.

108. Honig, *Baseball America,* 103.

109. Ibid., 104.

110. Herbert G. Gutman, *Work, Culture, and Society in Industrializing America: Essays in American Working-Class and Social History* (New York: Knopf, 1976); Harvey Green, *The Uncertainty of Everyday Life, 1915–1945* (New York: Harper-Perennial, 1992); Daniel Nelson, *Shifting Fortunes: The Rise and Decline of American Labor, from the 1820s to the Present* (Chicago: Ivan R. Dee, 1997).

111. Crepeau, *Baseball,* 8.

112. Riess, *Touching Base,* 65.

113. Betts, *America's Sporting Heritage,* 251.

114. Lucas and Smith, *Saga of American Sport,* 314.

115. Lieb, *Baseball as I Have Known It,* 113.

116. Riess, *Touching Base,* 233.

117. Smith, "The Black Sox Scandal," 24.

118. Novick, *That Noble Dream,* 52.

119. Chamberlain, "Old Men Die," 60.

120. Michel-Rolph Trouillot, *Silencing the Past: Power and the Production of History* (Boston: Beacon Press, 1995), 158.

Chapter 5: Idyll and Iconoclasm

1. C. Vann Woodward, *The Future of the Past* (New York: Oxford University Press, 1989), 235.

2. Tom Wolfe, "The Years of Living Prosperously," *U.S. News and World Report,* Dec. 25, 1989–Jan. 1, 1990, 117.

3. Robert W. Creamer, "It's So, Joe: The Black Sox Scandal Has Come Out Swinging as an Opera," *Sports Illustrated,* Aug. 3, 1981, 6.

4. Richard Pioreck's *Say It Ain't So, Joe!* was performed at the Arena Players Repertory Theatre in East Farmingdale, Connecticut, in March 1983. Lawrence Kelly's *Out!* ran at the Judith Anderson Theatre from July 11 to July 27, 1986. *Out!* was described as "an off-Broadway joy. Poignant, intelligent, funny and morally alert, it shows what the theater can do far better than TV or movies in dealing with historical material: bring characters alive by letting them explain their dilemmas directly to the audience." William A. Henry III, "The Boys of Sixty-Seven Summers Ago," *Time,* July 21, 1986, 77.

5. The exhibit's curator, Robert I. Goler, says it was "a casual decision" to run the Black Sox scandal show, that it was part of a series of exhibits, including shows on Frank Lloyd Wright and O'Hare International Airport. The society's Black Sox scandal exhibit featured approximately 250 artifacts, including bats, baseballs signed by the expelled players, gloves, catcher's equipment, photographs, oil and water color paintings, ticket stubs, score cards, pennants, player contracts, baseball cards (Cicotte, Gandil, Felsch, Weaver, Risberg), newspapers, editorial cartoons, buttons, press pins, court records (subpoenas for Eddie Cicotte and Arnold Rothstein and a copy of the jury's verdict), props from *Eight Men Out,* and Joe Jackson's home run ball from game eight of the series, among other items. According to the White Sox historian Richard C. Lindberg, this "stylish looking exhibit evokes the look and feel of the period," but represents the scandal "as an isolated event, which was certainly not the case." Jay Pridmore of the *Chicago Tribune* offered the following assessment: "Ultimately, it suggests that the eight Sox players who were banned from baseball were victims as well as being culprits. By showing an array of clippings, contracts and court papers, it also shows that Sox owner Charles Comiskey played a more complex role in the affair than commonly thought." Telephone interview with Robert I. Goler, Oct. 15, 1997; Richard C. Lindberg, rev. of "'Say It Ain't So, Joe': The 1919 Black Sox Scandal," *Journal of Sport History* 17:1 (Spring 1990): 120; Jay Pridmore, "A New Look to Historical Society Shows Faith in the Past," *Chicago Tribune,* Oct. 14, 1988, sec. 7, p. 8; Jerome Holtzman, "A Homecoming for the Black Sox Scandal," *Chicago Tribune,* Dec. 15, 1988, sec. 4, p. 6; Robert I. Goler, "Black Sox," *Chicago History* 17 (Fall–Winter 1988–89): 42–69.

6. There were also many articles about the scandal in the eighties, including Michael C. Malmisur, "Say It Ain't So, Joe: Sociology of Knowledge Analysis of the Black Sox Scandal," *Journal of Sport Behavior* 5:1 (Mar. 1982): 2–11; Pete Dexter, "Black Sox Blues," *Esquire,* Oct. 1984, 265–67; James Kirby, "The Year They Fixed

the World Series," *American Bar Association Journal,* Feb. 1, 1988, 65–69; George F. Will, "Black October: The Year the Series Was Fixed," *Washington Post,* Oct. 6, 1988, A25; Paul Galloway, "It Ain't So Sixty-Eight Years Later: Fans Seek a Pardon for Shoeless Joe," *Chicago Tribune,* Oct. 20, 1988, sec. 5, pp. 1–2; Nicholas Dawidoff, "Too Good to Be Left Out," *Sports Illustrated,* June 12, 1989, 118; William Plummer, "Shoeless Joe: His Legend Survives the Man and the Scandal," *People Weekly,* Aug. 7, 1989, 99–101; and Bob McCoy, "Amazing Glimpse into the Past," *Sporting News,* Oct. 16, 1989, 12.

7. George F. Will, *Suddenly: The American Idea Abroad and at Home, 1986–1990* (New York: Free Press, 1992), iv.

8. Garry Wills, *Reagan's America: Innocents at Home* (Garden City, N.Y.: Doubleday, 1987), 2.

9. In 1984, at a breakfast prayer meeting held during the Republican National Convention in Dallas, Reagan said: "The truth is, politics and morality are inseparable. And as morality's foundation is religion, religion and politics are necessarily related. We need religion as a guide. We need it because we are imperfect, and our government needs the church because only those humble enough to admit they're sinners can bring to democracy the tolerance it requires in order to survive." Haynes Johnson, *Sleepwalking through History: America in the Reagan Years* (New York: Doubleday, [1991] 1992), 209.

10. Frank Ardolino, "*Rocky* Times Four: Return, Resurrection, Repetition, and Reaganism," *Aethlon: The Journal of Sport Literature* 11:1 (Fall 1993): 149.

11. Thomas Byrne Edsall, *The New Politics of Inequality* (New York: W. W. Norton, 1984); Kevin Phillips, *The Politics of Rich and Poor: Wealth and the American Electorate in the Reagan Aftermath* (New York: Harper and Row, 1990).

12. Johnson, *Sleepwalking through History,* 243.

13. Victor Bondi, ed., *American Decades, 1980–1989* (Detroit: Gale Research, 1996), x.

14. Shelly Ross, *Fall from Grace: Sex, Scandal, and Corruption in American Politics from 1702 to the Present* (New York: Ballantine Books, 1988), 269.

15. Roderick Nash, *The Nervous Generation: American Thought, 1917–1930* (Chicago: Rand McNally, 1970), 128.

16. Johnson, *Sleepwalking through History,* 149.

17. Charles C. Alexander, *Our Game: An American Baseball History* (New York: Henry Holt, 1991), 313; Marvin Miller, *A Whole Different Ball Game: The Sport and Business of Baseball* (New York: Simon and Schuster, [1991] 1992), 287.

18. Benjamin G. Rader, *Baseball: A History of America's Game* (Urbana: University of Illinois Press, 1992, 215; John Bloom, *House of Cards: Baseball Card Collecting and Popular Culture* (Minneapolis: University of Minnesota Press, 1997).

19. Alexander, *Our Game,* 311.

20. Both periods followed a war that gave rise to notable disillusionment. Both had a curious combination of officially dictated moralism and social license to act freely. Both included tremendous tumult in terms of race and gender relations. And

both witnessed an extraordinary concentration of wealth and a widening gap between rich and poor. Haynes Johnson, however, argues that the eighties, unlike the twenties, was "not a romantic period, and it's doubtful that the characters who gave it special flavor will be remembered with nostalgic affection. Oliver North and Ronald Reagan, Michael Milken and Ivan Boesky, Jim and Tammy Faye Bakker, Arthur Laffer and his curve, the yuppies and the LBO kings, the hustlers and the quick-buck promoters—all typified a self-indulgent and imitative age when entertainers became public leaders and when celebrities, not pioneers, scientists, or artists, became cultural heroes." Johnson, *Sleepwalking through History,* 461.

21. Timothy Morris, *Making the Team: The Cultural Work of Baseball Fiction* (Urbana: University of Illinois Press, 1997).

22. Richard N. Current, "Fiction as History: A Review Essay," *Journal of Southern History* 52 (Feb. 1986): 77.

23. Warren A. Beck and Myles L. Clowers contend, "More Americans have learned the story of the South during the years of the Civil War and Reconstruction from Margaret Mitchell's *Gone with the Wind* than from all of the learned volumes on this period." Warren A. Beck and Myles L. Clowers, *Understanding American History through Fiction* (New York: McGraw-Hill, 1975), ix.

24. Russell Hollander, "Father and Son in 'Shoeless Joe,'" *Nine: A Journal of Baseball History and Social Policy Perspectives* 8:1 (Fall 1999): 84.

25. David McGimpsey, *Imagining Baseball: America's Pastime and Popular Culture* (Bloomington: Indiana University Press, 2000), 36.

26. W. P. Kinsella, *Shoeless Joe* (New York: Ballantine Books, 1982), 3.

27. The genesis of the novel probably accounts for some of its awkwardness. The novel's first chapter was originally a short story published in *Aurora: New Canadian Writing 1978,* ed. Morris Wolfe (Toronto: Doubleday Canada, 1978). As Kinsella tells it, "a young editor in Boston with Houghton Mifflin, named Larry Kessenich, saw the two-line mention [of the short story in a review of the anthology] and wrote me on the strength of it. He was right out of editors' school and didn't know that editors can't be bothered finding new writers, that they wait for them to come through the door. And he wrote me and said, 'We're all baseball fans here, and this idea of this man building a baseball diamond in his cornfield sounds so wonderful that if it's a novel we'd like to see it, and if it isn't it should be.'" After corresponding with Kessenich, Kinsella agreed to expand his story into a novel. According to Kinsella, "*Shoeless Joe* was just like a baby. I wrote it in nine months. And it was virtually unedited." See "The Spitball Interview: W. P. Kinsella," in *The Best of Spitball,* ed. Mike Shannon (New York: Pocket Books, 1988), 56–58.

28. According to Pellow, what is important about "Kinsella's novel, an importance almost completely absent from the film, is that Ray Kinsella feels that Shoeless Joe needs to be exonerated, just as he feels that he still owes something to his father, the proto-typical advocate of Jackson. Therefore, he is psychologically and politically pre-disposed to desire a miraculous resurrection. But both these strands of motivation are abandoned in the film." Pellow is correct, up to a point. Certainly the film

mutes the sense that Ray is a man in search of justice trying to "right an old wrong" and accentuates his vision quest, but in the novel and the film reconciliation is the ultimate end. Despite slightly divergent routes, both narratives arrive at the same conclusion: father and son are reunited, and Jackson is returned to a state of grace. C. Kenneth Pellow, "Shoeless Joe in Film and Fiction," *Aethlon: The Journal of Sport Literature* 9:1 (Fall 1991): 19–20.

29. August J. Fry, "The Return of Joseph Jefferson Jackson: A Study in American Myth," in *A Centre of Excellence: Essays Presented to Seymour Betsky,* ed. Robert Druce (Amsterdam: Rodopi, 1987), 100.

30. M. I. Finley, *The Use and Abuse of History* (New York: Viking Press, 1971), 16.

31. Richard Alan Schwartz, "Postmodernist Baseball," *Modern Fiction Studies* 33:1 (Spring 1987): 144.

32. Bryan K. Garman, "Myth Building and Cultural Politics in W. P. Kinsella's Shoeless Joe," *Canadian Review of American Studies* 24:1 (Winter 1994): 57.

33. A renaissance scholar and former president of Yale University, Giamatti believed that baseball was "the Romantic Epic of homecoming America sings to itself." As for Will, though he aspires to examine baseball from an "antiromantic" perspective, he nonetheless argues that to be a knowledgeable baseball "fan is to participate in something. It is an activity, a form of appreciating that is good for the individual's soul, and hence for society." A. Bartlett Giamatti, *Take Time for Paradise: Americans and Their Games* (New York: Summit, 1989), 95; George F. Will, *Men at Work: The Craft of Baseball* (New York: HarperPerennial, [1990] 1991), 2.

34. Garman, "Myth Building and Cultural Politics," 58.

35. Deeanne Westbrook, *Ground Rules: Baseball and Myth* (Urbana: University of Illinois Press, 1996), 168.

36. The most comprehensive examination of Mathewson's life is Ray Robinson's *Matty: An American Hero, Christy Mathewson of the New York Giants* (New York: Oxford University Press, 1993).

37. Eric Rolfe Greenberg, *The Celebrant* (New York: Penguin Books, 1983), 260.

38. Allen E. Hye, "The Baseball Messiah: Christy Mathewson and *The Celebrant,*" *Aethlon: The Journal of Sport Literature* 7:1 (Fall 1989): 41–49.

39. See Daniel A. Nathan, "Touching the Bases: A Conversation with Eric Rolfe Greenberg," *Aethlon: The Journal of Sport Literature* 7:1 (Fall 1989): 10.

40. For an interesting discussion of assimilation and *The Celebrant,* see Morris, *Making the Team,* 32–40. Also see Eric Solomon, "Eric Rolfe Greenberg's *The Celebrant:* The Greatest (Jewish) American Baseball Novel," in *Sports and the American Jew,* ed. Steven A. Riess (Syracuse: Syracuse University Press, 1998), 256–83.

41. Morris, *Making the Team,* 33, 40.

42. Peter C. Bjarkman, "Six-Pointed Diamonds and the Ultimate Shiksa: Baseball and Jewish-American Immigrant Experience," in *Cooperstown Symposium on Baseball and the American Culture (1990),* ed. Alvin L. Hall (Westport, Conn.: Meckler, 1991), 306.

43. Nathan, "Touching the Bases," 17.

44. Harry Stein, *Hoopla* (New York: St. Martin's Press, 1983), 5.

45. Schwartz, "Postmodernist Baseball," 143.

46. Peter Carino, "Novels of the Black Sox Scandal: History/Fiction/Myth," *Nine: A Journal of Baseball History and Social Policy Perspectives* 3:2 (Spring 1995): 284.

47. McGimpsey, *Imagining Baseball,* 56.

48. Carino, "Novels of the Black Sox Scandal," 283.

49. Schwartz, "Postmodernist Baseball," 142.

50. Brendan Boyd, *Blue Ruin: A Novel of the 1919 World Series* (New York: W. W. Norton, 1991).

51. Diane Cole, rev. of *Blue Ruin, New York Times Book Review,* Oct. 27, 1991, 20.

52. Marylaine Block, rev. of *Blue Ruin, Library Journal,* Aug. 1991, 140–41.

53. Carino, "Novels of the Black Sox Scandal," 286.

54. Linda Hutcheon, *A Poetics of Postmodernism: History, Theory, Fiction* (New York: Routledge, 1988), 114.

55. Eliot Asinof, *Bleeding between the Lines* (New York: Holt, Rinehart, and Winston, 1979), 105.

56. David Streitfeld, "A Place of Their Own," *Washington Post,* Mar. 15, 1992, Book World sec., p. 15.

57. According to Eliot Asinof, "the fact that this was a shatteringly dishonest venture did not escape him [Sullivan]. Curiously enough, he found the immorality of the scheme momentarily more troublesome than any fear of its consequences. It barely occurred to him that he was in any way vulnerable to the law, even assuming that something should happen to expose the fix. He could take this position not out of ignorance, but out of precedent. He knew of no case in which a gambler had gotten into serious difficulty for this kind of manipulation. Sullivan had always laughed at the workings of law and politics, for he had all the connections he needed to stay out of trouble." How Asinof knows this is unclear. Eliot Asinof, *Eight Men Out: The Black Sox and the 1919 World Series* (New York: Henry Holt, [1963] 1987), 9.

58. Ray Gamache, rev. of *Blue Ruin, Aethlon: The Journal of Sport Literature* 9:2 (Spring 1992): 177.

59. Gary E. Dickerson, *The Cinema of Baseball: Images of America, 1929–1989* (Westport, Conn.: Meckler, 1991); Hal Erickson, *Baseball in the Movies: A Comprehensive Reference, 1915–1991* (Jefferson, N.C.: McFarland, 1992); Howard Good, *Diamonds in the Dark: America, Baseball, and the Movies* (Lanham, Md.: Scarecrow Press, 1997).

60. Robert A. Rosenstone, *Visions of the Past: The Challenge of Film to Our Idea of History* (Cambridge, Mass.: Harvard University Press, 1995), 46.

61. Ibid., 77.

62. David Thomson, "Killing Time," *Esquire,* June 1998, 56.

63. David Thomson, *A Biographical Dictionary of Film,* 3d ed. (New York: Alfred Knopf, [1975] 1996), 440–41.

64. Dickerson, *The Cinema of Baseball,* 136.

65. According to Stephen C. Wood, J. David Pincus, and J. Nicholas Den Bonis, "there are nearly two dozen identifiable and notable variations between Bernard Malamud's book and Barry Levinson's movie." Kevin Thomas Curtin nonetheless argues that we should not "compare the film with Malamud's novel; this comparison would be a complete distraction, for the film makers clearly set out [to create] something very different." Stephen C. Wood, J. David Pincus, and J. Nicholas Den Bonis, "Baseball: The American Mythos in Film, *The Natural,*" *Nine: A Journal of Baseball History and Social Policy Perspectives* 4:1 (Fall 1995): 150; Kevin Thomas Curtin, "The Natural: Our Iliad and Odyssey," *Antioch Review* 43:2 (Spring 1985): 225. For more complete (and contradictory) discussions of the novel's adaptation into film see James Griffith's "Say It Ain't So: *The Natural,*" 157–63, and Peter Turchi's "Roy Hobbs's Corrected Stance: An Adaptation of *The Natural,*" 150–56, both of which are in *Literature/Film Quarterly* 19:3 (1991).

66. Gerald Early, *The Culture of Bruising: Essays on Prizefighting, Literature, and Modern American Culture* (Hopewell, N.J.: Ecco Press, 1994), 138.

67. When asked what he thought about the film version of *The Natural,* Bernard Malamud responded cryptically: "Those who read the book know what it means." Tim Purtell, "Apples and Oranges: Movie Concepts, before and After," *Entertainment Weekly,* Mar. 24, 1995, 75.

68. Bernard Malamud, *The Natural* (New York: Avon Books, [1952] 1980), 214.

69. David Denby, "The Neutral," *New York,* May 21, 1984, 95.

70. Griffith, "Say It Ain't So," 162.

71. David McGimpsey is probably correct, however, in noting that "fans pay well enough for the privilege of seeing [former Major Leaguer] Rob Deer strike out; they'll be damned if they'll pay to see Robert Redford strike out." McGimpsey, *Imagining Baseball,* 76.

72. George Lipsitz, *Time Passages: Collective Memory and American Popular Culture* (Minneapolis: University of Minnesota Press, [1990] 1991), 163.

73. If that was indeed the case, the film should be considered a success: by mid-January 1985 its gross receipts stood at $25 million. Dickerson, *The Cinema of Baseball,* 123.

74. Sayles continues: "I don't think Bernard Malamud was too thrilled with the new ending. You know, there's a story that Elmore Leonard called him up and said, 'So how do you feel after *The Natural* came out?' And Malamud said, 'I stayed in my apartment for a week.' And Elmore Leonard said, 'Well, I just saw the movie of my last book, and I'm leaving the country for a year.' So you don't have to be a historian to feel the record has been distorted." Interview with Eric Foner, in *Past Imperfect: History according to the Movies,* ed. Mark C. Carnes (New York: Henry Holt, 1995), 15.

75. Pauline Kael, "The Candidate," *New Yorker,* May 28, 1984, 101.

76. Ron Fimrite, "A Star with Real Clout," *Sports Illustrated,* May 7, 1984, 103.

77. Ibid., 103–4.

78. Mark Matousek, "Barry Levinson," *Interview,* July 1984, 56.

79. The literary critic Deeanne Westbrook notes that Levinson and his associates "bowdlerized the novel, stripped the protagonist of complexity, and transformed the novel's essentially tragic-ironic structure into a quest romance." According to Westbrook, "the filmmakers have produced a version with wider popular appeal than could have been possessed by one that attempted to convey the ironic integrity of the novel; that is, the film does not startle with its vision, stun with its beauty, or in any sense disturb our universe. For the most part it reiterates old assumptions, reassures, and serves rather than transcends the social and political interests of the 'tribe.'" Westbrook, *Ground Rules,* 75, 289–90.

80. Dickerson, *The Cinema of Baseball,* 137.

81. Kael, "The Candidate," 101.

82. Thomson, *A Biographical Dictionary of Film,* 152.

83. Ann Knight, "Baseball like It Ought to Be," *American Film,* May 1989, 76.

84. Janet Finch, rev. of *Field of Dreams, American Film,* May 1989, 62.

85. James M. Wall, "A Playing Field for the Boys of Eternity," *Christian Century,* May 17, 1989, 515.

86. Wilfrid Sheed, "Outtakes: Field of Dreams, Fields of Do-Do," *Baseball and Lesser Sports* (New York: HarperCollins, 1991), 155. Also, Robinson's Joe Jackson bats right-handed and throws left-handed, the opposite of the historical Jackson, a detail that could have been corrected and irks some baseball fans.

87. Erickson, *Baseball in the Movies,* 152.

88. Ibid., 151.

89. Brian D. Johnson, "A Bases-Loaded Hit," *Maclean's,* May 1, 1989, 66.

90. Harlan Jacobson, "Born Again Baseball," *Film Comment,* May 1989, 79.

91. Erickson, *Baseball in the Movies,* 152.

92. Ron Rosenbaum, "What Is It with Guys and Baseball?" *Mademoiselle,* July 1989, 68–69.

93. Jacobson, "Born Again Baseball," 78–79.

94. Pellow, "Shoeless Joe in Film and Fiction," 22.

95. Johnson, *Sleepwalking through History,* 197.

96. Bill Brown, "The Meaning of Baseball in 1992 (with Notes on the Post-American)," *Public Culture* 4:1 (Fall 1991): 69.

97. Osha Gray Davidson, *Broken Heartland: The Rise of America's Rural Ghetto* (New York: Doubleday, 1990), 35.

98. Johnson, *Sleepwalking through History,* 427.

99. Larry Ballard, "Movie 'Field of Dreams' to Premiere in Dubuque," *Des Moines Register,* Mar. 29, 1989, 3M.

100. Sarah Barnes, "To Branstad, Movie Passage Is Heavenly," *Des Moines Register,* June 4, 1989, 6B.

101. William E. Schmidt, "Just as in the Dreams, They Come to the Field," *New York Times,* Aug. 16, 1990, A18.

102. This phenomenon is not unprecedented. See Jayne Clark, "Tourism and the

Power of Hollywood: If You Film It, They Will Come," *Chicago Tribune,* May 2, 1993, sec. 12, pp. 1, 13.

103. Ralph Novak, rev. of *Field of Dreams, People Weekly,* May 15, 1989, 14.

104. Diane Carson, ed., *John Sayles: Interviews* (Jackson: University of Mississippi Press, 1999), xvii.

105. David Scobey, rev. of *Eight Men Out, American Historical Review* 95:4 (Oct. 1990): 1144.

106. Asinof was pleased with the adaptation: "I like Sayles. Two things really impress me about him. One is that he didn't try to steal the book—he's the first person who ever paid me in full and put my name on the fucking thing. Secondly, he got the whole book into one movie. Amazing. Very complicated story. I never thought it possible." Bruce Buschel, "Damn Black Sox!" *Gentlemen's Quarterly,* June 1988, 262.

107. Ben Henkey, "Real American Tragedy Unfolds in Sayles Script," *Sporting News,* Sept. 26, 1988, 12.

108. Scobey, rev. of *Eight Men Out,* 1143.

109. Carson, *John Sayles: Interviews,* 127.

110. David Bernstein, rev. of *Eight Men Out, Journal of American History* 77:3 (Dec. 1990): 1113.

111. Joe Pollack, "Baseball Season Has Two Big Hits," *Sporting News,* Sept. 26, 1988, 13.

112. Alexander, *Our Game,* 348.

113. Ring Lardner Jr., "Foul Ball," *American Film,* July–Aug. 1988, 47.

114. Quoted in Carnes, *Past Imperfect,* 18.

115. Jerome Holtzman, "Movie about Black Sox?: This Time, Nobody Will Say It Ain't So," *Chicago Tribune,* Nov. 15, 1987, sec. 3, p. 2.

116. John Sayles and Gavin Smith, *Sayles on Sayles* (Boston: Faber and Faber, 1998), 147.

117. Erickson, *Baseball in the Movies,* 128.

118. David Denby, "Fouling Out," *New York,* Sept. 19, 1988, 87.

119. Tom O'Brien, "A Tripleheader," *Commonweal,* Oct. 7, 1988, 529.

120. Buschel, "Damn Black Sox!" 264.

121. Scobey, rev. of *Eight Men Out,* 1143–44.

122. "Eight Men Out," *Premiere,* Oct. 1988, 76.

123. Nathan, "Touching the Bases," 16.

124. Roger Angell, "No, but I Saw the Game," *New Yorker,* July 31, 1989, 50.

125. Sayles explains, "filmmakers have more freedom when they work with low budgets." Quoted in Carnes, *Past Imperfect,* 14.

126. C. Vann Woodward, "Help from Historians," in *Ken Burns's* The Civil War: *Historians Respond,* ed. Robert Brent Toplin (New York: Oxford University Press, 1996), 5.

127. Giamatti, *Take Time for Paradise,* 90.

128. In 1988, an arbitrator's decision awarded those players affected by the own-

ers' collusion a $280 million settlement. See Miller, *A Whole Different Ball Game,* 350–53, 399–400.

129. Ron Fimrite, "Pete Rose," *Sports Illustrated,* Sept. 19, 1994, 63.

130. Will, *Men at Work,* 228–29.

131. Tom Callahan, "For Pete's Sake, He Cried," *Time,* Sept. 23, 1985, 61.

132. Fimrite, "Pete Rose," 63.

133. Thomas Boswell, *Cracking the Show* (New York: Doubleday, 1994), 17.

134. The investigation is known as the Dowd Report because its author is the former Department of Justice prosecutor John M. Dowd; see the online version at <http://www.dowdreport.com> to examine both the summary and the full text of Dowd's findings. In *The Baseball Book 1990,* Bill James offers a lucid and compelling critique of the investigation: "The Dowd report is, in fact, biased against Pete Rose to an almost bizarre extent. Every piece of evidence is interpreted against Rose to the maximum possible degree, even if to do so it must be twisted around to where it makes no sense, and even if Rose's explanation is far more plausible. The Dowd report is bloated with irrelevant information, distorted by strange characterizations and interpretations, and systematically denuded of any material or explanation which would tend to support Rose or cast doubt on his accusers." According to Robert Pitcairn Jr., one of Rose's attorneys, the Dowd Report "is no more than the bellicose, repetitive arguments of a prosecutor who knows he cannot make his case but is trying to confuse the jury with speculative, tainted evidence. In fact, most of the information you describe as circumstantial evidence is not evidence at all and would never be admitted into evidence in a court of law. . . . What puzzles me is why you would engage in a hatchet job after you assured us repeatedly that you were conducting a fair and impartial investigation. The Report goes beyond mere bias on your part. It shows desperation to provide support for action Mr. Giamatti apparently wants to take. If this Report is your idea of fair play and natural justice, I feel sorry for you." Bill James, *The Baseball Book 1990* (New York: Villard Books, 1990), 128–29, quoted in James Reston Jr., *Collision at Home Plate: The Lives of Pete Rose and Bart Giamatti* (New York: Edward Burlingame Books, 1991), 293.

135. Roger Kahn, "Story without a Hero," *Games We Used to Play: A Lover's Quarrel with the World of Sport* (New York: Ticknor and Fields, 1992), 262.

136. "Giamatti Turns down Shoeless Joe Jackson," *New York Post,* Aug. 11, 1989, 65.

137. Geoffrey C. Ward and Ken Burns, *Baseball: An Illustrated History* (New York: Alfred A. Knopf, 1994), 454.

138. Fimrite, "Pete Rose," 63.

139. Charles Leerhsen, "The End of the Affair," *Newsweek,* Sept. 4, 1989, 58–59.

140. Ibid., 59.

141. Boswell, *Cracking the Show,* 24.

142. Mike Lupica, "Goooood Morning, Cooperstown," *Esquire,* Sept. 1992, 135.

143. The Pete Rose matter came to a head (again) during the 1999 World Series

when Rose was honored as one of Major League Baseball's greatest players of the century. After being introduced before the second game of the series, writes Thomas Boswell, "Rose got more applause than anybody else. Then, support rolled in for him after Jim Gray's right-question-at-the-wrong-time TV interview. Emboldened by all this, Rose has been beating the drum recently for reinstatement into baseball and a place on the Hall ballot." The incident with NBC's Jim Gray ignited yet another round of debate, especially in Cincinnati, concerning Rose's ineligibility for the Baseball Hall of Fame. Thomas Boswell, "As Fisk Enters, Rose Should Wait outside the Hall," *Washington Post,* Dec. 12, 1999, D5; John Erardi, "Will Rose Furor Make Difference?" *Cincinnati Enquirer,* Oct. 26, 1999, D1.

144. Elliott J. Gorn, "The Fall of Charlie Hustle," *The Nation,* Jan. 22, 1990, 95.

145. James D. Smith III, "Five Old Timers Recall 1919 and the Series," *Elysian Fields Quarterly* 12:1 (1993): 64–66.

146. *USA Today,* Aug. 25, 1989, 8A.

147. Hal Bock, "One Man's Rise and Fall Stand Tall," *Los Angeles Times,* Dec. 23, 1989, 3C.

148. Wilfrid Sheed, "One Man Out . . . Too Long," *Gentlemen's Quarterly,* Aug. 1990, 215.

149. Ira Berkow, "The Hall, Rose, and Shoeless Joe," *New York Times,* Aug. 4, 1990, 43.

150. Scott MacGregor, "Rose Reinstated?: Think Again," *Cincinnati Enquirer,* Feb. 22, 1998, D4.

151. Miller, *A Whole Different Ball Game,* 395.

152. Bill James notes the outpouring of fan interest regarding Rose's Hall of Fame fate. Nearly all the fan letters he excerpts make the connection between Rose and Jackson. James himself believes "very strongly that Pete Rose got a raw deal from baseball. John Dowd's investigation of Rose's behavior, which claimed to be fair and impartial, was a mockery of those words. Dowd leapt to the conclusion that Rose was guilty, and twisted and bent the facts to support that conclusion." Yet James argues "that the people who want to put Joe Jackson in the Hall of Fame are baseball's answer to those women who show up at murder trials wanting to marry the cute murderer." Bill James, *The Politics of Glory: How Baseball's Hall of Fame Really Works* (New York: Macmillan, 1994), 21, 355, 358. For more on the Pete Rose controversy, see Michael Y. Sokolove, *Hustle: The Myth, Life, and Lies of Pete Rose* (New York: Simon and Schuster, 1990); Matthew B. Pachman, "Limits on the Discretionary Powers of Professional Sports Commissioners: A Historical and Legal Analysis of Issues Raised by the Pete Rose Controversy," *Virginia Law Review* 76:7 (Oct. 1990): 1409–39; Roger I. Abrams, *Legal Bases: Baseball and the Law* (Philadelphia: Temple University Press, 1998); Scott MacGregor, "Pete's Pain: Life in Exile," *Cincinnati Enquirer,* Aug. 22, 1999, A1, A16–A17; and Sean Lahman, "The Pete Rose FAQ," *SportsJones Magazine,* Oct. 25, 1999, <http://www.sportsjones.com/rose.htm> (Oct. 31, 1999).

153. Boswell, *Cracking the Show,* 31.

Chapter 6: Dreaming and Scheming

1. Lyn Riddle, "Shoeless Joe's Pen Is Even Mighter than His Bat," *New York Times,* Oct. 9, 1993, 9.

2. Harvey Frommer, *Shoeless Joe and Ragtime Baseball* (Dallas: Taylor, 1992); Joe Thompson, *Growing Up with "Shoeless Joe": The Greatest Natural Player in Baseball History* (Laurel Fork, Va.: JTI, 1997); Irving M. Stein, *The Ginger Kid: The Buck Weaver Story* (Dubuque, Ia.: Elysian Fields Press, 1992); David Pietrusza, *Judge and Jury: The Life and Times of Judge Kenesaw Mountain Landis* (South Bend, Ind.: Diamond Communications, 1998). Also, Donald Gropman's *Say It Ain't So, Joe!: The True Story of Shoeless Joe Jackson* came out in a revised second edition during the decade (Secaucus, N.J.: Carol Publishing Group, [1979] 1999).

3. Charles C. Alexander, *Our Game: An American Baseball History* (New York: Henry Holt, 1991); Dan Gutman, *Baseball Babylon: From the Black Sox to Pete Rose, the Real Stories behind the Scandals that Rocked the Game* (New York: Penguin Books, 1992); Benjamin G. Rader, *Baseball: A History of America's Game* (Urbana: University of Illinois Press, 1992); Richard C. Lindberg, *Stealing First in a Two-Team Town: The White Sox from Comiskey to Reinsdorf* (Champaign, Ill.: Sagamore, 1994); Daniel E. Ginsburg, *The Fix Is In: A History of Baseball Gambling and Game Fixing Scandals* (Jefferson, N.C.: McFarland, 1995); G. Edward White, *Creating the National Pastime: Baseball Transforms Itself, 1903–1953* (Princeton: Princeton University Press, 1996); Richard C. Lindberg, *The White Sox Encyclopedia* (Philadelphia: Temple University Press, 1997); Jonathan Fraser Light, *The Cultural Encyclopedia of Baseball* (Jefferson, N.C.: McFarland, 1997); Leonard Koppett, *Koppett's Concise History of Major League Baseball* (Philadelphia: Temple University Press, 1998).

4. Staci Sturrock, "'Shoeless Joe' Hits a Home Run," *Greenville News,* Sept. 17, 1995, 2A; <http://www.zuty.com/blacksox.shtml> (May 23, 2000); Louis R. Hegeman, *The Trial of Buck Weaver and Shoeless Joe Jackson,* Joe Jackson Folder, National Baseball Library and Archive, Cooperstown, N.Y.

5. Trevor D. Kramer of TDK Publishing explains that the *Shoeless Joe Jackson Times* "began in 1992 with a few thoughts on a couple of pieces of paper which were sent to a few family friends. Today we have grown to a printed subscription count in the hundreds and well over a thousand individuals have visited our web site so far. Our on-line petition has been signed by over one hundred people since its inception two months ago. Our goal is to one day see Joseph Jefferson Jackson take his rightful place in the Hall of Fame and to educate baseball fans about who Ty Cobb said was the greatest natural hitter of all time." "Shoeless Joe Jackson Times," Jan. 20, 1997, personal e-mail message. See also *Shoeless Joe Jackson Times* 1.1 (Winter 1992) <http://blackbetsy.com/sjjtimes/newsletter1.1.html> (July 7, 2000).

6. James O. Clifford, "Mock Court Rules to Reinstate 'Shoeless' Joe," *Iowa City Press Citizen,* Aug. 21, 1993, C4.

7. A week later, Ira Berkow of the *New York Times* noted that some White Sox fans

"have long believed that a hex was put on the team because of the Black Sox." Perhaps there is: in 1993, the favored White Sox lost the AL Championship Series to the Toronto Blue Jays; they have not reached the postseason since. Joey Reaves, "What a Blast!: Sox Clinch on Bo's Bomb," *Chicago Tribune,* Sept. 28, 1993, sec. 1, p. 8; Ira Berkow, "Is There a Hex on the Sox?" *New York Times,* Oct. 5, 1993, B13.

8. Jay Bennett, "Did Shoeless Joe Jackson Throw the 1919 World Series?" *American Statistician* 47:4 (Nov. 1993): 241–50.

9. Lea Sitton, "He's Sure It Ain't So, Joe," *Philadelphia Inquirer,* May 31, 1994, B2. See also Frederick Klein, "Amnesty for Black Sox Third Baseman?" *Wall Street Journal,* Jan. 17, 1992, A9.

10. "Hall of Famers Support Jackson," *Miami Sun-Sentinel,* Jan. 20, 1998, 2C; Ted Williams, "Shoeless Joe: It's Time to Open the Door," Mar. 1998, <http://www.sabr.org./archive/williams.shtml> (May 15, 2000).

11. Mark Gillespie, "Baseball Fans Want Pete Rose in Hall of Fame, but Say No to Shoeless Joe," *Gallup Poll Monthly,* July 1999, 28.

12. Jerome Holtzman, "A Homecoming for the Black Sox Scandal," *Chicago Tribune,* Dec. 15, 1988, sec. 4, p. 6.

13. See Shoeless Joe Jackson's Virtual Hall of Fame at <http://www.blackbesty.com./joestuff.html> (June 22, 2000). Other Web sites worth noting are <http://www.gingerkid.com>, <http://www.chicagohs.org/history/blacksox.html>, <http://www.findagrave.com/reunions/blacksox.html>, and <http://www.middlebury.edu/ac400b/>.

14. *The Barry Halper Collection of Baseball Memorabilia: The Early Years* (New York: Sotheby's, 1999), 215.

15. Dave Kindred, "Field of Dreams: Part 2," *Sporting News,* July 31, 1995, 6.

16. Arthur Hirsch, "In the Town of True Believers," *Baltimore Sun,* Aug. 2, 1998, Arts and Society sec., 8F–9F; Michael Hirsley, "Going to Bat for Shoeless Joe," *Baltimore Sun,* July 26, 2000, 2A.

17. The seven-acre Shoeless Joe Memorial Park includes an early 1900s-style ballpark and a granite memorial to Jackson. The first phase of the park cost $200,000 to complete. Melinda Gladfelter, "Park to Honor Shoeless Joe," *Greenville News,* Apr. 30, 1995, 2B; Frank Fitzpatrick, "One More Indignity for 'Shoeless Joe,'" *Philadelphia Inquirer,* Sept. 17, 1996, E3.

18. See the Shoeless Joe Jackson Society at <http://blackbetsy.com/society.htm> (June 22, 2000).

19. "House Urges Honor for 'Shoeless Joe,'" *Milwaukee Journal Sentinel,* Nov. 9, 1999, Sports sec., p. 2; Associated Press, "Politicians Press Shoeless Joe's Case," June 14, 2000.

20. Thomas R. King, "In Which Our Reporter Ponders What Hollywood Did to Iowa, and Vice Versa," *Wall Street Journal,* July 27, 1995, B1.

21. Many years before, it is worth noting, another Iowa farmer plowed under some of his crop to build a ballfield. In the early thirties, Bill Feller decided to clear his pasture and build a baseball diamond complete with a backstop and a small grand-

stand, according to his son, the Hall of Fame pitcher Bob Feller, so that he and local farm boys could organize teams and have a place to play. The Fellers "cleared the land and leveled it. We cut down saplings along the river to support chicken wire in front of our circus seats. We got real baseball bags from Des Moines and put up a scoreboard. We decided that 35 cents wasn't too much for the baseball and view." Prefiguring the Field of Dreams in Dyersville, the Fellers' ballfield was "a happy, exciting place for several years." Bob Feller, *Strikeout Story* (New York: A. S. Barnes, 1947), 11–12.

22. David Young, "'Field of Dreams' Economic Diamond," *Chicago Tribune,* May 25, 1992, sec. 4, p. 2.

23. Reidel was instructed that the filmmakers were interested in a "traditional all-American farm, set apart by itself with a long drive, . . . [that would] more-or-less come across as a one-man operation with a barn. . . . It was to be surrounded by and set within gently-rolling hills for location lighting and a sense of overall coziness." Nick Vetter, "A Glance Back," *Low and Inside* (Minneapolis: Nick Vetter), 6, quoted in Charles Fruehling Springwood, *Cooperstown to Dyersville: A Geography of Baseball Nostalgia* (Boulder: Westview Press, 1996), 129.

24. Young, "'Field of Dreams' Economic Diamond," 2.

25. Chuck Offenburger, "Filming of 'Field of Dreams' Was like Heaven for Dubuque," *Des Moines Register,* Apr. 23, 1989, 6B.

26. Gene Raffensperger, "Knee-High Corn Too Short to Shoot in Cinematic Scenes," *Des Moines Register,* June 18, 1988, 1A.

27. Rogers Worthington, "It's No Dream: Fans Still Coming to Cornfield Turned Ball Diamond," *Chicago Tribune,* Mar. 30, 1990, sec. 1, p. 6.

28. Jeff Sanders, "Can of Corn," *American Film,* Sept. 1989, 15.

29. Carol Rose, "Fielding Dreamers on Movie Site," *Des Moines Register,* June 17, 1989, 14A.

30. Stephen D. Mosher contends that, "in spite of their attempts to articulate their reasons for coming, most people conceded that they did not know why they had come" to the Field of Dreams. Stephen D. Mosher, "Fielding Our Dreams: Rounding Third in Dyersville," *Sociology of Sport Journal* 8:3 (Sept. 1991): 276.

31. Rose, "Fielding Dreamers on Movie Site," 14A.

32. Worthington, "It's No Dream," 6.

33. Springwood, *Cooperstown to Dyersville,* 129.

34. Ibid., 1.

35. Ibid., 112–13.

36. Bill Brown, "The Meaning of Baseball in 1992 (with Notes on the Post-American)," *Public Culture* 4:1 (Fall 1991): 69; Cheryl Temple Herr, *Critical Regionalism and Cultural Studies: From Ireland to the American Midwest* (Gainesville: University Press of Florida, 1996), 178.

37. Young, "'Field of Dreams' Economic Diamond," 2.

38. W. P. Kinsella, press conference, Iowa City, July 1991, quoted in Herr, *Critical Regionalism and Cultural Studies,* 183.

39. Springwood, *Cooperstown to Dyersville,* 20.

40. Ibid., 143.

41. Springwood notes that "for someone to be a Shoeless Joe dissenter at the Field of Dreams would be like someone hating Mickey Mouse at Disney World." Ibid., 123.

42. Debora Wiley, "Ghost Players Are Still Dreamin'," *Des Moines Register,* Apr. 12, 1996, 5M.

43. Andrew Zimbalist, *Baseball and Billions: A Probing Look inside the Big Business of Our National Pastime* (New York: Basic Books, 1993), xvii, 85.

44. Rader, *Baseball,* 200.

45. Zimbalist, *Baseball and Billions,* xvii.

46. Roger Angell, "Hardball," *New Yorker,* Oct. 17, 1994, 68.

47. Mark Maske, "The Evolution of a Major League Disaster," *Washington Post,* Sept. 18, 1994, D1.

48. Paul D. Staudohar, "The Baseball Strike of 1994–95," paper presented at the Eighth Annual Cooperstown Symposium on Baseball and American Culture, June 1996. Staudohar explains that "by voting to reopen negotiations the owners showed their intention to take a proactive stance of effecting change."

49. Ross Newhan, "Baseball Owners Open Door to Talks," *Los Angeles Times,* Dec. 12, 1992, C1.

50. Murray Chass, "Owners Terminate Season, without the World Series," *New York Times,* Sept. 15, 1994, A1.

51. Shirley Povich, "For Years, the Game Changes; Now, It Has Stopped," *Washington Post,* Sept. 15, 1994, B4.

52. Chass, "Owners Terminate Season," A1.

53. Walter Shapiro, "Bummer of '94," *Time,* Aug. 22, 1994, 71.

54. Mike Lupica, "Throwing the Last Pitch," *Sporting News,* Aug. 22, 1994, 7.

55. Thomas Boswell, "Wolves in Owners' Clothing," *Washington Post,* Sept. 9, 1994, C1.

56. Thomas Boswell, "A Sign of the Times: Sold Out," *Washington Post,* Sept. 15, 1994, B1.

57. Ibid., B4.

58. Ibid.

59. Albert Kim, "The Filmmaker behind PBS' 'Civil War' Steps Up to the Plate with His Epic 'Baseball,'" *Entertainment Weekly,* Sept. 16, 1994, 41.

60. Ken Fuson, "Show Has a Strike against It," *Des Moines Register,* Sept. 18, 1994, 3TV.

61. Gary Edgerton, "Ken Burns—a Conversation with Public Television's Resident Historian," *Journal of American Culture* 18:1 (Spring 1995): 1.

62. "Ken Burns," *Current Biography Yearbook* (New York: H. W. Wilson, 1992), 100.

63. Paula Span, "'Baseball': The Windup and Now the Pitch," *Washington Post,* Sept. 30, 1994, F1.

64. Gary Edgerton, "Ken Burns's America: Style, Authorship, and Cultural Mem-

ory," *Journal of Popular Film and Television* 21:2 (Summer 1993): 52. For the film's reception, see Robert Brent Toplin, ed., *Ken Burns's* The Civil War: *Historians Respond* (New York: Oxford University Press, 1996).

65. Edgerton, "Ken Burns—a Conversation," 6.

66. Ernst Breisach, *Historiography: Ancient, Medieval, and Modern* (Chicago: University of Chicago Press, 1983), 388–91.

67. David W. Blight, "Homer with a Camera, Our *Iliad* without the Aftermath: Ken Burns's Dialogue with Historians," *Reviews in American History* 25:2 (June 1997): 353.

68. Richard Zoglin, "Homer Epic," *Time,* Sept. 12, 1994, 78.

69. David Thelen, "The Movie Maker as Historian: Conversations with Ken Burns," *Journal of American History* 81:3 (Dec. 1994): 1040, 1047.

70. Kim, "The Filmmaker behind PBS' 'Civil War,'" 41.

71. George B. Kirsch, rev. of *Baseball, Journal of American History* 82:3 (Dec. 1995): 1314.

72. Span, "'Baseball': The Windup and Now the Pitch," F1.

73. Thelen, "The Movie Maker as Historian," 1037.

74. In its place, the film claims that at Comiskey Park one afternoon "Jackson was surrounded by a crowd of men and boys. One boy called out, 'It ain't true, Joe, it ain't true.' Others joined in. Jackson kept walking to his car, the fans followed in the distance. Jackson never said a word."

75. Holtzman adds that in *Baseball,* "Comiskey is the heavy. Studs Terkel, a knee-jerk liberal who apparently never met an owner he didn't dislike, pegs Comiskey as the villain because his players were ill-paid. I have no doubt the White Sox players were not rewarded sufficiently, but neither were hundreds of others. So far as I know, a comparison of player payrolls of that time never has been published. . . . Comiskey was not without sin. But he has been hung for the wrong crime. He knew the fix was in from Game 1, also the identity of the eight fixers, but remained silent. The players were valuable chattel, and he was hoping they would remain in his employ." Jerome Holtzman, "Alas, Burns' 'Baseball' Provides Rest for the Weary," *Chicago Tribune,* Sept. 25, 1994, sec. 3, p. 15.

76. Steven A. Riess, "The Early Innings," *Journal of Sport History* 23:1 (Spring 1996): 65.

77. Edgerton, "Ken Burns—a Conversation," 8.

78. Ken Burns, keynote address, Sixth Annual Cooperstown Symposium on Baseball and American Culture, June 8, 1994, quoted in Springwood, *Cooperstown to Dyersville,* 2.

79. Linda Williams, "Mirrors without Memories—Truth, History, and the New Documentary," *Film Quarterly* 46:3 (Spring 1993): 20.

80. John Sayles, interview with Eric Foner, in *Past Imperfect: History according to the Movies,* ed. Mark C. Carnes (New York: Henry Holt, 1995), 18.

81. Jill Godmilow, in conversation with Ann Louise Shapiro, "How Real Is the Reality in Documentary Film?" *History and Theory* 36:4 (Dec. 1997): 84.

82. "Say It Ain't So." *Wall Street Journal,* Sept. 19, 1994, A10.

83. Mike Bass, "The Grand Old Game Withstands a Wallop," *Sporting News,* Oct. 17, 1994, 40.

84. Harry Stein, "Baseball Strike Is Symbolic of an Epidemic: Selfishness," *TV Guide,* Oct. 22, 1994, 47.

85. Letter to the editor, *Sporting News,* Mar. 6, 1995, 10.

86. Donald Kaul, "Greatest Sports Stories of the Century," *Des Moines Register,* Mar. 22, 1995, 9A.

87. Paul D. Staudohar, *Playing for Dollars: Labor Relations and the Sports Business* (Ithaca: Cornell University Press, 1996), 51.

88. Steve Wulf, "An Unwhole New Ball Game," *Time,* Apr. 17, 1995, 48.

89. Staudohar, *Playing for Dollars,* 49.

90. Reuters News Service article, Apr. 28, 1995.

91. Larry Dorman, "Finally, Strikes Have Connection to Plates," *New York Times,* Apr. 26, 1995, B11.

92. George Vecsey, "Fans Await Privilege of Paying," *New York Times,* Apr. 26, 1995, B9.

93. Letter to the editor, *Sports Illustrated,* June 7, 1995, 7.

94. Bill Gallo, "Dead Ball Era," *Icon,* 26 Jan.–1 Feb. 1995, 4.

95. Robert McG. Thomas Jr., "Clubs May Just Have to Replace Fans, Too," *New York Times,* Feb. 28, 1995, B9; Tom Verducci, "Anybody Home?" *Sports Illustrated,* May 8, 1995, 18–23; Claire Smith, "Plenty of Good Seats Available, Fans," *New York Times,* May 28, 1995, sec. 8, p. 1; David Greising, "America's Pastime. Yeah, Right," *Business Week,* June 5, 1995, 40.

96. Letter to the editor, *Sports Illustrated,* June 7, 1995, 7.

97. Greising, "America's Pastime. Yeah, Right," 40.

98. Charles Krauthammer, "The Trouble with Baseball," *Washington Post,* May 5, 1995, A25.

99. Bill James, *The Bill James Historical Baseball Abstract* (New York: Villard Books, [1985] 1987), 124.

100. Ken Sobol, *Babe Ruth and the American Dream* (New York: Ballantine Books, 1974), 135.

101. Asinof, *Eight Men Out,* 275.

102. See Richard C. Crepeau, *Baseball: America's Diamond Mind 1919–1941* (Gainesville: University Presses of Florida, 1980), and Benjamin G. Rader, "Compensatory Sport Heroes: Ruth, Grange, and Dempsey," *Journal of Popular Culture* 16:4 (Spring 1983): 11–22.

103. Warren I. Susman, *Culture as History: The Transformation of American Society in the Twentieth Century* (New York: Pantheon Books, 1984), 148.

104. Verducci, "Anybody Home?" 20.

105. Mark Maske, "Ripken's Streak of Burden," *Washington Post,* Apr. 7, 1995, C1.

106. Ibid., C7.

107. Mat Edelson, "Cal on the Verge," in *The Best American Sports Writing 1996*, ed. John Feinstein (Boston: Houghton Mifflin, 1996), 314.

108. Heywood Hale Broun, "The Twin Symbols of Baseball's Timeless Virtues," *New York Times*, Sept. 3, 1995, sec. 8, p. 13.

109. Curry Kirkpatrick, "The Pride of the Orioles," *Newsweek*, Sept. 11, 1995, 79. Mickey Mantle, the iconic former New York Yankees centerfielder who died of cancer a month before Ripken reached 2,131, was a foil for Ripken due to his well-documented carousing. According to the sports columnist Ira Berkow, late in his life Mantle discussed "how he could have played beyond age 36 if he had not 'wasted' the talents God had given him. He confessed to being an alcoholic, a poor father and husband, and to a profligacy wrapped in self-absorption." Ira Berkow, "Much More than Just a Hall of Famer," *New York Times*, Aug. 14, 1995, C4.

110. Kirkpatrick, "The Pride of the Orioles," 79.

111. The record was set in the fifth inning, rather than in the first, because only then did the game become official.

112. In Arlington, Texas, for example, the Texas Rangers and the Chicago White Sox delayed their game to watch a live feed from Baltimore on the stadium's JumboTron screen. "Streak Scene," *Baltimore Sun*, Sept. 7, 1995, 8C.

113. "Five Million Watch Ripken Set Record," *Des Moines Register*, Sept. 8, 1995, 2S.

114. Tim Kurkjian, "Touching 'Em All," in *2,131: Cal Ripken Jr. Stands Alone*, a 1995 special collector's edition issue of *Sports Illustrated*, 15.

115. Jerome Holtzman, "2,131—and Counting," *Chicago Tribune*, Sept. 7, 1995, sec. 4, p. 1.

116. "Streak Scene," 6C. Ripken may have been purposefully vague in referring to "Robinson"; he may have meant the Hall of Famer and former Brooklyn Dodger Jackie Robinson, who broke the Major League's color line in 1947, the Hall of Fame outfielder and former Orioles great Frank Robinson, who was the first African American manager in Major League history, or the former Orioles third baseman, Hall of Famer, and local legend Brooks Robinson. The latter two were in attendance. It is also worth noting that Earl Weaver, Ripken's former manager, is reported to have once said, "I want nine guys named Robinson."

117. Kurkjian, "Touching 'Em All," 8.

118. "Streak Scene," 10C.

119. Buster Olney, "Players Throw Support behind Streak," *Baltimore Sun*, Sept. 7, 1995, 4D.

120. Harvey Araton, "Great Day for Baseball in the 90's," *New York Times*, 7 Sept. 1995, B19.

121. John Steadman, "This Sentimental Journey for the Ages," *Baltimore Sun*, Sept. 7, 1995, 1C.

122. Murray Chass, "Orioles' Ripken Goes to Work and Steps into History Books," *New York Times*, Sept. 7, 1995, B19.

123. Bob Verdi, "A Run for Glory Puts Finishing Touch on Run for Record," *Chicago Tribune*, Sept. 7, 1995, sec. 4, p. 5.

124. Murray Chass, "Reluctant Baseball Owners Approve Pact with Players," *New York Times,* Nov. 27, 1996, A1. After the owners and ballplayers finally reached a collective bargaining agreement, the historian Richard C. Crepeau commented during his weekly radio show:

> They called him The Old Roman. In 1919 Charles Comiskey, owner of the Chicago White Sox, so angered his players with low salaries and his cheapskate ways that they turned on him and fixed the World Series. In 1996 White Sox owner Jerry Reinsdorf so angered his fellow owners by his high salaries and wild spending that they turned on him, reversed their vote of the previous three weeks, and approved the new baseball collective bargaining agreement. Maybe they should call Reinsdorf the New Roman, or Roman Nouveau.
>
> Seventy-seven years after the Black Sox scandal a White Sox owner once again precipitated a series of events that could lead to a new commissioner for the game and a new era in the sport and business of baseball. Acting Commissioner for Life Bud Selig has said there would be a new commissioner after the collective bargaining agreement was approved and the situation in baseball stabilized. If all continues on course we will reach that point soon.

Broadcast of "Sport and Society," Dec. 6, 1996, WUCF-FM 89.9, Orlando, Fla.

125. E. J. Dionne Jr., "Baseball's Ordinary Hero," *Washington Post,* Sept. 5, 1995, A17.

126. Tony Kornheiser, "Sportsman of the Year: No Contest," *Washington Post,* Dec. 7, 1995, B2.

127. "Ripken's Record Is the Sports Story of the Year," *Des Moines Register,* Dec. 27, 1995, 1S.

128. Thomas Boswell, "Quiet Cal Speaks Volumes," *Washington Post,* June 30, 1996, D1.

129. Buster Olney, "At Crossroads, Party Is Over for O's," *Baltimore Sun,* Sept. 10, 1995, 10D.

130. James C. Roberts, "Home Base Is Where the Heart Is," *Washington Post,* Mar. 28, 1995, E1; see also Vince Winkel, "Thousands Still Dreaming on Iowa's 'Field of Dreams,'" *Christian Science Monitor,* Sept. 1, 1995, 1.

131. Richard Jerome, "Foul Territory," *People Weekly,* Aug. 30, 1999, 62.

132. Michael Hirsley, "Still a Field of Pleasant Dreams," *Chicago Tribune,* Oct. 1, 1995, sec. 3, p. 5.

133. Ibid.

134. In July 1996, that tension came to the surface. "The Field of Dreams near Dyersville," reported Deborah Wiley, "has become a field of divided philosophies between the two farm families who own the 7-year-old ball diamond." Apparently, Lansing was unhappy with the firm the Ameskamps had hired to manage their part of the ballfield and its efforts to "over-commercialize the property." Over the years, the tension has persisted and has occasionally intensified. Debora Wiley, "A Field Divided: In Heaven There Would Be Harmony," *Des Moines Register,* July 4, 1996, 1A. See also Pam Belluck, "A Battlefield of Dreams for Iowa Farmers," *New*

York Times, Aug. 6, 1999, A1, A12; and Richard Jerome, "Foul Territory," *People Weekly,* Aug. 30, 1999, 60–62.

135. Hal Erickson, *Baseball in the Movies: A Comprehensive Reference, 1915–1991* (Jefferson, N.C.: McFarland, 1992), 152.

136. Rose, "Fielding Dreamers on Movie Site," 14A.

137. Hirsley, "Still a Field of Pleasant Dreams," 5.

138. Springwood, *Cooperstown to Dyersville,* 151.

139. Span, "'Baseball': The Windup and Now the Pitch," F1.

140. Richard Corliss, "An Empty Field of Dreams?" *Time,* Aug. 8, 1994, 65.

141. Andrew Zimbalist, "Field of Schemes," *New Republic,* Aug. 15, 1994, 11–12.

142. Bill Hendrick, "Still Controversial?: Say It Ain't So, Joe!" *Atlanta Journal and Constitution,* Feb. 6, 1997, A3.

143. Jesse J. Holland, Associated Press article, Feb. 6, 1997.

144. Ted Curtis, "Ruling No Curve Ball," *American Bar Association Journal,* Nov. 1997, 28.

Conclusion

1. Ira Berkow, "From 'Eight Men Out' to eBay: Shoeless Joe's Bat," *New York Times,* July 25, 2001, C21.

2. "Shoeless Joe's Black Betsy Bat Nets $577,610," *New York Times,* Aug. 8, 2001, D3.

3. Steven Biel, *Down with the Old Canoe: A Cultural History of the Titanic Disaster* (New York: W. W. Norton, 1996), 226–27.

4. Ronald Story, "The Greening of Sport: Jackson, Dempsey, and Industrial America," *Reviews in American History* 8:3 (Sept. 1980): 389.

5. "Say It Ain't Sumo!" *Sports Illustrated,* Feb. 21, 2000, 24; Rich Eisen, "This Is SportsCenter?" *ESPN the Magazine,* May 1, 2000, 46.

6. To cite but one example, the historian Warren Goldstein argues that we "need to recognize that competing versions of baseball history have been part of the way the game has been played, watched, and thought about ever since its earliest years." Warren Goldstein, *Playing for Keeps: A History of Early Baseball* (Ithaca: Cornell University Press, [1989] 1991), 11.

Index

Abbo, Cliff, 29–30
Adams, Henry, 145
Adelman, Melvin L., 37, 76, 123, 126–27
Alexander, Charles C., 43, 64, 106, 152–53, 179
Algren, Nelson, 77, 81–84, 105, 153; *Chicago: City on the Make,* 83; 1959 World Series and, 103, 247n42; "The Silver-Colored Yesterday," 76, 83; "The Swede Was a Hard Guy," 82–83, 110, 241n107
Ali, Muhammad, 121
Allen, Frederick Lewis, 14, 113
American Baseball: From the Commissioners to Continental Expansion (Voigt), 120; critique of, 123–27, 134–35
Ameskamp, Al, 192–94, 215, 274n134
Ameskamp, Rita, 192–94, 215, 274n134
Angell, Roger, 183, 195–96
Anti-Semitism, 12, 32–36, 218
Aparicio, Luis, 102
Ardolino, Frank, 151
Arnold, Benedict, 5, 30, 79, 83, 86
Asinof, Eliot, 16–17, 47, 49, 63–64, 71, 78–79, 83, 88, 92, 119, 123, 126, 130, 132–33, 147, 178, 191, 204, 209, 219, 226n28, 241n107, 247–48n62, 248n63, 261n57; biography of, 106, 117; *Bleeding between the Lines,* 138, 249n83; *1919: America's Loss of Innocence,* 249n83; response to film version of *Eight Men Out,* 264n106; on Watergate, 138–39. *See also Eight Men Out*
Associated Press, 27, 63, 143, 188, 213
Attell, Abe, 33–36, 82, 116, 164, 166, 202, 204
Austrian, Alfred, 3–4, 109
Axelson, G. W., 45
Axthelm, Pete, 137

Baltimore Colts, 121
Baltimore Orioles, 210
Barron, Rob, 149
Barrow, Edward, 72
Barzun, Jacques, 6
Baseball (Burns), 191, 215–16; critique of, 199–207
Baseball, Major League: gambling in, 15–16, 28, 43, 64–65, 108, 124, 129–30, 132, 135, 136–38, 144, 148, 185–90, 195, 265–66n143; histories of, 15–16, 119–35, 140–48, 251n18; reserve clause and, 15, 121–22, 144; strikes, 152, 184, 191, 195–200, 207–14, 216
Baseball: The Golden Age (Seymour), 120; critique of, 128–35
Baseball Digest, 76–77, 136, 246n39
Baseball Magazine, 226–27n33
Becker, Carl, 75
Bell, James ("Cool Papa"), 176
Benton, John ("Rube"), 3
Berkow, Ira, 188, 267–68n7, 273n109
Betts, John Rickards, 122, 146
Biel, Steven, 217
Bjarkman, Peter C., 159
Black Sox scandal: blackness vs. whiteness in depictions of, 23–24, 53; cleanliness vs. contamination in depictions of, 12, 24–28, 53, 112; college basketball point-shaving scandals vs., 136; Cook County grand jury testimony, 1, 3, 20, 22, 25, 31, 34, 64, 109, 203; in editorial cartoons, 21–23, 25, 27, 31, 40; in fiction,

67–69, 81–84, 93–99, 153–69; in film, 169–82; genesis of, 114; history of, 1–5; as masculine narrative, 12, 59, 73–77; as news story, 16–57; nostalgia for players in, 82–83, 207; in photographs, 22, 30, 44, 58; as a phrase, 23; race in depictions of, 24, 27, 36, 117, 121, 124, 157, 175–76, 231n139; on stage, 149, 190, 257n4; Teapot Dome scandal vs., 138–39; on television, 104; television quiz show scandal vs., 102–5; as tragedy, 19, 113, 115, 123–25; Watergate vs., 9, 138–40, 149, 150, 163, 180
—in magazines: *New Republic,* 45, 216; *Newsweek,* 78, 100, 137, 187, 210; *New Yorker,* 78, 171; *Time,* 104, 216
—in newspapers, 16–57; Associated Press on, 27, 63, 143, 188, 213; *Atlanta Journal,* 21, 27, 30, 41, 44; *Baltimore Sun,* 21, 212–13; *Boston Daily Globe,* 21–22; *Boston Evening Globe,* 46; *Boston Globe,* 137; *Brooklyn Eagle,* 28; *Chicago American,* 70; *Chicago Daily News,* 21, 23, 27, 44, 136; *Chicago Herald-American,* 67; *Chicago Herald and Examiner,* 4, 17, 21–23, 28, 30, 40–42, 44–47, 49–50, 55–56, 69–70; *Chicago Sun-Times,* 102–3; *Chicago Tribune,* 21–22, 24–25, 28–29, 31, 37, 42–44, 46, 52–55, 76, 100, 102, 136, 190, 204, 212, 234n209; *Cincinnati Enquirer,* 22, 25, 26, 31, 40, 42–43, 46–47; *Cleveland Plain Dealer,* 21–22, 26, 31, 47; *Dearborn Independent,* 34–35; *Des Moines Register,* 22, 193, 207; *Detroit Free Press,* 28, 137; *Greenville News,* 243n128; *Kansas City Star,* 47, 50; *Los Angeles Times,* 21, 46; *New Orleans Times-Picayune,* 21–22, 29; *New Republic,* 45, 216; *New York Daily News,* 20, 27, 40, 52, 163; *New York Evening World,* 18, 39, 41, 227n33; *New York Sun,* 87; *New York Times,* 20, 25, 27–28, 39, 64, 69, 71, 85, 100, 131, 138–40, 165, 188, 212; *New York Tribune,* 20, 22–23, 25, 29, 43, 49–50; *New York World,* 14, 17, 20, 25, 158; *New York World-Telegram,* 71–72, 104; *Philadelphia Bulletin,* 41; *Philadelphia North American,* 3; *Pittsburgh Post,* 30; *St. Louis Star,* 23; *USA Today,* 188; *Wall Street Journal,* 207; *Washington Post,* 21, 26, 42–43, 88, 137, 196–98, 210, 213, 229–30n104
—in sports publications: *Baseball Digest,* 76–77, 136, 246n39; *Baseball Magazine,* 226–27n33; *Sport,* 246n39; *Sporting News,* 28, 33, 58–59, 70, 76–77, 87, 131, 140, 176, 178, 207, 226–27n33, 237n35; *Sports Illustrated,* 100, 128, 136, 185, 209–10, 213
Blake, Morgan, 27, 30, 41, 44
Blight, David W., 201
Bloom, Harold, 79, 241n95
Blue Ruin (Boyd), 184, 219; critique of, 164–69
Blum, John Morton, 120
Bock, Hal, 188
Borus, Daniel H., 13
Boston Braves, 142, 172
Boston Red Sox, 45, 65, 72, 142, 223n3
Boswell, Charles, 104–5
Boswell, Thomas, 186–87, 189, 198–99, 213, 266n143
Boyd, Brendan, 153, 164–69, 183; *Blue Ruin,* 164–69, 184, 219
Brigham, Henry H., 26, 37–38
Broeg, Bob, 140
Brooklyn Dodgers, 93
Broun, Heywood Hale, 210
Brown, Bill, 176
Brown, Warren, 70, 76
Bull Durham (film), 173, 180
Burke, Robert F., 47
Burns, Bill ("Sleepy"), 3, 82, 116, 164, 202
Burns, Ken, 191, 199–207; *Baseball,* 191, 199–207, 215–16; *The Brooklyn Bridge,* 200; *The Civil War,* 200–201

California Angels, 211
Campanis, Al, 152
Candelaria, Cordelia, 5
Capra, Frank, 174
Carey, James W., 12
Carino, Peter, 162–63, 165
Carradine, Keith, 204
Cartwright, Kent, 96, 99
Carver, Raymond, 164
"Casey at the Bat" (Thayer), 171–72
The Celebrant (Greenberg), 141, 149, 184–85; critique of, 157–61
Chamberlain, Charles, 148
Chandler, Raymond, 164
Chase, Hal, 18, 25–26
Chass, Murray, 197, 212
Chicago: City on the Make (Algren), 83

Chicago Cubs, 3, 42, 102, 109
Chicago Historical Society, 131, 149, 191, 257n5
Chicago White Sox: 1917 World Series and, 128; 1919 team, 125, 128–29, 202, 233n186; 1919 World Series and, 1–3, 78, 202; 1920 season, 3; 1959 team, 102; nostalgia for 1919 team, 82–83, 207. *See also* Black Sox scandal; *individual players*
Cicotte, Eddie, 2–5, 20–23, 25, 38–39, 41, 58, 72, 78, 82, 91, 95, 109, 158, 257n5; Cook County grand jury testimony of, 26, 29, 43, 46, 123, 126, 129, 138, 203, 248n66; fictional portrayal of, 179; National Baseball Hall of Fame and, 84; support for, 111
Cincinnati Reds, 1–2, 102, 104, 111, 185–87, 203
Cleland, Alexander, 85
Cleveland Indians, 3, 21, 26, 65, 87–88, 100
Cobb, Ty, 65, 128, 185, 187, 237n37, 252n28, 267n5
Coffin, Tristram P., 62–63
Cohan, George M., 3, 23, 164
Cohen, Morris R., 15
Cole, Diane, 165
Collins, Eddie, 2, 36, 43–45, 51, 125, 233nn176 and 186, 238n38
Comiskey, Charles A., 2–3, 16, 21–22, 25, 27, 29, 36, 42–43, 45–48, 51, 53, 63, 76–78, 80, 82, 88, 109, 111–12, 116, 118, 124, 132, 135, 146, 178; alleged culpability for Black Sox scandal, 108, 125–27, 130, 205, 271n75; criticism of, 45, 144, 271n75; fictional portrayals of, 104, 178; historical representation of, 144; knowledge of game fixing, 108, 119, 203, 247n62; obituaries of, 69–71, 239n57; parsimony of, 100, 104, 107–8, 125–26, 130, 144, 202, 215, 256n102, 274n124; possible alliance with Arnold Rothstein, 109; as victim, 125, 131
Comiskey, Louis, 239n57
Condon, David, 102, 136–37
Conkin, Paul K., 134
Connell, Evan, 7
Cook County grand jury, 1, 3, 20, 22, 25, 31, 34, 64, 109, 203
Cooperstown, N.Y., 84–85, 188, 192, 194. *See also* National Baseball Hall of Fame
Cooperstown to Dyersville: A Geography of Baseball Nostalgia (Springwood), 194
Costner, Kevin, 173, 175
Counter-memory, 86, 91, 242–43n121. *See also* Memory
Cowley, Malcolm, 81
Crepeau, Richard C., 52, 143–45, 274n124
Cronje, Hansie, 220
Crusinberry, James, 228n53
Cultural meaning, production of, 219, 221
Current, Richard N., 153

Daley, Arthur, 85, 100
Daniel, Dan, 87–88, 243n131
Darnton, Robert, 9, 11, 51, 235n225
Davidson, Cathy N., 51
DeMint, Jim, 192
Denby, David, 171, 180
Detroit Tigers, 65, 102, 136–37, 254n74
Dexter, Pete, 239
Dickerson, Gary E., 170, 172–73
DiMaggio, Joe, 90, 211–12
Dionne, E. J., Jr., 213
Doctorow, E. L., 94, 165
Dolan, Albert ("Cozy"), 64–65, 237n35
Donald, David Herbert, 127
Douglas, Mary, 25, 236n13
Douglas, Phil, 64
Drew, Betina, 81
Dryden, Charles, 23, 30, 42
Dubuque, Iowa, 176–77
Dulles, Foster Rhea, 122
Durant, John, 119
Dusenberry, Phil, 170

Early, Gerald, 170
Eckford Club, 16
Edgerton, Gary, 200
Edgren, Robert, 39
Edson, Richard, 178
Edwards, Harry, 121
Eight Men Out (book by Asinof), 16, 78, 83, 88, 92–93, 99, 119–20, 125, 128, 131–32, 141, 177, 179; critique of, 106–18, 248n72; influence of, 135, 147, 167, 182, 204, 218–19
Eight Men Out (film by Sayles), 139, 149, 159–60, 169, 204, 219; critique of, 177–82
Einstein, Charles, 76
Eisen, Rich, 220
Eisenhower, Dwight D., 104
Erickson, Hal, 174, 180

ESPN (Entertainment and Sport Programming Network), 5, 211, 220

Faber, Urban ("Red"), 242n118
Falls, Joe, 137
Farrell, James T., 43–44, 52, 101–2, 105
Fehr, Donald, 198–99, 213
Feller, Bob, 90, 98, 191, 245n8, 268–69n21
Felsch, Oscar ("Hap"), 2, 4, 5, 21, 39, 72, 82, 91, 101, 125, 252n28; fictional portrayal of, 156; support for, 111
Fiedler, Leslie, 81
Field of Dreams (baseball field in Dyersville, Iowa), 177, 191–95, 214–16, 269nn23 and 30, 274n134
Field of Dreams (Robinson), 142, 149, 154–55, 159, 169, 178, 180, 188, 191–92, 194–95, 215–16, 219; critique of, 173–77
Fimrite, Ron, 48, 185–87
Finley, M. I., 156
Fitzgerald, F. Scott, 33–34, 67–69, 77, 84, 153, 165, 238n51; *The Great Gatsby,* 33, 67–69, 76, 202, 238n47
Flood, Curt, 121
Ford, Henry, 34–35, 162
Foucault, Michel, 242–43n121
Fox, Nellie, 102
Freeman, Buck, 124–25
Frick, Ford, 106
Friend, Hugo M., 31, 230n106, 248n64
Frommer, Harvey, 6
Fry, August J., 156
Fullerton, Hugh, 3, 16–19, 32–33, 40–41, 47–48, 95, 108, 123, 129, 202–3, 247–48n62; criticism of, 226–27n33; as ethical hero, 226n28; fictional portrayals of, 158–59, 178

Gallo, Bill, 208
Gambling: Denny McLain and, 136–38, 148; Major League Baseball and, 15–16, 28, 43, 64–65, 108, 124, 129–30, 132, 135, 144; Pete Rose and, 185–90, 195, 265–66n143
Gandil, Arnold ("Chick"), 2, 4–5, 82, 100–101, 105, 107–8, 111, 125, 158, 164, 233n176, 246n33; fictional portrayals of, 156, 166–67; as game-fixing organizer, 114–15, 166–67, 202, 205
Garman, Bryan K., 157
Gedeon, Joe, 5, 131
Gehrig, Lou, 90, 209–12
Geiger, Edward, 69
Gerlach, Larry R., 122
Giamatti, A. Bartlett, 157, 184, 186–87, 189, 260n33
Gibson, Josh, 176
Giles, Bill, 209
Ginsburg, Daniel E., 16, 65
Gleason, Bill, 75–76
Gleason, William ("Kid"), 2, 16, 69, 71, 74, 108, 111, 202, 247n62
Godmilow, Jill, 206
Goldstein, Warren, 38, 121, 275n6
Goler, Robert I., 257n5
Gorn, Elliott J., 121, 188
Gould, Stephen Jay, 1, 6
Grabiner, Harry, 119, 132
The Great Baseball Mystery (Luhrs), 111, 119, 131, 248nn66 and 67
Great Depression, 67, 69, 80–81, 85
The Great Gatsby (Fitzgerald), 33, 67–69, 76, 202, 238n47
Greenberg, Eric Rolfe: *The Celebrant,* 141, 153, 182–84
Greenfield, Meg, 60
Greenville, S.C., 71–72, 79, 87–88, 90–91, 192
Grella, George, 5
Griffith, Clark, 48–49
Griffith, James, 171
Gropman, Donald, 71–72, 111, 141–43; *Say It Ain't So, Joe!* 111, 141–43, 154, 255n94
Guttmann, Allen, 107

Hackenberg, Dick, 102–3
Halbwachs, Maurice, 60–61, 73, 236nn6 and 12
Harding, Warren G., 132, 164
Hearst, William Randolph, 14, 21
Henkey, Ben, 178
Henry, Harley, 98–99
Hern, Gerry, 233n176
Hershey, Barbara, 170
Herzog, Charles ("Buck"), 3
Heydler, John, 18, 25–26, 247n62; fictional portrayal of, 178
Himmelfarb, Gertrude, 132
Hirsley, Michael, 214–15
History: as discourse, 119, 220, 244n1
Hoiles, Chris, 212
Holliman, Jennie, 122
Holtzman, Jerome, 204, 271n75

Honig, Donald, 5, 45, 50, 143–44
Hoopla (Stein), 149, 159–60, 181–82, 184, 207, 217, 219; critique of, 161–64
Hoover, Herbert, 69, 239n57
Hornung, Paul, 136
Hoy, Suellen, 24
Hoyne, Maclay, 30, 248n63
Hühm, Peter, 31–32
Hulbert, William, 19
Hutton, Patrick H., 61

Jackson, Bo, 190
Jackson, Joe ("Shoeless"), 1–2, 5, 20–21, 23, 25, 38–39, 53, 71–74, 77, 79, 80, 82, 95–96, 99, 109, 138–42, 149, 158, 172, 177, 181, 186–88, 190, 194–95, 202–3, 215–16, 221, 245n8; Cook County grand jury testimony of, 4, 26, 46, 96, 123, 126, 129, 133–34, 203–4, 223n8, 248n63, 253n54; counter-memories of, 85–88; fictional portrayals of, 104, 154–57, 161–62, 174, 176, 180, 184, 263n86; interview with, 131; legal redress for, 125, 252n28; memorabilia related to, 191, 217, 257n5; National Baseball Hall of Fame and, 75, 78, 84, 141, 188–92, 195, 220, 266n152, 267n5; 1919 World Series performance of, 2–3, 96, 142; reminiscences of, 103; "Say it ain't so, Joe" courthouse exchange, 4, 40–41, 74, 101, 143, 197, 204, 271n74; support for, 111, 155, 191, 192, 219, 243n128, 255n94, 268n17; sympathy for, 110, 115, 118, 145, 155, 219, 243n131, 255n94
Jackson, Katie, 190, 201, 204
Jacobson, Harlan, 174–75
James, Bill, 265n134, 266n152
James, Clifton, 178
Jauss, Bill, 76–77
Jenkins, Keith, 8
Johnson, Ban, 3, 22, 25–28, 131–32, 178, 203, 237n37, 247n62
Johnson, Brian D., 174
Johnson, Haynes, 177, 259n20
Johnson, Lyndon B., 120
Johnson, Walter, 86
Jones, James Earl, 175
Jones, Paul, 39
Jung, Carl, 95

Kael, Pauline, 171, 174
Kahn, Roger, 186
Kammen, Michael, 244n142
Karras, Alex, 136
Katcher, Leo, 33–34, 113, 167, 238n51
Kauff, Benny, 64, 237n31
Kaul, Donald, 207
Kelly, Lawrence, 149
Kennedy, John F., 10, 116, 120, 143, 160
Kerr, Dick, 2–3
Kieran, John, 69
Kimmell, Michael S., 231n139
Kinsella, W. P., 103, 142, 153, 173, 183–84, 193–94; *Shoeless Joe*, 103, 142, 149, 154–57, 159, 161–62, 173–75, 177, 182, 184, 194–95, 219, 259n27
Kirkpatrick, Curry, 210–11
Klingaman, William K., 11
Kopf, Josephine Z., 68–69
Korean War, 97, 117
Kornheiser, Tony, 213
Kramer, Trevor D., 267n5
Krauthammer, Charles, 209
Krout, John Allen, 122
Kuhn, Bowie, 136–38, 191
Kurkjian, Tim, 211

LaCapra, Dominick, 111–12
Landis, Kenesaw Mountain, 1, 4–5, 7, 27, 31, 36, 48–51, 59, 62–67, 69, 72, 78, 87–90, 130–32, 134–35, 137, 145–46, 161, 190, 201, 203, 218–19, 234n209; Black Sox ruling of, 101, 124, 130; disciplinary actions of, 64–66, 237n37, 238n45, 239n67; as ethical hero, 146; as Major League Baseball commissioner, 48–49, 59, 124, 126, 130, 135, 189; as Major League Baseball's savior, 64, 131, 146, 209; reputation of, 48, 62–63, 234n210
Lansing, Becky, 214
Lansing, Don, 192–94, 214–15, 274n134
Lardner, John, 77–80, 100
Lardner, Ring, 14, 57, 79, 95, 98, 108, 162, 164, 241nn93 and 94, 248n62; fictional portrayal of, 178
Lardner, Ring, Jr., 179, 241n93
Lasher, Lawrence, 98
Latimer, Carter ("Scoop"), 87, 243n128
Lauricella, John, 67–68
Leerhsen, Charles, 187
Leonard, Hubert ("Dutch"), 65
Leuchtenberg, William, 113
Levine, Peter, 35, 230n117

Levinson, Barry, 169, 170, 172–73, 183–84, 263n79; *The Natural,* 138, 169–73, 262n65
Lieb, Fred, 143, 146
Liebling, Jerome, 200
Lindberg, Richard C., 252n28, 256n102, 257n5
Liotta, Ray, 174
Lipsitz, George, 86, 171, 242–43n121; *Time Passages: Collective Memory and American Popular Culture,* 86
Lipsyte, Robert, 139–40
Liston, Sonny, 121
Lloyd, Christopher, 178
Loomis, Fred, 24–25, 228n53
Los Angeles Dodgers, 102–3
Louisville Grays, 16
Lowenfish, Leo, 144
Lowenthal, David, 84, 92, 115
Lucas, John A., 146
Luhrs, Victor: *The Great Baseball Mystery,* 111, 119, 131, 248nn66 and 67
Lupica, Mike, 187, 198
Lupien, Tony, 144

Macbeth, W. J., 49–50
Mack, Connie, 128
Magee, Rusty, 149
Maharg, Billy, 3
Major League (film), 180
Major League Baseball Players Association, 121, 196
Malamud, Bernard, 92–99, 100, 106, 117, 153, 170–72; *The Natural,* 92–99, 116–18, 154, 160, 170–73, 245n8; response to film version of *The Natural,* 262n67
Mantle, Mickey, 210, 273n109
Masculinity: Black Sox and, 12, 59, 73–77; boys and, 29–30, 36–43, 49–50, 64, 73–77, 80, 83, 87, 112, 141–42, 144, 203, 218, 240n81; conceptions of, 36–51; crisis of, 36–37, 231n139; fathers and sons and, 141–42, 157, 175, 213, 260n28
Maske, Mark, 196, 210
Mathewson, Christy, 17, 160, 184, 248n62; fictional portrayal of, 158–60
Mattingly, Don, 191
Mauldin, John, 71
Mayer, Erskine, 230n117
Mayes, Elaine, 200
McCann, Richard, 87
McCarthy, Joe, 97, 117
McChesney, Robert W., 14
McDonald, Charles, 26, 230n106
McElroy, Mary, 96, 99
McGimpsey, David, 163, 262n71
McGraw, John, 25, 128
McGuire, Biff, 104
McKeever, William, 37
McLain, Denny, 136–38, 148, 254n74
McMullin, Fred, 5
Memory: counter-memory and, 86, 91, 242–43n121; theories of, 60–62, 73, 84–85, 89–90, 92, 244n142
Merlock, Ray, 142–43
Merriwell, Frank, 93
Messenger, Christian K., 7
Messner, Michael A., 36–37
M'Geehan, W. O., 25
Miller, Marvin, 121, 189
Mills, Dorothy Jane, 128, 133–34, 253n49
Milwaukee Brewers, 198
Montreal Expos, 185
Morehouse, Ward, 87
Morgan, Peter W., 139
Morris, Tim, 159
Mosher, Stephen D., 269n30
Murray, Eddie, 211
Musial, Stan, 90
Mussina, Mike, 212

Nardinelli, Clark, 237n37, 238n45
Nash, Roderick, 152
National Baseball Hall of Fame, 45, 75, 78–79, 131, 188, 192, 220, 242n118, 266n152; Eddie Cicotte and, 84; George Weaver and, 84; Joe Jackson and, 75, 78, 84, 141, 188–92, 195, 220, 266n152, 267n5
National Football League, 136
National Public Radio, 191
The Natural (book by Malamud), 116–18, 154, 160, 170–73, 245n8; Arthurian legend in, 94, 172; critique of, 92–99
The Natural (movie by Levinson), 138, 262n65; critique of, 169–73
Negro Leagues, 123, 176
Neily, Harry, 70
Nevins, Allan, 104, 127
Newspapers: Associated Press reportage in, 27, 63, 143, 188, 213; history of, 13–15. *See also* Black Sox scandal, in newspapers
New York Giants, 16–17, 25, 64, 100, 158, 184

New York Mets, 186
New York Mutuals, 16
New York Yankees, 3, 72, 191, 208, 273n109
Nixon, Richard M., 77, 121, 138–40
Nora, Pierre, 85
Nostalgia, 7, 75, 85; associated with pastoralism, 193; for Black Sox players, 82–83, 207; as commodity, 173, 176; for past, 157, for time of innocence, 104, 151, 156, 206, 214

O'Brien, James, 39
O'Brien, Tom, 180
Ochs, Adolph, 14
O'Connell, Jimmy, 64–65, 237n35
Okrent, Daniel, 202–5
O'Leary, James, 46
Olney, Buster, 212–13

Paige, Satchel, 176
Pallone, Dave, 186
Palmeiro, Rafael, 212
Parrish, Michael E., 90
Paulette, Gene, 64
Paxson, Frederic L., 122
Pegler, Westbrook, 57, 72–73, 100
Pellow, C. Kenneth, 155, 175, 259–60n28
Phair, George, 30–31
Philadelphia Athletics, 43, 88, 233nn176 and 186, 237n37
Philadelphia Phillies, 3, 64, 106, 121, 185, 209
Pioreck, Richard, 149, 257n4
Pittsburgh Pirates, 223n3
Postol, Todd, 97
Povich, Shirley, 88, 137, 197
Prell, Edward, 100
Pridemore, Jay, 257n5
Prindeville, Edward, 37
Pulitzer, Joseph, 14, 18, 20
Purchase, Ian, 90
Puscas, George, 137

Rader, Benjamin G., 121, 143, 195
Rath, Morrie, 16, 248n66
Rathman, Darby, 239n67
Ravitch, Richard, 196, 198
Reagan, Ronald, 150–51, 164, 168, 172, 258n9, 259n20
Reaves, Joey, 190
Redford, Robert, 138, 170, 172, 262n71
Red Scare, 124, 132, 145, 249n83
Reidel, Sue, 192, 269n23
Reinsdorf, Jerry, 198, 274n124
Replogle, Hartley, 118, 133
Reserve clause, 15, 121–22, 144
Rice, Grantland, 14, 29, 52, 57
Richman, Sidney, 97
Riess, Steven A., 15–16, 122, 134, 145, 204
Ripken, Cal, Jr., 209–14, 273n116
Ripken, Kelly, 211
Ripley, Robert, 142
Risberg, Charles ("Swede"), 2, 5, 65, 83, 125, 140, 158, 164, 252n28
Robards, Jason, 203
Robinson, Brooks, 212, 273n116
Robinson, Frank, 212, 273n116
Robinson, Jackie, 176, 212, 273n116
Robinson, Phil Alden, 142, 169, 173–77, 183–84, 192, 215; *Field of Dreams,* 142, 149, 154–55, 159, 169, 173–77, 178, 180, 188, 191–92, 194–95, 215–16, 219
Roosevelt, Franklin D., 72
Rosa, Francis, 137
Rose, Pete, 152, 185–90, 199, 265n134, 265–66n143, 266n152; Dowd Report and, 265n134, 266n152
Rosenbaum, Ron, 175
Rosenstone, Robert A., 169
Ross, Dorothy, 127
Rothstein, Arnold, 4, 33–36, 68–69, 82, 95, 109, 164, 202–5, 257n5; fictional portrayal of, 167–69; possible alliance with Charles Comiskey, 109
Roush, Edd, 1
Royko, Mike, 138
Runyon, Damon, 14, 26
Ruth, George Herman ("Babe"), 3, 38, 90, 99, 128, 162, 164, 172, 203, 214, 218, 220, 245n8; as Major League Baseball's savior, 131, 146, 202, 209–10, 213, 218
Rutner, Mickey, 106

Sand, Heinie, 64
Sandburg, Carl, 201
Say It Ain't So, Joe! (Gropman), 111, 141–43, 154, 255n94
Sayles, John, 139, 169, 177–84, 202–4, 206, 262n74, 264n125; *Eight Men Out,* 139, 149, 159–60, 169, 177–82, 204, 219
Schalk, Ray, 76, 242n118
Scheinin, Richard, 245n11

Schickel, Richard, 73–75, 77
Schmidt, William E., 177
Scholes, Robert, 56
Schudson, Michael, 7–8, 69, 84, 140
Schwartz, Richard Alan, 156–57, 163
Scobey, David, 178–79, 181
Scott, Sir Walter, 94
Selig, Allan ("Bud"), 188–89, 198, 213, 274n124
Seymour, Harold, 15, 48, 64–65, 120–22, 124–25, 128–36, 140, 144–45, 147–48, 237n31, 238n38, 250n7, 252n39, 253n42; *Baseball: The Golden Age,* 120, 128–35
Shapiro, Walter, 197
Sheed, Wilfrid, 188
Sheridan, John B., 28
Shoeless Joe (Kinsella), 103, 142, 149, 182, 184, 194–95, 219, 259n27; critique of, 154–57, 159, 161–62, 173–75, 177
Shoeless Joe Jackson Times, 190, 267n5
Shoeless Joe Memorial Park, 192, 268n17
Sinclair, Upton, 24
Smith, Dean, 143, 146
Smith, Leverett T., Jr., 143, 225n5
Smith, Red, 80, 140
Smith, Ronald A., 146
Smock, Diane, 190
Sobol, Ken, 209
Society for American Baseball Research, 152
South Georgia League, 87
Speaker, Tris, 65, 237n37
Spink, J. G. Taylor, 65–67
Sport, 246n39
Sporting News, 28, 33, 58–59, 70, 76–77, 87, 131, 140, 176, 178, 207, 226–27n33, 237n35
Sports Illustrated, 100, 128, 136, 185, 209–10, 213
Springwood, Charles Fruehling, 194–95, 215, 270n41; *Cooperstown to Dyersville: A Geography of Baseball Nostalgia,* 194
Starr, Bill, 240n81
Staudohar, Paul D., 196, 208
Steadman, John, 212
Stein, Harry, 107, 153, 161–64, 183–84, 207; *Hoopla,* 149, 159–60, 161–64, 181–82, 184, 207, 217, 219
Stein, Irving M., 88–89
Steiner, Jesse Frederick, 122
Stern, Gardner, 203–5
St. Louis Browns, 131
St. Louis Cardinals, 64, 121
Stone, Albert E., 8
Stone, Oliver, 201
Strathairn, David, 179
Strikes: in Major League Baseball, 152, 184, 191, 195–200, 207–14, 216
Stromberg, Roland N., 134
Sullivan, Joseph ("Sport"), 22, 33, 107, 114–15, 261n57; fictional portrayal of, 164–69
Sunday, Billy, 40
Susman, Warren I., 209
Susskind, David, 106, 138, 249n83

Tennes, Monte, 3
Terkel, Studs, 178, 202, 271n75
Thelen, David, 60
Thompson, Lewis, 104–5
Thomson, David, 169, 173
Thurmond, Strom, 192
Time Passages: Collective Memory and American Popular Culture (Lipsitz), 86
Towne, Roger, 170
Trouillot, Michel-Rolph, 148
Tucher, Andie, 14, 29
Tunis, John R., 98
Turner, Nat, 8, 10
Tygiel, Jules, 66, 131

Ueberroth, Peter, 195

Van Doren, Charles, 103–4
Veeck, Bill, Jr., 102, 119, 131–32, 176
Verdi, Bob, 212
Verducci, Tom, 210
Vietnam war, 120–21, 150
Vincent, Fay, 195–96
Voigt, David Q., 7, 19, 120–28, 130, 133–36, 140, 144–45, 147–48, 251n23; *American Baseball: From the Commissioners to Continental Expansion,* 120, 123–27, 134–35

Waitkus, Eddie, 172, 245n8
Wall, James W., 174
Walle, Alf, 74–75
Washington Senators, 48, 86, 237n37
Wasserman, Earl R., 95
Weaver, Earl, 273n116
Weaver, George ("Buck"), 2, 4–5, 39, 72, 75, 78, 82, 181, 190, 192; counter-mem-

ories of, 85–86, 88–89; fictional portrayals of, 161–64, 180; National Baseball Hall of Fame and, 84; 1919 World Series performance of, 2–3, 88; obituaries of, 99–100, 105, 246n31; professed innocence of, 125, 140; reminiscences of, 75, 103, 244n140; sympathy for, 110, 115, 118, 219, 244n140
Weeghman, Charles, 3
Wendt, Lloyd, 228n53
Westbrook, Deeanne, 158, 263n79
Weston, Jessie, 98
White, Hayden, 9, 112–13, 116, 248–49n73, 249n75
Whitfield, Stephen J., 104
Wilkinson, James, 62, 90–91
Will, George F., 6–7, 139, 150, 157, 185, 260n33
Williams, Claude ("Lefty"), 2, 4–5, 21, 82, 101, 109, 111, 123, 158; Cook County grand jury testimony of, 126, 129, 248n63
Williams, Joe, 104
Williams, Ted, 90, 191, 245n11
Wills, Garry, 150
"The Witness" (television program), 104
Wolfe, Tom, 149
Wolfsheim, Meyer, 33, 67–69, 202
Wood, Joe, 65
Woodruff, Harvey, 25, 42, 52, 228n53, 235n231
Woodward, C. Vann, 59, 149, 183–84
Woodward, Stanley, 127
World Series: cancellation of, 196–200; early history of, 223n3; of 1919, 1–3, 202, 242n118; of 1920, 129; of 1959, 102–3; television ratings of, 152
World War I, 5, 13, 53, 67, 131, 145, 158, 160, 202
World War II, 76, 81, 90, 106

Zelcer, David, 22
Ziegler, Ron, 138

DANIEL A. NATHAN is an assistant professor of American studies at Skidmore College. In 2001–2 he was a Fulbright scholar and taught North American studies at the University of Tampere, Finland.

Sport and Society

A Sporting Time: New York City and the Rise of Modern Athletics, 1820–70 *Melvin L. Adelman*
Sandlot Seasons: Sport in Black Pittsburgh *Rob Ruck*
West Ham United: The Making of a Football Club *Charles Korr*
Beyond the Ring: The Role of Boxing in American Society *Jeffrey T. Sammons*
John L. Sullivan and His America *Michael T. Isenberg*
Television and National Sport: The United States and Britain *Joan M. Chandler*
The Creation of American Team Sports: Baseball and Cricket, 1838–72 *George B. Kirsch*
City Games: The Evolution of American Urban Society and the Rise of Sports *Steven A. Riess*
The Brawn Drain: Foreign Student-Athletes in American Universities *John Bale*
The Business of Professional Sports *Edited by Paul D. Staudohar and James A. Mangan*
Fritz Pollard: Pioneer in Racial Advancement *John M. Carroll*
Go Big Red! The Story of a Nebraska Football Player *George Mills*
Sport and Exercise Science: Essays in the History of Sports Medicine *Edited by Jack W. Berryman and Roberta J. Park*
Minor League Baseball and Local Economic Development *Arthur T. Johnson*
Harry Hooper: An American Baseball Life *Paul J. Zingg*
Cowgirls of the Rodeo: Pioneer Professional Athletes *Mary Lou LeCompte*
Sandow the Magnificent: Eugen Sandow and the Beginnings of Bodybuilding *David Chapman*
Big-Time Football at Harvard, 1905: The Diary of Coach Bill Reid *Edited by Ronald A. Smith*
Leftist Theories of Sport: A Critique and Reconstruction *William J. Morgan*
Babe: The Life and Legend of Babe Didrikson Zaharias *Susan E. Cayleff*
Stagg's University: The Rise, Decline, and Fall of Big-Time Football at Chicago *Robin Lester*
Muhammad Ali, the People's Champ *Edited by Elliott J. Gorn*
People of Prowess: Sport, Leisure, and Labor in Early Anglo-America *Nancy L. Struna*

The New American Sport History: Recent Approaches and Perspectives
Edited by S. W. Pope
Making the Team: The Cultural Work of Baseball Fiction *Timothy Morris*
Making the American Team: Sport, Culture, and the Olympic Experience
Mark Dyreson
Viva Baseball! Latin Major Leaguers and Their Special Hunger
Samuel O. Regalado
Touching Base: Professional Baseball and American Culture in the Progressive Era (rev. ed.) *Steven A. Riess*
Red Grange and the Rise of Modern Football *John M. Carroll*
Golf and the American Country Club *Richard J. Moss*
Extra Innings: Writing on Baseball *Richard Peterson*
Global Games *Maarten Van Bottenburg*
The Sporting World of the Modern South *Edited by Patrick B. Miller*
The End of Baseball As We Knew It: The Players Union, 1960–81
Charles P. Korr
Saying It's So: A Cultural History of the Black Sox Scandal *Daniel A. Nathan*

REPRINT EDITIONS
The Nazi Olympics *Richard D. Mandell*
Sports in the Western World (2d ed.) *William J. Baker*

The University of Illinois Press
is a founding member of the
Association of American University Presses.

Composed in 10/13 Sabon
with Bodoni display
at the University of Illinois Press
Designed by Dennis Roberts
Manufactured by Thomson-Shore, Inc.

University of Illinois Press
1325 South Oak Street
Champaign, IL 61820-6903
www.press.uillinois.edu